מגילה

ArtScroll Judaiscope Series

A Path Through the Ashes

A Path Through

Collected from the pages of
The Jewish Observer
by

Rabbi Nisson Wolpin,
Editor

the Ashes

Penetrating analyses and inspiring stories of the Holocaust from a Torah perspective

Published by
Mesorah Publications, ltd
in conjunction with
Agudath Israel of America

FIRST EDITION
First Impression ... January 1986
Second Impression ... February 1996

Published and Distributed by
MESORAH PUBLICATIONS, Ltd.
Brooklyn, New York 11223

Distributed in Israel by
SIFRIATI / A. GITLER
4 Bilu Street / P.O.B. 14075 / TEL AVIV 61140

Distributed in Europe by
J. LEHMANN HEBREW BOOKSELLERS
20 Cambridge Terrace / Gateshead
Tyne and Wear / England NE8 1RP

Distributed in Australia and New Zealand by
GOLD'S BOOK & GIFT CO.
36 William Street / Balaclava 3183, Vic., Australia

Distributed in South Africa by
KOLLEL BOOKSHOP
22 Muller Street / Yeoville 2198, Johannesburg, South Africa

ArtScroll Judaiscope Series / "A PATH THROUGH THE ASHES"
© Copyright 1986
by MESORAH PUBLICATIONS, Ltd.
4401 Second Avenue / Brooklyn, N.Y. 11232 / (718) 921-9000

The essays in this volume have been adapted
from articles that have appeared in the pages of
THE JEWISH OBSERVER
published by Agudath Israel of America.
Copyright and all rights reserved by The Jewish Observer, New York City.

No part of this book may be reproduced **in any form**
without **written** permission from the copyright holder,
except by a reviewer who wishes to quote brief passages in connection with a review
written for inclusion in magazines or newspapers.

THE RIGHTS OF THE COPYRIGHT HOLDER WILL BE STRICTLY ENFORCED.

ISBN
0-89906-856-1 (hard cover)
0-89906-857-X (paperback)

Typography by CompuScribe at ArtScroll Studios, Ltd.
4401 Second Avenue / Brooklyn, N.Y. 11223 / (718) 921-9000

Printed in the United States of America by Moriah Offset
Bound by **Sefercraft, Inc.,** Brooklyn, NY

This book is dedicated
in honor of
Mrs. Anna Rosner שתחי׳
and in loving memory of her late husband
Leo Rosner ע״ה

Noble philanthropist and colorful personality, Leo Rosner's name is enshrined in the leading institutions of the Torah world here and in Israel.

May his memory ever be a blessing.

Through the generosity of Mrs. Anna Rosner and her dear children, the Holocaust Study Program has been established to create programs of education and enlightenment for students of the entire Day School Movement, to learn and understand the events that took place in the darkest period in our time.

Through the inititative of Anna Rosner, the LIFE Center for Holocaust Studies is dedicated in memory of Herman and Mary Hershkowitz ע״ה, her beloved parents.

May their memory ever be a blessing.

Table of Contents

Introduction — A Call on the Shofar/
[Rabbi Benyamin Kamenetzky]   15

I. Approaching the Cataclysm

Galus: Why Are We Destined to Wander?
[Rabbi Meir Simcha of Dvinsk] Gershon Dubin   20
The Redeeming Features of "Galus Awareness"
[Rabbi Yaakov Kamenetzky]   24
The Loss of Europe's Torah Centers
[Rabbi Eliyahu Eliezer Dessler] Rabbi Yehoshua Leiman   26
Questions Without Answers ... Faith Without Questions ...
[Rabbi Avrohom Wolf] Rabbi Nosson Scherman   32
"Holocaust": A Rosh Yeshivah's Response
[Rabbi Yitzchak Hutner]
Rabbi Chaim Feuerman / Rabbi Yaakov Feitman   39
A Path Through the Ashes / [Rabbi Mordechai Gifter]   56

II. The Surviving Generation Looks Back

Shall We Tell Our Children?
Rabbi Moshe Sherer   66
The Destruction of European Jewry:
A Churban of Singular Dimensions
[Rabbi Yaakov Weinberg]   69
Our Generation: Churban Plus-One
[Rabbi Yaakov Perlow]   74
An Understanding of the Holocaust in the Light
of Moshe Prager's "Sparks of Glory"
Rabbi Nosson Scherman   84
The Last Mashgiach of Slobodka
Rabbi Hillel Goldberg   94
Bikrovei Ekodeish: The Six Million Kedoshim
A. Sheinman   97

III. Of Enemies and Friends

Where Evil is Spawned / Dr. Henry Biberfeld   104
The Master Race and The Chosen People
Rabbi Yaakov Feitman   109

An Apology for "the Silence of Pius XII"
Rabbi Joseph Elias 122
The Catholic Church and Nazi Germany
Rabbi Yaakov Jacobs 126
A Voice from Beyond:
The Kedoshim Ask Some Burning Questions
Aharon Jeruchem 131
Dateline 1976: In Search for Polish Jewry
Rabbi Elkanah Schwartz 136
Where are the Scars? / *Rabbi Hanoch Teller* 145

◆§ IV. Heroes of the Spirit

The Bluzhever Rebbe Remembers: Embers Midst the Ruins
Rabbi Nosson Scherman 152
Why Didn't They Fight Back
Joseph Friedenson 163
My Father's Survival in the Warsaw Ghetto
Joseph Friedenson 168
A Shabbos Choice in the Warsaw Ghetto
[*Moshe Prager*] 175
Eyeball to Eyeball
[*Moshe Prager*] *Rabbi Nosson Scherman* 179
The Song of Shlomo
[*Moshe Prager*] *Rabbi Nosson Scherman* 184
Sparks Beneath the Smokestacks
Joseph Friedenson / Rabbi Shmuel Unsdorfer 189
The Festival of Freedom in Block 20 ...
Mauthausen, Germany: 1945
Abraham Krakowski 192
The "Dumb" Child / *Asher Lazar* 197
A Shabbos in Siberia / *Sorah Mermelstein* 202
Mechel the Provider / *Aaron Hish* 207

◆§ V. Resistance and Rescue

The Mirrer Yeshivah's Escape from Europe
Rabbi Chaim Shapiro 210
"Never Again" — Who Can Say It?
Rabbi Nisson Wolpin 218
" — Like Sheep"? / *Yisroel Sapirstein* 237
Setting the Record Straight / *Gershon Kranzler* 242

Why Auschwitz Was Never Bombed
Lewis Brenner 252
Heroic Efforts, Fatal Failings / *Rabbi Joseph Elias* 258

◆§ VI. A Guide to Remembering

When Remembering is a Mitzvah
Rabbi Dovid Cohen / Rabbi Shmuel Unsdorfer
Rabbi Chaim Segal / Joseph Friedenson 270
Heroes: Remembering and Understanding
Rabbi Nisson Wolpin 274
Focus on Remembering / *Rabbi Nisson Wolpin* 280
Heroics and "Remembrance" — a New Jewish Religion?
Joseph Friedenson 283
Straw Hat in a Sea of Black / *Dr. Bernard Fryshman* 287

◆§ VII. Through the Eyes of the Media

The Real Elie Wiesel / *Rabbi Nosson Scherman* 290
Dealing with "Churban Europa" / *Rabbi Joseph Elias* 301
"Holocaust" — At Least They Know
Rabbi Nisson Wolpin 317

◆§ VIII. In the Aftermath

The Phenomenon of Reconstruction
Rabbi Avrohom Chaim Levine 322
Waiting for the Geulah: A Guide to Reconstruction
[Rabbi Elya Svei] Rabbi Mendel Kaufman 324
After the Churban: Being Judged by the Martyrs
[Rabbi Elya Svei] 330
After the Churban: A Groundswell of Love
[Rabbi Avrohom HaKohein Pam] Rabbi Shimon Finkelman 339

Glossary 347

Contributors to this volume:

Dr. Henry Biberfeld of Montreal, a distinguished scientist, author and lecturer is author of several works including the well received *David, King of Israel*.

Rabbi Lewis Brenner resides in Brooklyn, where he is active in communal affairs.

Rabbi Eliyah Eliezer Dessler זצ״ל (5652/1892 — 5714/1953) was a founder of the Yeshivah of Gateshead (England), where he served as *Mashgiach*. He later was *Mashgiach* in the Ponovezh Yeshivah in Bnei Brak, Israel. A master teacher and thinker, his lectures and letters have been published in the four volume *Michtav MeEliyahu*.

Rabbi Joseph Elias is menahel of the Yeshivah Rabbi Samson Raphael Hirsch High School for Girls and the Rika Breuer's Teachers Seminary. He served as editor of the Jewish Pocket Book Series, is a member of the Editorial Board of *The Jewish Observer*, and is author of the translation and commentary of the ArtScroll Haggadah.

Rabbi Yaakov Feitman, Rabbi of the Young Israel of Cleveland Heights, Ohio, is a well-known author and lecturer.

Joseph Friedenson, editor of *Dos Yiddishe Vort*, was the general secretary of the Agudath Israel organization which was established in post-war Germany by the liberated Jewish refugees, and is a member of the editorial board of *The Jewish Observer*.

Dr. Bernard Fryshman, associate professor of Physics at the New York Institute of Technology and executive director of the Association of Advanced Rabbinical and Talmudical Schools, is a frequent contributor to *The Jewish Observer*.

Rabbi Mordechai Gifter, Rosh Yeshivah of Telshe in Wickliffe, Ohio, is a member of the Moetzes Gedolei HaTorah (Council of Torah Sages) of Agudath Israel of America.

Rabbi Hillel Goldberg is editor of The Intermountain Jewish News in Denver, and author of *Rabbi Israel Salanter: Text, Structure, Idea*.

Aaron Hish, a musmach of an American Yeshivah, lives in Brooklyn.

Rabbi Yitzchak Hutner, זצ״ל (5664/1904 — 5741/1980), Rosh Yeshivah of Yeshivah Rabbi Chaim Berlin-Kollel Gur Arye, was a member of the Moetzes Gedolei HaTorah of Agudath Israel of America.

Rabbi Yaakov Jacobs is a former editor of *The Jewish Observer* whose essays often appear in various Jewish journals.

Rabbi Aharon Jeruchem is a prominent Talmudic scholar who came to America in 1940 from Vienna, where he was the Rabbi of the famed Ahavas Torah Schul. Among his publications are a study on *Rambam, Lo Sishkach* (in Yiddish) and *World Lost* (in English).

Rabbi Yaakov Kamenetzky, Rosh Yeshivah of Mesivta Torah Vodaath, is a senior member of the Moetzes Gedolei HaTorah of Agudath Israel of America.

Rabbi Mendel Kaufman is Rabbi of the Young Israel of Briarwood (Queens, NY) and is assistant principal of the Beth Jacob High School of Yeshivah Rabbi S.R. Hirsch (NYC).

Abraham Krakowski, a Holocaust survivor, was a student of various European yeshivos, and is currently engaged in business in the United States.

Dr. Gershon Kranzler, author of a number of children's classics on Jewish themes, as well as "Williamsburg" — a sociological study, was a Hebrew Day School principal for twenty years. He is a professor of sociology in Towson State College and Johns Hopkins University, Baltimore.

Asher Lazar is an Israeli Journalist, whose writings have appeared in *Digleinu* and other periodicals.

Rabbi Yehoshua Leiman of Brooklyn, is editor of *The Light* and a well-known lecturer, writer, and translator.

Rabbi Meir Simcha HaKohein זצ״ל (5603/1843 — 5686/1926), Rav of Dvinsk, Latvia, was an outstanding Torah scholar and communal leader during the first quarter of this century. His *Ohr Someach* on *Rambam* and *Meshech Chachma* on Torah are key works in their field.

Mrs. Sorah Mermelstein lives in Lakewood, NJ, where her husband is member of the Kollel of Beth Medrash Govoha. Her father, subject of her article in this volume, is a well-known Rosh Yeshivah.

Rabbi Avrohom Pam, Rosh Yeshivah of Mesivta Torah Vodaath, in Brooklyn, is a member of the Moetzes Gedolei HaTorah of Agudath Israel of America.

Rabbi Yaakov Perlow, the Novominsker Rebbe, heads the Yeshivas Novominsk Kol Yehuda, in Brooklyn.

Moshe Prager ז״ל (died, Tishrei 5745/September 1984), a distinguished Israeli journalist and historian, was editor of the Hebrew-language *Beth Jacob Journal*, and wrote widely on the Holocaust.

Rabbi Yisroel Saperstein, formerly a member of the Kollel of Yeshivas Mir in Brooklyn, resides in Monsey, NY.

Rabbi A. Scheiman, an American-born member of a Kollel in Jerusalem, is a frequent contributor to *The Jewish Observer.*

Rabbi Nosson Scherman is co-editor of ArtScroll-Mesorah; edits *Olomeinu*, Torah Umesorah's magazine for children; and is a member of the editorial board of *The Jewish Observer.*

Rabbi Elkanah Schwartz, rabbi of Congregation Kol Israel in Brooklyn, is author of numerous articles and short stories.

Rabbi Chaim Shapiro, a resident of Baltimore, lived in Europe before and during World War II. He is author of a major portion of the ArtScroll Judaiscope Publication, *The Torah World.*

Rabbi Moshe Sherer is president of Agudath Israel of America; chairman of the World Agudah Organization; and a member of the editorial board of *The Jewish Observer.*

Rabbi Yisroel Spira, Bluzhever Rebbe, is a member of the Moetzes Gedolei HaTorah of Agudath Israel of America.

Rabbi Elya Svei, Rosh Yeshivah of the Talmudical Yeshivah of Philadelphia, is a member of the Moetzes Gedolei HaTorah of Agudath Israel of America.

Rabbi Hanoch Teller, a lecturer at various seminaries in Jerusalem, is author of *Once Upon a Soul* and *Soul Survivor*, collections of his essays and stories.

Rabbi Yaakov Weinberg is a Rosh Yeshivah in Yeshivas Ner Yisrael in Baltimore.

Rabbi Avrohom Wolf זצ״ל was the founding dean of the Beth Jacob Teachers Seminary of Bnei Brak. A number of his essays on Torah thought were published in *Hatekufah Ubayoseha.*

Rabbi Nisson Wolpin is editor of *The Jewish Observer*, as well as this and the other volumes of the ArtScroll Judaiscope Series.

The essays in this volume are based on lectures and articles presented over a period of thirty years. Note should be taken of the date of the initial appearance of each essay, as indicated in a footnote on its first page. In some cases, however, the phraseology has been updated (e.g., "two decades ago" has been changed to "four decades ago") to reflect the passage of time. Some themes and anecdotes are cited by several authors; they are left as originally presented to preserve the integrity of each essay. All of the chapters of this book appeared in *The Jewish Observer,* the monthly journal of thought and opinion published by Agudath Israel of America. Dr. Ernst L. Bodenheimer serves as chairman of the magazine's editorial board; Rabbi Nisson Wolpin as editor.

Introduction:
A Call on the Shofar

THE JEW IS history's child. For him, forgetting is tantamount to denying his identity. Not that the Jew lives in the past; he understands himself, today, on the basis of a continuum that stretches from Creation to the ultimate redemption. All events past contribute to his current status, and direct him toward a purposeful future, defining the steps he takes at his every juncture in time.

To be sure, some events in the past loom larger than others. And beyond doubt, no event in recent times rivals the Holocaust in sheer destruction, in challenge to thought and action, in cause for mourning, and in inspiration and hope. Yet, it is not for every interested party or every armchair historian to recall, interpret and teach *Churban Europe*. The Torah, which summons all children of Jewry to "Remember the days of yore," does not stop there. It goes on — "Ask your fathers and they will tell you, your elders and they shall inform you" *(Devarim 32:7)*.

Where others might see a flourishing civilization, the wise men detect ominous clouds darkening the horizon:

> While the assimilated Jews gloried in the cultural renaissance of the Weimar Republic of Germany in the 1920's, the saintly Chofetz Chaim would interrupt his prayers with a fearful cry: "Ten years from now I see a great conflagration burning! The twelve million souls killed in World War I will be child's play by comparison!"

Where some accused Jews of cowardice and passivity — "going like sheep to the slaughter" — others recognized formidable moral strength and courageous obstinancy. And where some saw bravery, others feared for reckless foolhardiness. How is one to know which events to look for and how to interpret them? "Ask your fathers and they will tell you, your elders and they shall inform you."

◆§ The First Step: Across the Abyss

From the vantage point of the 80's, we try to assess what must be studied, and we look across an abyss of close to a half-century: It began with a decade of mounting discrimination in the early Thirties escalating to oppression and arrests, and, as the decade advanced, culminated in torture and in an unprecedented deliberate, scientifically executed design for mass annihilation — a design that was carried out with nightmarish efficiency. The forty years that followed were preoccupied with rebuilding — rebuilding individual lives and, where possible, shattered communities.

But how can one take note of the loss and mourn for it without knowing what has been lost? We must look to the other side of that abyss, to a thousand-year civilization that was destroyed: an ongoing civilization, a continuum that reaches back, through a most prolific and colorful period to earlier times and places. The Poland of 3,000,000 Jews that was wiped out — a Poland that included Warsaw, the world's outstanding Jewish cosmopolis; Lodz, with a deeply rooted *chassidus* of its own; Cracow, still containing the seminary building of Sara Schenirer, while in the older section of the city, one finds reminders of the Rama (Rabbi Moshe Isserlis, 16th century codifier); and Lublin of Reb Meir Shapiro, innovator of the Daf Yomi ... of the 18th century chassidic leader — the *Chozeh* (the "Seer") ... of the 16th century *Maharam* whose glosses are published in the Talmud; and countless villages and hamlets of piety and devotion.

Lithuania, of the saintly Vilna Gaon, whose grave is situated alongside that of the Righteous Convert of Vilna ... Radun, where the legendary Chofetz Chaim taught the world continence in speech ... and Brisk, where Reb Chaim Soloveitchik exemplified the rarest of commodities; pure logic — that same Brisk of Rabbi Yoel Sirkes (the 16th century *Hagaos Habach*), and other towering predecessors.

White Russia and Ukraine of the Baal Shem Tov and his myriad followers; Hungary of the Satmar Rav who battled against false Messiahs, of the Yismach Moshe, chassidic leader of the 1800's ... of the Chasam Sofer, whose definitive halachic decisions guide us to this day ... Rumania of the Vizhnitzer *chassidus*, stretching back to Reb Yaakov Kopel Chassid, who was the *baal tefillah* for the Baal Shem Tov ... the Galicia of Belz, of Bobov, of Bluzhev ...

Frankfurt, in Germany of old: Remember the towering leadership of Rabbi Samson Raphael Hirsch; a century before, the guidance of the *Hafla'ah* in the late 1700's, the *Pnei Yehoshua* in the early years of that century ... journeying back to the Germany of the Baal Shem of Michelstadt; earlier yet, to the depths of the Dark Ages, when Rabbi Meir of Rothenberg illuminated Jewish life with his vivid lessons ... the France of Rashi and the Tosafists, and their noble communities that fell victim to the rampage of the Crusaders.

Our first step, then, would be to scan at least a few peaks in the endless range of towering Torah personalities, each associated with his individual teachings, his classic *seforim*, his G-dliness, his battles for integrity of Judaism, and his legacy in terms of disciples and communities that led up until just the other side of that fifty-year abyss.

Before European soil was drenched with Jewish blood a half a century ago, it was saturated with a thousand years of Jewish piety, scholarship, and spiritual grandeur — from Kobrin on the edge of Siberia to Lisbon on the Portuguese Atlantic ... Once we take stock of this, we can begin to understand the enormity of the loss our nations suffered, beyond the incalculable human tragedy that the Holocaust represents.

~§ The Facts and the Spirit Within Them

Six million of our brethren — our fathers, grandfathers, uncles, aunts and cousins — went to their death. Were the victims guilty of complicity with the perpetrators of this crime against humanity, as the late Hannah Arendt had claimed? Or did the spirit actually triumph, while the dehumanizing Nazis only desecrated the bodies of *Klal Yisrael*?

From where are our children, our colleagues — from where are *we* to get our feeling for what transpired? — from TV specials that humanize the Nazis and romanticize the Americans, allowing all but a few intermarried Jews to slip through the cracks of history, leaving only assimilated victims to represent the six Million? Or will we learn from those who witnessed the transcendental power of the Jewish soul, and saw how the flickering candle of *emunah* stubbornly illuminated that blackest of nights in recent history?

Obviously, the fathers of our people, the elders of our time must be sought out to report, to interpret, to challenge, to inspire, and to direct. Only they can teach us this chapter in our history.

In these pages, we have sought out the rabbis, the *yeshivah* deans, and the teachers of our generation, as well as some from previous generations, to help us approach the Holocaust. Their spoken words have been transcribed, their written words have been studied and translated, their silent acts have been recorded.

The great chronicler of the Holocaust, Moshe Prager, tells of a humble *shamash* (sexton) who smuggled a *shofar* into a death camp, organized a *minyan* on Rosh Hashanah, and blew the *shofar*. The guards came running and decided to make a spectacle of the sexton. They whipped him endlessly, mercilessly, and all the while he continued chanting the prayers out loud: וּבְכֵן צַדִּיקִים יִרְאוּ וְיִשְׂמָחוּ, *The righteous will see and rejoice ... and all wickedness will vanish like smoke, for You will have removed the evil kingdom from the earth.*

That *shamash* blew his *shofar* and dropped it, and it lay in the dust. Our task is to pick up that *shofar* and renew its call to memory, to *teshuvah*, and to redemption. This book is a call on that *shofar*.

Rabbi Benyamin Kamenetzky
Dean, Yeshivah Toras Chaim at South Shore

This publication was made possible through
THE LIFE CENTER FOR HOLOCAUST STUDIES
884 CENTRAL AVENUE
WOODMERE NY 11598
(516) 295-1130

I.
Approaching the Cataclysm

Rabbi Meir Simcha HaCohen of Dvinsk זצ"ל

Translated by Gershon Dubin

Galus: Why are We Destined to Wander?

וְאַף גַּם זֹאת בִּהְיוֹתָם בְּאֶרֶץ אֹיְבֵיהֶם, לֹא מְאַסְתִּים וְלֹא גְעַלְתִּים לְכַלֹּתָם ... כִּי אֲנִי ה' אֱלֹקֵיהֶם.

And even with all that when they will be in the land of their enemies, I will not have degraded them, nor will I have rejected them, to annihilate them ... for I am HASHEM, *their G-d (Vayikra 26:44).*

THE HISTORY of the Jewish People through this current *galus* (exile) is truly awesome. It is a two-millennia chronicle of almost unrelieved suffering due to hostility, oppression, ostracism and eventual exile from lands where only years before Jews had found refuge. Who, at the time of the destruction of the *Beis Hamikdash* and the dispersion of the Jewish People, would have imagined the people to survive over such a long painful period, through so storm tossed a destiny, still loyal to its Divine mission, with its integrity of purpose still intact? Indeed, the mere survival of the Jewish People through two thousand years of cruelty and oppression can of itself provide the clearest evidence of the centrality of *hashgachah* (Divine direction) in the course of history.

Once one accepts Divine guidance of history, however, one can ask, as have so many Jews through the years: *Why have we been made to endure such unparalleled suffering? Is there any purpose in these seemingly endless wanderings?* A key to this puzzle may lie in the pattern this suffering has followed: *Jews arrive in a new land. They and their children gradually prosper*

This essay, translated from *Meshech Chochmah* (published posthumously in 1927), appeared in *The Jewish Observer* of September 1973.

and become important citizens of their adopted country. They organize into communities to build and maintain their own institutions. With the passage of time, they become more deeply involved in the culture of their surroundings. Acclimation leads to assimilation, as the Jew abandons his Divine mission and his hope for spiritual salvation in favor of the seductive glitter of the non-Jewish world. After a time, the host country turns against its Jewish citizenry, and several hundred years after its founding, this Jewish community is completely destroyed by the unleashed wrath of its erstwhile hosts. The survivors, impoverished and broken in spirit, once again return to their Redeemer and with His help escape to a more hospitable country to rebuild in an atmosphere of relative peace — until they are again subjected to harsh treatment.

The Drive for Change

The purpose of this cycle in the ultimate realization of Israel's destiny can best be understood by delving into the causes for each stage in the process. A universal characteristic of every generation is the desire to change and hopefully to improve upon the accomplishments of its predecessors. In the realm of worldly achievement, this can be of greatest value. After all, secular knowledge is the product of human intellect. As such, its theories and conclusions are subject to constant revision with the discovery of the heretofore unknown and its correlation with the already proven. This process of adaptation and revision absorbs the energetic compulsion for change of each succeeding generation. The thirst for newness can always be well met.

By contrast, Torah is G-dly wisdom, and does not have any such allowances for adaptation and revision. Yet before Israel was driven into *galus*, it too enjoyed opportunities for meeting this inherent drive for change in a constructive manner. The thirteen rules of exegesis were open for each *beis din* (religious court) to interpret the Torah in accord with its understanding. The choice to circumvent the law in cases of special need *(hora'as sha'ah)* was a viable power in the hands of our wise men. In addition, the guidance of prophecy and, later, of *ruach hakodesh* (Divine Spirit) prevailed in each generation in accordance with its needs — pinpointing new areas of special concern and concentrated effort.

While the Torah itself remained immutable, its application to the exigencies of the times remained for each generation to determine for itself. There was thus a constant process of renewal and an ever-pervading air of fresh accomplishment.

Once the Jews were driven into *galus*, however, the situation changed radically. The Age of Prophecy had ended with the destruction of the First *Beis Hamikdash*, and the *ruach hakodesh* that prevailed during the Second *Beis Hamikdash* was never since equaled. The concentration of scholars devoted to Torah study, which had characterized both Commonwealths, also remained unmatched. With the dispersion of the Jews in *galus*, the standard of Torah scholarship fell greatly. The result, as the *Rambam* (Maimonides) explains in the introduction to his *Yad Hachazakah*, was that the *beis din* no longer possesses the authority to institute new laws or to re-examine certain old ones. Since this avenue of expression for the need to innovate has been closed, new ones are always sought.

Thus the Cycle

The cycle of Jewish settlement in the *galus* can now be understood. When Jews enter a strange country, they are relatively ignorant of Torah as a result of the distraction caused by the insecurities that plagued them in their old country and their migrations to the new. They then experience a reawakening of the Divine Spirit within them, which impels them to return to Torah. Their Torah scholarship improves gradually until it peaks at an unusually high level — a level that nonetheless falls short of the attainments of earlier scholars. At this point the new generation does not conceive of any opportunities for progress. How can they possibly add to the accomplishment of earlier generations? So the need for change expresses itself in criticism of the status quo. This in turn leads to eventual denial of the worth and substance of their ancestral heritage. The Jew of this final generation abandons his religion and national identity in favor of the mores of his adopted country. He thinks of Berlin as his Jerusalem and learns to behave in a manner typical of the lower elements of the host society. A storm of destruction follows which uproots him and deposits him in a distant land, where the language and customs are unknown to him, his ears still echoing with the pejorative: *Jew! Who made you into a personage?* This brings him to the realization that his adopted culture and language in truth were foreign to him, and that his essence is that he is a Jew. His intrinsic "culture" is the Torah, his language is *lashon hakodesh* (the holy tongue, Hebrew) and his sources of comfort are the prophecies of the *Nevi'ei Hashem* (God's prophets). Any attractions other than these are to be regarded at most as temporary coverings to be shed when they present any conflict to the way of life ordained by the Torah ... This has been the pattern of Jewish existence over the centuries.

And this is the meaning of G-d's words of comfort:

"*I will not have degraded them*" — referring to the low level of achievement in Torah and Jewish consciousness.

"*[nor] will I have rejected them*" — referring to the expulsions and forced wanderings from land to land ...

"*to annihilate them*" — to the degree that they should completely abandon Torah and reject their heritage ...

"*for I am Hashem, their G-d*" — My bond with them is never annulled.

The degradation and rejection are not wanton, nor are they ever consummated. They are carefully modulated measures of maintaining the Jews' awareness of their special relationship with "*I, Hashem their G-d.*" Not *despite* wanderings and sufferings, but *because* of them, does the Jewish People remain alive.

Rabbi Yaakov Kamenetzky

The Redeeming Features of "Galus Awareness"

קוֹל דּוֹדִי הִנֵּה זֶה בָּא, מְדַלֵּג עַל הֶהָרִים, מְקַפֵּץ עַל הַגְּבָעוֹת.
The voice of my beloved, behold it comes, leaping over mountains, skipping over hills (Shir HaShirim 2:8).

AS WE CONTINUE TO endure our millennia-long *galus*, is it best to shut this condition out of our consciousness, or are there benefits to be gained from a deep-felt realization of our estrangement from the ideal status of being at peace in our own land, under the open protection of G-d's love and concern?

"Leaping over mountains," says the Talmud, refers to the merit of the *Avos* (Patriarchs) of our People, while "skipping over hills" refers to the merit of the Matriarchs *(Rosh Hashanah)*. In their merit, the *galus* in Egypt was shortened from four hundred years to two hundred and ten.

Why, then, does Scripture continue to refer to "the four hundred years of *galus*," beginning the count from the birth of Yitzchak, instead of from Yaakov's entry into Egypt? If the length of the *galus* was indeed reduced, the duration should correctly be recorded as two hundred and ten years. On the other hand, if *galus* actually did begin with Yitzchak's birth, why does the Talmud credit the merit of the *Avos* with shortening the *galus*?

The key to these questions lies in understanding the purpose of *galus*, and its fulfillment, which is dependent upon how the people suffering *galus* perceive their situation. If they are aware of their status as strangers, alienated from their life source, they need no further oppression to remind them of their being in *galus*.

This essay, based on an address at the 62nd national convention of Agudath Israel of America, appeared in *The Jewish Observer* of February 1985.

Thus, there was no need for the physical enslavement of the Jewish people in Egypt to begin until all of the twelve *Shevatim* (Yaakov's sons) had died. As long as any one of them was alive, they recognized that merely being in Egypt constituted *galus*. After their passing, however, the successor generation was not as sensitive as the *Shevatim* had been, and because of their complacency and sense of comfort in Egypt, they required some degree of oppression, so that they, too, could realize that Egypt is *galus*.

✥ Yitzchak's Heightened Awareness

When *Chazal* (the Rabbis of the Talmud) tell us that the count of four hundred years of *galus* begins from the birth of Yitzchak, that is because Yitzchak had a deep awareness of his *galus* status. For instance, when his wealth grew, it aroused the envy of the Philistines, who told him: "Leave us, you are far more powerful than we are" (*Bereishis* 26: 16). Thus, instead of becoming complacent from his successes, he became more aware that he was not "at home," even in the Holy Land. "Leaping over the mountains," then, refers to the towering spirituality of the *Avos*, which equipped them to recognize that they were, indeed, in *galus* when others would not have realized it.

Morai verabosai! I have, in my lifetime, lived during three distinct epochs: Torah in its glory during the years prior to the First World War; the years from World War I through the Second World War, which witnessed the progressive decline and near destruction of the dominion of the Torah in Jewish life; and the current war until the advent of *Moshiach* (the Messiah), when the primacy of Torah is mounting once again ... when the Torah institutions both in America and in *Eretz Yisrael* are blossoming, and people estranged from Judaism are finding their way back.

The forty years since the destruction of Europe have indeed been years of growth for *Yiddishkeit* (Judaism), but even as we witness continued advances, we must never lose our awareness that we are in *galus*. For if we fail to recognize it, Divine Providence has ways of reminding us of this even as we engage in rebuilding Torah institutions and communities, for only in this way will we merit our speedy redemption.

Rabbi Eliyahu Eliezer Dessler צז״ל
adapted by Rabbi Yehoshua Leiman

The Loss of Europe's Torah Centers: A Lesson for Our Generation

THE WAYS OF Providence are beyond our comprehension: we know only that His ways are just. Nevertheless, we must study those ways to determine what duties they may teach us. In this light, we will examine the subjects of *galus* (exile) and *churban* (destruction) to determine what obligations the events of our own epoch impose upon us.

Why did G-d permit the destructions of Torah centers and allow Torah scholars and teachers of Torah to be ruthlessly murdered? This severely lowered the spiritual level of our generation. Why then did it happen? It is clear that physical pain and the tribulations of *galus* expiate our sins; but what purpose can there be in the destruction of our spiritual resources? Rabbi Moshe Chaim Luzatto poses a similar problem.

> We know that all Hakadosh Baruch Hu does to the Jewish People is for their benefit. Yet how can it be beneficial ... when the nations of the world do not allow them to study Torah, as in those places where the Inquisition banned the study of Talmud? (*Igros Ramchal* 50)

He explains that this punishment comes to offset the sin of idolatrous thinking: the mere thought of serving any force other than *Hashem*. On this subject, Yechezkeil (14:5) prophesied, "to

---

This essay, adapted from the Hebrew original which was published in the Bais Yaakov Journal (Teves 5722), appeared in *The Jewish Observer* of September 1968.

bring Israel to repent the sins of its heart," and our Sages taught (Kiddushin 39b) that merely thinking of worshiping other forces is considered an actual deed.

Since the sin of idolatrous thought is an internal sin, for the very thought is a sin, so must its expiation — by the principle of *midah k'neged midah* (measure for measure, i.e., the punishment must be appropriate for the sin) — be internal, with no help at all from his environment. For example: a man finds himself in a sound spiritual society where everyone is bound to spirituality and labors at it. If a person in such an environment is drawn to spirituality, it is possible that his behavior is superficial, for it is motivated by external forces — the influence of his environment — and does not originate in the depths of his heart. While in the course of time he may rise to the level where his actions are internally motivated, this takes a great deal of effort and travail.

But if a person lives in an environment where he is forbidden to learn Torah, where our enemies rule over Torah, where the entire environment is hostile to spirituality, and there he rises to spirituality and faith in *Hashem* and in His Torah, that person's faith and service are clearly internally motivated. Only such internally motivated service of *Hashem* can expiate internally motivated sin.

⇨ The Value of Internally Motivated Service

Internally motivated service of *Hashem* has unique value: it not only makes no use of external forces, but the person so motivated stands in opposition to the external environment. The value of such inner spirituality is inconceivable to anyone who has not experienced it. This explains the words of our Sages:

"The vision of Ovadyahu: This is what Hashem said to Edom ..." Why was Ovadyahu chosen for Edom? [As he offered no other prophecies, why was he chosen for this prophecy over other prophets?] Rav Yitzchak said: Hakadosh Baruch Hu reasoned: Let Ovadyahu, who lived with two wicked people [Achav and Izevvel], and did not adopt any of their ways, prophesy about Eisav, who lived with two righteous people [Yitzchak and Rivkah] and did not adopt any of their ways.

(Sanhedrin 39b, brackets are from Rashi)

Ovadyahu was raised and trained in an environment dominated by two great evildoers, Achav and Izevvel, and did not adopt any of their ways. As a result, he knew at first hand the greatness of internally motivated spirituality in opposition to its external environment, and could fully fathom the depths of Eisav's degradation and the enormity of his wickedness in living with two saintly people, yet not learning any of their ways but turning to evil — in opposition to his environment. This qualified him to prophesy Eisav's end and the extent of his punishment.

He who allowed himself to be drawn into evil despite a sound environment has only one remedy; he can amend his sins only in the same manner as he transgressed. In other words, he must confront an evil, materialistic environment and yet cling to good. For only then will his penance be genuine and of sufficient weight to offset his sin.

The destruction of a spiritual environment as punishment for the entire nation is a subject spoken of by the Prophets and elaborated by our Sages:

> And the L-rd said: Because this people sought to approach Me with their mouth and honored Me with their lips, yet was his heart far from Me, and fear of Me was at the order of men who taught them how to look pious: therefore, I will shock this people with one shock after another; the knowledge of its scholars will be lost and the comprehension of its wise will be hidden (Yeshayahu 29:13-14).

And our Sages comment:

> Hakadosh Baruch Hu considers the removal of the righteous worse than the ninety-eight curses and the destruction of the Beis Hamikdash. Of the curses it is written, "Hashem will shock you with punishments," while of the removal of the righteous it is written," one shock after another." And why is "shock"repeated here? Because "the knowledge of its scholars will be lost."
>
> (Eichah Rabbah 1:7).

The sin Yeshayahu warns about is the fulfillment of Torah and the observance of *mitzvos* (commandments) not for their own sake — lip service; acting for various external ends such as wealth and honor, or simply out of habit, without a thought for the sake of Heaven. And the removal of the righteous is a punishment for their having *"honored Me with their lips."*

❧ What Purpose in the Punishment

But this poses several questions: Did our Sages not say: "From acting *shelo lishmah* (not for the sake of Heaven), one will ultimately act *lishmah* (for the sake of Heaven)?" Why should the people then be punished? Would their lip service not ultimately bring them to heart service? And why so severe a punishment — "worse than the ninety-eight curses"? And what purpose can this punishment serve? Once the righteous are gone, their generation, bereft of leadership, will find itself even more in the dark. How will the people's failure to serve for *Hashem's* sake be amended?

Let us first analyze the spiritual situation of our generation. The Gaon of Vilna writes that the generation in which *Moshiach* comes will be externally motivated: a generation whose ideologies are superficial. This refers to their sins as well as to their worthy acts. The generation's sins will not result from analytical or philosophical heresy as in previous generations, but from an exaggerated desire for their material comfort, and from a general desire to throw off all discipline: *Eat and drink for tomorrow we die*. Similarly the good deeds of that generation will suffer from superficiality; they will be motivated by the external force of a sound spiritual environment. Great efforts will be required to rise beyond the external nature of things spiritual and to experience their internal nature.

It is axiomatic that Providence grants the aid and abilities needed for the achievement of spirituality to each generation according to its level. And it would then follow that our generation, the generation in which *Moshiach* will surely come, needs secondary — not-for-the-sake-of-Heaven — aids: that the *ben Torah*, the *lamdan* (learned man), and whoever it is who strives for spirituality, be respected; that he be elevated by the masses in order to survive spiritually and to strengthen the generation's spirituality. Yet, amazingly, we see the opposite prevailing. The value and the honor of the Torah and of the fear of *Hashem* are debased and the not-for-the-sake-of-Heaven attitude, always so much a part of spirituality, is far less in this generation than in previous ones. Why?

I have elsewhere explained (*Michtav Me'Eliyahu*, Volume I, pp.24-29) that since the sole purpose of *lishmah* is to help a person achieve *lishmah*, there is great danger that this generation, motivated by external factors and mired in materialism, will remain satisfied with the element of *lishmah* in spiritual matters, and will never attain *lishmah*. Therefore *lishmah*, the environment conducive to spiritual advancement, was taken from us, for its sole value is as a conduit to *lishmah*.

The truth is that the normal way to advance spiritually is

with the aid of *lishmah*, using external aids, to attain *lishmah*, internality. This is the way of spirituality: to first grasp at even the externals of spiritual matters and then, by constant effort, to achieve internality — clinging to *Hashem*. And so from step to step till one reaches the level of internal unity.

The *rav* who teaches his student provides him with the means to discover his own internality. Once the *rav* has transmitted the *"You are to know this day,"* it is the pupil's function to fulfill *"and take it to your heart" (Devarim 4:39)* — i.e., to place the words deep into his heart and to make them a part of his internality. Yet, should the student be content with having a great *rav*, with being in the atmosphere of a Torah environment, and thus ignore his internal needs — so that all his Torah and service remains external, superficial, and habitual aspects of *"the order of men who taught them how to look pious"* — then there can be no solution other than: *"The knowledge of its scholars will be lost and the comprehension of its wise will be hidden."*

✥§ A Generation Excluded from Graduation

There are generations — ours among them — whose situation precludes step-by-step advancement from externality to internality for the reason given above: there is the danger that instead of advancing from externality to internality, they will sink into externality, and never attain *lishmah*. In this case there is no alternative but to proceed as the physician who advises a dangerously ill man to undergo surgery, even though the surgery itself endangers his life. Given no other option, surgery must be risked. The same is true in spiritual matters. It becomes mandatory to perform an extremely dangerous operation: the removal of aids to spirituality, the removal of spiritual guides and influences, and the destruction of a sound, stimulating environment, for they are only means for the attainment of spirituality. The hazardous operation of removing the righteous who aid and support *Hashem's* service had to be undertaken. And now there is hope that whoever labors under his own power to achieve internality, his heart will be truly close to *Hashem* and his fear of Him will be pure and not simple habit.

The same is true for the burning of *Sifrei Torah* (Torah scrolls), outlawing of Torah learning, and the destruction of societies that fostered sanctity, purity, Torah, and fear of Heaven. Of course a tremendous decline in the generation's spirituality results. But those individuals who hear *Hashem's* call, who are privileged to turn their hearts heavenward despite the great and awesome darkness when the entire external environment of Torah is rocked and destroyed, who confront the great and awesome challenge not to be goaded on by the *yetzer hara* (evil inclination) that demands that one question *Hashem's* ways,* but to strengthen one's faith in Providence — these are the men of pure internality, pure without a single stain of externality.

⚜ So Far from Purity

This idea is of ever greater concern in our generation: an external generation — the generation preceding the coming of *Moshiach*.

We are far from the internal values of belief and faith, untainted fear of Heaven, purity of heart, and love of others. Yet we perceive with our own eyes that the *lishmah* of the honor accorded Torah has been diminished, and that the guidance of a great *rav* and a spiritual environment have been diminished. Every place in Europe where Torah blossomed has been destroyed. The Torah giants are gone: masses of Torah students and Torah sages sanctified *Hashem* in death. Can one help seeing that our generation has undergone a hazardous "operation," that the possibilities for internal advancement through external means have been minimized? How great is the danger to us if we do not now seek the means of arousing our hearts' internality to cling to *Hashem* — by constant devotion to the study of His Torah; by devotion to His service through prayer and *mitzvos*. For without this service — what will be our end?

The great leaders of past generations taught us the critical need for the study of the heart's service: prayer, *mussar* (ethics) and *chassidus*. Now we lesser people have almost no one to advise us how to serve, how to earn merit. So we must labor, and must begin internal service by setting aside fixed hours for the study of the heart's service. For the dangers are very great, and without internal service there is no hope. May *Hashem* aid us and open our hearts to serve Him in truth.

---

* As witness the well-known admonition of Rav Elchonon Wasserman הי"ד when he and his students were about to be killed by the Nazis. He told them to be careful to let no impure thought spoil the sacrifice each of them was to be for all Jewry. See p. 32.

Rabbi Avrohom Wolf צ״ל
adapted by Rabbi Nosson Scherman

... Questions Without Answers ...
Faith without Questions ...

THE WOUND OF THE HOLOCAUST — the loss of six million Jews — cannot easily heal. But even after some of the pain has been numbed by the passage of time, gnawing questions continue to hover over us like a dark shadow. They are most difficult questions, and they do not ever seem to leave us:

Why did the Holocaust happen? How could a Merciful G-d have allowed it to happen? What can justify the brutality inflicted upon the Six Million?

These questions are posed from two different sources. Some use them as a basis for challenging the existence of a Divine hand in history. Or as a canard against those whose trust is in the Torah and its leadership. Or as a fulcrum for tilting confidence in favor of secular-oriented "activists" over the leadership typified by the presumed "passivists" of the previous generation.

To questioners such as these we owe no explanations. Their questions are not questions, but answers — justifications for all they choose to do and all they elect not to do. Their decision to abandon their religious heritage is the cause of their questioning, not the result.

Others ask these same questions in fullest sincerity, seeking enlightenment while still maintaining loyalty to their Torah heritage. In truth, one might say to them that the best we can do is to remain silent. *Who are we that we may question the Divine plan, that we may seek to probe the Divine intelligence?* Since we have no answers, why open up discussion in the first place? Yet

---

This essay, adapted from *Hatekufah Ubayoseha*, appeared in *The Jewish Observer* of September 1973.

we *cannot* remain silent, for to do so would be to allow foes of Torah to ensnare the uninformed with rhetoric and irresponsible insinuation.

For guidance in formulating any kind of understanding we must turn to the best source, the great contemporary Torah giants and those of the recent past: the self-sacrificing *Roshei Hayeshivah* and chassidic *Rebbaiim*, who had deleted "personal comfort" from their vocabularies. Having made note of the irreparable loss of the Holocaust, they went on to build new homes for Torah and raise new legions to carry the banner of Judaism. Their response and comment can provide us with a scenario for our own reaction.

৩১ The Reaction of our Greatest: Triumph — even in Death

Throughout our history, Torah leaders have taught us more than the Law; they taught how to face life — and death — too. The Holocaust period revealed countless people of whom the heavens could exclaim, "You are fortunate, Avraham, Yitzchak, and Yaakov, that such grandchildren descended from you." It was almost impossible to escape the destruction, but there were those who *could* have escaped and refused the opportunity because they felt they had no right to forsake their people in the time of greatest need — men like Rabbi Menachem Ziemba of Warsaw, Reb Elchonon Wasserman of Baranovich, and Rabbi Yosef Carlebach of Hamburg.

There were others who had no choice, but who died gloriously and inspired hundreds to face the end with Jewish pride and repentance. One was Reb Avrohom Grodzenski, *Mashgiach* (dean) of the *yeshivah* in Slobodka. Toward the end, he and Reb Elchonon Wasserman, together with their students, were in the same ghetto. The execution date had arrived and they spent their last hours together. Rabbi Grodzenski asked Rabbi Wasserman to deliver a Talmudic discourse on *Kiddush Hashem*, the commandment to sanctify G-d's Name in death. Rabbi Wasserman was surprised at first, but he acceded to the request. When he was finished, Rabbi Grodzenski delivered his last *mussar* discourse, and the group surrendered their souls from a spiritual summit far above Nazi ability to profane.

Reb Elchonon Wasserman's last moments have been recorded by an eyewitness, Rabbi Ephraim Oschry of New York:

> *In the heavens they seem to consider us great tzaddikim* (righteous men). *It seems that we have been chosen to atone*

for our brethren. If so, we must repent, sincerely and fully ... We must realize that our sacrifice will be a more perfect one if we hallow ourselves. In that way we will save the lives of our brothers in America ...

He continued until the end. He belonged fully to his students — and to his brothers in America and everywhere else. He could not even spare a moment for a last farewell to his beloved son, Naftali.

The chassidic Rabbi, Reb Klonymos Kalmish Shapiro of Piachena, was one of the powerful spiritual forces of the Warsaw Ghetto. He exemplified the type of courage that is so often overlooked by those who are fond of describing Jewish reaction to Hitler in terms of passivity and resignation.

There is a courage that is different from that exemplified by militants and freedom fighters. And it is deeper, too. It is the kind that was displayed by people like Reb Klonymos Kalmish who would not allow the Hun to dehumanize and de-Judaize them. He trained his disciples in the ways of spiritual strength that would sustain them to the death. He wrote a *sefer* (book) made up of the Torah discourses he delivered during the ghetto years, and buried it just before the extermination; it was found and published several years ago under the apt title *Holy Fire*. During Purim 1941, he told his disciples that the *Zohar* likens Purim to Yom Kippur because, just as a Jew must fast on Yom Kippur whether he likes it or not, so must he rejoice on Purim even if there is nothing to be happy about!

In a similar vein, the grand rabbi, Reb Shlomo of Slonim, looked for a way to dance on a Purim when he was a prisoner in a concentration camp. He challenged his Nazi guards to a dancing contest. They showed their prowess. Then the rabbi danced as though he were in another world, singing the Purim song: "*Shekol kovecho lo yevoshu* ... those who place their hopes in You will never be shamed and humiliated."

Perhaps the most amazing incident of all involves Rabbi Aharon Rokeach, the late Belzer Rebbe. When he was told that the last known survivor of his immediate family, his oldest son Reb Moshe, had been thrown into a burning synagogue and gone to a fiery death, the Rebbe exclaimed, "The Creator in His mercy has allowed me to share in the sacrifices of my people!"

Conventional wisdom sees the Nazi era as a horrible aberration of history — a nation gone berserk without rhyme or reason. Our giants of the spirit did not see it that way at all. They remained strong until the end no matter what the horrors and provocations. Their loyalty to G-d did not waver, because they saw His Hand everywhere, whether or not they understood the reason It smote. They saw no accident; only Divine judgment — so they accepted it.

Ten Years Before

Ten years before World War II — in 1929 — someone commented to the Chofetz Chaim on the tragedy of World War I, when twelve million people across the world had lost their lives. Hitler was still four years away from power; genocide was a term that could be found only in dust-covered unabridged dictionaries. And the Chofetz Chaim said, "Twelve million? That is child's play! The real thing will begin in ten years."

"What can we do in ten years?" asked his guest.

"*Eretz Yisrael* — there, it will be safe."

The Chofetz Chaim explained with a parable. Two villages shared in the cost of a fire engine. It was stationed in one of them, but if a fire broke out in the other village, the fire engine would come speeding to the rescue. Once a fire broke out and the apparatus was called. The answer was, "We can't come now. *Our village is burning. As soon as the fire is put out here, we will come to help you.*" In the same way, in ten years the fires will be burning everywhere. G-d will see to it that it is safe in *Eretz Yisrael*, because that is His village.

Military historians are indeed at a loss to explain why Rommel, most brilliant of military leaders, conqueror of Egypt and Libya, did not swoop down on *Eretz Yisrael* as it lay helpless before him. The Chofetz Chaim foretold why: "*G-d will see to it that it is safe in Eretz Yisrael, because that is His village.*"

The Chofetz Chaim's questioner was astounded. "That means that our generation will see a miracle! Why are we worthy of it?"

"*Hashem* will be testing us," was the answer.

No, our greatest saw no accidents in history. *History is G-d's tool, not His master.*

In the Aftermath: What Are We to Do Now?

In the aftermath, too, the faces of Torah leaders were fixed toward the future. The Holocaust was not a starting point for recrimination and hopelessness. Rebuilding the world of Torah was of greater importance than philosophizing on the theology of destruction. Of course there were looks backward, as well, but only to identify the seeds of destruction so that they would not again take root. Lesser men could consecrate themselves to deciphering the reason why; the truly great ones echoed the Chazon Ish. Upon being questioned on the reasons for the Holocaust, he responded:

> Can someone blithely dismiss a difficult Tosefos if he can barely translate a Mishnah? The layman might be infuriated when he sees a tailor cutting good material; he is simply too ignorant to understand that the tailor is making a new garment. It is true that we are too small and puny to understand the ways of G-d, but we must recognize that even history's most incomprehensible and barbaric eras are but a part of the Divine plan. Could we but see the complete design, we would understand each of its parts.

The worst of the Nazi fury was visited upon Polish Jewry; over ninety-five percent was wiped out. Yet soon after Victory in Europe in 1945, its greatest surviving leader, the Gerrer Rebbe — old, sick, alive only through miracles — wrote to his followers in America and Europe:

> Nation of G-d, be strong despite the suffering and be confident that He will be good to us. In the worst of days, look ahead to better times that once were and that will be again. We must hope that good times will come from now on.
>
> The main thing is to know that just as the curses of the Torah come to pass, so too its blessings and consolations will be fulfilled, as Rabbi Akiva remarked when he saw the ruins of the Beis Hamikdash. G-d is testing us by concealing His Divine Presence from us; He will reward us for withstanding this difficult test. Have faith in G-d and strengthen your Torah study and prayer. Then G-d will surely give you strength.

The Gerrer Rebbe did not offer philosophical speculation. He ordered a positive way of life just as a rabbi will decide a question of concrete halachic application. His letters made no attempt to answer the question: *"Why did it happen?"* Instead he was concerned with: *"What are we to do now?"*

◆§ The "Why" of the Holocaust

But the "Why?" remains a haunting question. The Talmud says that a wise man is superior to a prophet and, indeed, some wise men in the prewar period saw thunderclouds forming in the Jewish sky. And their origin was Berlin — not Hitler's Berlin, but Mendelssohn's Berlin.

The Maggid of Kelm said, "*Because of this sin of Geiger's Reform Code of Jewish Law, another law will emerge from Germany. It will say that every Jew, without exception, must die. May G-d protect us!*"

Reb Chaim Ozer Grodzenski of Vilna wrote:

> Faith in G-d has weakened in our time. Reform began in Western Europe and its influence has spread eastward. Our nation has suffered increasing persecutions, but instead of learning our lesson and returning to Torah, the irreligious are growing in number and audacity. As they refuse to repent, our suffering increases. And people wonder that this is our lot!

Twenty years before the war, the Rabbi of Dvinsk, Reb Meir Simcha Hacohen, wrote a most illuminating commentary on the lengthy catalog of Divine punishment in the twenty-sixth chapter of *Vayikra*. His prescience is awe inspiring as he draws a pattern of Jewish history. His presentation deserves detailed study.*
Among other things, he says:

> Modern man thinks that Berlin is Jerusalem, but the fierce storm of destruction will emanate from Berlin and leave but a scant remnant. The survivors will disperse to other countries and Torah will strike new roots and young scholars will produce undreamed-of accomplishments.

Others, such as Reb Dovid, the chassidic Rebbe of Chortkov, and Rabbi Yoel Teitelbaum, the Satmar Rav, looked beyond Berlin. They saw Jewish secular-nationalism and Zionism. In seeking to be "like all the nations," these ideologies have corrupted the ideal that must set the Jewish nation apart. We are *not* like the nations. We were different at our conception and we are required to remain different lest we forfeit our right to exist. It might be comforting to our latent chauvinistic instincts to hear the State of Israel described as the world's third military superpower, but we dare not delude ourselves into believing that we were granted nationhood by G-d and "chosen" to demonstrate superiority in the military and political arenas.

---

* *A translation of the full piece appears as the first essay in this volume.*

≈§ "Entirely beyond Human Comprehension"

But these are only attempts to find a glimmer of understanding in the events of *Churban* Europe. Each of these Torah luminaries gained an insight and shared it with us; would that we could learn from them. But no one can pretend that we know all the reasons or have anything even approaching a total understanding of what and why. In conclusion, the words of Maimonides always should be kept uppermost in our minds. They are quoted by *Tosefos Yom Tov* at the end of Tractate *Berachos*:

The time for Divine retribution comes: G-d devises ways to provoke men to violate the Torah so that the ensuing punishment is understood to be deserved. This is so deep and complex a concept that it is entirely beyond human comprehension. The Scriptures bear witness that the Divine mind is as far above ours as heaven from earth. All His ways are just and His justice is completely proper.

Rabbi Yitzchak Hutner צ"ל
prepared for publication by
Rabbi Chaim Feuerman and Rabbi Yaakov Feitman

"Holocaust"

A Rosh Yeshivah's Response

◆§ The Questions

(1) Is the term שׁוֹאָה, *Shoah*, (lit. Holocaust) acceptable in describing the *Churban*, the destruction of European Jewry during World War II?

(2) Should the Holocaust be taught separately, as many schools are now doing or planning to do, or should it be incorporated into the regular Jewish History courses and taught as part of the studies on this particular time period?

(3) If the latter, where indeed does the Holocaust "fit in" with the rest of Jewish history?

◆§ The Response

In order to determine the appropriateness of any term, one must first thoroughly understand what one is trying to define. Therefore, before we attempt to designate a name for the

---

In response to a request for guidance in establishing criteria for a Holocaust curriculum in *yeshivos* and day schools, Rav Hutner delivered a *shiur* (discourse) to a gathering of approximately one hundred *menahelim* (principals and educational administrators). The *shiur* focused both on specific questions raised by the *menahelim* and on significant aspects of the *Churban* that were hitherto either little known or studiously avoided. When the above authorized English rendition of Rav Hutner's *shiur* first appeared in *The Jewish Observer* in October 1977, it inspired a large volume of letters, questioning and challenging, much in the manner of the traditional oral *shiur*. In January 1978, these were published, followed by a *chazarah* — an in-depth analysis and review of the original *shiur*, with some expanded clarifications, prepared by Rabbi Yaakov Feitman. Some excerpts of the *chazarah* are presented here in the form of numbered footnotes.

shattering events of 1939-1945, we must examine the significance of those events in their historical context. For our present purpose of identification only, we shall refer to the term "Holocaust" only when we discuss the Nazi destruction of European Jewry during World War II. As we shall see, this in no way signifies the acceptability of this term.

It should be made clear at the outset that we shall not merely discuss history this evening. Our orientation toward Jewish history must reflect an attitude toward *kedushah* — approaching that which is most holy and sacred. This sanctity stems from the fact that "יִשְׂרָאֵל וְאוֹרַיְיתָא חַד הוּא" — *the Jewish people and the Torah are one*" (Zohar, Acharei Mos 73), thus intimately relating the proper study of Jewish history with the study of Torah. Yet, unfortunately, just as in the study of Torah itself we are familiar with the phenomenon of "מְגַלֶּה פָּנִים בַּתּוֹרָה שֶׁלֹּא בַּהֲלָכָה" — *those who distort and misinterpret the meaning of the Torah*" (see *Avos* 3:11), so is there an even more subtle danger from those who distort the meaning of Jewish history. It will be our task this evening to untangle the web of distortions about recent Jewish history, which has already been woven, and uncover the Torah perspective which has been hidden from us.

To be sure, it will not be easy to regain this perspective. The thoughts that we will explore this evening will be difficult to digest because of our long subsistence upon the forced diet of public opinion. The creators of the powerful force of public opinion are beyond the realm of our control and the mind-numbing results of their influence are largely out of our hands. In order to achieve any hold upon the truth, we will first have to free ourselves from the ironclad grip of their puissance and open our minds and hearts to the sometimes bitter pill of truth.

⊷ The Origins of the Term

As in all quests for the truth, we must return to origins. The term *Shoah* was coined by the founders of *Yad Vashem* in Jerusalem, since they were convinced that the tragedy of European Jewry was so unique in its proportions and dimensions that no previous phrase could encompass its meaning. Undoubtedly, to a certain degree they were correct, for indeed the destruction of hundreds of thousands of Jewish communities *was* unique in its proportions and dimensions. Yet, by singling out the quantitative differences of this particular *Churban*, those who sought a new terminology for these events missed the essence of their uniqueness. It is not just the proportions and dimensions of the Holocaust which define its quintessence, but its establishment of a new and significant pattern in Jewish history. At the same time it must be stressed that this pattern, far from coincidental, is intricately related to the basic pattern of Jewish history itself and profoundly affects our entire vision of recent history and indeed current events.[1]

By placing the Holocaust in its historical perspective, we shall uncover two new directions in recent Jewish history with reference to the gentile persecution of Jews. Whereas our entire history has been replete with various instances of persecution by different civilizations, empires and nations — varying only in intensity, means and ferocity — recent history has shifted dramatically in two new areas.

The Era of Disappointment

The first of these epochal changes involves the shift from generations of gentile mistreatment of Jews, which, if unwelcome, was nevertheless expected and indeed announced by our oppressors, to an era where promises of equality were made and then broken, rights were granted and then revoked, benevolence was anticipated, only to be crushed by cruel malevolence.

This change in our historical pattern, although it has hitherto gone largely unnoticed, is nevertheless a seminal movement in our progress toward *Acharis HaYomim* (the End of Days), the

---

1. To place something into a larger context is not to remove its uniqueness. Every major historical event has a character of its own, yet, as the article explains, it must belong to the pattern as well. Many note that the *Churban* Europe was singular in that it was the only time a complete apparatus was designed and put into motion whose sole purpose was a Haman-like: לַהֲרוֹג וּלְאַבֵּד לְהַשְׁמִיד — total destruction of a nation from young to old; men, women, and children. Surely this is the determining factor in assigning a "character" to the events of World War II. Where else had centuries-old communities been so totally decimated that they could never be rebuilt again!

At the same time, a careful reading shows that the *Rosh Yeshivah* has dealt with this aspect of *Churban* Europe, carefully placing it in its *tochachah* context. Only here does the Torah mention the terrifying punishment of becoming consumed by our enemies. This reference is to the words וְהָיָה לֶאֱכֹל — "and they will become consumed" — which is the direct follow-up to "fall prey to the lure of strange nations and trust in them." Such a dire prediction, as we must realize today, exactly corresponds to *Churban* Europe down to the most literal meaning of those awesome words הָיָה לֶאֱכֹל, as survivors have painfully attested. Thus, in its execution, this *Churban* was unique because of the extent and mechanics of its destruction. However, to dwell on this point, in seeking to plumb the depths of the *Churban's* meaning for us, is to settle for a shallow exploration when there are miles of unfathomed churning waters to probe.

inevitable culmination of history in absolute redemption.

The recent examples of these disappointments may be readily brought to mind, and indeed some are yet fresh with the pain of unfulfilled anticipation:

— The French Revolution, in that first eighteenth-century burst of dedication to equality and freedom, had granted equal rights to Jews *as citizens*, although nothing to Jews *as Jews*. The Treaty of Versailles had gone even further and granted rights to minorities *as minorities*, including Jews *as Jews*. Of course, these promises were later nullified or retracted, and heard from no more.

— In Russia, too, Lenin signed in 1917 the Soviet Minority Rights Law, granting a kind of Jewish self-government in the form of a Jewish soviet. This, too, was soon abolished in the 1920's by Stalin, dashing those bright hopes that had been kindled.

— England, too, entered the twentieth century by granting and then revoking a promise made to Jews in the form of the Balfour Declaration. In November 1917, Jews danced in the streets because Britain had declared that "His Majesty's Government views with favor the establishment in Palestine of a national home for the Jewish people." The declaration was accepted at the Conference of San Remo in 1920; yet, by June 1922, Winston Churchill, the British Colonial secretary, was qualifying that the declaration did not mean the "imposition of a Jewish nationality upon the inhabitants as a whole, but the further development of the existing Jewish community." Of course, a long and bitter period followed where a British hand held the gun of the age-old oppressor of Israel.

Thus it becomes clear that the trend of anti-Jewish phenomena of the first half of the twentieth century was characterized, not so much by persecutions and pogroms as in the past, but by the legalized retraction of existing laws granting sundry privileges. Although these reversals are dramatic and telling enough of themselves, they pale in the face of the retractions and total turnabouts made by the Germans in the 1920's and 30's.

— On March 11, 1812, Prince Karl August von Hardenberg had issued his famous edict emancipating Prussian Jews, but a century later, in 1919, as a supplement to the German translation of the so-called *Protocols of the Elders of Zion*, Gottfried Zur Beek (Ludwig Miller) used Hardenberg's definition of a Jew in drafting proposals for anti-Jewish legislation. These proposals culminated in 1935 in the so-called "Nuremberg Laws" which legitimized anti-Semitism and legalized anti-Jewish bigotry. These *Rassengesetze*, which forbade marriage between Germans and Jews and disenfranchised non-Aryans, exactly paralleled earlier rights and privileges legally granted to Jews. Thus the cycle was diabolically complete. What had been given legally was equally as legally taken away, leaving the Jewish people with a growing and ultimately inexorable disillusionment with the promises and even legal enactments of the gentile world.*

Let us restate clearly the pattern we have discovered in recent Jewish history: Jews have always been beaten by gentiles; only the means and instruments of torment have varied. The innovation of recent times has been that for long periods Jews were deluded into trust in the gentiles by a series of laws and regulations in their behalf, only to have that trust shattered by the rescission of those very laws. This historical period culminated in the Holocaust, the largest-scale annihilation of a people in history, yet resulting not from lawless hordes but flowing directly from legalized and formal governmental edicts. The end result of this period for the Jewish psyche was a significant — indeed, crucial — one. From trust in the gentile world, the Jewish nation was cruelly brought to a repudiation of that trust. In a relatively short historical period, disappointment in the non-Jewish world was deeply imprinted upon the Jewish soul.[2]

---

* Of course many works have been devoted solely to the German anti-Jewish legislation which preceded and legalized the murder that was to follow. An idea of the vastness of the literature may be gotten from the fact that *Die Gesetzgebung Adolf Hitlers* (Hitler's Legislation) takes up thirty-three volumes (ed. Werner Hoche, 1933-39). As early as May 27, 1924, the Nazis introduced a motion to "place all members of the Jewish race under special legislation (*sonderrecht*)." And from then on, every bit of terror perpetrated against the Jews was, with German thoroughness, preceded by meticulously worded legislation. It is perhaps significant that where anti-Jewish violence broke out in German streets before laws had been enacted to that effect, Wilhelm Frick, Minister of the Interior, and Reichsbank President Hjalmar Schact condemned and ordered a stop to the "illegal actions" (see Lucy S. Dawidowicz's *The War Against the Jews*, New York: Bantam Books edition, 1976, p. 83).

---

2. It has been pointed out that there have been periods of disappointment in erstwhile benevolent gentiles, long before the *Churban* Europe epoch. Pharaoh, Cyrus and others have been mentioned. However, as in many aspects of Jewish history, a distinction must be made between Biblical and post-Biblical times.

From the time of the close of Scriptures until the 1930's, no such comprehensive retraction of previously granted rights had ever taken place. Of course, individual monarchs had, for their own personal gain, temporarily

◆§ Torah Source for the New Era

As we delve more deeply into the Torah view of these awesome events, we shall find that they certainly are not coincidental, but reflect the greater cosmic plan of the Creator of the universe. If we find in world history an era where Jews move from the expectation of persecution by gentiles to a period of disappointment in those very people, this change must be reflected in the Torah. As we said earlier, since the Jewish people and the Torah are one, what happens in one must have a counterpart in the other. Therefore, let us study together the passage where this monumental turn of events is reflected:

וַיֹּאמֶר ה׳ אֶל מֹשֶׁה, הִנְּךָ שֹׁכֵב עִם אֲבֹתֶיךָ, וְקָם הָעָם הַזֶּה וְזָנָה אַחֲרֵי אֱלֹהֵי נֵכַר הָאָרֶץ ... וְהִסְתַּרְתִּי פָנַי מֵהֶם, וְהָיָה לֶאֱכֹל, וּמְצָאֻהוּ רָעוֹת רַבּוֹת וְצָרוֹת; וְאָמַר בַּיּוֹם הַהוּא, הֲלֹא עַל כִּי אֵין אֱלֹקַי בְּקִרְבִּי מְצָאוּנִי הָרָעוֹת הָאֵלֶּה.

> *And Hashem said to Moshe: "Behold you will soon pass on and this nation will arise and fall prey to the lure of strange nations and trust in them ... And I will hide My face from them, and they will become as food [for their enemies], and great evils and troubles will come upon them; then shall they declare: 'It is because my G-d has not been in my midst that these evils have befallen me'" (Devarim 31:16-17).*

We must first establish what is meant by the phrase אֱלֹהֵי נֵכַר הָאָרֶץ. It should be noted that we translated it as "the lure of strange nations and trust in them," and not as the "worship of strange gods." This interpretation follows *Onkelos*, who translates טַעֲוַת עַמְמֵי אַרְעָא, literally "the temptation of the nations." This translation, rather than the more obvious one of "idol worship," reflects the sense of the passage, for we know (*Yoma* 69b) that the *yeitzer hara* for idolatry has long been eliminated by the *Anshei Knesses Hagedolah* (the Men of the Great Assembly). We can only appreciate the gravity of the sin of straying after "the lure of strange nations" when we realize that only here does the Torah mention the terrifying punishment of becoming consumed by our enemies. Even the *tochachos* — the

---

granted certain privileges to Jews and later revoked them. But the total pattern of official, legislated rights being eradicated by formal legislation, as discussed in detail in the article, is a phenomenon uniquely epitomized by Nazi Germany.

portions of the Torah where G-d rebukes His nation for its sins and warns of the terrible consequences of evil — do not allude to such a dire punishment. The "great evils and troubles" which are the direct result of trusting and relying upon the gentile world signify the impetus for the next immediate stage in Jewish history, a unique point in the *teshuvah*-repentance process: *Then shall they declare: it is because my G-d has not been in my midst that these evils have befallen me.*[3]

✑ The First Steps Toward Teshuvah

When we now carefully study the Torah passages quoted, we will be struck by the Jews' response to the "great evils and troubles" which befell them. We know that the *viduy* — enumeration of sins — associated with true repentance necessitates the declaration that "I have sinned" in addition to the specifics of the transgression. Here, there seems to be *teshuvah* (repentance); yet, no real admission of wrongdoing has been made. In effect, what we encounter in this passage, unique in the Torah, is a kind of *teshuvah*/non-*teshuvah*, a leaning toward *teshuvah*, yet not quite reaching the point of *teshuvah gemurah*, the complete penitence required by the Torah.

The *Ramban*, in his explication of this passage, grants us the key to this paradox. He explains that it reflects the very first stirrings of *teshuvah* in its nascency. The lowest rung of evil is the disavowal of wrongdoing. Thus, as *Ramban* quotes, "Behold I do judgment with you for saying 'I have not sinned' " (*Yirmiyahu* 2:35), because this is the total rejection of guilt. We know that the essence of *teshuvah* is *viduy*, admission of wrongdoing and enumeration of sins. Yet, the prophet proclaims that punishment

---

3. There are two forms of idolatry: following the gods of strange nations and falling prey to the lure of those nations themselves. We learn from the *Targum* upon the words אֱלֹהֵי נֵכַר הָאָרֶץ which is: טָעֲוַת עַמְמֵי אַרְעָא, that in *Chumash*, what might be taken to be pure idol worship אֱלֹהֵי נֵכַר הָאָרֶץ — in truth refers to the temptation to follow the ways of the nation itself.

Not elaborated upon in the article is the fact that this *Targum* translation is not limited to this passage in *Vayeilech*. The *Targum* in general, except for the phrase אֱלֹהִים אֲחֵרִים in the Ten Commandments, is טָעֲוַת עַמְמֵי אַרְעָא. Thus, the significance of the *Targum* and the *Rosh Yeshivah's* interpretation hold true throughout. The phrase in the article, "reflects the sense of the passage," was used only because the wider ramifications of this *Targum* were not under discussion.

Why indeed is the *Targum* different in the Ten Commandments? The *Rosh Yeshivah* discussed this publicly on another occasion (one evening in the *succah*). The essence of his talk at that time was that since the terrible decree of *galus* was not given until after the occurrence of the *Meraglim* — the spies who

will not come because one has not said, "I have sinned," but because — infinitely worse — one has declared, "I have not sinned." Once the repudiation of innocence has been accomplished, the *teshuvah* process has begun. Even if one has not yet arrived at the positive point of *viduy*, the implicit significance of no longer claiming innocence is that the road to repentance has been cleared and one is ready for formal acceptance of guilt and positive commitment of the future. This, then, is a stage of *teshuvah*, a kind of *teshuvah*-readiness that *Knesses Yisrael* will reach in future days before it achieves total repentance.

This stage of *teshuvah* will come about as a direct result of the "great evils and troubles" which — as we interpreted according to *Onkelos* — come upon them because of their trust in the nations. The effect of the great calamities of those days, far from merely being a punishment for wrongdoing, will be to correct the previously misplaced trust and prepare the way for true *teshuvah*. As we have seen, the "great evils and troubles" did indeed come upon us from those very gentile nations who had gained our confidence and trust.

Thus, there is revealed to us both the chronology and the impetus for the *teshuvah* of *Acharis HaYamim* (the End of Days). The very first step will be reached by *Klal Yisrael* through their very repudiation of their earlier infatuations with gentile ways. In our terms, this is when the Jewish people move toward repentance because of disappointment in the gentiles. This can only come about through promises rescinded, rights revoked, and anticipations aborted. The pain and anguish at the time of these shattered illusions is all too real and tragic; yet the events themselves serve to bring us to the recognition that "it is because

---

misled *Klal Yisrael* concerning the Land of Israel — which was a direct outgrowth of the shattering of the *Luchos* (Tablets of Law), we must distinguish between two completely separate times in Jewish history. At the moment of the giving of the *Luchos*, there was not yet a decree of exile upon the Jewish people. When the Jews heard the first two of the Ten Commandments, they were not yet destined for *galus*. Therefore, the *Targum* on אֱלֹהִים אֲחֵרִים could not refer to the *galus* phenomena and was an exhortation against paganism itself. Only later with the pronouncement that the Jewish people would be "strewn among the nations" (see *Tehillim* 106:23-27) that the decree of Exile came directly from the sin of the *Meraglim*) did the danger of "following the lure of the nations" become an actual threat. Therefore, only in translating the Ten Commandments themselves does the *Targum* refer to literal idol worship. From the moment those first unique *Luchos* lay shattered, our history took a different turn and our concerns became involved with assimilation among people rather than the trepidation of falling into idol worship.

my G-d has not been in my midst that these evils have befallen me." This the *Ramban* sees as the necessary prerequisite to the final step of *teshuvah* when "they will add to their earlier regret the complete confession and total penitence."

✥ Children of the Violators

Our new understanding of the essence of our era allows us some comprehension of the phenomenon of our "age of *baalei teshuvah* (returnees to Judaism)." It has oft been noted that *teshuvah* seems to "be in the air," and indeed the many movements currently succeeding to an unprecedented degree in bringing Jews closer to Judaism are but a reflection of the fact that the very climate is permeated with a kind of *teshuvah*-readiness. This climate is the result of the disappointment in gentiles, which demolished the first stumbling-block to *teshuvah*, and forced the recognition that "it is because my G-d has not been in my midst" that the awesome events of recent times have occurred. Of course, this is not to say that each individual *baal teshuvah* has experienced a personal disappointment in gentiles. There are characteristics and trends common to an entire epoch that eventually affect each individual in his own way.

I had occasion to elaborate on this point when by a combination of circumstances I found myself in *Eretz Yisrael*, in the company of a group of extreme leftists on Ben-Gurion's *yahrzeit*. I was asked to say a few words in honor of the day and felt it worthwhile to relate the following to them:

> Ben-Gurion often used to tell people that now was not the proper time to resolve the controversy between the religious and the anti-religious. When opportunities arose for resolving such issues, he made sure they were tabled until a future time. Undoubtedly, his reasoning — conscious or subconscious — was that time was on the side of the secularists. The experience of Ben-Gurion's generation was that the number of observant Jews was steadily decreasing, and a Judaism empty of Torah seemed on the ascent.
>
> In so calculating, Ben-Gurion made a grave error. In that group of leftists, there were representatives of many prewar cities from various types of Jewish communities all over Europe. I asked each of the assembled in turn, "Do you recall a *mechalal Shabbos* — a non-observant Jew — in your city who had a son who became *Shomer Shabbos*?" Each of them answered with the same emphatic "No." Yet, I pointed

out to them, today there are thousands of *baalei teshuvah* whose parents knew virtually nothing of their faith. Ben-Gurion in his time seemed to be correct, but he could only calculate chronological time and knew nothing of the eschatological movement of generations. The era of disappointment tore a generation from the clutches of the טָעֲוַת עַמְמֵי אַרְעָא (*Targum* for אֱלֹהֵי נֵכַר הָאָרֶץ) *and prepared the way for an era of true teshuvah.*

So much for the first new direction in Jewish history in relation to gentile persecutions.

∗§ Public Opinion vs. Truth

Before we explore the second of the new directions in detail, it is important to establish a clear distinction between any common approach to world events and *daas Torah*, a Torah view of the world. "Public opinion" and any but the Torah approach is by definition colored by outside forces, subjective considerations and the falsehood of secular perspective.

An example of how public opinion can be molded — indeed, warped — at the whim of powerful individuals can be taken from a study of Russian history textbooks published during the respective reigns of Lenin, Stalin and Khrushchev. During each period, the textbooks hail the then-current leader to the exclusion of all his predecessors as the savior of Russia and hero of his people. Undoubtedly, "public opinion" during each period, once children's minds had been suitably molded, reflected the thinking and wishes of the state. While more subtle in form, this ability to direct public opinion exists in democratic countries as well. Thus, we already pointed out at the beginning that we must make every effort to free ourselves from the powerful grip of public opinion, and must be ever on our guard that our opinions of the true nature of world events be shaped only by Torah views seen through Torah eyes.

Sadly, even in our own circles, the model for shaping public opinion lies in the hands of the State of Israel. An appropriate example of this dangerous process of selectively "rewriting" history may be found in the extraordinary purging from the public record of all evidence of the culpability of the forerunners of the State in the tragedy of European Jewry, and the substitution in its place of factors inconsequential to the calamity which ultimately occurred.

To cover its own contribution to the final catastrophic

events, those of the State in a position to influence public opinion circulated the notorious canard that *Gedolei Yisrael* were responsible for the destruction of many communities because they did not urge emigration. This charge is, of course, a gross distortion of the truth, and need not be granted more dignity than it deserves by issuing a formal refutation. However, at the same time as the State made certain to include this charge as historical fact in every account of the war years, it successfully sought to omit any mention of its own contribution to the then-impending tragedy. What the State omitted in its own version of history is the second of the above-mentioned new directions in recent Jewish history. It is that phenomenon which we must now examine.

East and West Meet

For centuries, indeed millennia, gentile persecution of Jews took one of two forms, but the two never worked simultaneously. Either Jewry had to contend with the *Yishmael* nations of the East or was persecuted and expelled by the nations of the West. Never in our history did the nations of the Occident join forces with those of the East for the purpose of destroying Jews.

With World War II, this long epoch was brought to a crude and malevolent close. In 1923 Hitler wrote *Mein Kampf* spelling out his belief that the Jewish people should be wiped out. This was read by Haj Amin el-Husseinu, the Grand Mufti of Jerusalem, who joined with Hitler to found one of the most significant alliances of modern times. There is ample documentation that not only did the Mufti visit Hitler and his top aides on a number of occasions, but indeed with Adolph Eichmann he visited the Auschwitz gas chamber incognito to check on its efficiency.*

The extent of the Mufti's influence upon the Nazi forces may be seen in a crucial decision made by Hitler at the height of the war. Railroad trains were much in demand by the Axis, and Hitler's troops badly needed reinforcements in Russia. Yet, soon after he landed in Berlin in November 1941, the Mufti demanded that all available resources be used to annihilate Jews. The choice:

---

* Detailed documentation of the Mufti's activities may be found in Simon Wiesenthal's *Grand Mufti — Agent Extraordinary of the Axis* (who relates that Haj Amin also visited Majdanek); Maurice Pearlman's *Mufti of Jerusalem*; and, most recently (1965), Joseph B. Schechtman's *The Mufti and the Fuehrer* (translator's note, Y.F.).

Juden nach Auschwitz or *Soldaten nach Stalingrad* was to be resolved his way ... Two months later (January 20, 1942) at the Wannsee Conference, the formal decision was made to annihilate all Jews who had survived the ghettos, forced labor, starvation, and disease.[4]

Of course, the Mufti was serving his own perverted fears, which were the influx of millions of Jews into Palestine and the destruction of the Mufti's personal empire. Yet, there can be no doubt that through their symbiotic relationship, Hitler and the Mufti each helped the other accomplish his own evil goal. Eichmann simply wanted to kill Jews; the Mufti wanted to make sure they never reached Palestine. In the end, the "Final Solution" was the same ... At one point, Eichmann even seemed to blame the Mufti for the entire extermination plan, when he declared, "I am a personal friend of the Grand Mufti. We have promised that no European Jew would enter Palestine any more."*

The Mufti's First Step

The Mufti's trip to Berlin was the first ominous step in the joining of the anti-Jews of the East with those of the West to accomplish their diabolic design. This second of the new directions in Jewish history reached a climax of sorts in 1975 when Yassir Arafat, avowed destroyer of the State of Israel, stood before the United Nations, and received a standing ovation by nations of East and West alike.

From the purely secular historical standpoint, there is no connection between the two directions we have discussed. The Moslem world never granted privileges that it later retracted, and

---

* Quoted by Pearlman, pp. 71-72 and Schechtman, p. 158.

4. Questions have been raised concerning the Mufti's actual influence upon the Nazis and the degree of his power even among the Arabs. First of all, the article in no way exonerates, by one iota, the culpability of the Germans themselves. The Nazis surely needed no instructions in anti-Semitism nor outside motivation for their evil plans.

Even had the "Final Solution" been implemented without the Mufti's urging, however, there can be no question that in a war which was being inexorably won by the Allies, precious time was lost by the Mufti's machinations behind the scenes to speed up the murderous process. As to the Mufti's influence among the Arabs in the 1930's and early 1940's, a glance at almost any page of Schechtman's or Pearlman's books will be eye opening. As to his prestige among the British, it is enough to quote the British Secretary for the Colonies, who announced at the St. James Conference of February 7, 1939, concerning a thorny issue, "I shall have to consult my Mufti — the Prime Minister" (Schechtman, p. 89).

thus never disappointed the Jews in its midst. What, then, joins the two trends which seem to have coincided so significantly in our generation? A passage from the Torah can give us the answer:

וַיֵּלֶךְ עֵשָׂו אֶל יִשְׁמָעֵאל, וַיִּקַּח אֶת מַחֲלַת בַּת יִשְׁמָעֵאל בֶּן אַבְרָהָם אֲחוֹת נְבָיוֹת עַל נָשָׁיו לוֹ לְאִשָּׁה.

> *And Eisav went unto Yishmael and took Machlas the daughter of Yishmael, Avraham's son, the sister of Nevayos, in addition to his other wives, for a wife (Bereishis 28:9).*

Since the actions of the Patriarchs are a sign of what would happen later to the children and every action in *Chumash* is eternally significant, we may learn from this passage that it was inevitable for the forces of Eisav and Yishmael to combine. We are now living in the midst of that pivotal moment in Jewish history.

It should be manifest, however, that until the great public pressures for the establishment of a Jewish State, the Mufti had no interest in the Jews of Warsaw, Budapest, or Vilna. Once the Jews of Europe became a threat to the Mufti because of their imminent influx into the Holy Land, the Mufti in turn became for them the מַלְאַךְ הַמָּוֶת, the incarnation of the Angel of Death. Years ago, it was still easy to find old residents of Yerushalayim who remembered the cordial relations they had maintained with the Mufti in the years before the impending creation of a Jewish State. Once the looming reality of the State of Israel was before him, the Mufti spared no effort at influencing Hitler to murder as many Jews as possible in the shortest amount of time. This shameful episode, where the founders and early leaders of the State were clearly a factor in the destruction of many Jews, has been completely suppressed and expunged from the record. Thus it is that our children who study the history of that turbulent era are taught the fabrication that *Gedolei Yisrael* share responsibility for the destruction of European Jewry and learn nothing of the guilt of others who are now enshrined as heroes.[5]

---

5. It is painful to be confronted by the accusation of Zionist leaders that our Rabbinical leaders of the previous generation were contributing factors in trapping European Jewry in the Hitler-purgatory in which they perished. They claim that these Torah giants, the selfless leaders of *Klal Yisrael*, counseled their followers not to abandon their homes and traditional surroundings.

Rabbi Hutner has pointed out that, unpleasant as it may be, this is merely an illustration of the pernicious molding of public opinion by those upon whose

✡ Coming to Terms

We may now return to the original questions. "Is the term *Shoah* acceptable?" The answer is CLEARLY NOT. The word *Shoah* in Hebrew, like "Holocaust" in English, implies an isolated catastrophe, unrelated to anything before or after it, such as an earthquake or tidal wave. As we have seen, this approach is far from the Torah view of Jewish history. The *Churban* of European Jewry is an integral part of our history and we dare not isolate and deprive it of the monumental significance it has for us.

In truth, the isolation of one part of Jewish history from another, the separation of one part of Torah from another, has caused much of the inability to deal with events such as *Churban Europe*. Much of our education has been permeated with the "sunny side of Judaism," resulting from cowardice and failure of will to deal with the misfortunes of *Klal Yisrael*. Yet, here is one of the sources of our uniqueness. We are happy to teach our children of our "chosenness" in *mitzvos* and our closeness to G-d. Yet, at our peril, we ignore the fact that there are three different portions of *tochachah*, rebuke and promise of punishment in the Torah *(Bechukosai, Ki Savo,* and *Nitzavim-Vayeilech)*. We must learn these parts of the Torah with our children as well as the "sunnier" portions. These portions must become as much a part of the Jewish psyche as the *mitzvos* we strain so hard to imbue. Thus, when a Jewish child — or indeed, adult — hears for the first time of *Yiddishe tzaros* (the suffering of the Jewish People), he will not be shocked by a contradiction to what he has learned, but will see the living proof of the Torah he has absorbed.

---

shoulders a causal relationship to the Hitler-cataclysm has recently been documented, who then found themselves in a position to poison Jewish minds and hearts by indicting our great Rabbinical figures.

Should one ask why we suddenly seem so preoccupied with the causes of this latest catastrophe in Jewish history, and concerning earlier ones (such as Chmelnitzky's pogroms of *Tach V'Tat* — 1648) we offer no such causal relationships, the answer is simple. The *Rosh Yeshivah's* discourse was in no way an exercise in seeking to *place* blame, but to *remove* it from those who deserve better from us. Concerning the terrible events of *Tach V'Tat*, it has never dawned upon a single Jewish mind and is unthinkable to place blame at the doorstep of the *Shach*, the *Taz*, or other *gedolim* of that period. Suddenly, in the twentieth century, it has become fashionable to blame the true Torah *manhigim* (leaders) of the age. This is unprecedented in Jewish history. Never before was the Jewish mind poisoned with distrust of his *gedolim*, thus undermining the entire time-honored edifice of "ask your elders and they will tell you."

Some have commented that there seems to be a lack of *ahavas Yisrael* (love for

Thus we have exposed graphically the mistake of the founders of *Yad Vashem* who felt compelled to find a new term for the destruction of European Jewry because of its proportions and dimensions. Ironically, the artificially contrived term they finally applied empties the *Churban* of its profound meaning and significance. In appropriating a term that signifies isolation and detachment from history, they did not realize that the significance of the Holocaust is precisely in its intricate relationship with what will come after. The pattern of Jewish history throughout the ages is חוּרְבָּן גָּלוּת גְאוּלָה, *Destruction*, *Exile*, *Redemption*, and no event requires new categories or definition.[6] The answers to questions 2 and 3 are therefore obvious and need no further elaboration.

---

the Jewish people) displayed in the article. To be sure, they are correct. For those for whom *ahavas Yisrael* is identified with equanimity towards the undercutting of *kavod gedolim* (honor of great men), the criticism is quite fitting. However, they should be aware that the discourse was not meant for them in the first place.

It should be added that nowhere is there mention of terms such as "punishment" or "guilt" in discussing the trend of trusting in the gentile world until that trust was forever shattered. Of course, there does exist a causal relationship here but not one of sin-retribution. A simple example may be taken from the beginning of the Book of *Shemos*. The Jewish people multiply and fruitfully bear many children, and Pharaoh responds by torturing them with even more arduous labors. A number of levels may be seen to be operating simultaneously. The fact that the Jews are fulfilling the *mitzvah* of "be fruitful and multiply" is a direct cause of Pharaoh's treacherous new work orders. Although there is an obvious cause-and-effect at work here, surely the enslavement is not a punishment for the immediate cause, the fruitfulness ... Cause and effect, yes; sin and punishment, no.

6. Like human beings, words have a יִחוּס בְּרִיךְ — a history, a source, and indeed a genealogy. As stated, the word to be substituted for *Churban* — be it "Holocaust," "Shoah" or whatever else — is less important than the fact that the secular establishment (through the agency of *Yad Vashem*) sought a substitute at all. For millennia, Jewish children have grown up knowing of the *Churban Beis Hamikdash*, *Churban Yerusholayim*, *Churban Betar*, among others. Imbued with the concept of *Churban* as an integral part of Jewish history, they were not shaken in their *emunah* — their faith — if they learned of a new *Churban*.

However, the term *Shoah*, which was not coined in the time-forged mint of Torah experience, confronted a new generation with a psychologically devastating quandary. Not only were post-World War II Jews faced with an overwhelming tragedy and destruction; those who interpret events by redefining them denied the survivors the consolation of being part of a historical continuum by removing these links from the eternal chain, banishing them to the purgatory of free fall. Symptomatic of this attitude is the convening of a special day as *Yom Hashoah* rather than marking the tragic era along with other national tragedies on *Tishah B'Av*.

Indeed, once the historical pattern was broken, the ground was ready for the insidious seeds of unbelief, blasphemy and "alternatives" to the Torah view. By contrast, "*Churban*" is rooted in that holy terrain where suffering and tragedy lead to *geulah*, redemption.

✍ Tochachah vs. Specific Guilt

It should be needless to say at this point that since the *Churban* of European Jewry was a *tochachah* phenomenon, an enactment of the admonishment and rebuke which *Klal Yisrael* carries upon its shoulders as an integral part of being the *Am Hanivchar*, G-d's chosen ones, we have no right to interpret these events as any kind of *specific punishment for specific sins*. The *tochachah* is a built-in aspect of the character of *Klal Yisrael* until *Moshiach* comes and it is visited upon *Klal Yisrael* at the Creator's will and for reasons known and comprehensible *only to Him*. One would have to be a prophet or a Talmudic sage to claim knowledge of the specific reasons for what befell us; anyone on a lesser plane claiming to do so tramples in vain upon the bodies of the *kedoshim* who died *al Kiddush Hashem* and misuses the power to interpret and understand Jewish history.[7]

For other reasons, too, one must be careful of sudden and popular "awakenings" to different aspects of Jewish history, such as "Holocaust Studies." Nachum Goldmann, head of the only international secular Jewish organization not directly

---

7. Perhaps the most basic question in the post-*Churban* Europe era is "What does it mean for us?" From those whose *emunah* is less than totally secure, we receive answers from the extreme of radicals who have created a post-Auschwitz theology — that belief in G-d is no longer possible — to those who claim to have grappled courageously with the "problem" and concluded that it is meaningless to us. From yet others, whose *emunah* is such that they can leave no event untouched by detailed interpretation, we receive specific, painful correlations between sin and punishment: this for that, tit for tat.

As the *Rosh Yeshivah* states, not only is the former unacceptable, so is the latter. While every individual is permitted, even required, to search his personal actions in time of trouble [אִם רוֹאֶה אָדָם שֶׁיִּסּוּרִין בָּאִין עָלָיו, יְפַשְׁפֵּשׁ בְּמַעֲשָׂיו, *If one experiences travail, he should search his deeds (Berachos 5)*] to ascertain the cause of the Divine displeasure, this concerns each person's relationship with his own soul and his Creator. No mandate has been given any human being in today's times (the era of prophecy and Talmudic sages being over) to recognize, interpret and draw matching lines between sin and punishment.

The ways of Divine retribution are mysterious and operate across gulfs of time and space. To claim to have the keys to such esoteric knowledge is to assert an omniscience which no one can claim today. An example of the inscrutable paths of sin and its consequences is the tragedy of the *asarah harugei malchus* — the Ten Great Sages who perished horrendous martyrs' deaths at the hands of the Roman government (see *Eichah Rabbah* 2:2 and *Sotah* 48b). Our Sages (*Tanchuma Yashan, Vayeishev* 2; *Yalkut Mishlei* 929) reveal to us that the death of the Ten was an atonement for the ten sons of Yaakov who participated in the sale of Yoseif. Imagine the possible perversions in understanding the Divine Will if anyone attempted to attribute the deaths of Rabbi Akiva, Rabbi Chanina ben Tradyon and their holy colleagues to specific sins and transgressions, when in reality the Ten Martyrs were deemed by G-d as being *worthy enough* to atone

subservient to the Jewish State, has stated that the weakening of sympathy for the State was the result of a lengthy period of time after the Holocaust having passed and the resultant forgetting by the world at large. Undoubtedly, the State, taking advantage of the arbitrary figure of thirty years, seeks to reawaken interest in what it now termed the *Shoah* to regain some of that lost sympathy of the late 40's and 50's.

This aspect of the current widespread interest in the World War II years should only serve to alert us once more to the often duplicitous sources of public opinion. Of course, this in no way impugns the motives of those who have genuinely dedicated themselves to the study of that epochal time, especially the *she'eiris hapleitah* who feel the scars on their own bodies and who cry out in pain to the world not to forget. It does, however, give us an idea of the tremendous pitfalls on the road to a clear understanding of the true patterns of Jewish history. Only through a rededication to sole use of the Torah as guide through the byways of history will we be sure to arrive at the truth we all seek.

---

for those giants of *kedushah*, the שִׁבְטֵי קָהּ, the sons of Yaakov! We, too, dare not set ourselves up as arbiters of the Creator's mysterious ways in dealing with His creatures.

Jewry's status as a special child to our Creator exists across the barriers of time and space, as does his Father, who conducts His affairs with the infinite wisdom which only He possesses. Thus, for *ourselves*, each of us can seize the moment and awaken his own motivation for repentance and self-improvement. For *them* — who, like the Ten Marytrs, died the deaths of holy sacrifices — we can say nothing but *Kaddish* and *Yizkor*. About them, we dare say no more than: "May their memories be a blessing."

Rabbi Mordechai Gifter

A Path Through the Ashes:

Some Thoughts on Teaching the Holocaust

◆§ "Emunah" and the Historical Continuum

PRECEPTS OF JEWISH THOUGHT are closely tied to everyday realities. The individual Jew can strengthen his *emunah* and *bitachon* (belief and trust in G-d) through the daily occurrences that befall him. Primary means for the transmission of fundamental principles in *emunah*, however, have been left undeveloped. Jewish history is such an uncharted field. Secular sources have been permitted to tread this land with familiarity and to interpret it with an assumed authority from their own perspective, while we have defaulted. We read their writings, accept their "facts," and in the process unconsciously become products of their outlooks. It is precisely in this field of Jewish history that a non-Torah orientation can be the most detrimental to Jewish thought.

We do, indeed, have an approach of our own: In *Parshas Ha'azinu*, the Torah gives us guide lines for the viewing and understanding of history from a true perspective: זְכֹר יְמוֹת עוֹלָם בִּינוּ שְׁנוֹת דֹּר וָדֹר, *Remember days of yore, understand the years of every generation (Devarim* 32:7). If one wishes to comprehend an event in history, one cannot look at it in the limited scope of the finite here and now; rather, one must understand the event as having a place in the historical continuum. A historical occurrence extends itself beyond the isolation of time and space, and reaches towards the past and the future, to acquire true significance. But one must invariably begin with Creation and the

---

This essay, based on an address delivered at a conference of *yeshivah* teachers — sponsored by Torah Umesorah — appeared in *The Jewish Observer* of June 1974.

Creator. As the *Vilna Gaon* explained, to understand "the years of every generation," one must first "remember the days of yore" — the Six Days of Creation. For in those days lies the complete plan of the development of the universe and humankind in it. This, the *Gaon* taught, is the only way to understand history.

Secular sources view history in perspectives of their own, predicated on economic, social, and political principles. By contrast, the Torah directs us to view history as the unfolding of the Divine plan: History is the metamorphosis of man through the stages of destruction and redemption, continuing toward his final redemption in the days of *Moshiach*. And all such events, the redemptions and the destructions, are perceived as fundamental testimony to the presence of G-d in this world, and are understood as experiential units in *hashgachah peratis*, the active force of the Hand of G-d.

Children of the Holocaust

Redemption and destruction — familiar themes in Jewish history, and we, too, know them well. We, today, are all children of the Holocaust. Some have lived through it and some were born afterward. But all of us are deeply affected by it. Yet, the Holocaust has been left untapped as a resource in the teaching and imbuing of *emunah* in the hearts of those who came after it.

We are one generation removed, and this awesome occurrence somehow slipped out of the consciousness of most people. People forget, either due to preoccupation with daily matters, or because of inability to view the Holocaust in its true perspective and to reconcile it within themselves.

We are late in dealing with the Holocaust. *Chazal* explain the corrosive effect time has on the experiential quality of an occurrence. A *midrash* on *Megillas Eichah* (the Prophet Yirmiyahu's Lamentations on the destruction of the *Beis Hamikdash*) comments on the verse: *Hashem destroyed without mercy*. *Chazal* say that a hundred years after the *Churban* (destruction of the Second *Beis HaMikdash*), Rabbi Yochanan was able to explain this verse in sixty different ways, whereas *Rabbeinu Hakadosh* R' Yehudah HaNasi who lived one generation before him, was able to explain it in twenty-four ways. The Sages tell us that because *Rabbeinu Hakadosh* was one generation closer to the *Churban*, even though he did not live in the time of the *Churban* itself, he and his colleagues felt the intensity of the lamentation and the sorrow that much more deeply. After explaining the *pasuk* in twenty-four different ways, he would break down and weep. He did not have the emotional stamina to continue. Rabbi Yochanan and his companions, who lived one generation later, were that much more removed from the *Churban* and could therefore deal with it at greater length.

We are only one generation removed from the *Churban* of European Jewry, and yet the memory fades from our minds. Our emotional bankruptcy permits us to speak about it casually, in a detached manner, and even forget about it.

◆§ The "Churban" Fountainhead

We cannot permit the *Churban*, which has destroyed so many of our people and so much of our spiritual life, to pass into oblivion. We must reach out to it and grasp it before too much time elapses. Every detail is, of course, of utmost importance. But first, we must approach the entire concept of *Churban* at its harshest, and attempt to determine what it signifies in our relationship with G-d.

Truly understanding this most recent *Churban* does not begin with a particular event of a generation ago. It must begin with works written 2,500 years ago. Yirmiyahu the Prophet had written *"Hashem destroyed without mercy,"* regarding the destruction of the First *Beis Hamikdash*. Yet, this *pasuk* has been understood to extend beyond that *Churban* to include *Churban* in all times. The *Churban* of the *Beis Hamikdash* becomes the paradigm for all future *Churbanos*, and the Lamentations which the Prophet wrote with Divine inspiration encompass all sorrow, pain and mourning. All cries of loss and despair are united: *Chazal* interpret Yirmiyahu's outcry of "עַל אֵלֶּה אֲנִי בוֹכִיָּה" — *For these do I weep,"* as referring to events that occurred during the destruction of the Second Temple, even though the Prophet lived at the time of the First Temple ... we lack the power to make *kinos* (lamentations) of our own, so our lamentations find voice through the words of the *Navi*. His words are a vehicle for us to view and to understand the events of our time in the broad historical continuum, through an *emunah* perspective.

When referring to *Tishah B'Av* (the day the Temple was destroyed) the Prophet Yirmiyahu calls the day *Moed*, a word that usually refers to a festival. The Telshe Rav, Horav Reb Avraham Yitzchak Bloch, explains that the word *moed* (מועד) is derived from the word *vaad* (ועד), appointment. It is a time of appointment of *Hashem* with the world, when His greatness is manifested.

This greatness can be seen from two aspects: through the miracles of redemption, joy and happiness — the exodus from Egypt; or through destruction, pain and sorrow — the exodus from Jerusalem, a destruction so great that it could only have been administered by Divine plan ... two separate moments in the history of *Klal Yisrael: Geulah* and *Churban*, redemption and destruction. From the time the Second Temple was destroyed through the present, and on until the final redemption, we are caught in one long moment of "going out of Jerusalem," punctuated by especially harrowing experiences, such as the Holocaust.

"Churban" as a Father's Punishment

How does one approach these moments of anguish in the history of the Jewish People? What brings about this destruction? The *Navi* explains that the exile from Jerusalem is a result of sin, in a relationship of crime and subsequent punishment, whether we understand the sin or not. Punishment is not brought without sin and there is no *Churban* that is not punishment.

However, we are deeply troubled: *other nations also sin, and yet their punishment is not so severe.* But, when other nations sin, their actions do not make the imprint on the universality of history that the deeds of *Klal Yisrael* do *(Midrash Eichah)*. History is not impressed by insignificant individuals; only the great *Klal Yisrael* occupies a central position in history as the *Am Hanivchar* (Chosen Nation) whose chosenness is manifested through times of redemption and through times of destruction. *Churban* is testimony to the status of *Klal Yisrael* as the *Am Hanivchar*. *An orphan grows up wild and uncared for ... he has no one to reprimand him and chastise him for his errant ways. Not so the child with parents.* The *Churban* should thus become a source of inspiration and encouragement for us. We are assured that we *do* have A Father in Heaven who cares for us and is concerned enough with our spiritual status to demonstrate His disfavor.

During times of destruction, it is written, "And G-d will cause your enemies to rejoice over you" — not that G-d is happy with the downfall of *Klal Yisrael*, for He only rejoices when He performs acts of kindness for *Klal Yisrael*. G-d weeps with us at times of destruction, as a father cries for the pain of his son upon whom he was forced to inflict a needed punishment ... He is very much with us in our suffering, and in His presence He shares our sorrow.

✍ The Prime Facet of "Churban"

Churban has many facets. When the European *kehillos* (communities) were destroyed, all aspects of their lives were destroyed, too: the economic life, social life, the organized structure of a thousand years' standing. We cannot begin to understand the extent of this *Churban* until we research extensively into Jewish life at that time. *What was the Polish community like? What was the nature of the Lithuanian community? the Hungarian? the kehillos of Berlin, Warsaw, Pressburg, Kovno, Lemberg?* When we have gathered the facts and have a genuine understanding of these communities, then we can begin to realize the magnitude of the *Churban*, how deeply we suffered then and how deeply we still suffer today.

There is one aspect of the punishment, however, that is so sweeping that it is apparently without any element of mercy whatsoever — the destruction of the spiritual life in Europe. "*Hashem destroys without mercy all the dwellings* (נְאוֹת) *of Yaakov.*" The *Midrash* explains נְאוֹת as if it came from the root נָאֶה, *beautiful*, i.e., the *beauty of Yaakov*, the *talmidei chachamim*, the great Torah Sages, who lost their lives and the empires of Torah life that they had built, *al kiddush Hashem*. We weep at the uprooting of hundreds of years of spiritual growth, which was lost with their destruction, at the uprooting of the centuries of tradition and scholarship that had found its full flowering in prewar Europe. The towering personalities who had led these spiritual empires had even more than *yeshivos* and *kehillos* to their credit. These people were of pivotal importance to the spiritual development of the entire world. The *gaon* and *tzaddik* Reb Daniel Movshavitz of Kelm once pointed out that at the very same time that the *Vilna Gaon* was studying Torah in Vilna and illuminating great Divine truths to the world, Emmanuel Kant was in Berlin expounding on the ethical imperative, arriving at truths by human thought. His truth was not developed at parlor discussions and street-corner arguments, but as a direct result of the study of the *Gaon* in a small, dimly lit room secluded from the world. Through his study of Torah and his findings, vibrations of truth were created which penetrated the halls of learning in Berlin, making it possible for Kant to arrive at his philosophical projections. Every truth in the world comes from the truth of

Torah; every Torah scholar brings this into the world, making it more accessible to secular thinkers. These are people of historical significance, the leaders of *Am Hanivchar*, the "dwellings of Yaakov," the source of the inner splendor and glory of our people.

Thus the loss of *Churban* Europe was of a scope even broader than the six million *kedoshim* (martyrs). With their death, great sources of truth also went up in smoke.

⋑ The Response to "Churban": The Faithful Do Not Ask

Sometimes *Churban* reaches such proportions that the fear is evoked that *Hashem* has turned away from us. We fear, not that *Hashem* is smiting us too severely, but that He has abandoned us ... When the decree was issued for the slaughter of the *asarah harugei malchus* — the ten Rabbinical giants, including Rabbi Akiva and his colleagues killed by the Romans after the destruction of the Second Temple — Rabbi Yishmael ascended to the heavens to inquire if this decree was indeed from *Hashem*. He was answered: "The decree has been issued from before Me. Go and accept it."

The fundamental concept of *Churban* is that it is a decree issued by *Hashem* for the achievement of an ultimate purpose. When one has become so overwhelmed by destruction that he feels *Hashem* has left him, he must not turn away from Torah in frustration and anger, but should turn to the Torah to seek reassurance that whatever occurs "has been issued from before Me."

> *In the early days of Hitler's rise to power, we were confused and frightened, not knowing what the next day would bring. Then, someone reprinted and distributed the comments of Reb Meir Simcha (of Dvinsk) on Bechukosai from his sefer Meshech Chochmah — his predictions of the great destruction that would emanate from Berlin. The accuracy of his remarks was frightening — and yet reassuring ... He was gone since 1926, but he had looked into the Chumash and he knew ...*

This essay from *Meshech Chochmah* should become part of every *yeshivah's* curriculum.*

The Nitra Rav, in a telegram to the *Vaad Hatzalah* (rescue committee) of the *Agudas Horabonim* (Union of Orthodox

---

* A translation appears as the first essay in this volume.

Rabbis of United States) during World War II, remarked: *For those who doubt and ask, there are no answers. For those who do not doubt, there are no questions.*

From our vantage point, we must also respond to this terrible *Churban* with *"Sit in loneliness and be silent"* — not asking questions, but contemplating our condition: *How lonely we are without feeling the reassuring presence of Hashem's recognizable acts of kindness.* But we must remember at the same time, *"He will not forsake us forever."* Thinking into the depth and breadth of this *Churban* heightens one's understanding of this concept. For if, Heaven forbid, *Hashem* would have forsaken us, this *Churban* could never have occurred. The *Churban* itself is evidence and testimony to the fact that "we have a Father in Heaven."

❧ The Perspective: The World in an Incident

All that has occurred has its place in the Divine plan of *"Remember the days of yore."* A whole world of facts lies in the events of this *Churban* and these facts are infinite in number. It is our duty to find pertinent facts and to collate the proper material. The little that I know revealed entire worlds of insight to me ... random incidents that the children of the Telshe Rav related to me.

When the Nazi beat the Telshe Rav upon the head with hammer blows and taunted him: "Where is your G-d, Herr Rabbiner?", the Telshe Rav replied, "He is not only my G-d, He is your G-d; and the world will yet see this."

This was might and *Kiddush Hashem*. How would the others interpret his actions? — as a weakness?

At the time when the Nazis took the Telshe community to their intended slaughter at the lake nearby, the Telshe Rav said in a drashah (homiletic commentary): "If we will be scrupulous in kashrus, in Shabbos, in taharos hamishpachah (laws of family purity), the enemy will have no dominion over us." And from that day on plans were changed; they were taken away from Telz and were confined in a ghetto. The entire community suffered no harm until the first breach in kashrus.

Were we abandoned? Do we have a *Tatteh in Himmel* (Father in Heaven)?

When the Rav could no longer stand on his feet, not having enough strength to carry even a Gemara, he directed his young daughter (the sons were gone) to take out the Gemara Sanhedrin, to open it up to the topic of *Kiddush Hashem*, and to begin reading ... Such was their preparation.

Are these cowards? Or are these *"valiant men of might performing His words"*?

I see these events as Jewry in a microcosm, not just isolated incidents that occurred in Telshe. But Telshe is where I begin, and this is what I know of Telshe. And just as Telshe had a brand of *Kiddush Hashem* all its own, so did Kovno ... So did Satmar and Pressburg ... so did Warsaw and Lemberg. But how does one discover the individuality of each community? Each person generalizes from his own experiences, from what he witnessed, from what he heard, to gain insight into the character of his particular community and its heritage. From what each saw and heard, a man from Warsaw understands Warsaw, the survivor of Kovno understands Kovno, and he who observed his own *Rebbe* could understand the strength of Reb Menachem Ziemba.

There is so much to be researched. And when this is done and collated, it must be taught through a perspective of *emunah*. Then, out of the *Churban*, children will emerge fortified, understanding the significance of the *Tishah B'Av: Moed* as an encounter with G-d ... they will emerge fortified, understanding that the vow "He will not forsake us" is indeed binding forever.

After all, we are dealing with but a moment in history, and all moments together lead up gradually to that final moment for which we all wait longingly — "When *Shiloh (Moshiach)* will come."

II.
The Surviving Generation Looks Back

Rabbi Moshe Sherer

Shall We Tell Our Children?

AGAIN AND AGAIN, the "Six Million" are on the front pages of our newspapers. Periodically, as if propelled by a Divine design to jolt sluggish memories, the Nazi bestiality that decimated our people hits the headlines: The dramatic Eichmann capture and trial in Jerusalem in the 60's, the hair-raising trial in Frankfurt of the Nazi officials of the infamous Auschwitz death-factory in the 70's, the Goldberg Commission in the 80's.

For the adult Jew who lived through the war years, these recurring "shock treatments" serve to revive from the subconscious strata grim memories of an appalling holocaust that spared no family, and left us a nation of mourners. But do these unspeakable crimes against the Jews have any *real* meaning for our children? Are *they* aware of the full impact of what occurred during those nightmarish years, and do *they* personally identify with the tragic victims of the crematoria and gas chambers of Auschwitz and Dachau?

If the authors of history books for children would have their way, the psyches of the youngsters born in the last two decades would never be disturbed and tormented by these "dreadful horror stories." A survey by a New York daily revealed that the history textbooks used in schools have condensed the story of the vilest crime in the annals of humanity into a brief paragraph, and sometimes even into a terse sentence. One history book shamelessly downgrades the entire episode, by lumping the Jewish tragedy in an odd hodgepodge: "A large number of Communists, Socialists and Jews were despoiled of their

---

This essay appeared in *The Jewish Observer* of January 1964.

property, arrested and tortured in concentration camps or put to death." Period.

Our Historic Experience: Only Sweetness and Light?

Of course, the Jewish children in religious homes, who do attend *yeshivos*, do obtain a superficial knowledge about Jewish martyrdom, which they glean from the *Chumash*, Prophets, the Talmud, the fast days and holidays. But, breathing the free air of a democracy where they are spared harsh racial indignities, all these tales of Jewish suffering seem remote and abstract to their young minds. To American Jewish children, black nights of persecution of their people are like bad dreams from the days of yore, before the world was blessed with civilization and emancipation. They are taught that we are still in *galus*, but they cannot conceive that atrocities and barbarism could be the lot of the Jew in a modern world. They simply do not relate, in a personal way, to these events.

We shelter and overprotect our children from the full dimension of bestiality unleashed against our people in the twentieth century. "Horror stories will only create unpleasant traumatic experiences for my child," one parent argues, rationalizing this policy of gloss and silence. And an educator explains: "We must teach our children positive values, the joy of Jewish living."

As a result, so many of our youngsters are given a dream world image in which Jewish life is a potpourri of numerous pleasantries: the relaxed tranquility of a *Shabbos tisch*, the mouth-watering *latkes* of Chanukah, the unbridled gaiety of Purim, the festivity of a Pesach *Seder* and so on. In addition, the fact that our children are taught reliance on the humanitarianism of the modern world gives them a false sense of Jewish security.

Preparing Our Children for Every Eventuality

For our children's sake, we must not allow an exclusive sweetness-and-light, lollipop image to be the only dimension of Jewish life that they conceive. If they do not comprehend the truth of Jewish life in *galus*, where the specter of persecution stalks our path, they lack the inner fortitude and spiritual strength to cope with the uncertain realities of Jewish fate. How can we expect our children to be trained with a genuine sense of *emunah* and *bitachon* when they do not feel that their faith may some day be put to the test in crucibles of fire?

Rabbi Samson Raphael Hirsch develops this thought poignantly: "The Jew who knows his task and his history is not surprised by anything that happens, he is never thrown off his balance or dazzled. He has only to look back in the mirror of his past which G-d is ever presenting to him ... and he steers calmly, whether over a smooth sea or through storm and fire, towards the goal to which G-d is leading him. He is prepared for everything. He trusts no moment and fears none ... An undeserved piece of good fortune cannot elate him, an unmerited suffering cannot crush him" *(Judaism Eternal,* translated by Dayan I. Grunfeld).

If we want our children never to be thrown off their balance, let us tell them, each in accordance with his absorbtive capacity, the blunt truth about the Jewish facts of life. Let us spell out for them all the brutal details of the intense pain and suffering endured by our people in a "civilized" society which exploited scientific knowledge to devise heinous methods to slaughter 1,500,000 innocent children. Let us tell it to them again and again, until the term "Six Million" is no longer a cliche, but a meaningful symbol of *their own* flesh and skin.

As parents and educators we owe it to our children to portray for them how the uprooted Jews did not lose their Divine image even when the Nazi savages attempted to transform them into wild animals. We should relate the numerous acts of *Kiddush Hashem* that illuminated that dark era: of the Jews in concentration camps who risked their lives to put on *tefillin;* of the Jews who covertly read the *Megillah* (Scroll of Esther) and had arranged a clandestine *Seder* in dingy bunkers in the shadows of the smokestacks of Buchenwald.

Let us expose them to the full panorama of Jewish destiny, the "good fortune" *and* the suffering.

There is a Jewish lesson to be learned from the statement of our Rabbis in the Midrash, that Mordechai impressed coins for his generation: on one side a golden crown was engraved, and on the other, sackcloth and ashes. What a symbolic depiction of the long, tortuous road of Jewish history!

Rabbi Yaakov Weinberg

The Destruction of European Jewry: A Churban of Singular Dimensions

✥ Churban — a Primal Loss

THE DESTRUCTION of European Jewry a generation ago was one of those singular occurrences in Jewish history that left the Jewish people permanently changed in both substance and image. It falls in the category of such national tragedies as the *Churban Bayis Rishon* — the destruction of the First Temple, which brought to a close an era when G-d's immediate presence had been felt in every moment of every Jew's life; and the *Churban Bayis Sheini* — the destruction of the Second Temple, which also diminished the status of *Klal Yisrael* in ways that affected its essence, removing from Jewry the vital contact with the Divine provided by the daily *avodah* (sacrificial service).

These changes did not merely affect *Klal Yisrael* in degree, but in essence. Loss of the *Beis Hamikdash* not only reduced the number of *mitzvos* that Jewry could perform, but struck at the quality of Jewish existence. So affected, *Klal Yisrael* responded to these events by convening the seventeenth of *Tamuz* and the ninth of *Av* as days of fasting and mourning; not merely for the loss of millions of lives that took place on those days, but for the loss that was suffered in our national existence, and in all Creation, as well.

And so we will continue to mourn this loss until the coming of *Moshiach*, when the *Beis Hamikdash* will be rebuilt and Israel will be returned to its once and future perfection.

This essay, based on an address delivered at the 53rd national convention of Agudath Israel of America in November 1975, appeared in *The Jewish Observer* of June 1976.

✺ The Many Incidents of Churban

Since the *Churban* nineteen centuries ago, *Klal Yisrael* has passed through many vicissitudes: pogroms, oppresions, expulsions, and slaughterings. There is no forgetting them, for each of them — the expulsion from Spain, Chmelnitzky's murderous raids, the Crusades — has left its mark on *Klal Yisrael*. Each experience in its time was internalized by us as Jews — not only in our *tefillos* and in our remembering those who were lost during each of these periods, but in terms of our own perspective, our perception of what we are. For each event, there was a spontaneous reaction from within *Klal Yisrael*: *Klal Yisrael* had understood the nature of its essence and it lived accordingly. Thus it reacted to each of these horrors as a *Klal Yisrael*, with a recognition that each event — no matter how tragic — had its place in the continuum that began at Sinai, that had its roots in the Covenant made between the Almighty and His people.

Each of these oppressions reflected the horrors of the *tochachah*, wherein G-d foretold us at our very inception as a nation that as a G-dly people we would suffer these terrible oppressions. Thus, in the wake of each of these events, with all their attendant horrors and sufferings, the Jews were in fact strengthened by seeing clearly the direct hand of G-d in their lives. Accepting His chastisement as an expression of His concern and closeness, they reacted with a recognition of a need for *teshuvah* (repentance), with a recognition that they were treading on the road that leads to *Moshiach;* that these sufferings are the signposts that tell us of the eventuality of the day of G-d's ultimate reign.

No questions were asked, because the answers were clear before a question could be uttered. We knew the "Why"; we knew it in our being, in our minds, in our hearts, in our souls. It was not necessary for us to articulate it, for we lived with the knowledge that the "Why" was the ongoing of our special relationship with G-d. Thus Jewry could face tragedies with a confidence that they were a source of strength, ultimately leading to the full redemption.

✺ Churban With a Difference

The most recent *Churban*, however, is unique in many ways. It is the first time since the *Churban Bayis* that a tragedy has befallen *Klal Yisrael* that has permanently affected its very essence; since 1945, *Klal Yisrael* can never again be the same. Our areas of function, the nature of our problems, the methods we employ to solve them, even our very feelings have all undergone a permanent change because of *Churban* Europe. Not only has the focal point of *Klal Yisrael* been transferred from Europe to *Eretz Yisrael*, which brings with it a host of challenges, problems and shifts in perspective; not only have we lost the centers of vibrant Jewish life, with all the ramifications this must have on ourselves and our children for all generations to come; but we have lost our prime source of living *Yiddishkeit*. We must now struggle on a different level not only to understand the *hashkafah*, the philosophic outlook of Torah, but even to properly experience the simple awareness of our existence as Jews. Thus, our children are more impoverished than all preceding generations, for they cannot draw from this reservoir of a continuous, ongoing Jewish existence *per se*. The continuity was weakened and we must now recreate it.

The Wrong "Why"

Even worse, however, is the extraordinary phenomenon that for the first time in its existence, *Klal Yisrael* did not recognize with its customary clarity, certainty, and self-awareness that it was to react to events as an *Am Hashem*, a Torah nation. For the first time the question "Why" is posed because of loss of that clarity of insight. *Klal Yisrael* failed to recognize instinctively that this *Churban* also has its place in the continuity of its destiny, that its very horror is a part of our ongoing relationship with G-d, and that its very uniqueness is the truth of G-d's agonizing love for us.

Ironically, never since the *Churban* of nineteen hundred years ago has it been so abundantly clear that all that had occurred is the workings of the direct hand of G-d. Nonetheless, the question "Why" was posed: Not the "Why" of our Rabbis of old, "Why was the land destroyed?" — the search for the specific sin that earned destruction, which only G-d could pinpoint; but the "By what right?" — subjecting G-d Himself to our judgment, wherein human intelligence presumes to evaluate Divine justice.

Amalek Unmasked

Perhaps the uniqueness of this strange response can cast a light on a major theme underlying this *Churban*. Indeed it is one with the very problems that we find ourselves facing today, thirty years later.

The *Churban* brought to the fore the total bankruptcy of the belief that Man can fulfill his potential of greatness without cognizance of G-d's existence and His demands. This, in effect, is the Amalek approach, and never before was it so clearly revealed and then so roundly defeated. This Amalek — which had been manifest through Haman and his single-minded obsession to wipe out all of Jewry — was incarnate in Hitler and his murderous designs. In the earlier confrontation with Amalek, in the days of Mordechai and Esther, the Jews were worthy of the Purim miracle wherein Amalek was defeated, Haman was destroyed, and not one Jew suffered harm. To some extent, it was the same during this most recent *Churban:* Amalek had wanted to destroy the totality of *Klal Yisrael* — not as a mere by-product of his desire for power, but as Hitler's primary goal. He was prepared to conquer a world to destroy *Klal Yisrael*. But there the similarity ends. For the first time, Amalek succeeded in doing as much as it did. And if, again, we witnessed a miracle that in the end saw Amalek's destruction and *Klal Yisrael's* survival, at what price was this victory bought!

The degree of Hitler/Amalek's success and his final defeat would seem to put this recent epoch in the category of seminal events recorded in *Tanach* (Scripture) — except that we have neither the Prophets to explain the events to us nor the wise men with *ruach hakodesh* to guide us in our response to them.

Yet undeniably, Amalek in its ugly reality was unmasked for us. For what is Amalek but total denial of G-d-given criteria for human conduct? This was the essence of Amalek when it first accosted the Jews in Refidim when they were newly redeemed from Egypt — a militant challenge to G-d's rule on Earth. And it was the hallmark of the world view that came to full fruition in Nazi Germany. Indeed, this unique *Churban* crowned an era when Man's conduct was determined by man-made ethics, formulated by his own understanding of right and wrong ... an era when Man believed in the greatness of his own scientific thought, his own creativity, and his own instinct for goodness.

৵ A Truth Still Evident

Surely it was Divine *hashgachah* in recent events that displayed so unequivocally that he who depends on his own understanding and feelings rather than on G-d's command to determine good and evil will ultimately shed every semblance of human dignity, totally losing his *tzelem Elokim* (Divine image). It was surely obvious in 1940 that Man cannot depend on Man, Jews cannot depend on Man, and Jewry cannot depend on other nations — not on their humanity, their innate goodness, their sense of justice, nor on their sense of human dignity. After all, even those who did not join in the atrocities of Nazi Germany did join in the silence of complicity that viewed them, and with very few exceptions, managed to avoid even a minimal expression of outrage.

Perhaps the era of good will that followed World War II allowed some of us to forget the graphic and painful lessons of the bankruptcy of a G-dless humanity. But surely it is as apparent again today as it was then, during the war. For is human dignity built on the basis of man's understanding on a higher level today than at that time? Are the concepts of truth, right, justice and ethics held by men today any more acceptable than they were then? Is it not obvious, or have we yet to learn with even greater clarity, that *only* through G-d's Torah and His *mitzvos* can man ever be more than the beast!

It is essential — not only for Jewry to be Jews, but for mankind to function as humans — that we declare our total submission to Divine wisdom and Divine rule. Until we accept that there is no other source of truth, no other source of right, no other criterion for human behavior, we will continue to face the very same crises affecting all phases of human existence, awakening alienation and disaffection among all segments of humanity.

We are guilty of neglecting to learn what that entire epoch was about. For our own sake and for the sake of our children, we must reaffirm that truth and justice stem only from G-d's Torah and our submission to Him. This is the only source of hope for Jewry and for all mankind.

Rabbi Yaakov Perlow

Our Generation: Churban Plus-One

◆§ To Dare to Comment

CHURBAN EUROPE is a topic that terrifies the imagination, for it is a topic that rests upon the ashes of millions, on the trauma of an entire people. For one who was not there, to talk about *Churban* Europe is indeed a bit pretentious. One must therefore begin by asking forgiveness of the dead and of the living for venturing to tread on this painful path; for entering a field hallowed by the *neshamos* of *kedoshim u'tehorim* (the souls of pure and sacred martyrs); for violating the deep wounds of the living who still carry the scars of agony on their bodies.

But, perhaps precisely because I did *not* suffer, because my compatriots knew nothing but comfort in those black years, I may indeed take the courage to offer a few thoughts on this awesome subject. We are the generation who is, or should be, beset with a certain unspoken anxiety, a mixture of guilt, tension, and bewilderment, who must *especially* seek a way to re-evaluate ourselves and our tasks in the wake of the recent *Churban*.

Ultimately, after the entire frightful unit has been thoroughly studied, and all the commentaries have been given — if this can *ever* be done — our attitude is then reduced to one of צִדּוּק הַדִּין (acceptance of Divine judgment): *"Hashem has given, Hashem has taken, Blessed be the Name of Hashem"* (Job 1:21).

G-d blessed His people with a civilization of *kedushah* (sanctity) for one thousand years in Europe — a millennium that produced the spiritual giants and Torah culture that will nourish

---

This essay, based on an address delivered at the 53rd national convention of Agudath Israel of America in November 1975, appeared in *The Jewish Observer* of June 1976.

our people until the end of days. Suddenly, it was His will that the hand of destruction descend upon that glorious civilization, and it perished before *our* eyes. "I am the man who has seen affliction by the rod of His wrath *(Eichah* 3:1)." We weep with the prophet because *we* are the generation who saw this calamity befall us, because even a generation later our spirits have not yet fully adjusted to those frightful events. We are still yearning for consolation and comfort, but "I have no comforter to restore my soul (ibid. 1:16)." The sense of despair is still with us, and so we feel we must be mutely content by accepting the decree with deep trust, forever expressing our conviction in G-d's true justice as "faithful, without distortion, for He is righteous *(Devarim* 32:4)."

✥ To Learn to Live

But is this enough? Have we, the first post-*Churban* generation, acquitted ourselves by merely accepting the tragedy as the grave verdict of Divine justice and then depositing it in the annals of perennial Jewish suffering? Should not this cataclysmic event remain with us forever? Should it not have an ongoing impact and lasting effect on our lives and on the lives of our children?

By "impact" I do not mean continued grief and lamentations. *Aveilus* (mourning) has its limits and may not be overdone. But *aveilus* can have another message, besides grief and mourning for the dead: "It is better to go to the house of a mourner than to the house of revelry, for it is the end of all man, and he who is alive will take it to heart *(Koheles* 7:2)." When one goes to a house of mourning he is, of course, reminded that one day he too shall pass away. Reb Mendele Kotzker, however, drew from this passage another teaching as well: "He who is alive ... should then remind himself that *he* lives yet." Our task, our challenge, after the plague of death, is to learn how to *live;* to *study* the plague of death and turn it into a teacher of life.

Of course, we will continue to exist and multiply and be productive in body and spirit. This is after all what the Prophet Yirmiyahu implored *his* generation to do in their period of exile: "Build houses ... plant gardens ... raise families (29:5,6)," continue to live! But I would submit that these houses that we build, the families that we raise, indeed this very new society that we are hopefully building *b'ezras Hashem* (with the help of G-d) in this country and in *Eretz Yisrael — all this dare not be done* without a conscious sense that we are building *with* the ashes and *upon* the ruins of old castles. This means that the *new* generation cannot be permitted to remain untouched spiritually by the events of the preceding generation.

A generation ago we were overtaken by grief and suffering. Today we must *direct* that grief and suffering towards specific spiritual ends.

As Rabbeinu Yonah of Gerudni wrote in *Shaarei Teshuvah*:
> In the crisis of anguish, one who has true faith sees in the very darkness itself the seeds of new light, as it says: "Do not rejoice over me, my enemy; even though I have fallen, I shall arise. When I sit in darkness, G-d is a light for me" (Michah 7:8). Our Rabbis said, "If I did not fall, I would not arise. If I did not sit in darkness, G-d would not be a light for me."

Only when darkness leads to new light and decline becomes a harbinger of fresh growth, may one say that the darkness and decline have achieved moral redemption. The calamity of the six million will find its consolation and its ultimate restitution only when it begins to serve as a teaching source to enrich and direct our lives in the new era.

How does one draw spiritual direction from the *Churban*? Primarily by being confronted *by* the *Churban* with a challenge to recognize the true image of *Klal Yisrael*, by being compelled to face up to the real purpose of Jewish existence. Modern Jewish history is indeed difficult to comprehend because so much of it is wrapped up in the mysteries of *kavshi deRachmona* and *ikvesa deMeshicha* (the era immediately preceeding *Moshiach*), but we cannot seek guidelines for the future if we do not attempt to understand a little about the past. Thus, we must go back a bit in Jewish history.

৺§ The Alien Attraction

The French Revolution and the ensuing emancipation had toppled the ghettos and exposed *Klal Yisrael* to the so-called humanism of the new era. Some welcomed the opportunity. Many resisted the change. But the universal effect of emancipation was a newly found respect and undisguised deference for the culture of the nations of the world.

Never were Jews more intellectually at ease with the tenor of society than were the Jews of Germany in the century before Hitler. In Eastern Europe, as well, the liberalism and refinement of the "intelligentsia" was held in quiet but high esteem and even the religious masses and *yeshivah* students were being overtaken by a creeping, pervasive inferiority complex. A chassidic Jew who spoke German was viewed with a certain degree of deference even in many a corner of Eastern Europe.

Gedolei Yisrael always recognized the fatal consequences of such trends. Study the well-known *Meshech Chochmah* on *Parshas Bechukosai* (it appears in the first essay in this volume) and see the prophetic insight with which Reb Meir Simcha illuminates the sad pattern of the times. Then history itself came along and pointed its tragic finger at us.

Those very countries that symbolized *Kultur* and humanism were the first to become de-humanized. The fires that ravaged our people originated in those very societies with whom Jews had achieved such cultural comfort.

In another part of Europe where the ideology of Marx and Lenin had captured the imagination of the young and oppressed, where the Red flag was proudly waved as the great hope of a new era, where the Jews were in the forefront of the Revolution — for they actually were its intellectual elite — it took just a few short years to discover that this great new hope had given birth to a wild beast. The most awesome fact of our century, it would seem, is the spectre of two monsters, Hitler and Stalin, as the predominant figures of world history.

⇜§ The Lesson of Self Pride

If the European *Churban* has any message that we can perceive, it is the bankruptcy of alien culture. If the *Churban* has any instruction for us, it is that we must stop revering the alien intellectual. Our entire sense of awe for the heritage of western civilization has left us with a malaise of religious insecurity and weak posture. It is long overdue that we begin to regain our balance and spiritual pride. (This does not touch at all upon the need for secular education and the merit of the philosophy of *Torah Im Derech Eretz*. That is quite another matter. That approach, properly understood, seeks to adapt to the *needs* of the general society, to take from it whatever elements are considered worthwhile, and, on the contrary, to master them with the values of Torah and *mitzvos*. The emphasis of this discussion is the need to eliminate from our individual and communal psyches the false notion that *Vernumft* and *Wissenschaft* of other nations possess moral virtue. Our sense of awe and our devotion, after the

Churban, must turn *exclusively inward to our culture and our heritage.*)

Let the pride of Yaakov that He so loves finally emerge from within us in the joy of our service, in our praying and waiting for Moshiach, in our life as a Chosen People.

We are a nation of orphans after the catastrophe, but we will not find solace in the largesse of other nations or in the high councils of the U.N. — *only* in G-d and His Torah. *This* is the primary lesson of *Churban* Europe.

But there are other lessons, other demands.

To Complete Their Assignment

The destruction of the Six Million was a cosmic blow to the *neshamah* of our people as much as it was to the nation's physical existence. The redemption of the *Churban* will not be achieved by people of little vision and limited scope. The redemption demands an era of heroic responses. It demands that the *neshamah* of *Klal Yisrael*, so drained, so ravaged by pain and torture, be resuscitated and brought back to health. It demands that our lives and deeds replenish the treasuries of sanctity laid waste by the murders. It demands of our diminished people, of the still more diminished communities of Torah-committed Jews, that their *Yiddishkeit* and their actions must consciously replace that of our perished brethren. It demands that we continue *their* unfinished work, that we be *their* replacement.

The *Churban* of the European *yeshivos* must convey to every *yeshivah* student the constant reminder that *Klal Yisrael* can ill afford today — if it ever could — any apathy or sluggishness in devotion to Torah study. Every *ben Torah* today must live with the compelling realization that *his* learning has to make up for that of ten like him whose lives were swept up in the flames.

So great is the awesome *moral* challenge of *Churban* Europe, that it is, I think, the most pervasive existential factor of our lives today. If this *Churban* does not somehow awaken a more profound attachment to *spiritual* living in ourselves, in our families, in our *yeshivos*, in our organizations, then the *Churban* is tragically not yet over, the wasteland is still with us. The ringing words of *Yeshayahu:* וּבָנוּ חָרְבוֹת עוֹלָם, שׁוֹמְמוֹת רִאשׁוֹנִים יְקוֹמֵמוּ, וְחִדְּשׁוּ עָרֵי חֹרֶב, שׁוֹמְמוֹת דּוֹר וָדוֹר, *And they will rebuild the age-old ruins, restore the desolations of ancient times; they will renew the ruined cities, the desolations of every generation* (61:4).

These are the demands that *Churban* Europe imposes upon us — as individuals and as a community of Torah Jews.

⚡ To Relive the Glories

Rabbi Aharon Kotler זצ״ל was an individual who was, perhaps more than anyone else, responsible for the renaissance of Torah in America. He considered it his mission to replant Kletzk, Lithuania, and the *yeshivah* empire of Europe on new soil. This was the unspoken meaning of his life and work in this country, to which he was truly an ordained emissary of Providence.

We small people, however, cannot allow ourselves the privilege of unspoken deeds. The education of our children and our own spiritual re-enforcement make it imperative that we *articulate* and repeatedly *retell* the tragedy of European Jewry. But not only of the horrors and killings should we be speaking, but also of the glory and richness of that great authentic civilization.

I envision a father, one of those who escaped from Poland, telling his son about the ghetto and death camps. If that story, however, begins and ends there, and does not depict and relive the society that preceded the death camps, then only a half-truth has been told; and that father has done his son a grave injustice. The story of Jewish death must be placed in the panorama of Jewish life, to which death was only the tragic finale. What preceded Auschwitz and Treblinka were the Jewish Sabbaths and festivals, the vibrancy of the Warsaw *navlohkess*, the *chassidus* of the Lodzer *shtiblach*, the beauty and vigor of a dynamic Jewish world.

I recall an old chassidic Jew, reminiscing about his years in Poland, suddenly saying: "The *Shabbosos* and *Yomim Tovim* that I saw — you'll never see the likes of them. Perhaps, however, in your lifetime, you may yet catch a taste, a semblance, a whiff of the *amol'ige kedushah* of old that we experienced.¹

It is this vision of the *kedushah* of old that I never saw which sustains my *Shabbos* and *Yom Tov* today, and which I hope I can impart to my children, as well.

For this reason, the *she'eiris hapleitah* — the survivors of *Churban* Europe — have such a vital, educative duty to fulfill in our day.

---

1. אזעלכע שבתים און ימים טובים ווי איך האב געזעהן וועסטו שוין קיינמאל נישט זעהן. אפשר וועסטו נאך אבער אין דיין לעבן מרגיש זיין עפעס א טעם, א מעין, א רוח פון די אמאליגע קדושה וואס מיר האבן נאך מיטגעלעבט.

*We, the younger generation, never had the opportunity to see that "amol'ige kedushah," but you, as eyewitnesses, did experience the glory of European Jewry, and you can better comprehend the meaning of this disaster. Thus, you have a special obligation to us of the new era. Realize that twenty, thirty years from now there will hardly be anyone to tell what it was like in Jewish Lublin, the batei midrashim of Cracow, the yeshivos of Lithuania, the kehillos of Germany. You, then, have a sacred obligation to edify us with your reminiscences, and to inspire us with your impressions of this world that no longer exists. You must continuously teach this to your children, and to our children, "When you sit in your house, when you go on your way, when you repose, and when you arise."*²

✥ The Legacy of Greatness

How often have we, fathers and teachers, spoken directly to our children and students about *Churban* Europe? Have we ever told them about the last days of Reb Menachem Ziemba and Reb Elchonon Wasserman (May G-d avenge their blood!)? How much do our older *yeshivah bachurim* and *kollel* fellows know about the physical *mesiras nefesh* (devotion to the point of risking one's life) and *kiddush Hashem* of these towering figures? ... It seems to me that if a *yeshivah bachur's* acquaintance with Reb Elchonon is limited to explanations in his *Koveitz Shiurim* and he has never heard or read about how Reb Elchonon lived, and how he went to the *akeidah* and died, and what he spoke in his last moments, the *chinuch* (education) of this *bachur* is deficient of a great inspirational model for how an *erlicher Yid* is supposed to live — and die, if need be. Fortunately, the latest edition of the *Koveitz Shiurim* records the last words of Reb Elchonon before he was shot, as remembered by living witnesses:

In heaven they seem to consider us tzaddikim, for it seems that we have been chosen to atone with our bodies for

---

2. מיר, דער אינגערע דור, האבען דאך נישט זוכה געווען צו זעהן די דאזיגע "אמאליגע קדושה," אבער איר, עדי ראיה, איהר האט דאך יא מיטגעלעבט דעם פראכט פון אירראפיישען אידענטום, איר פארשטייט דאך בעסער דעם אנדייט פון דעם פינסטערן חורבן. האט איר דאך א באזונדערע פליכט צו אונז אלעמען פון נייעם דור. אין א 30־40 יאהר ארום וועט דאך שוין נישט זיין כמעט ווער ס׳וואל דערצייילען ווי ס׳האט אויסגעזעהן דאס אידישע לובלין, די בתי מדרשים און קראקע, די ישיבות פון ליטע, די קהלות פון אשכנז. ליגט דאך אויף אייך א הייליגער חוב אונז אנצואווארימען מיט די זכרונות אונז מעורר צו זיין מיט דעם רושם פון די וועלט פון אמאל. איהר מוזט די דאזיגע פרשה לערנען כסדר, מיט אייערע קינדער און מיט אונזערע קינדער, "בשבתך בביתך ובלכתך בדרך ובשכבך ובקומך."

*Klal Yisrael. If so, we must repent, sincerely and fully, now, on the spot. Time is short. We must realize that our sacrifice will be a more perfect one if we hallow ourselves. In that way, we will save the lives of our brothers and sisters in America. Let none of us think an impure thought which would render us unfit as a korban. We are now able to fulfill the greatest of mitzvos ... 'You scorched her with fire and with fire You are destined to rebuild her'. The very fires that consume our bodies are the fires that will rebuild the Jewish nation.*³

Ribono Shel Olam (Creator of the World)! How many *mussar* lectures, how many essays on piety are contained in these last words of this saint! He urged his fellow *korbanos* to *teshuvah*, to concentrate on the *mitzvah* motive of their acts rather than on personal thoughts, to atone for their brothers and sisters in America, to save *Klal Yisrael*. Such a vast Torah of Jewish sanctity, of *ahavas Yisrael*, of sacrifice — ought not this episode and others like it be a part of our present-day Torah curriculum?

And what about the epic tale of the Lubavitcher *chassidim* who persevered not five years under Hitler, but thirty years under Stalin, who raised their children with purity and sanctity under the noses of the NKVD, who built *chadorim* (schools) and *mikva'os* literally with *mesiras nefesh* — with risk to their lives and the fullest measure of devotion? Their story has hardly even begun to be told.

When some of them managed to leave Russia in 1948, one of the elders remarked:

"You realize that we are leaving the world of truth and we are entering a world of falsehood."

"Leaving the world of truth"? Was there any greater world of falsehood than Communist Russia?

So he explained:

"Here if one was an erlicher Yid it was with emes — truth. One earned no money through it, no recognition —

---

3. אין הימעל האלט אונז מסתמא פאר צדיקים, וויל מען וויל דאך אז מיר זאלען מכפר זיין מיט אונזערער גופים פאר דעם כלל ישראל. דארפען מיר טאקע תשובה טאהן, יעצט, גלייך אויפן ארט. די צייט איז קורץ. דארפען מיר אין זינען האבען אז מיר וועלען זיין בעסערע קרבנות, אויב מיר וועלען תשובה טאהן און וועלען מיר אפראטעוועון אונזערע אמעריקאנער ברידער און שוועסטער. זאל חלילה ניט אריינפאלען ביי קיינעם אין מוח א פסול'ע מחשבה וואס איז פיגול און מאכט דעם קרבן פסול. מיר זענען יעצט מקיים די גרעסטע מצוה "באש הצתה ובאש אתה עתיד לבנותה." דאס פייער וואס ברענט אונזערע גופים איז דאס פייער וואס וועט צוריק אויפרעכטען דאס אידישע פאלק.

only tzaros and weariness. Here one served G-d with emes. But in the new world of freedom that awaits us, who knows? There, one can earn some money through his Yiddishkeit and one can gain a bit of recognition. There, all sorts of personal motives and interests creep in. There, I fear it can become a world of falsehood for us."[4]

Such was the thinking of these great Jews of simple purity. When comparing the quality of our lives today with theirs under Stalin, we may well shrink with shame. Their ordeals and the entire recent era of Jewish life and death should thus be for us one great *mussar sefer* — a vast volume of ethical imperatives.

✑ Between Darkness and Light

Churban Europe can be a natural, effective medium for *chinuch* in our homes and schools. The more we study it, the deeper it will touch us, the better Jews we will be. It will imbue us with a sense of humility and unworthiness. It will refine our character, deepen our *ahavas Yisrael*. It will uplift the quality of our *Yiddishkeit*. It will implore us to conduct ourselves with greater modesty, to curb the excesses of luxury and extravagance all too rampant today: When thousands are spent for flowers and other frills at *heimishe* Jewish weddings — sometimes by the very survivors of Auschwitz themselves — such conduct, aside from its moral arrogance, profanes the memory of the *Churban,* and is a betrayal of the ideals for which our parents and teachers lived and died.

Above all, the *Churban* must finally awaken within us — individually and as a community — a deep sense of history, an ever-conscious feeling that we are part of the greatest enigma of Jewish existence. We are the generation that must grope between darkness and light, between tragedy and hope! On our shoulders was placed the historic duty to mend the torn *Sefer Torah* and put on it a new beautiful mantle. We are the ones who have been chosen to carry the wounded, suffering "lost sheep, Israel" back to its eternal Shepherd. If we are worthy of the calling, if we succeed in our task, we shall then look back to the *Churban* and proclaim to the entire world:

---

4. איהר ווייסט מיר פארוון יעצט ארויס פון אן עולם האמת און אריין אין אן עולם השקר. ארויס פון אן עולם האמת! דא אז מ'איז געוואן אן ערליכער איד איז דאס געוואן מיט'ן אמת. קיין געלט האט מען נישט געמאכט דערביי, קיין כבוד נישט געקראגגען, נאר צרות און מאטערניש, דא האט מען געדינט דער אויבערשטן מיט'ן אמת, אבער אין די נייע פרייע וועלט, ווער ווייסט? דארטן מאכט מען פון אידישקייט אביסעל געלט, מען פארדינט דערביי אביסל כבוד. דארטן כאפען זיך ארויס נגיעות און פניות. דארט, האב איך מורא וועט פאר אונז זיין אן עולם השקר.

אַל תִּשְׂמְחִי אוֹיַבְתִּי לִי כִּי נָפַלְתִּי קָמְתִּי, כִּי אֵשֵׁב בַּחֹשֶׁךְ ה' אוֹר לִי, *"Do not rejoice enemies of Yisrael! Indeed I have fallen but I have arisen again"* True, *"I did dwell in the darkness"* but *"Hashem is my ultimate light"* (Michah 7:8). He will bring us back to life and lead us on to *geulah*.

כִּי עִמְּךָ מְקוֹר חַיִּים. בְּאוֹרְךָ נִרְאֶה אוֹר
*"For with You is the source of life.
In Your illumination will light appear"*

Rabbi Nosson Scherman

An Understanding of the Holocaust in the Light of Moshe Prager's "Sparks of Glory"

~§ Historian of the Holocaust

MOSHE PRAGER, A WARSAW JEW descended from the *Chidushei HaRim*, was an established young journalist when World War II broke out. He was one of the pillars of the Orthodox Jewish press in Poland — an institution inspired by his cousin, the Gerrer Rebbe זצ"ל — which served as a powerful educational and social force in restructuring the Torah community after the ravages and dislocations of World War I. With the Nazi invasion, Prager became a secret correspondent for the Joint Distribution Committee (often referred to as the Joint) and convinced the American-based organization that, as an agency under the legal protection of a still neutral power, it was in a unique position to carry on relief and *hatzalah* (rescue) operations. Meanwhile, the Gerrer Rebbe was the Germans' Public Enemy Number One. Following their pattern wherever

---

Reb Moshe Prager ז"ל was one of Jewry's most important and — in the English-speaking world — least-known writers. He was recognized as one of Israel's leading authorities on the Holocaust and Nazi anti-Semitism. A prolific writer, he published over twenty works, nearly all of them on the World War II era, and his extensive scholarly analysis, "anti-Semitism in its German Manifestation" in the Hebrew Encyclopedia (Israel's equivalent of the Brittanica), has survived unchanged through twelve printings as the definitive work on the subject. His works have been translated into seven languages, but only in recent years has he been published in English, the language spoken by more Jews than any other.

The English version of *Nitzotzei G'vurah*, first published in Israel in 1952, is called *Sparks of Glory*. It was first published in English in 1974, by Shengold, and an expanded version was published by Mesorah Publications Ltd., in 1984. The following appreciation was written in June, 1974.

they conquered Jewish communities, the Nazis first tried to destroy the religious life of the then-helpless victims by burning and pillaging synagogues and *yeshivos*, and killing, torturing, or imprisoning the religious leaders. The Rebbe was in hiding from the Gestapo.

An old and intimate friendship with Stephan Porayski, director of the Warsaw Office of the Italian shipping firm Lloyd Triestino, made Prager a key figure in the attempt to smuggle the aged, ailing Rebbe out of Poland under the noses of the Gestapo. Prager approached Porayski asking him to arrange papers and passage. The Pole agreed, but only on the condition that Prager, too, accept a ticket to Palestine and save his own life as well. He did not want to leave his family, but his father and wife insisted that the rescue of the Rebbe was too vital a cause to be jeopardized by family considerations. If Porayski wanted Prager to go, then Prager would have to go. The miraculous rescue of the Gerrer Rebbe was accomplished and it became the subject of one of Prager's later books. The results of that daring feat are still unfolding in the rebirth of Ger in modern Israel, which began when the Rebbe arrived in Palestine.

∽§ "A Personal Mission: To Record ... "

Prager's family was wiped out in the Warsaw Ghetto, and it became a personal mission for him to salvage on paper the glorious history of Eastern European Jewry. During the war years he began carving a significant niche for himself in Israeli society. He was a very rare combination: an unusual literary and journalistic talent; a chassidic Jew steeped in the fervor and philosophy of Ger; a fighter in the Haganah; a brilliant thinker; a magnetic personality. He was perhaps the only one in the country who had entry without prior appointment to such disparate personalities as the sainted Gerrer Rebbe and secular political leaders such as David Ben-Gurion. He was a close confidante of such key figures in the secular life of the land as Shimon Peres, and, over the years, he has used his influence to the benefit of the Torah community.

Ben-Gurion saw him as the "symbol of the eternal Jew" and sought him out as a bridge to the Torah community. Prager was thus helpful in convincing Ben-Gurion that no Jewish state could survive unless it recognized its link with history. To build a totally secular state, he argued, would be to build a society without roots; such a society would wither and die. Prager's role was thus as "midwife" of sorts in bringing about the agreement between the religious community, represented by Agudath Israel's Rabbi Yitzchak Meir Levine, and the Jewish Agency on behalf of the proposed State of Israel, guaranteeing official recognition of *Shabbos*, *kashrus*, rabbinical control over personal status, and exemption of *yeshivah* students from conscription.

⋙ The Nazis: More Than Race Hatred

It was in Warsaw under the Nazis that Prager began to realize the underlying motive behind the Germans' sadistic brutality to the Jews: race hatred, to be sure; but more: *the hatred of what the Jews represented as a spiritual force, as well.* He began to understand this as a result of incidents like the following:

Prager was leaving Joint headquarters when he saw a Jew, an ordinary "amcho" man, walking down the street and appearing to be in great pain. The man was badly bruised and Prager took him into the building to ask him what was wrong and to see if he could be of assistance.

"It's nothing," the man said.

After much coaxing, he told Prager his story. He was walking down the street when two German officers accosted him and ordered him into an empty garage. There, for no apparent reason, they began beating him mercilessly. The Jew decided that he would endure the suffering without begging for mercy, without even screaming in pain. Mastery over his body might be denied him, but he would maintain his pride and dignity as a Jew. After a while, the Germans asked why he wasn't screaming. He remained silent. He realized that their purpose was to degrade him, to force him to scream and beg, and thus humiliate him. This doubled his resolve not to give them the satisfaction. The beating continued until finally his torturers themselves began screaming hysterically at him — almost begging him to cry out. Finally, they gave up and let him go. And it was very plain that he *had defeated* them.

Prager's research continued — on a personal, anecdotal level, as a questioner and collector of experiences — and on a deeper, philosophical level, as a historian who studied documents and looked for meanings in the senselessness that engulfed European Jewry. He came across many other bits and pieces of evidence that convinced him that he was on the right track.

A memo, sent by the Gestapo headquarters in Berlin to the Gestapo in Poland, said: the Nazis were willing to permit some Jewish emigration from Germany and Austria, because the assimilated, deJudaized Jews of Western Europe would simply blend into whatever country was willing to accept them; there was no danger that they would re-establish Jewish life in their new surroundings. From Eastern Europe, however, no escape was to be permitted. The OstJuden were too Jewish, too saturated with the values and ethics that Nazism was sworn to eradicate. They would rebuild their institutions and start all over again. This, Nazi Germany could not permit.

Prager cites, as further evidence, Hitler's letter written just before he committed suicide during the taking of Berlin. He wrote apologetically that he had not succeeded in carrying out the extermination of the Jews. *Not succeeded? He had carried out the most barbaric, most efficient campaign of genocide in history!* Yet he was apologizing for failure! In the light of Prager's thesis, Hitler's remorse is quite understandable. *The slaughter of the Six Million had not been sufficient to destroy Jewish influence and values because there were still enough Jews alive to rebuild.* True, we have not nearly recovered from the Holocaust, but Torah life has developed to an unimagined extent, and its influence has penetrated areas that were closed to it even before the Holocaust.

~§ Nazism: Destruction of Jewish "Conscience"

What then, is Prager's definition of German anti-Semitism? Firstly, it is not a new phenomenon. It is nothing more than the traditional hatred of the Jew that began when Avraham became recognized as the bearer of a unique set of values. The only truly new thing in Nazism was its harnessing of German efficiency and technology to the cause of anti-Semitism ... Zyklon B was merely the most effective tool yet invented for murdering Jews, but the cause it served was not at all novel.

Anti-Semitism was hatred of what the Jews represented. Friedrich Wilhelm Nietzsche, the nineteenth-century German philosopher, was not an anti-Semite, but his formulation of what the Jew represented became the raw material for the vile fumings of Hitler, Rosenberg, Streicher and their cohorts. Nietzsche differentiated between the "slave mentality" characterized by feelings of weakness, mercy, and kindness — as epitomized by the Jew — and the "master mentality" characterized by strength, courage, brutality — epitomized by the German. He saw Jews as the cultural force that had overthrown the natural order of Might Makes Right, the law of the jungle, and replaced it with a weakness. What is known as Western civilization and morality, he claimed, are in reality perversions of natural law and a violation of the ideal human order of domination by the strong for no other reason (for no other reason is necessary) than the fact of their strength.

Hitler, in his mad rantings, put it this way:

> *"It is true, we are barbarians. That is an honored title to us. I free humanity from the shackles of the soul, from the degrading suffering caused by the false vision called conscience and ethics. The Jews have inflicted two wounds on mankind — circumcision on its body and 'conscience' on its soul. They are Jewish inventions. The war for domination of the world is waged only between the two of us, between these two camps alone — the Germans and the Jews. Everything else is but deception."*

So the genocide of the Jews was not at all comparable to the genocide of the gypsies, because the Final Solution transcended race. That is why, in the closing year of the war, Hitler diverted troops and transport from his deteriorating front lines to speed extermination of the Jews. If unable to win the victory of the Thousand Year Reich, he could at least exterminate the "slave mentality," his ultimate philosophical enemy. And it was not enough simply to murder Jews. They had to be humiliated, dehumanized, stripped of their dignity and pride in order to discredit their creed and the philosophy of life they represented.

Seen in this perspective, the epitaph that "the Jews went like sheep to the slaughter" becomes all the more awful a distortion, because it implies that the Nazi atrocity is not told in the chilling words "Six Million" — it also indicates that the master race succeeded in demonstrating its spiritual superiority over the slave race.

❧ Biographer of the Soul

Against this background, Prager's work assumes a new dimension. He is more than a historian of the Holocaust; he is the biographer of the Jewish soul in its period of severest trial in many centuries, perhaps since the *Churban Bais Hamikdash*.

Prager's family was completely wiped out during the war. But, scholar, historian, and journalist that he was, he had the training and the tools to investigate the deaths and keep alive their memory and what they represented. And he had the unflagging will to do it. "I die every day and I am resuscitated again," he says. Fame, success, and prosperity did not dampen his determination to carry out his mission of capturing and preserving the truth of the past.

As soon as the war ended, he obtained permission to visit the Displaced Persons camps of Europe. Many people were doing so in those days, but none of them were hearing the stories of the emaciated remains of Eastern European Jewry, for they could not be interviewed. The agony through which they had lived was too horrible to tell: to tell it was to relive it — and how could one voluntarily enter hell again? Prager's method was different. He lived with the liberated prisoners. For six weeks he lived in Bergen-Belsen, listening and gently probing until he became one of them and was able to elicit their stories. Always he sought corroboration and refused to settle for less than the most accurate version of events obtainable.

His research has continued to this day and has resulted in scores of articles and a shelf of books. He was probably the most widely read historian of the Holocaust in Hebrew and Yiddish, and his popularity spans all shades of the Israeli cultural and religious spectrum. His tales are not happy — how could tales of the Holocaust be happy? Yet, Prager is popular despite the tragedy, pathos, and heartbreak of his stories. One reads him and feels drained — yet elevated. He explains it best:

> *I looked at the tragedy of the Holocaust and I saw the Jewish people enveloped in fire. But we were like the burning bush in which G-d first revealed Himself to Moshe.* וְהַסְּנֶה אֵינֶנּוּ אֻכָּל — *the bush was not consumed." No matter what the Nazis did to us, we were not consumed. They did not win the war; we did because they are gone and we have rebuilt.*
>
> *When I was last in the United States, I met the principal of a day school in Denver, Colorado. He told me that he was in Auschwitz when the war ended and for the last eleven days before the liberation, he lived by eating snow! He survived and he has been a mechanech (educator) for seventeen years. "The bush was not consumed." He symbolizes what the Nazis were trying to destroy, but he outlived them and he is bringing Toras Hashem to a new generation in America.*
>
> *That is what my stories are about. The Nazis could kill*

us, torture us, destroy our bodies — but their war was against our spirit and they could not destroy our spirit.

(From an interview with the author)

✍ "Sparks ..."

Prager's first collection of stories of *Kiddush Hashem* was *Nitzotzei G'vurah*, published in Israel in 1952. It was an immediate success and has gone through many printings. Chapters from *Nitztotzei G'vurah* have been printed in anthologies and are used in standard texts by all three Israeli school systems and by the Israel Defense Force. A long-overdue English translation, *Sparks of Glory*, has now finally appeared. *Sparks of Glory* contains twenty-eight chapters, all of them isolated stories of heroism. They show Jews — in nearly all cases, ordinary *amcho* people — reacting to desperate situations of hunger, danger, torture, pain, suffering. The more the layers of flesh were stripped away from them, the stronger their spirits became. As one of the countless unknown heroes of the book puts it, *"We thought that our bodies were keeping our souls alive, but our souls were keeping our bodies alive."* The book makes it clear that the Six Million did not go like sheep. They went like great men. They perceived that the conqueror wanted to destroy their spirit, so they responded by keeping their spirit strong and vibrant. Of course, they didn't rise up in physical revolt. How could they? But they did react with almost unbelievable bravery and strength of *neshamah*.

• *The Jews of Lublin were doomed to fall victim to SS Commander Glabochnik, a notoriously sadistic murderer. He herded them to the outskirts of the city until their backs were up against barbed wire. He ordered them to sing and ordered his troops to beat them savagely and push them backward against the barbed wire. Their flesh was torn as the barbs cut into them and they fell upon one another trampling each other. Then someone freed himself and began to sing: "Lomir zich iberbetten — Let us reconcile ... " but he sang alone.*
Then he improvised:
"Mir vellen zey iberleben, iberleben, iberleben,
Avinu Shebashamayim;
Mir vellen zey iberleben, iberleben, iberleben."
"We shall outlive them, outlive them, outlive them,
our Father in Heaven;

We shall outlive them, outlive them, outlive them."

The bruised and bleeding mob rose and began singing and dancing the refrain. Glabochnik roared with laughter until he realized they weren't accommodating him; they were defeating him. He ordered them to stop. They continued. He panicked and pleaded, but the singing and dancing continued. The SS troops plowed in swinging whips and clubs and still the singing continued.

• A simple Jew performed a miracle. All through the war he never missed a day of putting on *tefillin* even in the death camps. Once he was caught by a German guard. The infuriated German threw him to the ground, ground one iron-studded boot into his stomach while scraping the skin off his face with the other, as the Jew lay on the ground, sure he would never get up again.

"What did you think to yourself?" Prager asked this same Jew when he later related the story to him.

"What's the difference ... ? I don't know ... "

Prager pressed him until he finally answered, "All right, I said a verse from Psalms over and over again: 'See my suffering and my ordeal and forgive all my sins.' I repeated it over and over again, and it may be because of that that I was able to rise up and go on with my prayers ... "

• Little Shmulik was brutally whipped by a Polish policeman because he sneaked out of the ghetto to buy extra food for Shabbos. He hid his terrible pain from his parents, but against his father's wishes made his way to the secret subcellar where Shabbos prayers were held. The Germans punished public prayer with death and the Jews didn't allow children to come, to protect the safety of all. But Shmulik came and knocked. The men thought it was the Gestapo and agreed to open the door and face death bravely. But it was Shmulik. They were outraged and his father slapped him. Shmulik could endure his pain no longer.

"Will you beat me, too? Haven't I had my share of blows? I, too, am a Jew. I, too, want to pray!"

• A humble little *shamash* smuggled a *shofar* into a death camp, organized a *minyan* on Rosh Hashanah, and blew the *shofar*. The guards came running and decided to make a spectacle of the *shamash*. They whipped him endlessly, mercilessly, and all the while he continued chanting the prayers out loud.

"The righteous will see and rejoice ... and all wickedness will banish like smoke, for You will have removed the evil kingdom from the earth."

• Rabbi Shem of Cracow was among those chosen at random to be condemmed to a special torture jail. He comforted his fellow Jews by asking them, "If each of us were given the choice at this moment to be the victim or the victimizer, which would he choose? *Ribono Shel Olam*, is there one Jew who would like You to turn him into a murderous gentile?"

"Rabbi, Rabbi, I swear to you on the memory of my holy mother, even I would not want it."

It was the Jewish Kapo.

❧ Who Will Teach "Holocaust" to Our Children?

Who won? Who outlived whom? Was the bush consumed? There is agony and inspiration in *Sparks of Glory*, and the sum total is pride in Jews who faced death — and worse — like lions.

But it has enormous value for another reason, and it is to be hoped that we will not pass up the opportunity it presents us. The publicizers of the Holocaust have not been Torah Jews. The popular image that has been drummed into the minds of American Jews, and especially of our young people, is precisely the one that Prager fiercely opposes — that the Jews went like sheep to the slaughter. Many young people here and in Israel hold the Six Million in contempt for that reason, especially during this era when violence and militancy are as American as apple pie.

At the same time, the children in our *yeshivos* are virtually untaught about the Holocaust. The reasons for this are many. A large proportion of the parents and faculties of our *yeshivos* are survivors of World War II Europe. The suffering of that period left physical and emotional scars on them that make it difficult if not impossible for them to teach the history of this period to their children and students. Then, too, the unprecedented bloodletting and barbarism raise excruciatingly difficult questions of *hashkafah:* How could G-d allow it to happen? What sins could have justified such punishment? Why was the cream of religious Jewry decimated when the principal sinners were surely found elsewhere? The list goes on. We are living in an age that is not prepared to accept anything without a full explanation — but the ways of G-d are inscrutable. The response of many *Gedolei Yisrael* was outlined in the essay, "Questions Without Answers ... Faith Without Questions." But it is not a subject that is easy to teach and this is especially true when there is a distinct lack of English-language materials that are both literate and consonant with the Torah outlook.

For whatever reasons, however, the fact is that few of our young people have any knowledge of the behavior of their martyred brethren other than the sheep-to-the-slaughter stereotype. To further complicate matters, the non-Orthodox and left-of-center Orthodox have virtually monopolized the memory of the Six Million. It is they who commemorate the Warsaw Ghetto Uprising and *Yom Hasho'ah.* The Torah camp cannot subscribe to the tenor of their observance and the *"Never Again"* ironfisted philosophy it represents. Then, too, much of the enthusiasm for Holocaust observances comes from people who would substitute *Yom Hasho'ah* for Tishah B'Av when, to us, the Holocaust is an outgrowth of the historic Tisha B'Av. This has caused a backlash effect resulting in too many Torah Jews ignoring or belittling the significance of formally preserving memories of the Holocaust, an attitude that has the terrible effect of Jews refusing to learn lessons of Torah and *teshuvah* from the destruction of the Six Million.

Hillel Goldberg

The Last Mashgiach of Slobodka

A PROFOUND BUT SOMEWHAT OBSCURE Torah volume written in this century is *Toras Avraham*. I had not yet given it serious attention when its contents were first reviewed for me by a disciple of the volume's late author, Rabbi Avrohom Grodzenski.

"Rabbi Grodzenski was the last *Mashgiach* in Slobodka," said the disciple.

❧ ❧ ❧

In Eastern European *yeshivos*, a teacher rich in the Torah's wisdom and endowed with psychological insight served as mentor to students in the capacity of *Mashgiach*. This position represented an innovation of the Lithuanian *Mussar* Movement, which stressed the development of ethical and introspective capacities as well as intellectual abilities and Torah knowledge. The Movement began in the mid-nineteenth century and flourished until World War II when, together with most other expressions of Eastern European Orthodoxy, it was cruelly cut down by Nazism. The Movement spawned a number of educational centers, one of which was Slobodka.

❧ ❧ ❧

"Rabbi Grodzenski was the last *Mashgiach* in Slobodka," said the disciple.

A routine statement, a minor part of our conversation, I cannot explain why it had such an impact on me. For one thing, I had little knowledge of Slobodka in any of its connotations — as a

---

This essay appeared in *The Jewish Observer* of June 1976.

Lithuanian city, as a *yeshivah*, as a historical concept. I had never heard of the *Mashgiach* before. And all that I know about him now is that he was the last *Mashgiach* there.

Perhaps that's it — he was the last. Of course, I knew what that meant. Just as there had been a last Jew in Vilna, a last one in Kovno, in Bialystok, in Warsaw, so had there been a last one in Slobodka. And if there had been a last Jew there, then it only made sense that there had been a last *Mashgiach*, too.

A discordant term: "last one." An unprecedented term. A term that leaves the taste of ashes in your mouth and the throb of questions in your heart if you think about them at all, which of course you do.

You cannot express all of the questions. You cannot even conceive of all of them. But one question, to a religious Jew, takes form immediately, for it has been asked so many times that it has become a spiritual instinct: "Why did *tzaddikim* die?"

It's a strange question in today's context. People generally ask, "Why did *any* Jew die in a gas chamber?"

The religious Jew cannot always view it that way. His approach is not acceptable? Too bad — there is nothing he can do or intends to do about it. He's been trained that way. He's been asking the same questions, pursuing the identical quests, renewing the same values for longer than he can remember. All this may appear conceptually unchallenging, but it's far from easy in practice. Renewal means struggle, sorrow, exaltation, nitty-gritty: life. That's the way the religious Jew is.

Hence, the question endures, "Why did *tzaddikim* die? Haven't we been taught that there is absolute justice? Isn't the lot of *tzaddikim* supposed to embody that justice?"

As much as the question persists, the answer evades concretization. It's true, there are answers, but in their formulation, somehow, they cheapen the question rather than answer it. If our intellects can be satisfied, our emotions cannot.

Whereupon the instinct shifts. The question persists, but the action, the struggle — the response — changes. Memorialization, replacing philosophizing, comes to the fore.

Not "Why did *tzaddikim* die?" — but, "They did not die!"

The response then is to preserve their memory, to chart their last steps, to ponder the secret of their beginnings. This means research, writing, publishing. It means books, articles. It means memorial foundations. It means fantasy. The dead will not rejoin us. The disfigured visages depicting their ugly demise — etched indelibly on our minds — cannot depart. The imponderability remains.

Yet, a new course of conduct has been fixed — to preserve — for to preserve means to carry on. It means, not that the dead are revived, not that their last steps are any less painful for us, not that the question is answered. It means that *we* are revived. *We* live again; *our* dignity is restored. The past — we have no choice but to pursue it. Yet as we do, we become ever more detached from it. As we reveal its treasures, they become ever more distant.

Distant, in their own reality. But in our sphere of reality, we become sure footed again. We become Jews with a straight back, and even a straight mind. More, the yearning for our Creator can emerge within us once again; the final *tikkun* (restoration) is achievable. We renew, revitalize the jubilance requisite to the proper celebration of His commands. The questions subsides; indeed, we persist in asking different questions: "Who was the last *Mashgiach* in Slobodka? What was his greatness? His legacy, his discoveries? How may we nurture them?"

For our own sake, we pursue such questions passionately. Don't we?

Rabbi A. Scheinman

Bikrovei Ekodeish: The Six Million Kedoshim

✥§ The "Kadosh" Paradox

NO PASSAGES WRITTEN ABOUT *Churban* Europe weigh so heavily on the heart of the religious Jew as those that see "no point, no faith, no Divine inspiration ..." in the death of the Six Million. We admire those who preserved their faith under the worst of circumstances. Indeed, we view the individual who is a *moser nefesh* — who risks his very life — to be *mekadesh shem shomayim* (sanctify G-d's name) as someone whose concept of life transcends the flesh and blood of a this-world existence. Thus, we revere the Jews of the Middle Ages — spiritual giant and simple Jew alike — who chose the stake over the cross; in their death we catch a glimpse of eternal life. Regardless of the nature of their previous life, their choice at the moment of truth branded each as a *kadosh*, and for all time to come their act is a beacon of inspiration.

But what about *"Churban* Europe"? What choices were the victims given? What merit could they have earned with death? Why do we call them all *kedoshim*, when so many of them had been vehemently anti-religious and had helped destroy the foundations of Torah in Europe? Consider, for example, the most ironic situation imaginable: a young Jew, born of Jewish mother and Catholic father, raised as a Catholic, is kneeling in a church, quietly murmuring his *paternoster*, perhaps even offering a prayer for the well-being of the brave German soldiers. In come two soldiers and drag him off to the death camps, while he

---

This essay appeared in *The Jewish Observer* of September 1980.

protests all along that he is a good Catholic, and not a Jew — is he also one of the six million *kedoshim?*

Without pretending to offer definitive explanations for an inexplicable tragedy, the following essay deals with the use of the term "kedoshim" in regard to those who lost their lives in *Churban* Europe.

The source of the confusion lies in the incorrect translation of *kedoshim* as "martyrs." While a martyr is usually someone who willingly gives up his life for a principle ("a person who chooses to suffer death rather than renounce his religion" — first definition, *Random House Dictionary*), "*kadosh*" has a far broader and deeper meaning. Let us begin by explaining *Kiddush Hashem* and *Chillul Hashem.*

~§ The Makings of Kiddush Hashem

G-d is immutable. He does not ever change in the least — neither in sanctity nor in its lack — regardless of any actions initiated by man. On the other hand, man can affect the degree of Divine revelation in our world — the degree of *gillui panim* and *hester panim* — that which permits man to perceive the Divinity, or veils Him from human perception. This can be understood on a simple level, in terms of psychological impact: if a person commits an *aveira* (sin) brazenly and with impunity, it can weaken faith in G-d on a broad scale, and should he perform a *mitzvah*, the positive, inspirational effect could be equally far reaching.

This can also be understood on a deeper level, as the *Nefesh HaChaim* elaborates: Every person is granted the power both to bring the light of Divinity to this world, or to block its illumination if he so chooses. Thus the description *mechalel Hashem* (desecrator of G-d's Name) applies to the person whose actions serve to dim the rays of *ha'oras panim* — His illuminating presence; and *mekadesh* (sanctifier) refers to the person whose action brings about *gillui haShechina* — revelation.

Kiddush Hashem can be achieved in two ways — actively and passively. The active approach is simple to envision: a person does *mitzvos* with great dedication, involvement, and *mesiras nefesh*, or he actually gives away his life for God's honor. The Mirrer *Mashgiach*, Rabbi Yerucham Levovitz, elaborates on this point in his classical *shmuess* (discourse) on *Ha'Avos Heim HaMerkava* (The *Avos* are the "chariot" upon which the *Shechina* (Divine Presence) entered our world). He explains that

Kiddush Hashem describes any action that serves as a vehicle to usher the *Shechina* into our domain. In other words — any action that makes G-d's truth more apparent is an act of *Kiddush Hashem*.

But what is "passive" *Kiddush Hashem?* To understand this, we refer to G-d's declaration of *Bikrovei Ekodeish* ("I will become sanctified through My close ones") in regard to the deaths of Aharon's sons Nadav and Avihu, who were consumed by holy fire during the consecration of the Tabernacle. Their transgression was so slight that commentaries have difficulty in pinpointing it. Their level of *kedushah* was so great that it surpassed that of Moshe and Aharon (see *Rashi* on *Vayikra* 10:3), and they — not their elders — were chosen to be the *kedoshim*. The *Gemara* explains that in our conception of things, G-d becomes elevated, awesome, and sanctified when He castigates *tzaddikim*, even though they did not perform any acts of *Kiddush Hashem per se*; through suffering Divine retribution, they become instruments of Divine revelation, and their status merits the description of *Ekodeish* — I will become sanctified — through them.

We encounter many examples of this type of *Kiddush Hashem*:

— A person who is *mechallel Hashem* is forgiven only through his death. He had lifted his hand audaciously, defying the existence of the Deity. Only when he himself crumbles into nothingness is a proper perspective restored.

— The *Gemara* explains: כִּי לְךָ תִכְרַע כָּל בֶּרֶךְ — זוֹ יוֹם הַמִּיתָה, "Every knee will bow before You — this is the day of death."

Chazal saw in death the ultimate prostration before the Almighty. The haughty, the mighty, the self-anointed deities persist in misleading the world, till the day their own knees buckle before their inevitable demise. Then their mortality is established, and the true state of affairs is once more reaffirmed — G-d's eternal immutability, in contrast to man's fleeting, transitory state.

— One says *Kaddish* after the passing of a close relative, for an intimate encounter with death brings a person closer to the realization that this world was created by the Almighty and is ruled in accordance with His will. The surviving relative expresses verbally his humility before G-d's eternal sanctity. If this death can help others comprehend G-d's omnipotence, it surely is a great *z'chus* (merit) for the deceased.

❧ The Corrective Kiddush Hashem of the Klal

This is the passive *Kiddush Hashem* of an individual. What is the passive *Kiddush Hashem* achieved collectively by *Klal Yisroel?*

The *Kiddush Hashem* of *Klal Yisroel* is the realization of: *And you[r] fate will be a shock to all the nations of the earth* (Devarim 28:25). Or: *And you will be a wonderment, a metaphor* [for suffering], *a legend among all people* (ibid. v. 37). Or: *All the people will say, "Why did G-d do this to this land? Why this great anger?" And they will say, "Because they abandoned the covenant of ... the G-d of their fathers"* (ibid. 29:23-24).

When *Klal Yisroel* is punished on so awesome a scale that one can almost see the Divine Hand manipulating its fate, we are forced to say, *"Why did G-d do this?"*

By the same token, *Churban* Europe can be attributed to no other cause than *Why did G-d do this?* The German-Jewish confrontation was not a case of two nationalities competing in a zero-sum-total situation, as existed with the Palestinians versus the Jews. Nor was it a situation of the Jew as the prospering middleman between the drunken estate-lord and the oppressed serf, as it was during the pogroms of the Middle Ages. We cannot even ascribe the Nazi campaign against the Jews to the madness of a psychopathic aggressor, for deep, deep in the war, when every bit of aggressive instinct should have been engrossed in waging the war on the battle fronts, major emphasis was on the meticulous planning to carry out the Final Solution to its fullest infamy.

Considering the events of that epoch in the light of the passages in *Devarim*, the question is not "Where was G-d at Auschwitz?" but *"Why* was G-d at Auschwitz?"

❧ G-d's "Corrective Action"

In a remarkably prescient essay, Rabbi Meir Simcha Hacohen of Dvinsk (the *Ohr Somayach*) wrote in the mid 19th century* of an impending *churban* due to the *haskala* (Enlightenment) — total assimilation to the host culture of Western Nations; Rabbi Avrohom Grodzenski (who was killed in the Grodno Ghetto) made a list of specific *aveiros* that in his view brought down G-d's wrath; but all this is of secondary

---

* In *Meshech Chochma* on *Bechukosai*. A free translation appears as the first essay in this volume.

importance. The primary point made must be that one way or another the destruction was a Divine corrective action for a long-standing accumulation of shortcomings on the part of *Klal Yisroel* over the ages.

> *My father, who was in the Kovno Ghetto with Rabbi Mottel Pogremanski (the Tavriger Illuy)* told me that Reb Mottel would say shmuessen during the closing moments of the Shabbos. A deep hush would fall on the crowded room ... Reb Mottel closed his eyes and began, in a haunting voice: "I see no German parading ... I hear not the bark of their rifles ... Passages from Tanach I do see ... I hear the Kol Hashem — the Voice of G-d — echoing from one end of the ghetto to the other ... אֶמְלוֹךְ עֲלֵיכֶם ... אִם לֹא בְּיָד חֲזָקָה, 'As I live' — said G-d — 'with a strong hand, an outstretched arm and a flow of wrath shall I rule over you ... I will gather you from the lands where you are scattered ... to a wilderness of a nation and I will wrangle with you there face to face' (Yechezkeil 20:33-36). Had we been deserving, we would have accepted G-d's rule — on our own; but we did not do so, and now he is forcibly imposing his dominion over us."*

Reb Mottel's words, seeming to reaffirm Reb Meir Simcha's predictions, echoed the anguished cry of the Prophet: *For saying, "Let us be like all the nations ..."* (did G-d vow), *"As I live ... with a strong hand ... and a flow of wrath shall I rule over you!'* (ibid. 32-33). The prophecy, the warning, and the searing lament at the brink of destruction all seem to suggest that *Klal Yisroel* had chosen to distort its collective image by emulating the nations, rather than pursuing its own sacred destiny. Meant to be a kingdom of priests, a holy nation, inhabiting the sacred soil of the Holy Land, it betrayed its charge. The "corrective action" for this was a brutal, massive rejection of Jewry by the most powerful of Western nations, the epitome of European culture — Germany. This terrible suffering was *Bikrovei Ekodeish* before the eyes of humankind as a whole: G-d is our King, ruling us by His determination, if not by our own elective volition. And the purest, the saintliest, the most learned, the most innocent were included in this terrifying enactment of *Bikrovei Ekodeish*.

---

* The Tavriger *Illuy* (genius) was an illustrious Torah personality, one of the greatest disciples of the *yeshivos* of Telshe and Slobodka. He was widely recognized for his Torah scholarship and original *mussar* thoughts, in addition to his exemplary *tzidkus* and piety. He survived the Nazi purgatory, dying in Paris shortly after the war.

~§ The Response and the Burden

The proper response? Perhaps this was most succinctly phrased by the *Sforno* in his commentary on וַיִּדֹּם אַהֲרֹן, *And Aharon was silent:* "He found comfort in the *Kiddush Hashem* that resulted from their death."

The burden resting on our shoulders, as the first generation after the Holocaust, is not the burden of self-defense; nor is it the wreaking of vengeance on the Germans. It is the burden of knowledge by a generation that witnessed *Bikrovei Ekodeish*, the בְּיָד חֲזָקָה אֶמְלוֹךְ עֲלֵיכֶם. If we sin, it is the sin of one who has seen the fury of Divine retribution. It is committed with the callousness of one who has peered into the depths of *Gehinnom*, seen the fires and heard the screams, and then continued on as if nothing had happened. As *Rashi* comments on the impact of witnessing the death of the sons of Aharon: should anyone sin in a like manner after their death, it would be comparable to having witnessed a man drink poison and die, and then drink more of the same potion himself. As surviving witnesses we are charged with an awesome responsibility.

# III.
Of Enemies and Friends

Dr. Henry Biberfeld

Where Evil is Spawned

WHEN THE DIVINITY of the Bible is repudiated, that is the point where evil is spawned. In the spring of 1902, there appeared in Leipzig a book with the curious title *Bible or Bable*. Its author was a professor of Assyriology, Friedrich Delitzsch. The book — a collection of lectures — caused a furor far beyond the circle of Biblical scholars. What it claimed was no less than this: All the great religious and moral teachings that Judaism had bequeathed to the world were, in truth, not a legacy of Judaism but of ancient Babylonia. A gigantic fraud had been perpetrated on an unsuspecting world. Cleverly adopting Babylonian wisdom, the Jews had then presented it to mankind as their own.

Today we might look at this whole incident as an absurd and isolated manifestation of a prejudiced mind; we would be grievously mistaken. Delitzsch's pamphlet was but a symptom of a lingering sickness, part of a ground swell of hidden resentment, the proverbial visible top of a huge submerged iceberg of hostility.

Friedrich Delitzsch's work was one, albeit perhaps the most outspoken one, in a long line of publications aimed at undermining the veracity of the Bible. Beginning with the writings of Ferdinand Astruc (who found support for his thesis in the works of Spinoza), continued and expanded by De Wette, Eichorn and culminating in Wellhausen's dissection of the Bible into literary fragments, there had spread in German universities the disastrous discipline of "Bible Criticism" — which treated the Bible simply as another ancient literary document.

This essay appeared in *The Jewish Observer* of September 1979.

Judaism's, and indeed humanity's, priceless heritage was subjected to an unending process of vivisection and dismemberment until it all but gave up its ghost. Highly skilled in their respective fields of archaeology, ancient languages, etc., these scholars were, however, quite ignorant of our classical Bible commentators, or willfully ignored them. As far as the fact of the literal fulfillment of Divine predictions in the Pentateuch and Prophets, made thousands of years ago, was concerned, they simply closed their eyes to it.

৵ Why 19th-Century Germany?

How can one explain this sudden concentric attack against "The Book" that had fathered the three major religions of the Western World? Why at that particular point in space — Germany, and at that particular point in time — the 19th century? Whence its widespread popularity?

We shall see that the answers to these questions will provide far more than an explanation of a theological controversy. They will throw a novel and revealing light on that great catastrophe of our time: the rise of National Socialism in Germany, an event that seems as inexplicable in the suddenness of its appearance as in the bestial brutality of its methods. A straight causal line connects the diligent activity of those German professors busily chipping away at the authenticity of the Bible and the sadistic excess of the storm troopers.

No historic occurrence exists in isolation; each is a link in the complex web of the Master's design. In order to understand the genesis of Bible Criticism, we have to know the historical context in which it arose.

The Germany that evolved during the 19th and early-20th centuries was one of a growing deep national sentiment. It was the age of Bismarck, the "Iron Chancellor," whose appeal to German unity led to the restoration of imperial Germany after centuries of fragmentation. The historian Treitschke held his students spellbound with his teachings of the supremacy of Germany as the true heir of the Holy Roman Empire. It was an age of a search for "National Glory and Military Success, of a collective descent into the German soul." Motivating this historical development was a keen intellectual and emotional fixation on the ideas of "Racial thought, German Christianity and Volkish nature mysticism" (George R. Mosse in *The Crisis of German Ideology*). The romantic authors of the period resurrected the German past in their writings and collections of ancient fairy tales and legends.

Racial Purity and National Destiny

Perhaps the most typical of the exponents of this era is that evil genius Richard Wagner who, with the bewitching power of his music, brought back to life the "Niebelungen Song," that ancient German saga of bloodshed, sorcery and deceit.

The philosopher Nietzsche was the eloquent spokesman of the movement. He may or may not have been an anti-Semite, but he provided some of the key ideas for the right of Germany to dominate the world. He claimed boldly that the German "Superman," "The Blond Beast," was destined to rule by a "Master Morality," above the restriction of ordinary human justice.

The world view of the Germans that evolved, based on notions of "a mystic communion with the soul, racial purity and a unique national destiny," excluded any influence that may have stemmed from the Jewish or Judaeo-Christian tradition. (We may note that Nietzsche, for one, was powerfully opposed to Christianity and its dominant influence on Western history.) Specifically, of course, the Jews and Judaism came under attack.

There was no possibility of compromise or harmonization between the Jewish teachings of universal justice, the brotherhood of all men and the ideal of humility, and those of the inherent right of the stronger, the superiority of the German race, the worship of the all-conquering hero.

Hence Judaism and its heritage had to be proven historically antiquated and morally inferior. It is, therefore, no coincidence that this era produced an entire literature of tendentious writings presenting the Old Testament as a second-rate adaptation of Babylonian epics and legal codes, the Talmud as a repository of a primitive morality.

Prime Target: The Bible

The attacks focused on the Bible. Talmud and Jewish Codes of Law might provide convenient targets to demonstrate the inferior character of the Jew, but it was the Bible, the common source of Judaism as well as Christianity, that was the real obstacle in the path of German glory. Its credibility as a source of morality had to be utterly destroyed. This, Bible criticism set out to do.

Much of the foundation of this assault against the Bible was rooted in the Graf-Wellhausen theory of the composition of the Old Testament. In fact, as a modern scholar, Erich Voeglein, recently wrote: "The critical work of the Wellhausen school moves methodologically in a haze, because it is insufficiently aware of the difference between empirical, philological work and the interpretation put on its results" (*Order and History*, Vol. I, p. 153); but many, and not only laymen, were taken in by Wellhausen's barrage of quotations and the peremptory assurance of his conclusions.

The Defenders

German Jewry was not quite unprepared for the onslaught. True, the majority of German Jews, assimilated as they were, were supremely disinterested in this conflict. But a small group took up the challenge. The great rabbinical scholar, Rabbi Ezriel Hildesheimer, founded in 1872 the Rabbinical Seminary of Berlin to train Jewish scholars to become familiar with the methods and results of modern science. He attracted to his staff Biblical and Talmudic scholars of world renown. The most brilliant of these scholars was probably Professor David Hoffmann, who published pioneering works in almost every sphere of Jewish learning. Of special interest here are his commentaries to the Pentateuch (originally written in German and recently published in Hebrew translation by Mossad Harav Kook).

In these commentaries, Professor Hoffman set out to disprove the theories of Bible Criticism, meeting them on their own ground. Gifted with an encyclopedic knowledge and razor-sharp intellect, he systematically demonstrated that Bible Criticism's theories were flimsy castles-in-the-air supported only by the will to believe.

And the effect of his writings? As far as the academic world was concerned: nil; he was simply ignored. His Biblical fundamentalism did not fit into a society nurtured on evolutionism and a Germanic Christianity.

That does not mean that Hoffmann's work (and that of his colleagues at the Seminary) was in vain. There were many, even among believing Jews, who were enticed by the persuasive phraseology, the scientific apparatus, the sheer mass of published material of Bible Criticism.

Hoffmann's and his confreres' works pointed out the weaknesses of the hypotheses of Bible Criticism and gave renewed confidence to many perplexed by this assault on faith and tradition.

But for the Germans, the road toward world domination was now cleared. If the Bible was fallible, then so were its ideals. In their place was set the rule that "Might makes Right." On the horizon loomed two World Wars and untold suffering.

Rabbi Yaakov Feitman

The Master Race and The Chosen People: — A Look at the Nazi Ideology in a Torah Light

HOLOCAUST ... SHOAH ... CHURBAN. After a third of a century, we have, at least in the literal sense, begun to "come to terms" with the devastating events of World War II. Torah Jewry has learned to discard the terms coined in grief or politics and accept the designation our sages have used for millennia to describe Jewish suffering: *Churban*.[1] Yet, whatever name we give to that awesome nightmare, our discussions and analyses of the destruction of European Jewry often take a dangerously self-torturing path. The ideological "right" agonizes over the alleged "sins" of this or that community which led to G-d's wrath; the "left" torments itself and desecrates the memories of these courageous Jews who were murdered, by obscenely condemning them for "going to their deaths like sheep."

Strangely, in all this flurry of recent Holocaust studies, the enemy is almost forgotten. Especially in Torah circles, the Nazi ogre is almost erased from the picture. We are taught to accept and to learn to repent from our past — and indeed, this is an essential part of the pattern of Jewish history. But it is crucial to remember that there was a particular villain here as well. The

---

This essay appeared in *The Jewish Observer* of June 1978.

1. See the essay on this subject based on a discourse by Rabbi Yitzchok Hutner זצ"ל, appearing earlier in this volume.

Nazis were not merely inert tools of Divine wrath[2] but conscious and diabolical servants of evil. It is now clear, although there were indications even then, that the malignancy infecting Nazi Europe traveled through a bloodstream poisoned by a specific ideology. Just as Pharaoh had to convince his people that the Jews were dangerous to the prosperity and even survival of the Egyptians, so too would Hitler's evil machinations have been impossible on such a mass scale without the tools of rationalization and justification.[3]

◆§ Concepts in Collision

Much has been written about the philosophical and ideological underpinnings of Nazi propaganda. Various antecedents — Nietzsche, H.S. Chamberlain, Schopenhauer — have been cited. Yet, for the Jew with that sensitive ear, the single concept in Nazi doctrine that proclaims itself the loudest is

---

2. It is noteworthy that as recently as the Eichmann trial, Dr. Servatius (Eichmann's defense counsel) used the "Divine purpose" argument in defense of his killer client. "The death of six million," he asserted, "was part of a higher purpose and in recompense for an earlier and greater crime against G-d, thereby joining the modern trial in Jerusalem with one held twenty centuries before."

Of course, we need not dignify Servatius' argument with a formal answer. However, for our own edification, it is worth knowing that the *Ramban* (Nachmanides) dealt with an apposite issue over seven centuries ago. I am grateful to Rabbi Mordechai Weinberg, *Rosh Yeshivah* of Yeshivah Merkaz HaTorah of Montreal, for pointing out the *Ramban's* answer (*Bereishis* 15:14) to the *Rambam's* (Maimonides) question concerning why Pharaoh was punished for afflicting the Jews when actually he was only fulfilling a Divine decree. After refuting the *Rambam's* own answer to this crucial question, the *Ramban* states: "Know and understand that [although] on the New Year a person has been inscribed and sealed for violent death, the bandits who kill him will not be guiltless [on the basis of the claim] that they merely have fulfilled that which had been decreed against him. *The wicked man shall die in his iniquity (Yechezkeil* 3:18), but his blood will be sought from the murderer." Rabbi Elchonon Wasserman is even more explicit in his interpretation of the *Ramban*, asserting that "no person can die unless the L-rd has decreed that it be so; nevertheless, the murderer is punishable by death" *(Koveitz Maamorim:* הכל בידי שמים חוץ מציגים ופחים).

3. According to the Gaon of Vilna זצ״ל, even the wicked Pharaoh, dealing with the wicked Egyptian people, could not simply enact as barbaric a decree as the killing of every male Jewish child. Thus, the Gaon explains, when the *Gemara (Sotah* 11b) states that Pharaoh gave the Jewish midwives a way of telling if the fetus was male or female, the implication is that only if they could make it appear as though the children were stillborn could Pharaoh "get away with it." This, although Pharaoh was an absolute monarch and surely a strong ruler! (*See Divrei Eliyahu: Shemos* 1:1.) Hitler, too, could not have involved an entire nation in his obscenities without a deep philosophical or practical motivation.

contained in the phrase: The Master Race. Indeed, one can hear in Aryanism a direct challenge to the concept: וִהְיִיתֶם לִי סְגֻלָּה מִכָּל הָעַמִּים, "And you shall be to Me the most treasured of all the nations" — the election of Israel.

The Germans openly recognized this diametric opposition between Nazi "Masterdom" and Jewish "Chosenness."[4] In fact, Himmler attempted to justify genocide as a perverted pre-emptive strike when he announced at Posen in 1943, "We had the moral right to wipe out this people bent on wiping us out."[5] For he, like other Nazis, recognized two prime powers in the world, the Jewish Nation and the German — as personified ultimately in the chosen elite of Aryanism.

If we become uneasy at the juxtaposition, we must nevertheless recognize its existence. As an example of the persistence of this problem in "post-Holocaust theology," a *Commentary* magazine symposium in 1966 posed five questions which it deemed crucial and pivotal to an ideological stance. Participating were fifty-five rabbis — Orthodox, Conservative, Reform, Reconstructionist, and unaffiliated. One of the questions was: *"In what sense do you believe that the Jews are the chosen people of G-d? How do you answer the charge that this doctrine is the model from which various theories of national and racial superiority have been derived?"*[6]

The very fact that a prominent group of editors and Jewish intellectuals should deem this question among the five most basic to Jewish belief is an indicator of the uneasiness of the secular Jewish mind with the concept of being chosen by G-d. Indeed, of the thirty-eight responses, almost all the Reform and many of the Conservative respondents attempted to wriggle out of terms such as "chosen" and "election of Israel" or "mission of Israel" by appealing to the Torah's fairness to gentiles, statements such as "Christianity is the true religion for Christians and Judaism is the true religion for Jews" (Solomon Freehoff), and other disclaimers of uniqueness.

Torah-true Jews readily accept both the yoke and the glory of being the *Am Hanivchar* (Chosen People). Apologetics are

---

4. This was expressed as early as 1873, in Wilhelm Marr's book, *The Victory of Jewry Over Teutonism (Germanentum)*.

5. Quoted by Hannah Arendt, *The Origins of Totalitarianism* (London, 1958), p. 429.

6. Published in book form as *The Condition of Jewish Belief* (New York: The MacMillan Company, 1966).

The Master Race and the Chosen People / 111

unnecessary and our suffering for our chosenness has more than compensated for any debt that perverse elements in the world would exact upon us for our pride in our status. Yet, as the phrase "Master Race" grates on our ear and offends our mind and heart, our own *Am Hanivchar* comes to mind and we may fall silent, not knowing exactly how to deal with the strange parallel. It is as if we see ourselves in an amusement park house-of-mirrors, one feature distorted out of all proportion — ugly, almost unrecognizable; but we still have the uncanny feeling that we are looking into a mirror.

The Definitive Difference

Rabbi Yaakov Kamenetzky deals with this sensitive issue in a published essay:

People mock us because of our self-concept as the Chosen People. I believe that George Bernard Shaw said the Nazis took anti-Semitism from the Jews; they just embellished it. But (he claims) the idea of racial superiority originated with the Jews' claim to chosenness ... The truth is, we cannot be racists. The Talmud asks, Why did G-d create man alone (unlike the animal kingdom where a male and female of each species were created)? So no man could say to another, "My father is greater than your father" (Sanhedrin 38a).[7]

Then what of our "Chosen People" concept? How are we different from the Nazis? The answer is, every person can become a member of the "Chosen People," while according to Nazi doctrine, you had to be born an Aryan; you could never become one.[8]

As Rabbi Hutner says, we ourselves have often forgotten (and indeed this is more pleasant to forget than to keep constantly in mind) that one of the paramount characteristics of our nation is in its pattern of *suffering*. Nowhere in our literature is there a claim that because we are "chosen" we deserve or demand more from the world than we give. On the contrary, our history reveals that blemishes and peccadilloes that would have been ignored in

---

7. On the Torah's strong statements concerning the brotherhood of man, see also *Yerushalmi Nedarim* Chapter 9, 41C; *Tosefos Yom Tov* on *Avos* 3:14; and *Seder Eliyahu Rabbah*, Chapter 18. It is clear from these and other sources that nowhere is chosenness seen as a privilege or "right' but as a moral yoke and *obligation* toward ourselves and mankind.

8. *Hamenahel,* Published by Torah Umesorah, Nisson 5736 (1976), pp. 17-18.

been ignored in another nation were the cause of severe punishment and chastisement to the Nation of Israel.

Undoubtedly, Rabbi Kamenetzky's delineation should have answered questions about the ostensible similarity between the racism of Aryan ideology and the concept of *Am Hanivchar*. Yet, the gnawing question remains about the presence of any similarity at all. What, after all, is the meaning behind this correspondence?

The Vexing Similarity

Two typical non-Torah treatments of this similarity come to mind, which are indicative of the dangers inherent in misinterpreting this important doctrine — one from a non-Jew, one from a Jew. Wyndham Lewis, one of the most prolific and influential "men of letters" of the twentieth century, is an excellent example of one who obviously bristled and was indeed angered by the Jewish claim of chosenness. Lewis had been influenced by Pound, Eliot and company for much of the 30's into thinking Hitler a saviour, at best — or harmless, at worst.[9] By 1939, however, he had "repented" and in *The Hitler Cult*, disavowed his earlier infatuation. Wishing to clear himself of charges of anti-Semitism and moral support for the enemy, Lewis then wrote a book praising Jewish contributions to the world. He sought to characterize the Jewish people as

> one who have many faults, like the rest of us (among which is an exasperating idea that they have been especially picked out by the All-father as His favorite race is not the least, and is not rendered any more endearing by reason of the Nazi Aryan imitation) but who nevertheless, as a race, have acted as a leaven very often, in the more stodgy and backward of the European societies, adding the lustre of

---

9. Lewis, like many intellectuals of the 20's, had fallen victim to the spell of Hitler's promise and anti-Semitism, publishing in 1931 a groveling and sycophantic ode to Hitler: *Hitler* (London, Chato and Windus). The book was originally published in 1931 as a series of pamphlets on Hitler and Hitlerism. The Nazi anti-Semitism is played down and Lewis seemed convinced that "Hitler would grow more tolerant of the Jews in time"(pp. 35-43, 48). It is perhaps well to remember that Ezra Pound, the intellectual "hero" of the day, was one of the century's most virulent anti-Semites. When he mistakenly thought that T.S. Eliot — an anti-Semite whose venom still infects much of modern literature — wrote a line sympathetic to Jews, he viciously slashed his disciple in print: "Eliot, in this book, has not come through uncontaminated by the Jewish poison. Until a man purges himself of this poison he will never achieve understanding" (quoted from Ezra Pound's *A Visiting Card*, London: Peter Russell, 1952, p.22).

their irrepressible wit to what would otherwise have been a grim, dull business.[10]

Once one has unraveled the tight strands of Lewis' prose, the parenthetical "exasperation" with the Jewish Nation for being preoccupied with its uniqueness can be seen as a subconscious and psychologically sound indictment of the Jews: "Don't complain to me; you brought it on yourselves."

Lewis, of course, did not consider his new charge anti-Semitism. He believed he was merely commenting on an unfortunate aspect of Jewish theology, which "had gotten them into trouble." However we characterize Lewis' earlier romanticizing of Hitler — pure anti-Semitism, stupidity, naivete — it is clear that his later "exasperation" was a weapon wielded by intellectual thugs such as Eliot, Pound, e.e. cummings, and others in their anti-Semitic machinations.

✥ The Conservative Rabbi and the German Priest

Perhaps Wyndham Lewis would have been a more ardent battler against Nazism had he not been "exasperated" with us; but the case of Richard Rubenstein is of greater concern. A Conservative rabbi who in his book *After Aushchwitz* claims to have been pushed by Auschwitz over the brink into "radical theology" (a pseudo-movement which utilizes events of modern times to promote various "G-d is dead" ideologies), Rubenstein records his strange, somewhat surrealistic discussion with Heinrich Gruber, Dean of the Evangelical Church of East and West Berlin.

A German cleric whose credentials as a non-anti-Semite are apparently secure,[11]

Gruber spoke of the ancient covenant between G-d and Israel and how Israel as the Chosen People of G-d was under

---

10. Wyndham Lewis, *The Hitler Cult* (New York: Gordon Press, 1972), p.19. Interesting, Father Walter Burghardt, a Jesuit priest, responding to the scathing indictment of Christianity by Rosemary Ruether, a fellow Catholic quoted later in this article, proposes a number of theological affirmations for Christians as "atonement" for centuries of anti-Semitism. One of these is: "The Jews were chosen by G-d as His special people, His people of election." (p.94 of *Auschwitz: Beginning of a New Era.*)

11. Gruber was sent to Sachsenhausen concentration camp and later to Dachau for his opposition to the Nazi regime. He was a witness at the Eichmann trial in Jerusalem in 1961, and on his seventieth birthday, the "Gruber Grove" was planted in Jerusalem. It is interesting to note, however, that his major effort was devoted to saving "Christians of Jewish extraction from Nazi persecution"(*Encyclopedia Judaica* 7:942).

a very special obligation to behave in a way which was spiritually consistent with Divine ordinance.

Rabbi Rubenstein apparently had difficulty accepting this, and Gruber had to insist with considerable emotion, "I don't say this about Israel; G-d says this in the Bible and I believe it."

After a lengthy exposition of his discussion with Dean Gruber on this subject, Rubenstein concludes his chapter:

As long as we continue to hold to the doctrine of the election of Israel, we leave ourselves open to the theology expressed by Dean Gruber, that, because the Jews are G-d's Chosen People, G-d wanted Hitler to punish them.[12]

Underlying Rubenstein's rejection of the *Am Hanivchar* concept is the fear of the elitist label. If we can ignore for the moment the shame of a Jew being taught our noble place by a gentile theologian, we must deal with Rubenstein's agony at being compared ideologically with the Nazis. Why, indeed, must this striking parallel exist?

From One Womb

In his published works, Rabbi Hutner has attributed the source of Eisav's power over Yaakov, whenever he has momentarily succeeded, to his status as Yaakov's twin. The significance of this circumstance of birth stresses the inner differences between the two nations by highlighting the superficial similarities — much as the two goats of Yom Kippur service (in the time of the Temple) had to be absolutely identical in a number of aspects, to accentuate the divergence in their ultimate destinations.[13]

Rabbi Hutner goes on to illustrate that although the Jews have always had enemies and perhaps even imitators, only the spiritual descendants of Eisav claimed to be the New Israel. The root source of Eisav's enmity is not merely his wish to destroy Yaakov or even jealousy over that which he himself does not have, but the burning desire to totally appropriate that which he had lost when he cravenly sold his birthright. This is the Eisav pattern throughout the ages and we must take note that it is an enmity of a kind of perverse brotherhood, not of xenophobic dissimilitude.

Yet, if this similarity will eventually result in the downfall of

---

12. Richard Rubenstein, *After Auschwitz*, pp. 52-58.
13. See *Pachad Yitzchak* on Purim, by Rabbi Yitzchak Hutner p.68 ff.

Eisav as the false pretender to the rights of the first-born — וְעָלוּ מוֹשִׁעִים בְּהַר צִיּוֹן, לִשְׁפֹּט אֶת הַר עֵשָׂו, *The saviors will ascend Mount Zion to judge Eisav's mountain (Ovadiah 1:21)* — it has also given Eisav incredible power and often ascendency over Israel. Let us, therefore, not be shocked, when the bloody hands of Eisav turn up to wreak vengeance upon Israel, that those same hands can imitate, in whatever perverted way, the eternal signs of Israel. Thus, if one of the watchwords of Israel is that it is the *Am Hanivchar*, the Chosen Nation, Eisav does not merely come along and declare, "I will destroy the chosen ones"; he first declares himself the "elect," the "super man" and then, of necessity, must attempt to destroy the other, the "pretender."

✥ The Deeper Elements of the Conflict

There is an even deeper, infinitely more sensitive element to this inner struggle between Israel and Nazism.

In his analysis of the place of Eisav in the modern history of the Jews, Rabbi Hutner recognizes in Christianity as a doctrine (not necessarily in its adherents) the descendant of Eisav. Just as Eisav had continually claimed to be the true descendant and sole spiritual heir of Avraham and Yitzchak, so did the church claim to be the New Israel. In the same vein did the church lay claim to our Holy Writings and declare them its own.[14]

We must therefore reexamine the Holocaust in terms of its religious and theological matrix: What is its relationship with Christian tradition and myth? How did the maniacal ideologies of Nazism anesthetize the German people to the horrors before their eyes? For only by using the murky aura of pseudo-religious propaganda and quasi-holy purpose can atrocities such as the Holocaust be justified to an ostensibly civilized people.[15]

Even a cursory examination of the historical record reveals two distinct patterns. The first one, more obvious, and perhaps therefore less dangerous, is typified by the Archbishop of Slovakia's words to a delegation of rabbis that had to come to intercede for Slovakian Jewry to prevent their "expulsion":

"This is no mere expulsion. There you will not die of hunger and pestilence. There — they will slaughter you all, old and young, women and children, in one day. This is your punishment for the death of our Redeemer. There is only one hope for you —

---

14. Ibid.
15. Cf. above, note 3.

to convert all to our religion. Then I shall effect the annulling of this decree."

> Rabbi Michael Ber Weissmandl, too, recalls the answer given him by the papal nuncio when Weissmandl begged him to intercede with Father Tisso, who could have helped the Jewish families waiting in a detention camp prior to their deportation to Auschwitz. At first, the cleric merely responded, "This, being Sunday, is a holy day for us. Neither I nor Father Tisso occupy ourselves with profane matters on this day." When Rabbi Weissmandl protested that the rescuing of innocent blood could not be considered profane, the nuncio replied, "There is no innocent blood of Jewish children in the world. All Jewish blood is guilty. You have to die. This is the punishment that has been awaiting you because of that sin."[16]

This attitude, multiplied thousands of times all over Europe (although with some noteworthy exceptions) and certainly not condemned by the Vatican, undoubtedly contributed to the death of six million.

Yet, infinitely more significant than the actions of a number of clerics was the subtle and invidious effect of two millennia of Christian canards against the Jews.

It is not my purpose here to explore the theological roots within Christianity for the Holocaust. These have been examined elsewhere in detail; to their credit, some courageous Catholic clerics have accepted, on behalf of Christianity, moral culpability for creating the atmosphere in which Hitler could operate. For one, Prof. Rosemary Radford Ruether has stated in no uncertain terms that "at its root, anti-Semitism in Christian civilization springs directly from Christian theological anti-Judaism."[17] Rather, this study centers only upon the theological "rivalry" which has its roots in the Yaakov/Eisav relationship. The seeds of the rivalry — in Christian eyes — of the "New and Old Israel" go back to Pauline statements in the gospels. But the concept of G-d punishing a sinful Israel for the death of "the Redeemer" goes back to Justin Martyr, who lived a hundred years after Paul.

---

16. Rabbi M.D. Weissmandl, *Min Hametzar*, p. 23-25.

17. Published in *Auschwitz: Beginning of a New Era* (New York: Ktav, 1977), p.79. Prof. Ruether has since expanded her study into a full-length work, *Faith and Fratricide: The Christian Roots of Anti-Semitism* (New York: Seebury Press, 1974).

Delighting in the perversion of Jewish symbols for his own insidious purposes, Justin writes of circumcision:

> *It was given as a sign ... that you alone suffer what you now justly suffer; and that your land may be desolate, and your cities burned with fire; and that strangers may eat your fruit in your presence and not one of you may go up to Jerusalem.* [18]

Clearly, the early Church Fathers, and many of their followers, took the Jewish *tochachah* and twisted its warnings to their own ends. The crucial point to note in many of these writings is the constant repetition of the theme that the Jews have been rejected — "*Old* Israel, *Old* Testament" — and been replaced — "*New* Israel, *New* Testament" — because of their sins. The sensitive ear easily detects in them the pretentious queries of Eisav, "How does one take tithes from salt and straw? How can I prove I am more religious than my brother Jacob?"

An Ancient Rivalry, Updated

A direct unbroken line can now be drawn from Justin to Hitler, where Jewish symbols are not merely ignored or excoriated, but *used* for ignominious and malicious purposes. One example of this centuries-old trend is the Nazi use of the Messiah concept. As early as 1919, many German anti-Semites were talking of "a Messianic Fuehrer, who would fulfill all prophecies and lead the *Volk* out of bondage."[19]

Other instances of the German people *thinking of themselves* as "a kind of Jewish people" are equally startling. Dean Gruber, in his conversations with Rubenstein, had dwelled long on this point:

"We are now in the same situation as the Jews. My church is in the East sector. Last Sunday I preached on Hosea 6:1 (*'Shuvah Yisrael!'*)." He pursued the analogy between Germany and Israel: "I know that G-d is punishing us because we have been the whip against Israel. In 1938, we smashed the synagogues; in 1945, our churches were smashed by bombs. From 1938, we sent the Jews out to be homeless; since 1945, fifteen million Germans have experienced homelessness."

Graduates of Auschwitz and Bergen-Belsen may not so

---

18. Justin Martyr, *Dialogue with Tryphon*, tr. A.L. Williams (London: SPCK, 1930), II, 107.

19. Robert Cecil, *The Myth of the Master Race* (New York: Dodd Mead & Company, 1972), p.71.

readily accept "homelessness" as equal atonement for the horrors they witnessed. The point to notice is that Gruber not only thought of Germany as *atoning*, but claimed this was done in an Israel-like fashion.

Hitler and Christianity: Love or Hate?

One question often brought up in discussions of the Holocaust is Hitler's apparent hatred of Christianity itself. There is, indeed, ample proof in *Hitler's Secret Conversations*[20] of his detestation of the then-existing Christianity. Yet, it is important to understand that Nazism's abhorrence of Christianity lay purely in the Nazi perception of Christianity as having been polluted by Judaic elements. Lagarde, the anti-Semitic author and propagandist of the late 19th century, had codified the Nazi doctrine that "Christianity was doomed to extinction because of the Jewish elements it has absorbed."[21] The Nazi reconciled the problem of condemning Jews for having killed their lord, while acknowledging his alleged Jewish ancestry, by "scientifically proving ... the probability of his non-Jewish descent."[22]

We thus come to the strangest paradox of the Nazi ideology. On the one hand, Christianity is utterly rejected because "it is, in fact, the main channel through which Jewish ideas infect the healthy corpus of Germanic thought" (Alfred Rosenberg).[23] On the opposite side, it is absolutely manifest that "without Christianity, the Jews could never have become the central victims" of the Holocaust. As Rubenstein writes, "The Judas tale is part and parcel of the Passion drama, which is told and relived by every practicing Christian during Holy Week. From the cradle to the grave ... the high point of the Christian religious calendar rehearses, amidst utterly magnificent music, frequently aesthetically overpowering architecture and ceremonial grandeur,

---

20. Octagon Books, 1972, pp.49-50, 62-65, 277-79, etc.
21. Quoted in *The Politics of Cultural Despair*, F. Stern (University of California, 1961), p.40.
22. Quoted by Cecil, op.cit,p.75. The concept of *true* Christianity having been perverted by Jewish elements is ubiquitous in Nazi writings. Dietrich Eckart, another misfit and former asylum-inmate turned Nazi ideologue, "demonstrated" in his newspaper that "Judaism, acting through Christianity, had given the death blow to the Roman Empire." In a later series of articles, Alfred Rosenberg, architect of Aryanism and author of such works as *Unmoral in Talmud*, claimed that the downfall of the Persian Empire began when "Mordechai secured authority."
23. Ibid.,p.91.

the terrible tale of 'Jewish betrayal' and the 'Jewish murder of the Jewish G-d.' "[24]

Secular writers on Nazi ideology often have trouble understanding and reconciling these two seemingly antipathetical strands in Nazism. Conspicuous on one side is the powerful strain of paganism and demonic barbarianism, which seems to lead directly back to the hordes of Attila. Historians seem to have difficulty relating this trend to the affinities the Nazis found with Christianity.

But we know. In the last phases of the *Galus Romi*, we are equally in the deepest throes of our eternal conflict with Eisav. If we find hands raised against us in murder which have just been used in pious prayer, we are not shocked, for we have met them before: "The hands are the hands of Eisav." If we sense not only hatred but some perverse jealousy in the Nazi ideologues, we can open a *Chumash* and read of that same jealousy: וַיִּשְׂטֹם עֵשָׂו אֶת יַעֲקֹב עַל הַבְּרָכָה אֲשֶׁר בֵּרְכוֹ אָבִיו, "*And Eisav hated Yaakov because of the blessings bestowed on him by his father*" (Bereishis 27:41). Not only is this history, but the Talmud (which, like the Torah, is a manifestation of Divine wisdom) states it as a definitive part of our outlook: הֲלָכָה הִיא בְּיָדוּעַ שֶׁעֵשָׂו שׂוֹנֵא לְיַעֲקֹב.

◆§ The Vindication of the Victim

As Rabbi Hutner teaches us, the *Churban* of European Jewry was a manifestation of the *tochachah* which *Klal Yisrael* carries on its shoulders. In many ways, this manifestation was worse and more potent than the past visitations of *Bechukosai* and *Ki Savo*, but our generation witnessed the culmination of a pattern, not the breaking of a chain. The villains of this *Churban*, too, were not simply isolated madmen wreaking random destruction. While they descended to the nadir of depravity and were aided by a horrible technology unknown in the past, the battle waged was an ancient one.

What difference does it make? All the difference in the universe. For as Reb Moshe Prager, survivor and chronicler of the *Churban*, relates; Hitler's final letter to his associates "apologizes" for not having succeeded in their goal: the total destruction of all the Jews, Heaven forbid.[25] If what is termed *Holocaust* is indeed seen as a grisly perversion of human history, merely the product of deranged minds and unleashed insanity,

---

24. Rubenstein, p.31.
25. Quoted by Rabbi Nosson Scherman elsewhere in this volume.

then what meaning can there be in the deaths of our beloved *kedoshim*?

But knowing that we — and more important, the *kedoshim* — have triumphed, is not only vindication or victory; it is the only *Kaddish* possible in place of the graves and monuments they were not granted in death. In perishing *al Kiddush Hashem*, they declared to a modern world unaccustomed to such declarations: "We know who we are, we accept our position in the world when it is exalted, or Heaven forbid, when it means death; and we know our children will complete the Divine pattern." We have suffered *Churban*; the survivors went into *Galus*. This pattern completes itself with *Geulah* — ultimate redemption. May we become worthy of seeing the final stage by being careful of *their* memories not only by refraining from condemnations — an obscenity perhaps unparalleled in any nation's self-appraisal — but by doing for them what they no longer can do for themselves: the Torah study and *mitzvah* performance our ancient enemy could not obliterate.

Rabbi Joseph Elias

An Apology for "the Silence of Pius XII"

◆§ Silent ... Even Though He Knew

"DURING THE PAST DECADE, scathing attacks on Pius XII — and equally impassioned counterattacks — have found their way into print"; this book "is designed to counteract the error of earlier interpretations by the use of well-founded argumentation based on documents never before used. Carlo Falconi reveals the reasons why a man of Pius XII's courageous character and vast power maintained almost total silence, even though he knew the immensity of Hitler's atrocities."

These words on the jacket of this book well define what its author set out to do. In the first place, he established — drawing in particular on the case of Poland — that the Pope was *fully aware* of the horrors perpetrated by the Nazis. Equally clearly he traces the *stubborn silence* of the Pope, in the face of constant requests and demands for him to intervene. He examines the justifications commonly given, that it would have been both dangerous and useless to speak up, and he finds them totally unsatisfactory: there was no danger in speaking up, and the great prestige and power of the papacy might have made such intervention quite effective; moreover, the Pope, claiming as he does a position of exalted authority, is under obligation to take a stand on great moral issues no matter what practical consequences might or might not follow.

Why, then, did Pius XII remain silent? His critics have drawn the conclusion that he was moved by cowardice or, even worse,

This review of *The Silence of Pius XII*, by Carlo Falconi (Boston, 1970; Little, Brown and Co.) appeared in *The Jewish Observer* of December 1970.

by an utterly reprehensible moral blindness and hope of practical utilitarian benefits to be gained by his silence. It is here that Carlo Falconi disagrees: "The fact that, in my belief Pius XII was silent not out of fear, but for respectable if inadequate motives, means that we cannot brand him with infamy, even if it does not absolve him from undoubted responsibility" (p. 15). But were Pius XII's motives really "respectable if inadequate"? Falconi utterly fails to establish this; on the contrary, the facts lined up in his book constitute a truly damning indictment.

Diplomacy Above Godliness

Falconi lists "various reasons, which had nothing to do with his character or with utilitarian motives," for the Pope's silence. There was what he calls "situational reasons":

• The Pope's pessimistic view that Catholics, in particular German Catholics, were psychologically unready for a strong papal stand (p. 92).

• His conviction that Communism would derive encouragement from any weakening of Nazism. In fact, Falconi declares that during the second half of 1941, after the German attack on the Soviet Union, papal intervention was very improbable because, "in whatever way Germany double-dealing might be judged on a political and moral level, it was bound to appear to the Vatican as one of those curious undertakings too dear to Divine Providence ..." (p. 91); and later in the war, papal intervention was out of the question because "Pius XII became literally paralyzed by the drama of advancing Communism" and the German armies' desperate resistance (p. 92).

• Most important of all, there was his preoccupation with guaranteeing the Church's survival all over Europe, and guaranteeing it " ... a decisive influence on the future of the Continent and the whole world once the war was over" (p. 93). Therefore Communism had to be defeated — and the Pope's good relations with the German masters of the continent had to be safeguarded!

In addition, Falconi lists two factors of a "sentimental-psychological" nature: the Pope's Germanophilia and, above all else, his profound and pathetic trust in diplomatic maneuvering. As a result, instead of rising above the world conflict, and responding to the moral challenge posed by it, he kept on trying to work within the confines and niceties of appropriate (and therefore cautious and inoffensive) diplomatic action. Hence careful neutrality between aggressors and victims, and prudent silence in the face of mass murder. "The victory of the diplomat over the man of G-d," in Falconi's view, is the deepest reason for the Pope's failure.

"Respectable, if Inadequate"

Can we accept Falconi's "situational reasons" as "respectable if inadequate" explanations of Pius' conduct? Can his preference for diplomatic caution over moral leadership be seen as anything but a disastrous weakness of character? Can we, in short, absolve Pius XII of the stigma of infamy? By Falconi's own evidence, this reviewer believes, the answer to these questions must be a resounding "no."

It should be added that the failure of the Vatican was of course symptomatic of that of the Western world in general. Arthur D. Morse's *While Six Million Died* and other studies have amply documented the cynical way in which the supposed national self-interest of the free nations at every turn blocked effective help for the victims of Nazism; when voices were raised in protest, it was all too often a matter of mere lip service or of propaganda capital to be made from the Jewish tragedy.

We should hardly be surprised by this. Man, and the institutions he has created for himself — from the Catholic Church and the parliaments of the world to every last bureaucratic establishment and political club — are not the embodiment of the pure virtue to which they would like to lay claim. Their reasoning and actions are inevitably and profoundly influenced by their self-seeking, in the narrowest sense of that word. Sometimes unaware, often quite consciously, they identify the definition of virtue with the path of greatest practical advantage. The result is always disappointing, all too often tragic.

This is a universal human weakness, yet it is essential to draw particular attention to the Church's falling prey to it and failing to rise to the challenge of Nazidom. After all, on the one hand, the Church lays claim to providing spiritual leadership to the world and, on the other hand, it has proven time and again that it is particularly outstanding in its moral blindness. Throughout its history it has sought to establish its authority by degrading the Jewish people and by causing untold suffering and martyrdom. Even after the last war, when quick and warm support for a Jewish Palestine was needed to help save the pitiful remnants of European Jewry, the Vatican hesitated — and still hesitates — not even because of sympathies for Arab refugees, but because of the Church's narrow calculations of its political and theological self-interest. All disinterested considerations of humanity fade away in the face of those hard-headed calculations, and so the Church once again aids in the rejection of the Jewish people from among the community of nations.

No Freedom from Tyranny

We should remember, and be prepared for, this attitude of the Church and of the world in general; and, as we said before, it should not really be a surprise to us. We have always known that freedom from the tyranny of man's weakness can only be found through Torah: "only he is a free man who engages himself with Torah," our Sages declared. We must be ever grateful that the Torah is our portion and always mindful that, to the extent to which the Jewish people disregard the guidance of the Torah, it too becomes a victim of human weakness.

Rabbi Yaakov Jacobs

The Catholic Church and Nazi Germany

THE NEW YORK TIMES headlined a story on a study of Catholic textbooks used in this country: JESUITS FIND BIAS IN CATHOLIC BOOKS. The study was conducted with the American Jewish Committee. "The report," the *Times* noted, "cited the following excerpt as a 'negative distortion' of the Crucifixion: *The chief priests took up a cry that put a curse on themselves and on the Jews for all times* ... The references to the Pharisees as the *'temple gang'* and as *'racketeers selling sheep and doves'* in the building were also criticized."

In a recent issue of *The St. Louis Review*, one of the finest liberal Catholic weeklies in this country, a Catholic professor of philosophy, in answering a question concerning Jewish guilt of deicide, wrote:

> The unjust accusation that the Jews (were guilty of deicide) ... has been the root of Christian anti-Semitism for nearly twenty centuries. It has caused Christians to hate rather than to love; it has given them an excuse for almost constant persecution of the Jews: and it *formed a ferment which had its ultimate result in Nazi extermination camps* (emphasis ours).

One need only turn to the pages of history to discover the sordid details of the Church's relationship to the Jew as expressed in the Crusades and Inquisitions, in the ever-recurring charges of deicide and blood-libels. A book published on June 15, 1964, brings the story up-to-date, at least as far as the activities of the Catholic Church in Nazi Germany. (Reinhold Neibuhr, the Protestant theologian, has expressed the hope that someone will do a similar study of the Protestant Church.)

In the preface to the book, *The Catholic Church and Nazi*

This review appeared in *The Jewish Observer* of June 1964.

Germany, (McGraw-Hill/New York) Guenter Lewy, a young American scholar who left Nazi Germany at the age of fifteen, writes that *"The relationship of the Roman Catholic Church and Hitler's Third Reich has for many years been obscured by what may justifiably be called an extensive mythology."*

In his chapter, "The Jewish Question," Professor Lewy writes (p. 269):

> ... the Nazis' ferocious assault upon European Jewry took place in a climate of opinion conditioned for such an outrage by centuries of Christian hostility to the Jewish religion and people. Numerous Christian theologians throughout the history of Christianity had painted the Jews as a people who had betrayed G-d and had called upon themselves a permanent curse by crucifying Jesus Christ. The historical accuracy of the cry, "His blood be upon us and upon our children," and the orthodoxy of a theological interpretation that saw in these words an acknowledgment of the guilt of all Jews for the death of Jesus have been successfully challenged by recent scholarship. But for many centuries Christian preaching and religious instruction derived their intensely anti-Jewish character from just such conceptions. In medieval times the recital of the Passion in Good Friday sermons was frequently followed by acts of violence against Jews, for whom this holy day became a day of dread. Hitler's racial anti-Semitism and its logical outgrowth, Auschwitz, a French-Jewish scholar (Jules Isaac) has concluded, appeared on ground which previous centuries had prepared: *"Without centuries of Christian catechism, preaching, and vituperation, the Hitlerian teachings, propaganda and vituperation would not have been possible."*

Professor Lewy, drawing heavily on German state papers recently made available and official Church archives, examines the role of the Catholic Church in Germany in the face of the rising strength of Nazism before 1933 and throughout the period of Nazi power.

What were the German clergy doing when it was slowly becoming clear that Hitler with his violent anti-Semitic doctrines would one day rule Germany? *"If in the course of proceeding against the Jews as a race some good harmless Jews ... will have to suffer with the guilty ones,"* wrote Curate Roth, an early supporter of the Hitler movement, who later became an official in the Nazi Ministry of Ecclesiastical Affairs, *"this is not a violation of Christian love of one's neighbor as long as the Church recognizes the moral justification of war, for example, where many more 'innocents' than 'guilty' have to suffer."*

ೂ§ Opportunity to Throw Off Jewish Yoke

Dr. Haeuser wrote in 1923, in a book which bore the *Imprimatur* (certification by the bishop of the area in which the book is printed that it contains no misstatement of Church dogma) that, in Lewy's words (p. 272), *"the Jews (are) Germany's cross, a people disowned by G-d, and under their own curse. They carried much of the blame for Germany having lost the war and ... the time had come to put them in their place ..."* Father Senn, a veteran National Socialist priest, termed the Hitler movement *"the last big opportunity to throw off the Jewish yoke."* While in isolated cases a bishop or a cardinal termed Nazi anti-Semitism "extreme," Lewy points out that

> a Church that justified moderate anti-Semitism and merely objected to extreme and immoral acts was ill prepared to provide an effective antidote to the Nazi's gospel of hate. The roots of the Church's failure to protest or act against the later National Socialist policy of extermination lie right here, in the highly ambivalent attitude of the Church toward the Jews which we can trace from the early days of Christianity up to Hitler's accession to power and beyond.

With documentation from official Church sources, Lewy writes (p. 279):

> ... And so it went on. The Jews had had a "demoralizing influence on religiosity and national character." The Jews as a spiritual community had brought the German people "more damage than benefit" ... "The Jews had been the first and most cruel persecutors of the young Church." The Jews had killed Christ and in their boundless hatred of Christianity were still in the forefront of those seeking to destroy the Church. These are some relevant examples of Catholic writings during the years 1933-1939, all published in journals edited by priests, or in books bearing the *Imprimatur*. From this ruthless intellectual onslaught upon the Jews it was but a small step to the position of Father Senn, who in 1934 hailed Hitler as "the tool of G-d, called upon to overcome Judaism."

The Church Stood By Silently

In one area, Lewy did find Church resistance to Nazi anti-Semitism. When the Nazi Ministry for Ecclesiastical Affairs asked permission to consult the diocesan files on conversions and mixed marriages, the Church withheld consent. In essence, when it came to persecution of Jews who had converted to Catholicism, the Church was prepared to assert itself. When the Nazis called for the dissolution of mixed marriages involving Catholics and Jews, again the Church spoke out, since dissolution of these marriages violated Church law. Yet, the mass extermination of Jews, which the German hierarchy was fully aware of, went unchallenged. "*The Church*" in Lewy's words (p. 295), "*custodian of Christian love and charity, stood by silently.*"

The New York Times, in announcing the publication of *The Catholic Church and Nazi Germany*, predicted that it would revive the debate surrounding the failure of Pius XII to condemn Nazi crimes against Jews. This prediction was borne out by the *Times* itself (June 18, 1964) in a dispatch from Washington reporting the release by the State Department of documents indicating that the United States government called upon Pius to condemn the Nazi atrocities. His reply was, as reported by Harold H. Tittman, representing President Franklin D. Roosevelt:

> *He explained that when talking of atrocities he could not name the Nazis without at the same time mentioning the Bolsheviks, and this he thought might not be wholly pleasing to the Allies. He stated that he "feared" that there was foundation for the atrocity reports of the Allies, but led me to believe that he felt there had been some exaggeration for purposes of propaganda.*

A careful reading of the chapter on "The Jewish Question" would show that the implications of the author's documentation are much broader. In a word, they make the entire question of Pius' silence academic and absurd in the light of the Catholic Church's encouragement of Hitler's anti-Semitic policies from the initial stages through the death camps. Indeed, Lewy himself seems to shy away from the logical result of his own documentation, when he speculates as to whether a declaration from Pius XII would have halted the extermination of Jews.

❧ Absolution Absurd

In the light of the facts marshalled in this significant work (as of the writing of this review there has been no official Church reaction though the book was available long before the official publication date) the discussion of the proposed statement by the Catholic Church "absolving" the Jewish people of the crime of deicide becomes equally absurd. The press reports periodically the ups and downs of the statement, and the Jew must consult *The New York Times* each day to determine his state of grace. But what is totally disregarded, particularly by the Jewish organizations who wait with baited breath for the Church absolution, is the paradox that while Jewish "guilt" is at the core of the proposed statement, the Church has indicated no willingness to speak of its own guilt.

The Church's willingness to even backhandedly admit a measure of guilt by the proposed *schema* offered to the first session of the Ecumenical Council has been systematically downgraded. The *schema* was never brought to the Council; from a *schema* it was reduced to the status of a statement by the Church Fathers. It is now indicated that the statement, if ever it is to be made, will omit reference to the false accusation of deicide. This has lead some to fear that the entire discussion will only strengthen the hostility against the Jew, since the Church's failure to act, even in a minimal manner, will lend credence to the basic element of Christian anti-Semitism.

It is a basic aspect of Catholicism that one who has committed a sin must first confess his sin and then do penance. There is little to be expected from an ecumenical spirit which seeks brotherhood and closer understanding, while attempting to cover up its own guilt by tempting its victim with a promise of "absolution."

Rabbi Aharon Jeruchem

A Voice From Beyond: The Kedoshim Ask Some Burning Questions

❧ "When You Were Children ..."

THIS MESSAGE comes to you from many generations of Jews who have lain in East European ground for centuries, and from the Six Million massacred who fell in the field of history's most savage slaughter. It is a collective call to all of you, living brethren, from all of us. We, that is, our "dry bones," turn to you; "all our bones speak" to you. Many among us shrunk to bones even before our lives were snuffed out. Hunger and horror, torture and terror reduced us to skeletons. Some of us arrived as piles of ashes, some went up in a column of smoke.

With this, our desperate outcry, we beseech you, to stir your hearts and minds. Pause for a moment; keep silent — listen to those who went "down into silence."

Four decades have passed since we were left alone. We understand the anxiety of the survivors to run from the bloody soil. But we do not comprehend that they never return to visit us, to abate our loneliness. Addressing ourselves to all of you, we wonder why none of you appears to find how we rest, to ascertain whether we still *are* in our resting places.

When you were children, we would come to you in the night to be sure that you were sleeping peacefully. Why do you not come to see how we sleep?

In the language of our Torah "to die" is to be "gathered to one's people." To us, death has meant separation, isolation *from our people.*

This essay appeared in The *Jewish Observer* of September 1966.

Did it ever enter your mind to gather together the mass graves scattered over Eastern Europe? Did you once think of transferring the remains of the holy to the Holy Land?

Have you ever wondered what it is like to lie in strange lands surrounded by the people who helped the German murderers to kill?

The stones which marked our tombs were taken away, the fences which enclosed our burial sites are gone. We are exposed to invasion and abuse, subjected to desecration. Our graves are trampled by beasts of all sorts; cattle graze above our heads. Scavengers loot our abodes in search of gold teeth, as if the German hyenas missed anything.

We can do nothing to drive them away, and you seem not to care. No one disturbs those who disturb our slumber.

Like Job we thought, "If we would sleep, we would be at rest." Yet we sleep, we came to rest, and find no rest.

Near and above our graves rise parks, halls of entertainment, of joy and laughter, blackening ever more the darkness of the night.

We realize that it is too inconvenient for you to come to us. There are more pleasant places to go. But wherever you are, close your eyes for a while and project yourself into our position. Imagine you are alone, abandoned, cut off not only from life but also from the memory of the living. No one stops to whisper a prayer, to say a *Kaddish*, to drop a tear into your grave. Only vandals, barbarians pass your way, annoy, anger you, step on you, crush, crumble you. You are forgotten, forlorn, deserted. *"The ways of Zion are in mourning, because none come to the feasts, all her gates are desolate."*

How Can You Desecrate Your Homes?

A long time has gone by since the monstrous blood-bath. You who survived returned to business as usual, as if nothing had happened, as if the greatest flood of blood ever did not take place before your very eyes. In the course of the years, some of your own have departed. You interred them and placed stones on their graves. Often you come to express your sorrow. Every now and then, someone smears a swastika on a gravestone or throws it down; you become agitated and hasten to repair it. Our graves have nothing left to be defaced or knocked over. Not stones — bones, our very fragments are in jeopardy. This does not agitate, does not irritate you?

With Yehudah Halevi each of you should ask himself: *How can eating and drinking be sweet to me, while I see dogs rending at your young lions? Or how can the light of day be pleasing to my eyes, when I see corpses of your eagles in the beaks of ravens?*

How can you stand idly by, how can you build houses, decorate homes, water your gardens, knowing that we lie without protection, confronted with diverse elements of mutilation and abasement?

Say not, since we are dead and do not feel or know anything, it makes no difference what happens to us, or where we lie. How do you know that we do not know? Have you ever been dead? Do you already know all the answers of life, that you are so sure about the facts of death? Have you ever experienced them? Not having access even to all the secrets of the world you live in, you venture to claim knowledge about the mysteries of afterlife. Maybe your assumption in regard to the nature of death is one of the illusions man has about so many phenomena of being and non-being. Do you not, while sleeping, consider everything you see and think of in your dream as real? And it is not. Could it not be also that in the absence of empiric evidence your conjecture about the dead's ability to sense and to know is merely a product of your imagination? Who knows?

There are most competent sources which indicate that expiration of life does not mean abrogation of the capacity of knowing or feeling *(Berachos* 18a-b; *Bava Metzia* 84b). And also that the dead have their preferences and are sensitive as to where they are laid to rest. Did not Yaakov charge his sons: "Carry me out of Egypt"? And Yoseif pleaded to his brothers: "Carry up my bones from here."

And when the time of the Exodus arrived, people were busy accumulating wealth, as you do. Moshe *Rabbeinu* alone remembered the bones of Yoseif and his brothers, and took them with him. What remained of all the gold and silver the others were busy amassing? Nothing. Only Moshe's deed was of lasting value. Throughout their wandering in the desert the Jews carried with them the bones of Yoseif in a coffin resembling the Ark containing the Tablets of the Law. (Concerning the difference where one lies see also *Yerushalmi Moed Katan II*, 4; *Shulchan Aruch, Yoreh Deah* ch. 363.)

"For the living know that they will die" *(Koheles* 9:5). But you seem not to know it. Otherwise you would not behave the way you do. For, in case the hour of Resurrection, when "the earth shall cast out the departed" and "the dead will be brought to life again," is still far off, you too will be summoned sometime. Sooner or later you will be our guests. Then we shall put before you the question: What did you do in those long five years while we were systematically and pitilessly exterminated? And what did you do thereafter, when our bodies were the target of defilement, of humiliation?

... and Where are You Now?

Where were you during our awful ordeal, and where are you now? Till we breathed our last we kept on hoping you would come to our rescue, you will somehow manage to free us from the clutches of the bloodhounds. You disappointed us terribly. You did not meet the challenge. You failed the test then, and you fail the test now. You followed the course of the "democratic" Western powers. They did not speak out, and you did nothing to make them act. They were deaf and dumb toward our trial and so were you. They wrapped themselves in silence, and so did you.

When the Almighty gave the Torah, no bird chirped, no fowl flew, no ox bellowed, the Ophanim did not stir their wings, the Seraphim did not say 'Holy, Holy,' the sea did not shake, the creatures spoke not, the entire world kept silent and stood still (Shemos Rabbah ch. 29:9).

The same condition prevailed when the people of the Torah perished, when an Empire of Torah disappeared, vanished. The whole world stood still. All the humanitarians, even the Societies for the Prevention of Cruelty to Animals, exercised strict indifference. And when somebody tried to do something about it, he was silenced. *Haolam shosek*, the world kept silent; *umacharish*, it also silenced others.

As in the hour of Revelation so it was in the long years of devastation: *And all the people perceived the thunderings and the lightnings and the voice of the horn and the mountain smoking, and the people saw it and trembled and STOOD OFF AFAR.*

You pretended not to be quite sure; you refused to believe that the rumors were true. So you granted yourself graciously the benefit of the doubt, and decided to do nothing.

And when the black curtain went up, when the horrible acts of bloodshed were revealed; when your calls for your dear ones were met with dreadful silence; when you learned that the bitter facts far exceeded the previous reports, you resumed your passivity, your inactivity. For, even some work was left to be done ... to liberate the children that Jewish mothers, in their despair, before they were driven into crematories, turned over to non-Jews in the hope that after the war, our people would redeem them ... to save our remnants, those that were left of us.

Both tasks were not carried out by you. Our children were raised as Catholics; the orphans of holy martyrs bear crosses on their breasts. They have no idea who they really are and under which circumstances they came to be where they are. They were even inoculated with the anti-Jewish poison: *"Those that I had tenderly nursed and reared up, my enemy brought to their end" (Lamentations 2:22).*

And we, the dead, we are where and how we are.

What of the *mitzvos* of *pidyon shvuyim* (redeeming captives) and *kaved hamess* (honoring the dead)? Is this the treatment we deserve after all the anguish we underwent, after such a dreadful end? Is this the way you compensate us for all the inexpressible suffering and sacrifices? This is the reward you bestow upon us?

Rabbi Elkanah Schwartz

Dateline 1976:
In Search for Polish Jewry

✥ The Week of Mourning

EREV SHABBOS CHAZON, 5736 (Friday, July 30, 1976), we were on the way from Cracow to Auschwitz. We were a group of American youths, visiting the sites we had previously heard about but wished to know first hand, seeking "to remember the days of old." What time more fitting was there than the days preceding *Tishah B'Av!*

Less than forty years ago Polish Jewry sparkled as the crown of the Jewish people. Not only cities, but towns and villages, whose names and spirit live on in Brooklyn and Bnei Brak, and now are but empty echoes. *Where was my rebbe's Warsaw? my mother's Cracow? the Kattowice where the Chofetz Chaim and Reb Chaim Ozer led a mass gathering of Torah Jewry? the Lublin of Rabbi Meir Shapiro?* As Rabbi Yishmael *Kohen Gadol* is quoted as saying upon the murder of Rabban Shimon ben Gamliel: "Where is the tongue so quick to teach words of Torah? By our sins, how it now licks the dust."

✥ No Side Trip to Bendin

Before the trip, someone of Polish origin had asked if, while in Kattowice, we could visit her grandfather's grave in Bendin. He is buried among leading figures of the Gerrer chassidic dynasty. We arrived late at night in Kattowice and there was no time the next morning. On the way, our Polish guide pointed to a side road, indicating that Bendin was nearby. A road like all roads ...

This essay appeared in *The Jewish Observer* of December 1976.

... the same road fifty years ago heavily traveled by religious Jews on the way to their *Rebbe*, to hear *Divrei Torah* (words of Torah) we now study in print, the melodies we now listen to on cassettes. Now, only the cemetery lives in Bendin.

Warsaw: three of our group are not with us. One, whose parents came from Pabianitz, had gone with the others on a private excursion. Armed with a hand-drawn sketch of birthplaces, *shuls* and schools attended, relatives' graves, recalled from memory, for these people a name came alive, however briefly.

How many Jews are there in Poland today? How do you identify a Jew who hides his identity from others as surely as he could never hide it from himself? In Cracow, we were told: In a distant village live three Jewish families. Once a month, they bring in chickens for kosher slaughter. *What do they do for Rosh Hashanah and Yom Kippur? — come to Cracow?* No. Those Jews go to a nearby town, where others like them come and have a *minyan* ... Were they included in the official figures?

⋴§ Warsaw: A Beautiful Monument

Warsaw is a beautiful city. Leveled in the war, it was rebuilt to simulate what was destroyed. The resemblance to the days of the monarchies is impressive. Walking at night through the center of town is an aesthetic delight, with nothing to fear. (Except perhaps the black-market moneychangers. The vender just might be a plant.) But as one strolls through the streets of Warsaw, takes those steps, one cannot help but think of years ago. One is constantly confronted with smoldering remains of Jewish life, reflecting the varieties of prewar Jewry.

There is the Theatre Zydowski, where today the cast includes non-Jews, and the seats have earphones to provide translations.

In the same building, the Redakcja Folks Sztyme publishes a Yiddish-language newspaper.

In a public square, the Zydowski Instytut Historyczny has two divisions: an exhibit on the Warsaw Ghetto, and a library which includes over twenty-thousand *sifrei kodesh* (sacred books).

In a decaying building near the theater, the *Vaad Hakehillos Hakedoshos d'Polin* stocks records that give a meager representation to vanished communities in Warsaw, Cracow, Lublin, and Lodz.

Behind it, at Twarda 6, is the Nojzik *Shul*, the sole surviving Jewish house of worship in Warsaw. Obviously once a beautiful synagogue, it is undergoing renovations, as it has been for a number of years. A *minyan* meets there once a week, on *Shabbos* morning, with fifteen to twenty local Jews attending. And there are always tourists, Jewish and otherwise. Some local Jews come to the synagogue to meet other Jews and solicit contributions, or to offer to purchase dollars at high rates, or both. Some, like Reb Moshe Shapiro, come to do what is proper.

Reb Moshe is *shochet* (ritual slaughterer), *baal korei* (reader of the Torah), and *melamed* (teacher) for the few children in town. There is no rabbi in Warsaw, There is no rabbi in all Poland. The last one left Lodz three years ago to settle in Brooklyn.

৺ Meet Reb Nochum

In the building occupied by the *Vaad* live Reb Nochum, his wife, and two young daughters. I brought him regards from his brother in Boro Park. He had no advance notice of our coming — there were fourteen of us — yet, within minutes, he had vodka, egg advokat, Coke, seltzer, and home-made pickles on the table. Within another five minutes, given the nature of Polish vodka, we were singing ... Avraham's tent, giving food and comfort to wayfarers ... Soon we were dancing, finding our visit just cause for a *farbreng* on an otherwise ordinary Monday afternoon. His wife entered and turned, ran out, to bring back some people we knew:

(The previous year, our group had spent *Shabbos* in Warsaw. In the morning, a group of five young Dutch gentiles came into *shul*. They had volunteered their vacations to help the Jewish people by restoring dignity to the Jewish cemetery in Warsaw, which was in disrepair. After *davening*, all twenty-seven of our group went to Reb Nochum for *kiddush*. He took along Reb Moshe, and we took along the five Dutchmen.)

Now when Reb Nochum's wife saw us, she went to bring the Dutch contingent who were back in Warsaw. The attitude of this group was consistent with what we had seen in Amsterdam: the Anne Frank House, a tribute to attempts by non-Jews to hide Jews from the Nazis; and the Dockworker's Statue, in the park next to the Portuguese Synagogue, in tribute to the only instance in all of Europe of organized resistance by non-Jewish workers to Nazi deportation of Jews.

In the midst of our singing, the organizer of the Dutch group stood up, and with tear-filled eyes, said: "Friends, did we ever imagine that we would hear Jewish youth singing Jewish songs in Warsaw?"

In our visit to Reb Nochum, we learned two unforgettable things: the value of a Jew, as the bearer of his heritage even in isolation; and our own value, seeing what our presence meant to him and the others.

"A Small Candle Is Aflame"

One Warsaw Jew, not attached to any building, is an institution unto himself: Dr. Szymon Datner. He is a recognized authority on the Holocaust. The YIVO library in New York has a bibliography of his writings, and the Library of Congress also has a lengthy list of entries under his name. Dr. Datner had been head of the Zydowski Instytut, and still prepares articles for their publications. He was once an avowed Communist, but somehow in the Holocaust he found the validity of faith, and became religious. He is in *shul* every *Shabbos*, and spends Pesach *sedarim* with Reb Nochum.

We lunched together on a park bench. He spoke to us in a classic, almost prophetic Hebrew: "As long as there is a *minyan* in Warsaw, I will not abandon it ... A small candle is aflame here. I make no predictions that Jewry will once again flourish in Poland, but I caution you against predictions that it will not."

The Cemetery Lives

Ironically, Jewish life still lives in the vast Jewish cemetery. It is a massive legacy, mostly neglected. An old Jew sits inside the gate, waiting for the many tourists. To the extent there is anyone who knows where anything is, it is he — and he doesn't know much. During the war, partisans had hidden there. Overgrowth abounds, but every visitor, seeking his ancestors, cleans up a bit more ... We came across the Dutchmen, and invited them to our hotel for dinner ... In our meanderings over the messy terrain, the old Jew showed us the remains of the grave of Reb Chaim Brisker.

From the gate, Mordechai Anielewicz Street (named after the leader of the Ghetto uprisings) leads to Mila 18, where a monument marks the site of the bunker where the uprising was planned. Across the street, in a little park, is a two-sided monument to those who died there. These are surrounded by modern apartment buildings.

Our local guide, Swadek, escorted us to the remaining section of the Ghetto wall. Suddenly he stopped. He stared at a mound of rubble. "Only last week I was here," he said, "and it was standing." Not any more.

↩ Lublin

Reb Nochum accompanied us to Lublin. Approaching the city, we caught sight of the medieval castle in whose protective shadow Jews lived for centuries. Once this road had been crowded with pilgrims slowly making their way to the *Chozeh*. Now Lublin's main attraction is Majdanek concentration camp, within walking distance of the center of this thriving metropolis.

Lublin has one "*shul*," in a rented apartment, with a *minyan* once a week, Friday evenings. A *shochet* comes in from a nearby town for *Shabbos*. Reb Nochum keeps close touch with these people, maintaining a loose network of communication among the remnants.

In our hotel that evening, we read aloud from the first story of Moshe Prager's *Sparks of Glory* — "The Dance of Death": In Lublin, the Nazi leader Globochnik rounded up the Jews, and forced them to sing. They sang "*Lumir zich iberbeten*," and as they faltered in their singing, they were beaten. Then someone changed the words to "*Mir velen zey iberleben* — we will outlive them" and they so picked up in song that they were beaten to stop. Only they didn't. Globochnik was licked.

The familiar story suddenly cast our surroundings into another dimension. This lovely city — where road signs pointed to Chelm, where tourists come and go in large numbers — was the city of The Dance. And we saw Globochnik's picture on display in Majdanek. The people of the People's Socialist Republic of Poland view the Fascists as enemies, which is why Majdanek, like Auschwitz and Birkenau, are maintained as museums to defame the Fascists. We were sitting comfortably where the evil had taken place less than forty years earlier.

↩ Welcome to Majdanek

Majdanek, built as an "improvement" over Dachau, set the stage for the "grand achievement," Auschwitz. Yet, in certain respects, it is more incisive to view than are the others. Entering the camp along marked pathways, one can grasp the entire process: the four boundaries are seen, the sections identified, the scope of the system complete in one look — the remaining barracks now housing exhibits, the "bath and disinfection" buildings with their shower heads and gas chambers, the tall silent chimney at the distant end. It was a superb example of technological efficiency in service of the barbarianism of human extermination.

The people who conceived it, designed it, built it, and ran it too well were not drunkards. Nor were they stupid, or ignorant peasants. They did it because they believed in it, which is where the ghastly perversion lies.

Being surrounded by the barbed-wire fences we had known of, walking through gas chambers we had read about, touching crematoria ovens we had heard about, all converted the indescribable into an unbearable reality. Our presence testified that *Die Endlosung Der Judenfrage*, the Final Solution of the Jewish Question, was not achieved, just as we know it never will be. We hoped that our demonstration of a Jewry and a Judaism that is alive was a comfort to those who had agonized there, whose ashes lie heaped in a giant stone urn.

The Majdanek Exhibit

Among the exhibits, a showcase contains a *tallis*, a pair of *tefillin*, a *yarmulka*. In a collection of flags representing the nationalities of the victims, hangs one with the Star of David. Prisoners' uniforms and hats are displayed, to convey a sense of individuals rather than just numbers. Two of the barracks — long, low wooden buildings where inmates steamed in the summers and froze in the winters — contain shoes. Not placed carefully side by side, but piled, one over the other, like so many warehouse items. In one area cans of Zyklon B pellets are stacked. A sign tells their source: I.G. Farben factories. A sign in the building housing the gas chambers informs us: "Here the prisoners' hair was cut to be sold at the German firm, P. Reimann. The total of 780 kilograms of hair was sent out of Majdanek." Reciting a *"Molay"* (memorial prayer) was not an easy task.

Before leaving Lublin, we visited the Collegium Maius, the College of Medicine on Lubartovska Street. The building was not put up by the college, but was built almost fifty years ago by Rabbi Meir Shapiro as the *Yeshivas Chachmei Lublin*. A splendid structure. How many schools of Torah function around the world on the merit of what was begun there?

Reb Nochum bids us goodbye, returning to Warsaw, while we moved on to Cracow.

∼§ Cracow

The city's majesty castle looms as a reminder of bygone days of royalty; Cracow's Holiday Inn, the only one in Eastern Europe, reflects the city's present-day commercial role. To Jews, however, Cracow is the home of the *Rama* (Rabbi Moshe Isserles), *rebbe* of Ashkenazic Jewry for the past four hundred years. His burial place lies behind the synagogue bearing his name. A *minyan* still meets he ry Friday evening and *Shabbos* morning. Visitors from al the world flock to the *shul* to pray and to be inspired, recalling Cracow's distinctive role over the centuries as a major center of Torah study.

Within a few blocks, near the center of the town, is the old ghetto, containing the few remaining Jewish installations. The *Alte Shul*, dating from the fourteenth century, built like a fortress, was the seat of the chief rabbi. It still has an *Aron Kodesh* (holy Ark), a platform *bimah* surrounded by a high gate, a ladies' section, and a slot in the wall marked "*tzeddakah*" (charity). It serves as a museum by day and, because of its fine acoustics, as a concert hall in the evening. On the face of a building around the corner one sees engraved:

"ח"ק קובע עתים לתורה"

The Holy Society for Establishing Set Times for Torah Study. This building is no longer used for Jewish purposes.

A block away, in a courtyard behind a high wall, is the *Rama Shul*. Here visitors receive their first "*Sholom Aleichem*" from Jews maintaining the traditional practice of *shnorring*. These Jews also maintain the *minyanim*.

Cracow is blessed with two functioning synagogues. Around the corner is the large Templul. Services are also held here Friday evening and *Shabbos* morning. Beyond its courtyard is the *mikvah*, put to extensive use by visiting *chassidim*.

∼§ Poland Lives ... in America

Traditions die hard, even bad ones. Neither *shul* has a *minyan* on *Shabbos* afternoon. There are only enough people for one *minyan*, and they cannot agree on which *shul* to use. The same is true regarding daily services.

Mr. Meir Yakobovitz, who heads the community, is approached by people the world over who send in money to have graves repaired, cemeteries maintained. Mr. Yakobovitz takes care of the requests. Visitors like us, whose parents came from this region, inquire about all sorts of places, and this gentleman answers, much as a museum guide directs tourists to dead exhibits. Two of our group ask about the building where Sarah Schenirer opened the first Bais Yaakov seminary ... He directs them there.

I offered Mr. Yakobovitz some *siddurim* (prayer books) and other religious paraphernalia. He placed his arm around me and said: "We have *siddurim*, we have *Chumashim*. We only lack people ... like the ones with you."

Friday evening we attended the Templul, and one of our young men led the services as *baal tefillah* (cantor). Later, Mr. Yakobovitz asked him if he could serve as *baal tefillah* on the *Yomim Noraim* (High Holy Days).

Shabbos morning we attended the *Rama Shul*, and another of our young men was *baal tefillah*. Later, Mr. Yakobovitz asked him if he could serve as *baal tefillah* on the *Yomim Noraim*.

Because of us, the people arranged a *minyan* for the afternoon in the Templul. The *baal korei* from the *Rama Shul* was there, then disappeared. He refuses to *daven* there, but wanted to make sure that there was a *minyan*.

At a location where but recently our fathers could feast on a spiritual banquet, we were nibbling crumbs. It was *Shabbos Chazon*. The seventh verse of the *Haftorah* reads: "Your country desolate, your cities burned with fire" (*Yeshayahu* I) ... At *seudah shlishis* (third of the three traditional Sabbath meals), I had to find words of comfort and assurance to the few people there. I quoted from verse 24: "I will console Myself from My oppressors, and will avenge Myself from My enemies." I described what Cracow had meant to us, of all we had heard from our teachers and relatives; how we and our generation are carrying on this tradition.

The *shochet* cried. The *baal tokaya* (man who blows the *shofar)* kept repeating: *"Poilen lebt in America* — Poland lives in America."

◆§ The Auschwitz Experience

On Friday morning, we went to Auschwitz. We stood in the bright sun under the sign *"Arbeit Macht Frei,"* tourists of many nations passing by, listening to the guide tell us that "in this camp, and in Birkenau nearby, between three-and-a-half to four million people were killed." How is one to picture the faultless precision of trains, evacuating villages, towns, and cities on perfect timetables for "resettlement in the east"? How is one to believe that here, more than anywhere else, sheer madness made a way of life out of the ultimate in brutality?

Statistics are easy to quote. Absorbing the reality is something else. We do not speak. We walk quietly with the guide, feet scraping the pebbles, our faces pale. Barrack buildings have been turned into exhibit areas, marked by numbers to lead the visitors in their sequence. The enormity of it envelops us. "Numerous other calamities befell our ancestors throughout the generations." These were "the days of old" we have to remember. *"Where is the tongue so quick to teach words of Torah? — By our sins, how it now licks the dust."*

Polish school children in the area are required to visit the camp, to see what Fascism did. A group of them look at our *yarmulkas*, smile, and say nothing. Did they also think that there were no more of us?

In the communities where we live, we are nothing out of the ordinary. We take our religious way of life for granted.

No more. We gained an appreciation for what we are. The Jewish people is guaranteed to live; we learned that we are not merely isolated individuals, but an integral part of a continuum. We did not cry at the *"Molay"* at Birkenau. Instead, we stood erect — exhausted, but assured.

The most massive effort at the Final Solution had been mounted. It devoured six million of us. But ultimately it had failed.

For not only one enemy
has risen against us to destroy us,
but in every generation
they rise against us to destroy us
and the Holy One, Blessed is He,
saves us from their hand.

(*The Pesach Haggadah*)

Rabbi Hanoch Teller

Where Are the Scars?

❧ The Austrian Paradox

IN SOME WAYS, I still cherish memories of my boyhood visits to Vienna; how I walked the streets, rode the trolleys, and observed my fellow Austrians. One winter morning as I walked over the cobbled streets, I slipped on the ice and knocked over an old man as I fell. Within a few seconds, this old gent had lifted me up, handed me my hat, and brushed off my snow-covered shoulders. "*Gruss G-tt,*" he said, and was on his way. I was impressed — a bonafide *mentsch*.

The next summer I visited Vienna again, and once more was exposed to Viennese *mentschlichkeit:* I had descended from a trolly at Stepfansplant, Vienna's main shopping hub, and was followed by a woman waving her arms. She presented me with a hundred-shilling note that had fallen out of my pocket. Aside from the inherent kindness of her act, she now had to wait for another streetcar and pay her fare once more. I had never witnessed this on the I.R.T. Who doesn't admire a *mentsch?*

Several years have elapsed between that summer and my most recent visit this past winter. Since then, my affection towards Austrians has dwindled and my Jewish memory has expanded. I beheld more this time than I had in the past. Previously, every Austrian was my respected friend; now I kept asking myself that haunting question: *What was he doing during the war?* It occurred to me that the elderly man who had picked me up could be the very one who murdered my grandparents and that the considerate lady may not have been kind at all during the

---

This essay appeared in *The Jewish Observer* of April 1978.

war years. Were the Austrians any better than the Germans? Both were united in their servile barbarism. Together they had succeeded in perverting any potential humanitarianism. Their universities taught racial "science," their medicine exploited virulent doctors, their chemistry invented Zyklon B gas. They assembled orchestras to drown out Jewish screaming.

I was living in a paradox: I had witnessed their benevolence; I had read about their malevolence. My only comfort was in another contradiction. The characters are different but the dilemma is similar.

∞§ The Philistine Precedent

The dialogue between Avraham *Avinu* and Avimelech, King of Gerar, is rather perplexing: Avimelech took Sarah, Avraham's wife, assuming that she was his sister, as Avraham had said. Avimelech's behavior was just; as he put it: "In the innocence of my heart and the integrity of my hands have I done this" — scrupulous. When notified of his error, he speedily rectified the situation: "Avimelech took sheep and cattle and menservants and maidservants and gave them to Avraham, and restored Sarah his wife to him ..." He asked in return merely the answer to a justifiable question: "In what way did I sin against you that you have brought upon me and my kingdom such a great sin? Deeds that ought not be done you have committed against me. What then did you see that you did this thing?!"

Avraham *Avinu's* reply is, *prima facie*, puzzling. "*Because I said: 'There is no fear of G-d in this place, and they will kill me on account of my wife.'*" Avraham had not responded to the question posed nor did he acknowledge Avimelech's probity.

It was not until another visit to Austria that I could understand Avraham *Avinu's* response and meanwhile reconcile my personal paradox. Of course Avimelech was kind, generous, probably well educated and highly cultured. One can talk like a *mentsch* and act like a *mentsch*; however, it can still be a deception. Avraham *Avinu* was not deluded. Pick me up when I fall down, return my money, present me with sheep and cattle. But as long as "There is no fear of G-d in this place," I am afraid for my life.

∞§ No "Jews" at Mathausen

From Vienna, my wife and I drove 120 kilometers to the Mathausen Concentration Camp. Mathausen was one of the most demonic death camps; once he arrived there, no Jew survived for more than three days. The inmates there were forced to carry heavy rocks up the 186 steps of a granite quarry. This slave labor insured quick liquidation as a result of overwork and starvation. The camp prisoners were also murdered with phenol injections, gas chambers, and bullets shot precisely into the nape of the neck — rendered feasible by means of a special measuring-installation.

The village of Mathausen looks like a picture postcard: white Alps form the backdrop of this quaint, serene town. A steeple church stands at its center. As we approached the camp, we wondered how they would redeem from oblivion the destruction of hundreds of thousands of Jews. Certainly no place was more appropriate to bemoan the loss of European Jewry than a concentration-camp site. Here, for sure, the scars of guilt and feelings of contrition of the Germans and their Austrian allies would be brought to the fore ... Even those not directly involved in the mass murders were silent witnesses. This, too, demands some expression of mourning or remorse. So we started our pilgrimage.

Before the gate, we stopped to read a sign bearing the death tally: On the left-hand side was a list of countries, on the right-hand side was a corresponding list of numbers, generally five-digit ones, enumerating these respective countries' martyrs. We were surprised that the sign did not indicate that the primary victims were Jews.

I tried to open the gate but it was locked, *"Jahwohl es ist zugespert,"* said the attendant, *"Winterurlaub."* Winter vacation at a concentration camp? The Viennese Kuntzhistoriches Museums didn't have winter vacations.

The locked camp forced us to concentrate on the nearby memorial plaza. Every country whose Jews perished in Mathausen was entitled to erect a memorial in their memory. One Eastern European country's memorial depicted a man with his hands in the air, and bore an epitaph reading: "People be alert." France had erected a memorial *"Aux Liberales,"* along with a poem in French, German and English, the contents so abstract that it was meaningless to us ... Poland's monument paid tribute to the victory over Fascism ... A Russian memorial consisted of a bare-chested muscle-bound warrior, with one arm huddling a girl and the other arm chained to the wall. It bore the inscription: "The victims of Fascism." ... Luxembourg had put up a small stone slab with only the word "Luxembourg" engraved on it ...

Albania erected a statue of an Albanian soldier overpowering a helmeted SS soldier with the butt of his rifle ... Germany had the most ostentatious memorial. After all, she was the home team. There was a stone relief of a heavy woman, surrounded by a brick wall. Hewn into the wall was a poem by Bertold Brecht:
"O Deutschland bleich Mutter!
Wie haben deine Sohne dich zugerichtet ... "
O Germany pale mother,
In what condition have your sons left you,
That you sit among the peoples,
A mockery or a fear?

I then understood why the sign said *Poles 35,000, Czechs X amount, Finns Y amount*, as opposed to: *Polish Jews 35,000, Czechoslovakian Jews X amount, Finnish Jews Y amount*. Austria as well as her neighbors refuses to recognize Jews as a people and a nation. Therefore, it was Polish citizens who perished, not Jews. Is it not ironic that Jews earn citizenship posthumously? While Jews are denied equal rights during their lifetime and are the victims of venomous decrees, after their death they are dubbed citizens, and their particular Jewishness is totally obliterated. This is the current situation in Russia: Alive? — Jew ... dead? — Russian.

We desperately searched for some acknowledgment of the Jews' role as a Jew in this epoch. At the edge of the adjacent forest, beyond range of the memorial plaza, something caught my eye: From the distance it looked like an ordinary tombstone three feet in height. As we approached it, we discerned Hebrew letters. How apt — but why out here? Hewn into the marble were the words of the Almighty to Kayin who had just murdered his brother Hevel: "The voice of your brother's blood is crying: — erected by *Die Jüdische Jugend in Ostereich* (the Jewish Youth in Austria)."

✺§ The Terezin Counterpart

Four days after our Mathausen visit, we took a bus from Prague to Theresienstadt (Czech: Terezin). Theresienstadt is a ghetto which had held over 150,000 Jews between the years 1941-45. The Nazis deported Jews primarily from Western and Central Europe to Theresienstadt, in order to gradually transfer them to death camps, particularly Auschwitz. We descended from the bus in Terezin next to an army camp and asked one of the sentries where the concentration camp was. He pointed next door to an area that was covered with monuments and memorials. It seemed as if they did not miss paying homage to a single victim; we welcomed the change over Mathausen.

We passed this massive area and headed towards the camp gate where there was an influx of Czech tourists. Just inside the gate there were maps and explanations in various languages describing what had transpired there. The attendant and her assistant came over to us and explained in German that we were in the wrong place. We were most probably interested in the crematorium where the Jews were dealt with; this camp was used exclusively for political prisoners.

I questioned her whether there wasn't a crematorium in this camp. "Nein," she replied, this camp was for political prisoners; the only crematorium in Terezin is in the *Jüdische Konzentrationslager*. She gave us approximate directions how to reach the crematorium. As we walked through Terezin we could not help ponder the painful cognition that this village of three thousand was inhabited thirty-three years ago by back-to-back Jewish inmates. We had anticipated Theresienstadt to be restored like its hapless Terezin counterpart.

The Telltale Smokestack

We would not have found the crematorium had I not tripped over a railroad track almost buried by thirty-three years of growth. No doubt this was the means of the heinous transportations. The Jewish concentration camp also had a conflux of people but of a different type: boys were racing, girls were giggling and women were strolling with their baby carriages. This wasn't a concentration camp. It was a park, endless acres of green grass with plenty of shade. We beheld only four obstructions: A tiny white house with a chimney protruding, an ornamental hammer and sickle, a concrete *menorah* — the Jewish candelabrum — and a huge cross erected in someone's memory. But where was the camp? The gate? The crematorium, the barbed wire? Up the embankment were some buildings encompassed by walls. We speculated that this must be the camp. We trudged through a field of manure and discovered that these buildings were only a farm.

Below sat Theresienstadt. My great-grandmother perished there, but one could never tell. It was too pastoral and serene. A white house, hammer and sickle, a *menorah* and a cross — that is all there is. The smokestack of the white house should have given it away. Why would they paint such a nefarious building white? The front and back doors were locked. I was inflamed, my wife was speechless. I found scribbled in a window a note which read, "closed since October '77."

Behind the crematorium was an interminable row of identical memorials erected by countries whose Jews were extinguished in Theresienstadt. There weren't any monuments or epitaphs, but rather monotonous slabs of grey concrete upon which appeared the countries' names. At the end of this row, the hindermost point of the green, we found a black-and-gold monument: — "*lechavod zichron* — in honor of the memory," read the memorial, "of the thousands of saints who perished here by the iniquitous Nazi regime ... *Hashem yechonein efram.* — May the Almighty have mercy upon their ashes. — Erected by the Jews of Czechoslovakia." There weren't any attendants, any maps, any explanations ... but we didn't need any ... Avraham *Avinu* had already explained it.

IV.
Heroes of the Spirit

recorded by
Rabbi Nosson Scherman

The Bluzhever Rebbe Remembers: Embers Midst the Ruins

◆§ "G-d's Crown" in the Lublin Ghetto

IN THE BLUZHEVER RAV'S *beis midrash*, as in hundreds of others, each *Yom Tov* ends with *Neilas HaChag*, a soulful, joyful gathering of refreshment, song and Torah. But the Bluzhever *beis midrash* in Brooklyn is different. *Neilas HaChag* always concludes with a lively singing and dancing to the words of the prayer וְיֶאֱתָיוּ כֹל לְעָבְדֶךָ, *They all shall come to serve You*, from the Rosh Hashanah-Yom Kippur liturgy. That particular custom goes back to 1941 in the ghetto of Lublin. Tens of thousands of Jews were crowded together in the ghetto square waiting for their own Final Solution. The Bluzhever Rav was one

---
Rabbi Yisroel Spira, the chassidic Rebbe of Bluzhev, is heir to the dynasty of the B'nai Yisos'chor, Harav Zvi Elimelech of Dinov and the Grand Rabbis of Bluzhev. Before the war, Rabbi Spira was Rav of Prochnik. Then came World War II. His Rebbetzin, and their only child, a daughter, her husband, and their children were among the Six Million. Rabbi Spira suffered for nearly five years in a succession of labor, concentration, and death camps. His personal travail began in the ghetto in Lublin, a camp that was commanded by a notorious sadist. Out of perhaps half-a-million people who passed through the Lublin Ghetto, there are only fourteen known survivors.
   Rabbi Spira has many memories. They are a panorama of tribute to the Jewish people. They are tales of strength, courage, faith, resistance, self-sacrifice, holiness. They are expressions of people — great and simple, men and women, religious and non-religious — who knew that their cause, and not the murderers', would ultimately prevail; people whose great wish was that they not lose their inner strength and that they not be forgotten. This article, which appeared in *The Jewish Observer* of June 1978, recounts a few of those memories — just a few. They are isolated instances, perhaps, but they paint a picture in which pride overcomes pathos and light banishes darkness.

of them. The Gerrer Rebbetzin, wife of the late *Beis Yisroel* and her son Rabbi Leibel were there. They and other great and ordinary people spoke to one another, giving each other strength as they prepared to die together *al Kiddush Hashem*. (After the war, the Bluzhever Rav wrote to the Gerrer Rebbe informing him of the greatness of spirit with which his nearest ones faced their end.)

Another in that group was Rabbi Yehudah Leib Orlean who was one of the key figures in the establishment and growth of the Bais Yaakov movement.

Rabbi Orlean said to the Bluzhever Rav, "Tonight is Shemini Atzeres. We have no *Sefer Torah* with which to rejoice, but at least we can say the *Atto Horeiso* prayer."

With that, Rabbi Orlean raised his beautiful, powerful voice in the words that had always signaled the outbreak of joy, the tingle that was the prelude to the *hakafos* (Torah circuits) of Shemini Atzeres and Simchas Torah.

אַתָּה הָרְאֵתָ לָדַעַת, כִּי ה' הוּא הָאֱלֹקִים אֵין עוֹד מִלְבַדּוֹ "You have been shown to know that *Hashem* — He is the G-d. There is no other besides Him!"

Thousands of voices repeated after him in a crescendo of devotion. If this was indeed to be their last *Yom Tov*, then they would surrender their souls with the unflinching proclamation that there was none but Him; that though *Hashem*, the G-d of mercy, might assume the attribute of *Elokim*, the dispenser of uncompromising justice, He still remained the G-d of mercy whether or not we understood His ways.

The verses continued: first Rabbi Orlean, serving as cantor; the largest congregation he had ever led, repeating after him. Tears flowed like a river. *Atto Horeiso* was concluded, but Rabbi Orlean had another thought. Again he turned to the Bluzhever Rav.

"The Nazi soldiers saw us and heard us. They think we were crying because we fear *them*. Let us show them the truth."

He began singing וְיֶאֱתָיוּ כֹּל, *They all shall come*, with a lively infectious tune. What a beautiful liturgical poem! It foretells the End of Days when everyone, including the most distant of nations, will come to the Mountain of G-d to pledge their devotion to Him, to serve Him, to proclaim Him as King. It concludes וְיִתְּנוּ לְךָ כֶּתֶר מְלוּכָה, *and they will give You the crown of sovereignty*.

He sang and others joined. Hands clutched one another and

feet began to dance. It was Shemini Atzeres and Jews rejoiced. More — under the muzzles of German rifles they sang that even the hated murderers, the most degraded and bestial of men, would one day acknowledge the kingship of *Hashem*. They sang and danced until the SS commandant arrived and the death march began.

Hardly anyone survived that horrible night. But the Bluzhever Rav was spared, and the words, the dance and the tune are recalled at the end of every festival in the Bluzhever *Beis Midrash*.

◈§ Yom Kippur: Our Work Was Perfect

It was the Lemberg-Yanovsky labor camp, a few days before Yom Kippur. There, as in all the ghettos and camps, the Nazis appointed Jews to supervise the laborers and extract from them the last particle of endurance and strength. The chief *Ordenungsdienst* (work supervisor) in Lemberg was a Jew named Schneeweiss. Like many Jews in his position, his fawning desire to please his masters in return for an extra portion of bread or an extra day of life often made him seem even more cruel than they. The Nazis, in turn, enjoyed the spectacle of Jew persecuting Jew.

Now, Yom Kippur was on the way. Fasting could be managed. It would mean placing oneself in mortal danger, because food rations were below the subsistence level in any case and the labor required even more than the nourishment that had been normal in prewar days. The rabbis who were frequently called upon to decide such questions always answered in accordance with the *halachah*: "The Torah requires us to eat even on the holiest of fast days because to do otherwise is to invite death by starvation — and *Hashem Yisborach* wants us to exert every effort to live. We are forbidden to surrender to death even though we are too limited to understand the purpose of our living under such circumstances."

Nevertheless, there were always those to whom a Yom Kippur, a smuggled pair of *tefillin*, a blast of the *shofar* on Rosh Hashanah, a secretly baked morsel of *matzah*, a bit of oil for a Chanukah flame, a *minyan*, were worth an encounter with a bullet or, worse, a whip. A group of such people approached their spiritual leader in the Yanovsky camp of Lemberg.

"Rav Spira, Yom Kippur is coming. What are we to do? How can we desecrate the Holy Day working as if it were any other day?"

The rabbi was moved as he often was by the devotion of his fellow Jews. He would try to help them.

The Bluzhever Rav went to the hated Schneeweiss, "Herr *Ordenungsdienst*. As you know, it will soon be Yom Kippur. I am a rabbi and it is important for me to observe this day as properly as possible. A group of my disciples in the camp wish to do the same. We do not ask to be freed from labor, all we ask is that for that one day we be given work which will not force us to violate the law of the Torah. We are willing to do extra work on other days to make up for any labor which goes undone."

That simple request was in itself an act of great heroism, for Schneeweiss, no friend of observant Jews, had in his own hands the power of life and death. He could easily have used the "treasonous" request as a means of proving his loyalty to his SS mentors by turning in the "lazy rabbi who was prepared to sabotage the Master Race's war effort for the sake of his Holy Day foolishness." Schneeweiss asked for time to consider. The next day, he told the rabbi that he could choose a limited number of prisoners who would be assigned to clean the apartments of the camp's commanding officers. But the *Ordenungsdeinst* would guarantee them nothing nor would he defend them if the Germans sensed something wrong. And if there was so much as a speck of dirt to be found anywhere in the house, they would pay with their lives.

So it was that on Yom Kippur an unusual prayer service was held by Rabbi Spira and fourteen young men. The rabbi stood on a window sill polishing the glass while the men were sweeping, dusting, tidying — and all the while he led them in the solemn prayers as he had led congregations for many years in Galicia, but never had the Yom Kippur service been as fervent or as tearful.

At midday, a tray was brought in with food. It lay ignored on a table as the praying and cleaning continued. Then a few German officers entered to admire the work of their servants for the day. They examined the rooms and were pleased — until they saw the food.

"*Jüdische Hunde, freszt!* Stuff yourselves, Jewish dogs!"

The Jews could not ignore the order. What should they do? Rabbi Spira walked to the officers and explained:

"It is our Holy Day, the day when sins are forgiven. As you have seen, we serve you loyally, even on this sacred day, and our work is perfect. But we are required to fast today and we ask of you to excuse us from eating our meal today. Our work will continue and it will not be affected by hunger."

The officers were furious. They sent for Schneeweiss. Quaking, the *Ordenungsdienst* came to the room. "These dogs refuse to eat their rations. You are responsible for them. We shall return in two hours — and if all their food is not eaten, *you* will be shot."

Schneeweiss stood up straight and unbuttoned his shirt, baring his chest. "I will not force them to eat. I am fasting myself today. If you wish to shoot me, then shoot me now!"

An officer drew his gun and Schneeweiss stood firm. A shot. He was dead. Hated Schneeweiss had become holy Schneeweiss. Who can estimate the great heights to which every Jewish soul can rise? ... Then the Germans turned to the fifteen Jews who were ready for the same treatment.

"You will continue to work. The food will be removed and you will receive not a scrap to eat until tomorrow morning. Go back to work!"

※ ※ ※

One expects flashes of greatness from distinguished people, and crisis can call forth unfathomed heroism even from ordinary people. But what of the broad masses? Weren't they bitter? Surely they could not have risen to the challenge.

No, the Rav replies. In his nearly five years in the most inhuman conditions, he remembers no Jew who was bitter, regretting having been born a Jew. They were incredibly determined not to lose their dignity, the pride in their Jewishness. They refused to be broken.

☙ A Knife for a Mother

In one of the camps, the Bluzhever Rav was assigned to saw wood in an open field. As he wielded his saw, he witnessed one of the most barbaric scenes in the five years he had endured. An order had gone out that all women with infants less than four weeks of age were to be rounded up. The box cars had pulled into the concentration camp and were disgorging their pitiful cargo of sick, starved, weakened mothers who had but recently given birth, clutching their tiny, crying, hungry babies. One mother began to scream.

"A *messer*, a knife! A knife! Give me a knife!"

The Rav dropped his saw and ran to her.

"Don't even think such a thing. No matter how terrible the suffering, you dare not kill yourself. We must have faith in the mercy of the *Ribono shel Olam*. We must try to live. This suffering will not last ... "

He didn't finish talking. An SS guard sent him sprawling with a savage blow to the back of the head and another one to the face.

"Dog! Traitor! What were you plotting with her? Tell me the truth or I'll kill you!"

"I encourage no plots. The woman wanted a knife to kill herself. I told her our religion does not permit us to kill ourselves. We must try to remain healthy to do our work."

The guard went to the woman still holding her tiny infant. "What did he tell you?" he demanded.

"He said I should not kill myself. That I must try to live."

"Why did he think you wanted to kill yourself?"

"Because I asked for a knife."

The guard laughed. He pulled a knife from his coat and handed it to her. Then he stepped back to enjoy the sight of the cowardly Jewish woman murdering her baby and killing herself.

Gently she put the child down on the ground and undid his clothes. She looked up at the sky and said,

"Sweet Father, you gave me a pure Jewish child. Now he is eight days old and we are being taken to die. I return him to You as a pure and holy Jew."

She recited the *brachah*: "Blessed are You, *Hashem*, our G-d, King of the universe Who has sanctified us with His commandments and has commanded us concerning circumcision."

And she took the Nazi knife and circumcised her child.

৵ঌ The Private "Akeidos"

A pair of *tefillin* was smuggled into the camp and kept secret from the Nazis. To be found with them would mean death or torture, but people *waited in line* to don the *tefillin* and say a swift *Kriyas Shema* before passing them on to the next person. All the Jews knew, but there were no informers and the Nazis never knew. But when could one don those precious *tefillin*? The Jews were roused before dawn to go to their forced labor and they did not return to their barracks until after dark. It fell to the Bluzhever Rav to decide whether or a not a Jew should put on *tefillin* at night. He ruled that under the circumstances they should, and the little boxes and black straps infused countless Jews with the inspirational knowledge that G-d is One.

There were no *siddurim* in the death camp, but every now and then a prisoner would find a piece of paper and pencil, write down a prayer and paste it to a wall in some out-of-the-way spot where his comrades could surreptitiously recite it unbeknown to the guards.

There was no *shofar* in the camps, but how could Jews contemplate Rosh Hashanah without a *shofar*? Somehow, a *shofar* was smuggled into the camp and blown softly on Rosh Hashanah. There were places where the Jew who dared to blow a *shofar* was caught and publicly tortured to death, but that did not stop Jews from smuggling again and blowing again and listening again to the sound that proclaimed that one day *all* would know that He is One and His Name is One.

These people were the quiet heroes, the ones no one knew before the war and who, if they survived, became ordinary shopkeepers, businessmen, housewives, and clerks. But they had within themselves the legacy of Avraham, Yitzchak, and Yaakov — so in their own furnace, on their own *Akeidah*, and surrounded by enemies, they were not found wanting.

✥ "Shehecheyanu" in the Shadow of Death

When Chezkel Frankel returned from a visit to Warsaw, he brought regards to the Bluzhever Rav from a strange source, a non-believing former Polish-Bundist leader named Zomatchkovsky who said simply, "Tell Rabbi Spira that he saved me. He will understand." Frankel delivered the message and waited for an explanation.

On an *Erev* Chanukah in Bergen-Belsen, a random selection was made. The Germans went from barrack to barrack and pointed to prisoners. They were taken out of the barracks and shot dead without provocation. There was not enough time that afternoon to remove all the bodies, so all day long, the prisoners walked by and stepped over the grisly reminders of the morning's terror. But that night it would be Chanukah and a *menorah* must be lit. With what?

The prisoners wore wooden shoes that were dyed black by women inmates. The shoe dye was flammable and it could serve as oil; some was smuggled out of the camp factory. Threads were pulled from sweaters by the women and spun into wicks. The word spread in whispers. That night there would be a secret

Maariv minyan followed by the kindling of Chanukah lights. The Bluzhever Rav led the *Maariv* service. Then he recited the three blessings of the first light of Chanukah and lit the *menorah*. Thousands of Jews joined in the ceremony. They all knew the danger of discovery, but they were undeterred.

Zomatchkovsky approached the Rav and asked, "Rav Spira, there is one thing I do not understand. You said the prayers and upheld the tradition you believe in — good! But how could you bring yourself to say the blessing of *Shehecheyanu* — how dare you thank G-d for allowing us to live for this horrible time of torture, death, and hunger? Haven't you made a mockery of our suffering?"

The Bluzhever Rav answered, "You ask a very good question. I too was wondering how I could joyfully recite that blessing, but then I looked around and what did I see? Thousands of Jews gathered together to watch the kindling. They have a right to give up hope, but they insist on remaining Jews. Never have we seen such a demonstration of Jewish courage and strength. For that alone it is sufficient to thank the Creator for giving us the privilege to be alive and to see the greatness of our people! You see all these Jews and yet you persist in asking. You amaze me! You know our history. When you speak of Jewish suffering during the Inquisition and the Chmelnitzky massacres, you admire those Jews for having the courage to rebuild, yet you think that you have suffered more that they — that you have the right to surrender and give up hope. What makes you think that you have suffered more than any other Jew in history? No! We do *not* give up. We are proud that we have lived to see thousands of Jews who will *never* give up and who prove that we will rebuild again!"

Years later, the non-religious Bundist was still grateful to the chassidic Rebbe for giving him the strength to survive the war and rebuild in his own way.

✢ For Whom the Matzos?

It was two weeks before Pesach and there was no *matzah*. The Bluzhever Rav approached Commandant Hass of the death camp, with an audacious request:

"We wish to celebrate our religious holiday by baking *matzah*. We do not ask for extra rations. All we ask is that we be given flour instead of bread and that we be permitted to build a small brick oven for ourselves. All the work will be done outside of our regular working hours."

The officer said that the request would be fowarded to Berlin. To the amazement of all, the answer was not to execute the "dogs" who dared ask, but to grant them the privilege.

During those busy pre-Pesach days, one of the women in the camp went into labor. She was taken to a nearby hospital to give birth. With her, someone smuggled out a letter addressed to Switzerland. The letter described the inhuman conditions in the camp and begged that some way be found to send food packages to prevent starvation. Ordinarily, patients going to hospitals were able to find ways to forward letters, but this one could not. The letter was discovered on her person and sent back to Commandant Hass. He was furious and he was determined to vent his rage on the *Rabbiner* for whom he had just done a favor.

"Rabbiner Spira, I was kind enough to let you bake your filthy *matzos* and then you repay me by sending out this ungrateful lying letter!"

The Rav answered calmly that he knew nothing of the letter and had no hand in dispatching it.

"But you are the *Rabbiner*. Either you know who sent it or you can find out. If you do not inform me within twenty-four hours who is responsible for this letter, I will have you shot."

The Bluzhever Rav answered, "I repeat that I know nothing of the letter. If I did know or if I find out who is responsible I will not tell you. Therefore, you should shoot me now."

Hass turned to leave. Why the notorious murderer did not add one more victim to his list, no one knows. With his jackboot, he smashed the *matzah* oven and went his way.

Matzos had been baked, however. Now the question was how they should be divided. The preponderant opinion was that they should be given to adults who were required by the Torah to eat *matzah*. Children had no such requirement and therefore should not be permitted to deplete the scarce supply of *matzos*. There was a stray voice raised in opposition, however — the voice of a woman.

In the camp was a widow who cared for her two sons and three nephews throughout the war. She came from a distinguished family to which she personally added stature. "We must rebuild the Jewish people with our children," she argued. "*They* are precisely the ones who should receive portions of *matzah* for if we ever escape this *Mitzrayim* (Egypt), they are the future."

Responsibility for children was more than rhetoric to her. In the camp, she learned of someone who had a Bernfeld *Tanach* with German translation. She bought it for *three pounds of bread* — an enormous fortune in the currency of hunger and suffering — so that she could use it to teach the children, as indeed she did for over two years. Eloquent, passionate, persuasive — she carried the day and in *hora'as sha'ah* (an extraordinary decision) the children were given *matzah*. That *Seder* night, the Bluzhever Rav conducted a *Seder* for the children of the death camp. Instead of living in freedom and learning about slavery and redemption, he taught them, who were living in slavery, of the hope of redemption and freedom. He interpreted the Four Questions to reflect the concentration camp experience. He told them that the word עֲבָדִים *slaves*, is composed of the initials of דָּוִד בֶּן יִשַׁי עַבְדְּךָ מְשִׁיחֶךָ, David son of Jesse, Your servant, Your anointed. He told them that one day they would look back at the bitterest of exile-nights as the prelude of a new redemption. Today, those children, who had learned from a *Tanach* bought with bread and eaten *matzos* baked with tears, are leaders in the rebirth of Torah in America, England, and Israel.

◆§ Too Few For Rivalry

When the war ended, the Bluzhever Rav was totally alone, and broken in everything except spirit. He told his dear friend Reb Isaac Yaroslaver, "What does it matter — my children or *your* children? As long as there are still Jewish children and the nation has a future."

He recalled the passionate wish of the *Kedoshim* from among the Six Million that he knew. They wanted not to be forgotten. They wanted their *Yahrzeit* to be remembered and most of all, their bravery and determination to become part of the Jewish legacy. The Chanukah, the *matzos*, the *V'ye'esoyu*, Schneeweiss's final fast, the *tefillin* — the countless acts of devotion that surely led *Hashem Yisborach* to reaffirm that Israel is a unique nation on earth.

He had hoped that the survivors would gather to tell their tales and have them recorded. It happened only rarely, but he is grateful that there are stirrings now. Hopefully, succeeding generations will realize and marvel at the bravery and steadfastness the *Kedoshim* displayed in the midst of utter helplessness.

He had another hope and he prays that it not be frustrated.

He was sure that after the ashes were sifted and the few living sparks salvaged from the destruction, the surviving individuals and groups would rush to embrace one another in an unprecedented upsurge of *Ahavas Yisrael.* With so few left, how could there be room for rivalry and jealousy? He shakes his head sadly at the reality and prays that the madness will cease.

Joseph Friedenson

Why Didn't They Fight Back?

TIME AND AGAIN the cruel taunts are hurled. "Those Jews in the ghettos and camps were *galus* Jews, without fighting courage." "Why didn't they fight back?" "Why did they go to the camps and the ovens like sheep to the slaughter?"

The taunts are repeated often. The alienated American Jew and the Sabra estranged from Jewish tradition in Israel are at one in insisting: "It could never happen to us." And, "We are proud Jews, not servile ones, like those in the ghettos were." And even religious Jews, who should know better, become uneasy and apologetic when thus challenged. From the Eichmann trial through the appearance of Hannah Arendt's controversial book, the question has resounded repeatedly in books, periodicals, newspapers, in private and public discussion: "Why didn't they fight back?" Surely the challenge requires an answer.

Let it be said clearly. The question is asked either by non-Jews or by Jews who have taken over — lock, stock and barrel — the values of the gentile world.

Resistance, revolt — what meaning does it have? If resistance and revolt could have saved Jews, the challenge would have meaning. But the question is not posed in this sense. Those who pose the question know full well that such a possibility never arose; that during those years, even mighty armies were unable to resist the Nazis.

If the question seeks to ascertain why at the least some of the German murderers were not slain to "redeem" the Jewish blood they spilled, it would be a meaningful question. But this too is not its intent. All too often the militants who pose the questions have

---

This essay appeared in *The Jewish Observer* of September 1963.

no qualms about studying at the feet of Hitler's professors in German universities, or about spending their vacations in Germany in fascinated enjoyment of German music and art. Surely such as these do not experience the blazing desire for vengeance, which might properly fill a Jewish heart.

≈§ Heroism and Jewish Honor

The question concerning resistance and revolt is asked in a different sense: "Why did they not die with dignity and arms in hand?" or "Why did they desecrate our Jewish honor, and allow themselves to be led to the slaughter like sheep?"

Behind *that* question there stands a false, pagan conception of what is meant by Jewish honor, Jewish dignity and Jewish heroism; a non-Jewish conception which presently is desecrating an entire generation of sainted martyrs.

Certainly those who redeemed the blood of their murdered brothers and sisters were heroes. However, it is a horrible desecration of the memories of the millions of heroes — heroes of another sort — who were holy and pure, to say that only those who rebelled saved the honor of our people. Or, as a Jewish writer recently put it: "Without them (those who rebelled) we would have no right for further life as a people."

Certainly the uprisings in Warsaw and in Bialystok were glorious chapters in the martyrology of our people. No one, however, is presently capable of judging in whose resistance there was greater heroism — that of the Jew who fell with gun in hand, or that of the Jew in the Budzin concentration camp who, tranquilly and unresistingly walking to his death, called out to the terrified Jews all about him: "If only I could be an atonement for all of you."

≈§ Jewish Resistance at Every Step

The simple Jew in Budzin, who went to his death "without resistance," (of whom the Revisionist leader Dr. Wdowinsky spoke at the Eichmann trial) was not the only hero of his kind. Those who were there came upon numberless instances of Jewish resistance without arms, of Jewish courage without grenades, of incomparable Jewish heroism without guns.

They — the Germans — strove to transform their Jewish victims into animals even before they began their mass murders. But despite all, the Jews remained human beings who did not lose their Divine Image at the very edges of their mass graves. The

Germans wanted to transform Jews into cannibals who would devour each other, but as if for spite, Jews mutually helped one another, strengthened each other, often shared their last bite of bread with others. The Germans wanted to force Jews to forget their names, to forget the time, but thousands did not forget. They *davened*, and observed *Shabbos* and *Yom Tov*. They baked *matzos*, they sounded the *shofar*, even when to do so endangered their very lives.

One Who Symbolizes Many

Volumes could be filled with similar experiences, to which the camp survivors bear witness. For the moment, let an account be heard of only one of those many unsung sanctifiers of the Divine Name. What heroism was imbedded in that Hungarian Jew, Reb Binyomin, who slept near my cot in block 22 in Auschwitz-Birkenau, and who would rise early each morning for prayer! I do not speak of his *tefillin*, which he somehow wondrously managed to hide in his straw-sack, thereby endangering himself at the hands of both the Germans and the Polish Kapos.

I remember something different. In the morning, when saying the morning *Brachos* which precede the *Shacharis* service, he was wont to repeat — perhaps ten times — with devout concentration: "*Ashreinu* — Happy are we, how good is our portion, and how pleasant is our lot." He would utter each Hebrew phrase and lovingly translate the words into Yiddish again and again. How happy — how good — how sweet. Imagine it if you can. A Jew stands in Auschwitz. The chimneys burn, the air in the barracks is stultifying, the stomach is empty and tortured by hunger. The best that awaits him is another day of hard labor under whips and wild, ranting insults. And here the same Jew stands in the morning, upright and unafraid. Despite everything, he still takes pride and rejoices in his being a Jew capable of saying *Shema Yisrael* ... Was that Jew a coward?

I do not know whether Reb Binyomin knew how to handle a gun. I am not even quite certain whether he would have joined an uprising. But in my eyes he remained to this day a symbol of heroism.

A Piece of Bread and Jewish Honor

Another episode is recalled to memory.

In great haste, or better said, while being chased, I once

forgot my portion of bread on the cot on the way to the inspection and daily count. I need not, nor can I, describe that day in my life. If you were there, you know its meaning. If you were not there, you will, in any event, never understand. I had nothing to eat all day, and knew that that night I would go to sleep hungry. But when I returned to the barracks, Reb Binyomin came towards me with the bread. He had that day remained in the barracks. He had found the bread and hidden it.

"Believe me, it was a difficult test," Reb Binyomin told me. "You understand, after I finished eating my own portion, I was still hungry, and suddenly, another portion of bread. I had already held it near my mouth. But quickly, I remembered that here in the camp such miracles as extra portions of bread do not occur. I thought it must either be yours or Yanek's (Yanek was a Polish gentile boy who shared our cot). If yours, how could I eat it? And if Yanek's — I could accomplish a double purpose. Firstly, I could give him a new life, and secondly, I could sanctify the Divine Name. Let the non-Jews in the barrack know what it means to be a Jew who wears *tefillin*. A whole day I wrestled with myself. It is good that the day has passed, and I am now done with the test."

What heroism there was imbedded in that Jew!

When Reb Binyomin Collapsed

Only once I saw him shattered and without hope. It came suddenly. A day earlier he still appeared healthy and fresh. But in one day he collapsed. It happened after another kind of "selection" had taken place. Candidates were chosen for work in the crematorium. When he heard that such a selection was to be made, his whole body suddenly shrank. The thought alone that there was a possibility that he would have to be one of those who drive other Jews into the oven crushed him instantly.

I remember what he looked like at that "call." He seemed to have become a mixture of two colors, black and white. Black as the earth and white as chalk. He stood near me and shuddered convulsively. When the call ended with his not having been selected, he hardly managed to drag himself back to the barracks, and then fainted.

Reb Binyomin never recuperated. From that day on he was never the same. In a few days he shrank till he became a mussulman (the term used for those who had become thin as skeletons). Not long afterwards he fell a victim in a selection. One of the Jewish Kapos related that on taking Reb Binyomin out of the block, the latter said to him: "It is better for me to go today than it would have been then. It is easier to depart for the true world with clean hands."

I related these episodes because Reb Binyomin is the first one who came to mind. But his heroism was only one of countless such instances which await recounting.

Joseph Friedenson

My Father's Survival in the Warsaw Ghetto

WHEN MY FATHER, Reb Eliezer Gershon Friedenson, was killed by the Nazis (most probably during the Ghetto uprising in Pesach of 1943), he was only forty-three years old. Although relatively young, he was already famous throughout Poland and much of the rest of Europe as editor of two publications — *The Beth Jacob Journal* for adults and *Kinder-Garten* for children — besides contributing articles and advice to many other Agudath Israel publications. In addition, he ran the offices of N'shei and Bnos Agudath Israel, with close to three hundred branches. Besides this, he founded and supervised a vocational school for girls, was on the boards of tens of educational institutions, and even found time to edit textbooks for the Beth Jacob schools. He also served as "Speaker" of the Agudath Israel faction in the Lodzer *Kehillah*, and was a member of leading bodies of the World Agudath Organization.

Those were his official functions. His "unofficial" functions included being host to almost every great *Rav* (such as the Lubliner Rav and the Sanuker Rav) and *Rosh Yeshivah* (Reb Elchonon Wasserman of Baranovich, Reb Yerucham Levovitz of Mir, and Reb Dovid Blecher of Beis Yoseif, come to mind) as well as all the *meshulachim* (emissaries) from *Eretz Yisrael*, who passed through Lodz to raise money. He housed them, fed them, and gave them not only desk space in his tiny office but also his enthusiasm, his connections, and his expertise toward achieving their monetary goals. (Father himself set an example for richer men with his open-handed charities.)

This biographical sketch appeared in *The Jewish Observer* of March 1983.

That was not all. Father gave regular lectures and *shiurim* to Zeirei Agudath Israel, to Poalim, and to Bnos groups. He traveled the length and breadth of Poland in the interests of various causes — Agudath Israel, Bais Yaakov, Keren Hayishuv, Keren HaTorah — and campaigned in parliamentary and local elections.

We at home took all these facets of Father's busy life for granted — they were as routine as three-meals-a-day. But the real essence of Father, and what is worth noting and remembering, came to the fore in the dread years of the Warsaw Ghetto. These I remember with clarity, and choose to share with the reader.

The Welcome Mat in Warsaw

By present-day American standards we did not exactly live luxuriously, even in Lodz. In fact, through most of the Thirties we occupied only three rooms and a kitchen. Our apartment also served as the editorial office of Father's magazines, the meeting place of prominent *Askanim* (community activists). Yet I don't remember a weekday, not to mention a *Shabbos*, that we did not have guests at the table. (Besides mealtime guests, there were people who stayed with us for weeks, sometimes months at a time.) Great and humble, they passed through our place by the hundreds, all received by Father like long-lost relatives. Father pursued *orchim* (guests) like a single-minded businessman pursues customers. He often picked up an *orayach* on the train while returning from one of his frequent trips, and rejoiced with him as over a great bargain.

Once Father said to Mother: "*Hachnosas orchim* — the mitzvah of hospitality — isn't so much a matter of welcoming a great *rav*, the elegant Dr. Deutschlander from Vienna, or Mr. Harry Goodman from London — who wouldn't want to do that? It's more a matter of welcoming a poor, tired stranger who lies down, with his boots on, in my bed," which in fact, someone had just done.

After being tipped off that Father was on a Nazi "Wanted" list, we had to flee from Lodz to Warsaw. It took quite a few weeks just to find ourselves some living space. We ended up with a single room and a kitchen at Muranowska 40. Having arrived with only a few *zlotys* (which Mother had somehow managed to save and hide), we were forced to reduce our living standard in every conceivable way. And so we lived a very constricted life — except for *hachnosas orchim*, which was as expansive as ever.

Warsaw was full of refugees fleeing the Germans, and we

too were refugees. There was very little that Father could do for others — we soon needed help ourselves. And yet, for many who despaired of finding even just a listening ear into which to pour their bitterness of heart, Father's warm smile and his willingness to share his meager meals were a rare source of *chizuk* and encouragement. Even when, about a year after the outbreak of the war, the Germans sealed off the Ghetto and our situation became even more precarious, Father continued to bring home guests, especially for *Shabbos*.

Bands of beggars roamed the streets, and people in self-defense would lock their doors against them, because there was nothing left to give. Not so Father. When the apartment was emptied of both cash and food, he still courteously opened the door at every knock and explained that although now he could not help, when he could again he surely would.

One of the most heart-rending sights and sounds of the Ghetto was that of the homeless or orphaned children, ragged and barefoot, bellies swollen from hunger, crying in the Ghetto streets and begging for *"a pitzele broit"* (a crumb of bread). But what could anyone do? Who had a crumb to spare? ... Father could not just stand by. Cutting up bits of bread, he would wrap them in slivers of paper and throw them out of the window — there was a 7 or 8:00 P.M. curfew for adults, but the children were not affected by it and there they were, begging. Word was out that on our street a "rich man" gave out bread, and a crowd of children began to collect there night after night.

One evening, when the children, chanting their pathetic hunger-cry, gathered as usual, Father started cutting up our last loaf of bread in the house. Before too long, he had used up all the bread in the house. Not only did we have no bread left for the evening meal or for the next day's breakfast, we also had no money with which to buy more. Realizing what he had done, Father started humming the tune of an old little Jewish song that goes: *"Oif Morgen vet G-tt sorgen — Let the Good G-d take care of the morrow"*; and he sat us down, my brother Shimshon Raphael and me, to a *shiur* in *Hilchos Tzeddakah* (Laws of Giving Charity), the gist of which was that even the needy are obligated to give.

◆§ When History Can Wait

Father was always sprouting "ideas." It became a humorous byword among family and friends, and soon even Father would smile at himself as he announced happily a few times a day, "I have an idea!" Nevertheless, he took his ideas seriously, and would carry them out as quickly as humanly possible.

Father's ideas and energies centered both upon his "official" jobs (the publications, Agudath Israel, Bais Yaakov, Bnos, etc.) and also upon every aspect of Torah and *yeshivah* activity. Everything was his job; even after forty-eight hours of continuous work, Father did not complain of being tired.

When the Germans marched in, all such activity came to a dead halt. Communal life ceased to exist. When we fled to Warsaw, we found that not one address familiar to Father from his years of *askanus* was still open and functioning.

The early months in Warsaw were fearful times. The Germans snatched men off the streets, beat them bloody, and transported them to slave-labor camps. Yet Father never let the extreme danger, especially to him as a bearded Jew, stop him from his rounds. He ran through the streets at least every second day to Gryzbowska 26 to appeal to the officials of the Judenrat for one sufferer or another. (He never rode a rickshaw, the primitive means of transportation ghetto-dwellers were reduced to once the Germans confiscated all the horses, because he could not bear the thought of a fellow human pulling him through the streets.) In contrast to most other places, where the Germans installed low-class elements in the local Judenrat to lord it over their suffering fellow Jews, the Warsaw Judenrat was different. For some reason it was staffed by prestigious, experienced former *Kehillah* leaders, many of them known to Father from his active *askanus* days. And he went constantly from one clandestine meeting-place to another to help realize his "ideas": community kitchens for the refugees, underground schools and orphanages, lectures for former Bais Yaakov students, and various relief committees.

One place where Father went only with great reluctance was the Z.O.S. (Zydowska Samopomoc Spoleczna) or Z.T.O.S. (Zydowskie Towarzystwo Samopomocy Splolecne), the Jewish "Self-Help" Agency secretly financed by a representative of the Joint Distribution Committee and the International Red Cross. For some reason the Nazi administration of the Warsaw Ghetto treated this organization much better than the Judenrat; they were not harassed constantly, as the Judenrat office was. As a result, their officials sometimes functioned in oblivion to the people's suffering. Father therefore detested the dandified, Polish-speaking officials who staffed it, their assimilationist behavior and speech, their fancy titles (Dr. This and Dr. That), and what seemed to him their lack of empathy for their fellow Jew. He once quoted a *Gemara* to me that said people who continue business as usual at a time when Jews are suffering, סִימָן שֶׁאֵינָם מֵהֶם, to which Rashi says: סִימָן שֶׁאֵינָם מִבְּנֵי אַבְרָהָם יִצְחָק וְיַעֲקֹב — "They are not of Jewish extraction."

Once Father was so upset by the behavior of one of the officials toward a Jew who spoke to him in Yiddish that he ran to the second floor and stormed the inner sanctum of the famed historian of the Warsaw Ghetto, Dr. Ringelblum, head of the Z.O.S., and cried out in anguish: "You, Dr. Ringelblum — you are a Socialist! You're supposed to represent the masses! Can't you take the trouble to find a clerk who will speak to a poor provincial Jew in Yiddish?"

Rabbi Huberband, the young Orthodox historian who assisted Ringelblum, tried to calm my father, but Father would not be appeased. "Put away your dusty archives and go down to help that poor Yid!" he raged. "History can wait, but that man downstairs can't wait until your snob down there learns some Yiddish!"

⇥ Thundering Over the Luftwaffe

Father was ever the optimist and *baal bitachon* (man of faith), even when he found the going rough for his "ideas" and plans. He never knew despair, he never lost his ebullience and his joy of living, the chassidishe *ivdu es Hashem besimchah* (serve G-d with joy!).

It was hard to keep up this spirit in the ghetto-years. Outdoors, danger and death prevailed, while hunger and disease lurked within. Hitler's hordes were winning victory after victory. People used to flock to our place for an interpretation of day-to-day events, for some strength to go on. Hard as it was for him, Father was the one who supplied that necessary measure of optimism.

A Jewish neighbor, Mr. Domb, who had a Swiss passport, used to leave the ghetto and smuggle in Italian newspapers. These were somewhat different from the Nazi newspapers. Here and there, there were even occasional hints of Axis weaknesses. Father would expand upon these and interpret them to predict the inevitable downfall of the Nazis. Warned to restrain his enthusiasm because there might be informers in the group, Father waved away the danger. He refused to believe that any Jew could stoop so low as to inform on his fellows.

In our first two ghetto-years, there was a *shul* in our courtyard at Muranowska 40. Up to three hundred people gathered in the *shul* every Friday night at nine o'clock at great risk — it was after curfew — and Father would deliver a *drashah* on *Parshas Hashavua*. Once during the dark days of the Battle of Britain and the Nazis' merciless aerial bombardment, when the German press was full of Hitler's boasting that victory was at hand for the Third Reich, Father commented on the *pesukim* in Yeshayahu (14:13-15):

> "If you (Eisav) shall say to yourself, 'I have soared to the heights of Heaven ... I am likened unto the Deity' ... Know that you will be struck down into the lowest depths, the very bowels of the earth ... "

Raising his voice my father thundered:

> "The Germans may be soaring arrogantly over Britain and raining destruction on its cities, but G-d will bring them down in ignominy!"

To this day, a chill goes through me when I think of Father speaking so openly before hundreds of people, many of them strangers, while German gendarmes paced back and forth outside.

Epilogue

I am not sure that Father expected that he personally would survive the war. When I was smuggled out of the ghetto on December 31, 1942, his parting words were: "Who knows when we shall meet again ..." Nevertheless, his faith in the eventual downfall of the tyrant never wavered, and anyone who came into contact with him was infected with his contagious *emunah* and *bitachon* — his unshakable faith in the *yeshuah* (salvation).

On the day that I arrived in America, a Yiddish newspaper printed an article mentioning my father's name as one of the heroes of the Warsaw Ghetto uprising. *Did my Father die a hero's death?* Maybe. He was involved in some underground activities from early on, but I was not present at the end, so I can never know for sure.

In truth, I do not need any proof of his heroism. With or without his participation in the uprising, Father, like thousands of others, lived a hero's life. In the two-and-a-half years that we were together in the ghetto, I can testify that every day of Father's life was filled to overflowing with heroic acts of *chessed* (kindness) and *maasim tovim* (good deeds), of high-risk communal involvement, of *tzedakah*, *hachnosas orchim*, and *bitachon* — unbreakable links in an eternal chain of valor and heroism.

Moshe Prager

A Shabbos Choice in the Warsaw Ghetto

THE *SHABBOS* HAS BEEN a companion to the Jewish People from their early history. Under its protective wings, the downtrodden Jew becomes transformed into a king, joyous and arrayed in splendor. The Nazis methodically tried to destroy the Holy *Shabbos*, the very soul of the Jew. But the harassed, oppressed people steadfastly clung to their faith and kept the Seventh Day sacred. They did not neglect it nor did they desert it. They took it along with them into the cellars; they burrowed into the bunkers with it; they watched over its light and did not allow it to become extinguished.

A voice from one of the hidden, gloomy rooms of the crowded ghetto was heard, half pleading, half chanting, "Children, the Holy *Shabbos* is coming. Don't forget it, in G-d's Name." That was Mother, weighed down with sorrow and compassion.

It was Monday, the day on which one's existence during the entire week depended. It was the day that the tyrants, the oppressors of the ghetto, had chosen for handing out the week's ration of bread. Their inhuman plan was simple: the Jews who labored like beasts of burden would presumably consume the bread allotted to them in the beginning of the week, and they would not have anything left for *Shabbos*. "Here, take it, hungry Jews," they implied, "divide your bread for the entire week. Toil each day and eat your miserable bread. Count your morsels ... count your crumbs ... and if you cannot overcome your hunger and you consume more than your fixed amount for the day, the privilege of dying of starvation is yours."

This story appeared in *The Jewish Observer* of January 1965 under the title "A Warsaw Ghetto Tale."

The older folk were able to withstand temptation and divided their allotment into portions for each day. But the children, who were weak from hunger, clung to their mother and pleaded, "We can't do it! You divide the bread, please."

The mother, the most unfortunate of all the ghetto's miserable creatures, took this heavy burden upon herself and divided the bread of her children for the entire week. How difficult was her task! She cut the bread into as many slivers as possible, weighed the morsels in her hand, and all this time kept the thought in mind that she must leave something for the *Shabbos*. As she cut it, she spoke to them.

"Remember, children, the days pass quickly and the *Shabbos* will soon be here. It is almost knocking on our door. Remember, in G-d's Name!"

Poor Mother! How that responsibility weighed upon her! But a more difficult task was that of watching the bread and making sure that it lasted the whole week through.

"Listen, children! I'll take special care of the pieces we set aside for *Shabbos*. Each of us can take a little from his daily portion, whatever he wishes. These pieces will add up so that we will have more for *Shabbos*."

"We agree!" the children shouted in unison.

One child, who was sick in bed, spoke up hesitantly, "Mother, if all of us give you an extra piece, will you make the delicious *kiggel* that you made for us last *Shabbos*?"

"If G-d be but willing! Please, G-d, be willing!"

"What a wonderful *kiggel*! How did you make it?" another child asked.

"That's a secret; I can't tell," Mother answered with a wry smile. She felt ashamed when she thought of how she had made that *kiggel*. Mother did not reveal the secret. What was there to say? Could she tell them that she took an extra piece from her own minute portion each day and that these crumbs made the "wonderful" *kiggel*? Now that one child was ill and she gave him some of her own bread each day, how was she to save anything extra for the *kiggel*?

"If G-d wills it," and Mother's hand trembled as she wrapped the *Shabbos* portion of bread into a white napkin, "you shall have a *kiggel* this *Shabbos* also. I promise you! And a very delicious *kiggel* it shall be!"

Mother kept her promise. She made a *kiggel* the likes of which had never been made before. It was a *kiggel* fit for a king.

She took potato peelings that she had collected secretly, soaked them in water and washed them thoroughly so as to remove every speck of dirt and grime. Then she dried and ground them. Into the flour she added all kinds of spices: salt, pepper, dried herbs.

And one more ingredient she added: her scalding tears ... "May it be Your will, O L-rd," was her silent prayer, "that this dish is good to my children, that they find in it the savor of manna as did our holy forefathers in the desert. May it be Your will, dear G-d, that the work of my hands shall not desecrate the holiness of the *Shabbos*."

All the time that the unfortunate woman was preparing the *kiggel*, her thoughts kept distressing her. "Maybe this *kiggel*, a dish made of nothing but potato peelings, will prove to be a desecration of the *Shabbos* ... It would be nice to add few drops of oil to this unusual mixture. Oil would add much to its flavor. But, if I use up the oil for the *kiggel*, how will I light my *Shabbos* candles?"

Thus, the poor woman debated with herself. "Food and candles ... both in honor of the *Shabbos* ... What comes first? No doubt, candles come first, for there is a special prayer to say when lighting them ... a commandment and a blessing ..." However, the next moment she changed her mind. "What can a candle do for my sick child when he is dying of hunger? The oil in the *kiggel* may sustain his life."

Her heart was torn with uncertainty.

"This commandment, to light *Shabbos* candles, is also of importance to a sick child. The child depends upon the mercy of Heaven and there is no better time for prayer and supplication than at the moment of lighting the candles for the *Shabbos* Queen."

Suddenly, another thought struck her, a shattering one: she would make the blessing over the candles without oil!

"He who dwells in Heaven and sees all and understands our thoughts will know that I am sanctifying the bit of oil for the holiness of the *Shabbos*. There is consecration in my use of the oil; I will light the candles without it!"

Shabbos eve, at twilight, Mother stood before her candles — wicks without oil — and her lips moved in silent prayer.

"Oh Lord of the Universe, accept these candles without light. In Your infinite mercy, illuminate them with Your Heavenly radiance. O Lord in Heaven; forgive me — a woman rebellious and ashamed, who dares to steal the oil from the wicks, in order to light the joy of the *Shabbos* in the hearts of her little children who are starving before her eyes. If I have sinned and You cannot accept this prayer, I beg of You, O Compassionate Father, listen to the *Shabbos* songs of the children that will resound in my poor dwelling when I bring this *kiggel* to the table ..."

When the children ate the *kiggel*, it tasted of Paradise, and they burst out in chorus, "We will sing the *Shabbos* Song ..."

And what about Mother? She swallowed her tears — tears of joy and fear. How was she to know that the *Shabbos* Queen herself had spread her pure angel wings over these singing children, and was humming a song of her own, "Let us sing a song to the Jewish Mother?"

Moshe Prager
translated by Rabbi Nosson Scherman

Eyeball to Eyeball

IT WAS NOT LONG after Germany's lightning conquest of Poland. A group of Nazi officers, drunk with triumph, went carousing through the Jewish streets of Warsaw looking for amusement. It did not take them long to find it. It was one of the Intermediate Days of Succos and Jews proudly dressed in their holiday garb still prayed openly in their synagogues. As the officers careened down Twarda Street, they came upon a group of Gerrer *chassidim* just leaving their house of prayer. The Nazis pounced on them gleefully.

"Hey, Moses, let me have your pretty beard." One of them grabbed at the beard of an old man and cut it off with his bayonet. One after another, the officer pulled at the beards of the frightened old men and they stood there unresisting and humiliated, grateful that their lives were spared.

Then came a shout, "Shoot me! Kill me! I won't let you cut my beard!" The shout of defiance came from a heretofore quiet, meek, young man named Yaakov "Yanchie" Geffen. To back up his words he held tightly onto his beard with both hands and stood his ground as if daring the Germans to cross him.

"Damn Jew! I'll kill you on the spot!"

"Please, Yanchie, don't be so stubborn. We mustn't get them angry," one of the old men pleaded with Yanchie privately, but to no avail. Meanwhile the Germans were increasing in their anger, especially since they were totally unprepared for such a show of defiance.

"Blasted Jews! Let him go to blazes!"

The officer with the knife lost his composure and began

This essay appeared in *The Jewish Observer* of September 1973.

pleading with Yanchie. "Just a few hairs. Let me just have the long ones."

"Yanchie, have pity on your own life. You're too young to die!"

"Yanchie, stop it! They'll kill us all if you don't give in!"

"Let me have just the *tip* of your beard and then I'll let you go!"

Finally Yanchie gave in and still holding his hands tightly wrapped around his beard, he exposed a few hairs to the Nazi barber.

Infuriated, the Nazis chased away the *chassidim*. "Get out of here, you lousy Jews. No wonder the Fuehrer hates you so!"

Later on Yanchie was asked why he risked his life over something so trivial. His answer was simple: "I did it to show them that the whole world doesn't belong to them."

※ ※ ※

Yaakov Geffen, the quiet one, became a fierce and courageous leader during the most trying times. He left Warsaw to travel secretly to the ghettos where the Nazi boot stamped hardest. After Mattisyahu Gelman left Cracow never to be heard from again, conditions in the ghetto became steadily worse. Cracow was the headquarters of the Nazi military governor of Poland and it was there that the harshest regime existed for Jews during the early part of the occupation. Jewish life was an unending chain of fear, terror, and persecution. The chassidic group that Matti Gelman had put together — the Mattisovtzies — began to feel that in unity was danger. They decided to split up into small groups to ease concealment and avoid the chance that all would be caught at the same time. It was then that Yanchie Geffen arrived on the scene. His presence electrified the Gerrer group and gave them new courage. His first move was to get them all together again. Yanchie would not permit them to continue their scattered existence like frightened rats. They must all stay together in one hiding place and carry on their life of prayer and study without fear of the Germans. The location Yanchie chose was the top floor of an abandoned Talmud Torah building.

Once, after midnight, the entire group was immersed in Torah study when they heard the raucous voices of a German patrol coming down the street.

The soldiers stopped at the Talmud Torah and began pounding on the door, demanding admittance. The young *chassidim* inside listened in terror and their hearts stopped. *Had the Germans discovered their whereabouts? Had their lamps been seen through a crack in the covered window? Were the Nazis planning to search the building on a hunch?* Some of them immediately thought of escape — they could silently climb up to the roof and hide there. Perhaps they should separate and hide in the many rooms and closets of the deserted building. But standing over them was Yanchie Geffen, calm and serene as though the angels of death were not shouting obscenities and in the process of breaking down the door of their refuge. Yanchie motioned to the *Gemaras* and cast his fearless look on each of the young men. His bearing calmed them and gradually each one returned to the now-silent study — or, at least, maintained his self-control. They heard the crash of the broken door falling inward. The Nazis swarmed into the building cursing, laughing, shouting.

"They're here! They're here!" It was one of the Klein brothers, dashing in from the corridor, terror stricken. With an angry movement of his hand, Yanchie silenced him and directed him to be seated.

Time dragged on like an eternity. Finally the Germans were heard again, this time laughing and exulting as they left the building. Then it was quiet again. As the chassidic group learned later, the Nazis had discovered that the basement of the building had been used to conceal the valuables of a wealthy Jewish refugee. They came to loot and departed happily.

Then Yanchie turned to the Klein boy whose hysteria had nearly given them all away. He was furious, but not because Klein had endangered everyone. What he had to say was meant for all; it was the *raison d'etre* of the Mattisovtzies and their unique form of resistance.

> *You lost control of yourself! You made no astounding discovery — didn't we all know who they were? Didn't we hear them coming? And anyway — so what! What difference does it make if they come or not? That's what they want, isn't it? Isn't that why they make all that noise and commotion — so that we should lose our heads and panic? They want to break us and make us give up. Let them do theirs. We'll do ours. We'll never give in! The Scriptures say, "Fortunate is the man who trusts in G-d."*

That was the key to the way of life of the Mattisovtzies. They knew full well that the ultimate Nazi goal was to dehumanize their victims through terror and a blitzkrieg against the psyche. Fear and confusion were the Nazis' most formidable allies. The chassidic underground refused to be intimidated. By retaining their sense of purpose and self-respect they remained unconquered to the death.

※ ※ ※

In the slave labor camp of Plashuv, a Jewish prisoner was awakened one night by a conversation between two Kapos. The Kapos were concentration-camp police chosen from among the inmates themselves to carry out the orders of the Nazis. Their survival lay in proving their loyalty to the Germans by their compassionless cruelty to their own brethren. That there was always a supply of such people is a sad commentary on the human condition. That night in Plashuv, the bone-weary Moshe Brachtfeld was sleeping on the wooden shelf that served as his bed when he awoke and listened to the conversation of the two Kapos who were on guard duty.

One of them was crying and his comrade was astounded. After all, no cruelty was a novelty to a Kapo and sentiment had long since ceased being a part of their make-up.

"Why the tears? What happened?"

"Don't ask. Something happened today that depressed me terribly."

"What's wrong with you? I escorted my own father to his death. You watched your mother being shot. What could possibly bring us to tears?"

The weeping Kapo answered, "Today it was a different kind of thing. I was taking an old *chassid* to be killed and suddenly he stopped and looked at me and said, 'Yes, we deserve this horrible judgment. We are indeed guilty. If one Jew is capable of leading another Jew to the slaughter, then there is something wrong with the entire nation and we deserve even this punishment.' Whenever I think of that old man's words, my insides twist."

"And that's enough to make you despondent! Listen to what I saw with my own eyes a short while ago. You remember those young Gerrer *chassidim*? Well, when Commandant Goethe ordered them taken out to be killed, one of them asked for permission to say a few words of farewell to his friends. I was standing right there and I heard every word. His name was Yisroel Eisenberg and he was the leader of the group. He didn't say much, just that they were all about to die to sanctify the Name of G-d and they must all be happy. He grabbed them by their hands and said, 'The main thing is to be happy.' Then they all took hold of one another and started singing and dancing. They pulled their *payos* out from under their caps and kept on singing and dancing as if they were going to a ball. Such young people, about to die, and celebrating! I thought I would go mad. They kept on dancing until the bullets ended everything. Even the Gestapo officers knew they were in the presence of holiness. One of them said, 'They aren't human; they are angels.'"

The two Kapos fell silent for a few moments. Then both burst into sobs.

Moshe Prager
translated by Rabbi Nosson Scherman

The Song of Shlomo

Shlomo Zelichovsky was a young man who never sought followers, but had them just the same. In his quiet way he was the model of a Gerrer *chassid*. Shlomo was never without a smile — a real one — no matter what problems he might face. And his every free moment was spent studying Torah. His voice was of rare beauty and power, and he was a favorite of Reb Yossele Chantziner, the main *chazzan* of the Gerrer Rebbe and composer of Gerrer music. This music made the heart long for the Divine Presence, and could set the feet tapping in a happy march of joy for being G-d's chosen soldiers on earth. Shlomo Zelichovsky, just by being himself, created a circle of admiring young *chassidim* who saw him as an example and a goal because of dedication to Torah, the joy of his Jewishness, and the beautiful melodies that always accompanied him. When he stood before the *amud* (altar) to lead the congregation in prayer, the song, the words and his soul seemed to melt into one rapturous whole.

He wasn't a Mattisovtzy; he did it on his own. When the war broke out, Shlomo and his family went to the town of Zdanska-Volia to join his father-in-law. There he was part of an unconquered chassidic group much like the Mattisovtzies of other ghettos. And there he emerged as one of the war's greatest heroes, his bravery to be spread by the underground newspaper of the Warsaw Ghetto and memorialized in a Hebrew poem by the non-religious poet, Yitzchak Katznelson. He defeated the Gestapo and, by his example, he wrote a new definition of vengeance.

This essay appeared in *The Jewish Observer* of September 1973.

✢ ✢ ✢

It happened in 1943. The Nazis had a favorite method of mass mental torture. They would use Jewish holidays as an excuse to punish the entire Jewish community for some sin committed during its history. On Purim that year they assembled every Jew in town to witness a public hanging of ten Jews to avenge the death of the ten sons of Haman. Two days before Shavuos that year, ten more Jews were arrested. The official charge was sabotage and smuggling of food, but the ghetto knew it was to be a macabre spectacle "in honor" of Shavuos. This time, instead of gathering around a mountain to receive the Ten Commandments, the ghetto of Zdanska-Volia would gather around a gallows to witness the hanging of ten of their brothers. The ten criminals were picked at random and Shlomo Zelichovsky was one of them.

Meanwhile the official order went out: All Jews were to gather on *Shabbos*, the first day of Shavuos, in the Stanshitz marketplace. No reason was given, but the Jews knew. Once again they would be forced to stand and watch, horrified, humiliated, powerless, while their Nazi overlords reveled in the entertainment of the day. The soldiers of the army and the sadists of the Gestapo would turn out *en masse* for the spectacle. The officers would bring their wives and mistresses to watch the fun. That is exactly how it happened, but Shlomo Zelichovsky and his nine condemned comrades turned the tables; they were the victors and the Germans were the humiliated ones.

While they languished in prison waiting to go on as stars of the Gestapo's passion play, Shlomo would not allow his fellow prisoners to give in to despair. He raised their spirits to a summit as they joined him in preparing to sanctify the Name before every living soul in Zdanska-Volia. He proposed that they declare the day before their execution as their Yom Kippur, that they fast and pray the Yom Kippur service. He himself would lead the prayers, as he had done so often in the past with his sweet voice, unsurpassed fervor and the beautiful *nusach* (liturgical melodies) of Reb Yossele, the Gerrer *chazzan*. They all agreed, and that day became Yom Kippur. The prayers of the day penetrated even the hearts of the Jewish ghetto police, those unfortunate men whose temporary survival was bought at the price of extinguishing the spark of brotherly love, and turning their once warm hearts into icy rocks. Reb Shlomo led. The other condemned men sang and

The Song of Shlomo / 185

prayed with him. And even the ghetto police cried like children.

They began *Ne'ilah*, the prayer that closes the Yom Kippur service with a final passionate appeal for Divine mercy. Shlomo stopped in the middle; the last part of *Ne'ilah* would be said on the way to the gallows.

The next day, ten prisoners — hands tied behind their backs — were marched to the gallows. The Germans were there. The Jews were there. All were waiting to see ten cowering, broken men, fearful of their fate. The Germans waited with gleeful anticipation; the Jews with heartbroken trepidation.

The ten men came, heads high, all of them singing the concluding and most moving part of *Ne'ilah*, led by Shlomo's sweet and powerful voice: ... אֶזְכְּרָה אֱלֹקִים.

"*I remember, O G-d, and I tremble, when I see every city built up on its hilltop, and the city of G-d degraded down to the lowest depths. And despite all this, we belong to the Merciful G-d and our eyes look to the Merciful G-d.*"

They reached the gallows. The anguished people of the ghetto looked at them. They stood there, the ten of them ... an even line — backs straight — heads erect ... their eyes looking to heaven. And the Jews of the ghetto straightened up too, transfused with inspiration and courage. "*Despite all this, we belong to the Merciful G-d and our eyes look to the Merciful G-d.*"

There were ten gallows, each one with a bench beneath it. The condemned men would be placed on the benches, the nooses would be put around their necks, and the benches removed. But the Germans were in no rush. They wanted to prolong the fun. *Draw out the minutes, let the cowards beg for mercy, let the cowering spectators stand by and stew in their helplessness.* Shlomo Zelichovsky stood there and demanded of his guards,

"Well, aren't you ready?"

With that he stepped up onto the bench and the Stanshitz marketplace was filled with a familiar voice chanting for the last time,

"*Shema Yisrael* — Hear, O Israel, Hashem our G-d, Hashem is One."

Silently every Jew in Zdanska-Volia called out with the inner voice that carries to the heavenly throne, "Hashem our G-d, Hashem is One."

Then one of the ten shouted, "Fellow Jews, avenge our blood!"

The Gestapo had been robbed of the delicious pleasure of prolonging the agony. Shlomo and his comrades had defeated them. They continued with the closing words of *Ne'ilah*.

"*Shema Yisrael* ... *Blessed is the name of His glorious kingdom forever and ever. Hashem is G-d.*"

The benches were kicked away and their lips were stilled, but their fellow Jews still heard the words and the handful who survived the war remember them still.

❈ ❈ ❈

Mendel Yuskowitz was about sixteen when he witnessed the execution. At the time he thought that the cry, "*Fellow Jews, avenge our blood,*" was somehow ludicrous. "How could we take revenge? We whose lives hung on a hair, starving, weakened, frightened — what could we do?" Then he realized that they could indeed realize revenge — the very act of singing *Ne'ilah* and saying *Shema* was revenge. The Nazis chose Shavuos as an execution day for a reason: they wanted to execute the Jewish soul, to eradicate their faith in the Torah and in its Giver. Shlomo had publicly proven that the Nazi murderers had no power over the Jewish soul; our faith in G-d was beyond their power to uproot. What greater revenge could there be than to prove that the Jewish spirit was impervious to all the blitzkriegs Germany could unleash against it!

The very next day Mendel participated in his own little act of revenge. He took part in a secret *minyan* in the ghetto to recite the festival prayers of Shavuos. The Torah reading was read from a torn, slashed scroll, one that had been bayoneted by an enraged Gestapo officer when he discovered it at an earlier secret *minyan*.

Until the end of the war, Mendel carried within him the memory of Shlomo Zelichovsky, and that memory kept his faith strong no matter how great the suffering or apparent hopelessness.

A few months after the Shavuos execution, the Jews of Zdanska-Volia were herded to the town's Jewish cemetery. It was Shabbos, 25 Elul 5703 (September 25, 1943). The weather was hot and stuffy. For three days they were kept there without food or water. The thirst was unbearable. People fainted. They licked the gravestones to cool their parched tongues. Some bit their skin to drink their own blood. Mendel felt as hopeless as the rest when he made a discovery. There on the cemetery field, he found a pair of *tefillin*. Suddenly he felt strong again and he donned the *tefillin*.

Hurriedly he prayed so that he could pass the *tefillin* to a neighbor. Every Jew who wore those *tefillin* felt new strength surge up within him as he wrapped them on his arm, fixed them on his head, and renewed his bond with G-d. *"Fellow Jews, avenge our blood."*

Another time, Mendel was among hundreds of Zdanska-Volia Jews who were being shipped to the Lodz ghetto for their "Final Solution." They were crowded into a cattle car for a four-hour train ride. Fumes from the locomotive went into the cars and the trip was made twice as long as necessary so that as many as possible could die on the way. The people could not move; they could barely breathe. Many called out, "Down with Hitler. Long live Stalin." They were hoping to provoke the guards into shooting into the crowd, thus ending the agony. It did not help. The train lurched on.

Then Mendel remembered Shlomo Zelichovsky. He called out, "Fellow Jews, we are going to the gas chambers. Let us pray together our last *Maariv.*"

They prayed, and in praying avenged their brothers.

Sparks Beneath the Smokestacks

Selections from a Symposium

EVEN UNDER THE INFAMOUS chimneys of Birkenau-Auschwitz, which lit up the sky by night and choked us with their suffocating fumes by day, Jewish men maintained their spiritual dignity. Let me give you a few personal experiences:

※ ※ ※

In block 22 in Birkenau, a Hungarian Jew used to arise every morning and say the morning blessing aloud, giving us the opportunity to answer *Omein*. Then, coughing from the smoke from those chimneys, he'd continue the morning prayers, "*Ashreinu* — How fortunate we are, how good our portion, how sweet is our lot ..." One Monday was a German holiday, so we had more time, and he recited from memory the *V'hu rachum* (recited on Mondays and Thurdays): "*Look from heaven and perceive that we have become an object of scorn and derision among the nations; we are regarded as the sheep led to slaughter, to be killed, destroyed, beaten, and humiliated. But despite all this we have not forgotten Your Name — we beg You not to forget us.*"

※ ※ ※

One Sunday in the Hermann Goering factory in Staracharke, the German and Polish guards were not to be seen, so we stayed in our *Judenstube*. Someone remembered that it was Simchas Torah so he sang at the top of his lungs the *Mi Pi Kel* song of the holiday. "*No one is mighty like G-d, no one is blessed like Moshe son of Amram, there is no*

These vignettes appeared in *The Jewish Observer* of March 1985.

greatness like the Torah, and no one seeks it like Israel ... there are no wise ones like Israel."

Suddenly we became aware of the chief of our factory in the room, and the singer stopped cold.

"What is going on here? Tell me, Friedenson, what is he singing?" he asked me, since I was relatively fluent in German.

I explained that it was a Jewish holiday ... He was not singing, but praying, I added.

"But what do the words mean?"

Again I explained.

He was dumbstruck. *"Du glaubst das, Friedenson?* Do you really believe that?" he asked.

After a moment's hesitation, I started to stammer. A young fellow prisoner, quite unlearned, jumped to his feet and said, *"Ja, Ich glaube!* Yes, I believe!"

The German shook his head and muttered, *"Unglaublich!* Unbelievable! I am afraid the Fuehrer will never succeed with you people!"

"Despite all this we have not forgotten Your Name ..."

❧ ❧ ❧

Reb Yossel Novominsker, formerly a chassidic *Rebbe* in Warsaw, came across a Jewish Kapo beating another Jew.

"Don't hit him!" begged the *Rebbe.*

"*Rebbe,* stand back or I might hit you," warned the Kapo.

"*Schlog! Schlog! Schlog!* (Beat me! Go ahead, beat me!)" replied the *Rebbe.*

"Despite all this we have not forgotten Your Name ..."

❧ ❧ ❧

Three hours after the liberation in Buchenwald, two bedraggled, gaunt fellows — Reb Leibel Geliebter and Reb Leib Pinkosevitz — came rushing into our barracks, panting, "I hear that there's a pair of *tefillin* here! Where are they? Please give them to us!"

"Yes, despite all this we have not forgotten Your Name ..."

— retold by Joseph Friedenson

❧ ❧ ❧

When the Klausenberger *Rebbe* was in Bergen-Belsen, a Nazi officer delivered a blow to his back and knocked him over. "Are you still the Chosen People, *Herr Rabbiner?*"

"*Zicher*, to be sure," the *Rebbe* replied. "One hundred times may we be struck," said the *Rebbe*. "As long as *we* are not the oppressors, we are the Chosen People."

— retold by Rabbi Shmuel Unsdorfer

Abraham Krakowski

The Festival of Freedom in Block 20 ... Mauthausen, Germany: 1945

I ROLLED THE WHEAT KERNELS over in my hands. I had already popped one into my mouth and had made it last as long as possible. I ached for another, but I restrained myself, simply because of the bravado announcement I had so foolishly made in transit.

Our boxcar from Sachsenhausen lurched to a halt. The door slid open slightly and we saw an open car loaded with wheat kernels standing nearby. Within easy reach were hundreds of kernels. We scooped up several handfuls of the stuff before the train began to move again. Someone sighed ruefully.

"It's exactly thirty days to Pesach," I said, breaking the silence. "We ought to save these kernels — Who knows? Maybe we'll be liberated by Pesach, and we will use these for *matzos mitzvah!*"

The mere mention of liberation and the festival of freedom was heady stuff, and none of the religious members of our group dared chew any more kernels, at least publicly.

But that was weeks ago. Liberation had not come. No one received food packages, as we had in Sachsenhausen. And at Mauthausen the food was impossible. One loaf of bread was rationed for eight men. The daily soup was inedible. I had always managed to eat everything, even in Birkenau, but in spite of gnawing hunger I could not tolerate the Mathausen soup and vomited from it.

I was fingering the wheat longingly, weak, when Mendel Markus and the Rubenstein brothers approached me. The *Seder*

This story appeared in *The Jewish Observer* of March 1973.

night was two weeks away. I should ask the *Block Altester* (Senior), Atze Levin, and the *Stuben Altester* (Room Senior), Ernst Gottlieb, for permission to bake *matzos*, since I was on good terms with them. Markus and the Rubensteins would take care of the time and the place, using the washroom late at night so the SS would not find out. The only problem would be to heat the stove sufficiently so the baking could proceed quickly.

I could not share in their excitement. We were isolated slave-laborers in a prison camp, surrounded by the SS men on all sides. Our only value to our masters was our skills in handling counterfeit money, not as human beings. I could not see risking our lives further just to bake *matzos*. And then, what about the prisoners who sleep near the stove? Some were only "half-Jews" and "quarter-Jews." We were so crowded that we practically slept in a heap. They would never tolerate the overheated stove. What would we do if an SS officer would make a sudden appearance? And how would we beat the kernels into flour? (That was a job I would relish, but how would we do it?) The plan was simply too fraught with doubt and danger.

Markus would not soften his stand. *Is it only coincidence that these wheat kernels came into our hands a month before Pesach?*

We finally agreed that I would present our dilemma to Reb Avigdor Glanzer, a *talmid chacham* whose word we all respected. (Markus was not on good terms with Glanzer, but he agreed to accept his decision.)

I told Glanzer the entire story, and he agreed with me fully. When I brought back his opinion to Mendel Markus he spat out at me: "So now you'll have your way and we won't have *matzos*. Don't you realize that this is probably the last Pesach of our lives? You'll have some explaining to do in the next world."

His words hurt, and I had to struggle with myself not to punch him. "You're a scoundrel for rubbing salt in our wounds," I shot back at him. "If you can talk that way, your entire religion is phony! *I'm* not stopping *you* from baking *matzos*. Why don't *you* approach the *Block Altester* and *Stuben Altester*, the way you ask me to? I, personally, don't see any *mitzvah* in risking our lives."

More out of desperation than conviction I quoted the *Gemara* in *Pesachim* (43b, 91b) that draws a parallel between the obligation to eat *matzos* on Pesach and the prohibition against eating *chametz*. Anyone prohibited to eat *chametz* must eat *matzos.* "Could that apply to us?" I argued heatedly. "We couldn't live eight days without *chametz.* We'd starve. So we're not expected to eat *matzos,* either."

I realized the argument was faulty, so I added in parting, "Remember Chanukah? I didn't want to take chances then, either. So you lit candles on your own. Who's to stop you from baking *matzos* now?"

My answer to him was no answer to myself. I sought comfort from the Rubensteins and Glanzer. They were quick to agree with me that Markus was cruel, and that I should ignore his taunts. Glanzer was especially furious with Markus. Yet they voiced reservations.

"But still —"

"Maybe we could still manage —"

"After all, the grain — isn't it a sign from Heaven that G-d wants us to go ahead and bake *matzos?*"

"Look here," I insisted, "no one ever *thought* of baking *matzos* until I said it in that boxcar from Sachsenhausen. It was my idea, and now I say forget about it. As for G-d wanting us to eat *matzos,* His help can come in a flash, anyway. Let's just leave this to Him."

My retort quieted them, but not my restless thoughts. That night I slept fitfully. In my dream, my deceased father and I were visiting the Wonder Rebbe of Radomsk.

> *We stood at his table at which he usually sat. Next to him stood his son-in-law, Reb Moshe. (The Rebbe and his son-in-law had been killed by the SS in the Warsaw Ghetto in 1942, together with their wives. I had known that already.) The Rebbe asked me, "What are you doing about davening with a minyan? It is written:* דָבָר, וְלֹא חֲצִי דָבָר, *'A whole thing, and not halfway.' "*
>
> *I answered: "If it is at all possible, we see to it that when someone has to say Kaddish on a Yahrzeit (the anniversary of the death of a parent) that we get ten people together. We also manage an occasional Kedushah and Borchu."*
>
> *Suddenly my father was not there anymore. I realized while dreaming that my father was no longer of this world, and I began begging the Rebbe to look into our situation, and that he should pray to G-d to help us. Then I told him the entire story of the grain and how Markus had chastised me, insisting that we bake matzos. I told him about my answer, the Gemara I quoted, my argument. I asked him*

what he thought about the matter. He answered: "I shall tell you. As a matter of principle you are right, but you will remember how your dear father labored to bake matzos. And it is written: וְכֵן תַּעֲשׂוּ לְדוֹרוֹת, 'And thus you shall do for all your generations.'"

With that the dream was over.

The next morning I awoke full of hope that we would be freed. The words were echoing in my ears: "Thus you shall do for all your generations ... all your generations!" There would be more generations!

I could not wait to hear them call, "Everybody out of bed." I ran directly to Glanzer and all but shouted, "Glanzer, we'll bake *matzos!*"

He stared at me, and asked, "What happened all of a sudden?"

I told him the entire dream and the impression it had made on me.

"If that is the case, I have no counsel to offer and I am in agreement," he said, "— and very happy at that."

I went to Markus and the Rubensteins, and also told them the story, and that we would indeed bake *matzos*. I was so convinced that our liberation was at hand that no guns could scare me.

Glanzer, one of the Rubensteins, and I approached Atze the Block Senior for permission to bake the *matzos* in the evening after taps. He asked, "Where do you expect to do all that?"

We told him that the preparation would be done in the washroom, but we would like to have the stove in the room well-heated so the baking could be handled with speed. We assured him that the whole operation, from beginning to end, would take only half an hour. He went with us to Ernst Gottlieb, the Room Senior. Both realized that we were serious. They agreed, and added, "Think of us, too."

We quickly began the detailed planning on how to accomplish our task. We washed four towels and hung them to dry on the wall surrounding the yard. After they had dried, we wrapped the grain kernels in the towels and took four hammers (we had access to tools) and beat the grain until late in the afternoon. We did this out in the yard. The guards were puzzled by our actions, but they were not permitted to talk to us, nor we to them. But we could hear them asking each other: "What are they doing there?" As the grain became pulverized, we poured it into a piece of paper. After several hours of arm-aching work, we had collected about two hundred grams of flour.

During the course of the day we found a tin can which we heated through to make it *kosher* for Pesach use. By bedtime the stove was piping hot. When the light was turned off, some of those near the stove started to complain that it was too hot for them. Gottlieb raised his voice, "Krakowski is not to be disturbed in his work. Everyone quiet!" That was sufficient to silence the complaints.

We quickly went into the washroom. We prepared the dough in a bowl we had previously heated and cleaned, and whispering, with tears on our cheeks, we sang snatches from *Hallel*. The kneading and rolling took some ten minutes. We had a board for rolling out the dough, but we had to use an empty bottle as a rolling pin. I then stationed myself at the stove, and every minute or so, one of my co-workers brought me a *matzah* from the washroom. The stove was so hot that it took barely two minutes for six *matzos* to be done. I would slide one *matzah* on and take off another.

We stuck to our schedule, and the entire work was finished in less than eighteen minutes! We had baked sixteen *matzos*, each about the size of the palm of my hand. For the first time in years we went to bed happy.

The next morning we began writing down the *Haggadah* and its recounting of the Exodus from Egypt, piecing it together from whatever anyone could remember by heart.

In the evening, our *Seder* began. Again we slipped into the washroom. The previous evening we were six in the washroom; that night, fifteen. There were more who wanted to join us, but there was not enough room, and then, we were afraid that the SS might hear us. We started reciting the *Haggadah* very quietly. Some of us could not contain ourselves and broke into sobs. As for me, I could not utter a single word.

When I had quieted down a little, I reminded the others not to forget where we were, and to try to be quick. After we recounted the Exodus from Egypt, we washed our hands and ate a piece of *matzah*. I permitted myself to save a piece the size of a fingernail, as a talisman.

At the conclusion of our *Seder*, after the traditional "Next year in Jerusalem," we said in one voice, as if it were part of the text: "If G-d will only free us now, we will have to make an even greater *Haggadah*."

Asher Lazar

The "Dumb" Child

I DO NOT KNOW the name of the youth and I erred seriously at the time in not asking for his name, though I doubt if he would have given it to me, for he would not open his mouth for many days. The story happened as follows:

At the end of 1941 reports reached Jerusalem concerning the Nazi brutalities, wherever their hordes set foot. These were unconfirmed reports, and no one wanted them to be confirmed. The refugees, who till then succeeded in escaping from the areas of Nazi conquest, in the majority also did not know what was happening or, for some reason, did not tell what they sensed.

One of the British officers revealed to me in the beginning of February, 1942, that a small group of Jewish youths had managed to escape from the Warsaw Ghetto and had reached Budapest, Hungary. The matter was kept absolutely secret. And my informer warned me that if it were to become known that he had revealed the secret to me, his end would be bitter. I did not want to cause him harm, and did not divulge the matter to anyone. After several weeks I met him again and he told me that a group of youths — seventy-two in number — had succeeded in crossing the border and in reaching Belgrade. They were already approaching *Eretz Yisrael.*

After an hour's journey we met the youths, in two Arabian buses. The buses were driven by Arab drivers, and in each there were armed British soldiers, in addition to Lebanese policemen.

I introduced myself to the youths as a Jewish newspaperman from Jerusalem, that I had come to greet them. The older youths silenced the younger ones with warning, "frozen" glances. The boys and the girls were silent. At first I tried to speak Hungarian

---

This story appeared in *The Jewish Observer* of January 1964.

to them. It quickly became apparent to me that in the entire group there wasn't one who understood the language. I, on the other hand, knew no Polish or Russian. I tried to speak Yiddish to them, and they answered in a friendly manner. But under no circumstances would they tell anything about what had happened to them, nor even how they had managed to slip through the closed borders.

✑ The Tehillim and the Tefillin

I always carry a *Tehillim* and a small notebook in my pocket. When I asked one of the youths, who seemed to be the leader of the group, about the number of refugees in the group, as well as similar questions which were easily answered, he replied. On taking my notebook out of my pocket, my *Tehillim* accidentally fell to the ground. One of the youths saw the little *sefer*, picked it up from the ground, glanced inside, drew it close to his lips and kissed it. I thanked the boy and asked him his name. He did not answer.

"The boy is dumb," said the eldest of the group to me. "We know that he is a Jew, but we know nothing about him."

Like the other youths, this boy too had had his hair cropped close, without any trace of *peyos*. In an attempt to engage the group in conversation, I asked:

"How do you know that he is a Jew? He doesn't speak."

A meaningful smile spread on the face of the leader of the group. "Convince yourself."

He approached the child, lifted up the shirt he wore under a torn jacket and said to me: "Look and you will know!"

On the child's stomach I saw *tefillin* straps. I looked closely and saw a pair of hand and head *tefillin* bound around his body. I offered the child my small *Tehillim*. At first he motioned as if to decline, but then he took the small *sefer* from my hand and again brought it close to his mouth. This time his kiss was a longer one. Tears welled up in his eyes, but no sound escaped his "dumb" lips.

I do not know why, but the thought struck me that the boy was not dumb. I put my hand on his shoulder and said to him in Yiddish: "Have no fear. From now on you will be in *Eretz Yisrael*, amongst Jews."

The British border-patrol officer and the soldiers of the patrol stood close by, but did not interfere. I requested the officer to permit me to ride with the children in one of the buses till Atlit, and he could return in my auto by himself. The officer agreed and I entered the bus.

When I was alone with the youths, the "frozenness" on their faces seemed to thaw. "Where are they taking us?" almost all the children asked at once. The "dumb" child also asked the question, with his large feverish eyes, but his lips did not move. I told them that they would be taken to a temporary detention camp in Atlit, and that in several days they would be released, and would be free to travel in *Eretz Yisrael*. They asked me from which city I was. I said I had come from Jerusalem and that I lived there. I sat down near the "dumb" youth, who read, with his eyes, the pages of the *Tehillim*, and from time to time he wiped away a tear.

When the two buses loaded with refugees and the three British border-patrol cars reached Haifa, and the youths saw various Hebrew signs over store windows, their glances conveyed wonder: had their suffering and wandering finally come to an end?

☙ "Is the Rabbi of Ger Still Living?"

The "dumb" youth showed signs of being troubled. He rose, sat down, and again rose. He moved towards the door of the bus, and tried to open a window. I feared that he might make an effort to escape. Suddenly, without prior thought, I asked him if he had relatives in Jerusalem, if he had ever heard about Jerusalem.

"Is the Rabbi of Ger still living?" he responded.

I had been right. The child was not dumb. But now all the other travelers in the bus seemed dumbstruck. They had all thought, for many months, that the child was dumb, and had even suspected that he was mentally unbalanced. Now they suddenly heard him speak Yiddish with a clear Polish accent. After several moments, I told the child that the Rabbi of Ger was still alive and that I had met him, that the Rabbi was old, weak and sick, but that he resided in Jerusalem, in *Yeshivas Sfas Emes*.

The child's confidence was won, and he began to speak. Now his words came in a flow, rapidly, as if he had never stopped speaking. His story was terrifying. He had seen with his own eyes the Nazis enter his home in Warsaw, murder his father, mother, brothers and sisters. They had tortured his aged grandmother and murdered her. He had been bodily thrown into a truck with many others. "When the truck reached Majdanek I jumped off and tried to escape. A gentile who had known my parents caught me and hid me from the Nazi murderers. It was a week after my *Bar*

Mitzvah. When the Nazis entered our house I managed to take my *tefillin* bag, since I was sure that they were only chasing us out of our house. The *tefillin* were all that I had.

"The man who saved me cut off my hair and also my *peyos*, and said to me that I must not tell anyone that I was a Jew — that if I would tell, the Nazis would kill me, and him as well, for having hidden a Jew in his home. I knew that I had lost my parents, and my brothers and sisters. I knew that it was forbidden for me to reveal that I was a Jew. But I also knew that it was forbidden to lie. I told the man who had saved me that I would not lie, and that if it were decreed that I be killed, I would die a Jew. The man scolded me and said that I was stubborn like all the Jews, but promised that he would not take me to church. He would even try to obtain *kosher* food for me. Should he find a Jewish prayer book, he would bring me one, so that I might be able to pray to G-d. He did not find a *siddur*, or any other *sefer*. Once he brought me a fowl, and said that it was *kosher*. I knew he wasn't telling me the truth and I did not eat. All those months I ate only bread, onions and sometimes an apple.

"I lived in that man's house for about three months. Every Sunday he and his family attended church. He once suggested to me that I go along with him, in order that the neighbors might not suspect that I was not Christian. I did not know what to do. In the end, I decided not to go. I looked for excuses to avoid going. On *Shabbos* I was "ill," and would not leave my bed. Once a doctor who was brought to see me asked my name. My rescuer answered in my place, 'Stephen.'

ೞ§ "I Will Not Open My Mouth Till ..."

"That moment I decided that I would not open my mouth until G-d in His great mercy would save me. The physician said that I was in truth sick and wanted to have me taken to a hospital. I embraced my rescuer and begged him with my eyes. He shielded me and promised the doctor that he would take proper care of me. After that I no longer spoke even to my rescuer or to his family. They all believed that I had become ill and had really lost my speech.

"One day the man came home very sad. He entered a room with his eldest son and his wife. I sensed that they were talking about me and overheard that the Nazis were going from house to house looking for Jews in order to kill them. My rescuer knew that I had *tefillin* which I wore every morning, when I *davened*, in the cellar of the house. He was afraid that the Nazis might discover my *tefillin* in his home, and tried to prevail upon me to agree to burn the *tefillin*. At first he spoke gently to me, as a father would to his son. He explained to me that I had no right to cause him harm, in return for all the good he had done to me. I pressed the *tefillin* bag close to my heart. And finally they forcibly took the *tefillin* out of the bag. But at that moment I grabbed hold of the *tefillin*, and before their eyes tied the straps around my body. I covered them with my shirt and my jacket. And they let me alone.

"The Nazis entered the house one day looking for Jews. They examined every one of the members of the family, including myself. But they did not search under my clothing. 'Stephen is my wife's nephew,' said my rescuer, pointing at me. 'Stephen is a dumb child.' The Nazis believed him and let us alone.

"One day as my rescuer was walking through the street, the Nazis accidentally shot him to death. They were chasing a Jew, and he was caught in the line of fire. Shortly thereafter, his son fled briefly into the forest, but he soon returned home. He told us that in Majdanek the Nazis had erected a large concentration camp in which there were many Jews. There was also a factory in Majdanek in which Jews worked, manufacturing soap. He had brought home several bars of the soap, and gave me one of the bars. He said that the soap was *kosher*. It was Jewish soap, and had been made from Jews. 'Here is the Jewish soap' — the youth said, and took out of his pocket a yellow bar of soap on which three letters were engraved — R.J.S."

The youth became silent. He again took my *Tehillim* and began to read aloud: *"The children of men who dwell in darkness and the shadow of death, who are prisoners of affliction ..."*

I remained with the group in the camp at Atlit till evening. I returned to Jerusalem that night, wrote down what the "dumb child" had told me and conveyed the matter to the Tel Aviv newspapers. The following morning I went to the Rabbi of Ger and told his son-in-law Reb Yitzchak Meir Lewin the story of the child. Reb Yitzchak Meir immediately went to the camp and brought the youth to *Yeshivas Sfas Emes* in Jerusalem.

Sorah Mermelstein

A Shabbos in Siberia

SIBERIA, 1943. Among the thousands of exiles in this vast, frigid Russian interior were eighty-six students from the Kamenitzer Yeshivah. When Russia took control of Lithuania in June of 1941, all of Reb Boruch Ber Liebowitz's *talmidim* (pupils) fled and hid. Those that escaped and were not found by the Russians were eventually trapped by the Germans and perished; those that were caught by the Russians were banished to Siberia.

These eighty-six Kamenitzer *bachurim* found themselves in the company of the enemies of the Soviet empire: political prisoners, generals, ministers and clerics. This particular Siberian camp was largely for the "elite" of Soviet prisoners. Yet even among the better class of captives, the Kamenitzer young men wore a mark of distinction. Their honesty was so evident that prisoners who received a two-day supply of food stored it with the *yeshivah* students.

In the summer of 1943, when this incident took place, the war raged on with an intense fierceness. Even in this wilderness, in this vast expanse of isolated land, each prisoner understood the gravity of the battle. The *bachurim* knew that the supervisors would tolerate no slack in their effort, so they worked daily — even *Shabbos*, with the sanction of *pikuach nefesh*: the camp commander would surely kill them if they reduced thier productivity.

They were a weak group of young men who did not produce much. The rations they received were in relation to their work output, a system which in turn further weakened them physically.

This story appeared in *The Jewish Observer* of March 1985.

One *Shabbos*, the local group commander, who was himself a prisoner, selected twelve young men from the larger group of students. He instructed them to clear the river bed of all wood pieces, twigs, and branches, and throw them into the lake. These wood particles would then be washed ashore on the other side, and be carted away for industrial use. They were to begin work at seven in the morning and finish by three in the afternoon. Under the strong assumption that the local commander would leave for the day, the Kamenitzer boys produced a plan of action. Until now, the group commander always oversaw their work and they were not free to honor the *Shabbos*. But with his departure they would at least mitigate any desecration.

Carrying on *Shabbos* in a crowded metropolitan area constitutes a Biblical prohibition, a *d'oreisa*. Carrying twigs and branches in the Siberian wilds, which is a *karmalis*, constituted a Rabbinical prohibition, a *d'Rabbanan*. Yet these *yeshivah bachurim*, after two long years of Soviet labor, still searched for a way to minimize even a Rabbinical desecration of *Shabbos*. If two individuals share a load that each person could carry himself, this too lessens the severity of *chillul Shabbos* (desecration of the Sabbath). And, furthermore, if they would stop for a few moments every few steps, before walking four *amos* (approximately 85 inches), this minimizes it even further. So the group of twelve students divided themselves into pairs. Each twosome lifted a small twig and carried it on their shoulders. Then each pair marched a few steps and halted. The performance looked ludicrous, yet for eight hours the Kamenitzer *bachurim* rejoiced in the knowledge that in this limited way, they were glorifying the *Shabbos*.

Little did this small party realize that the commander did not leave the area, but was observing their activities from a nearby hilltop. His reaction, which was puzzlement at first, turned to suspicion and then rage: This group of young men who dragged heavy chains during the week were walking in pairs, carrying ridiculously small twigs and stopping every few feet. At the conclusion of the day, he approached the group and asked them innocently why so small an amount was collected. They replied that they could not accomplish more because of their weakened condition. He wrote down the amount of wood they had collected and dismissed them.

Late that evening, after supper, a loud bell resounded throughout the camp. The ringing sound at such a late hour could only indicate an emergency. The hundreds of workers assembled in the large hall. There, a makeshift courtroom had been set up. The twelve *bachurim* had been seated aside as the defendants, while the local commander acted as the court prosecutor. The chief director of the camp, the *natchalnik*, sat solemnly as the judge.

The local commander began by describing the day's events and the activities of the *yeshivah* students. As he portrayed their performance, the courtroom exploded in laughter. The scene threatened to become a comedy. The chief director remained seriously composed. He asked the students to speak in their own defense. One of the group, who spoke Russian fluently, spoke on their behalf. He explained to the courtroom that they were diligent workers who toiled earnestly all week. Without going into the intricacies of Talmudic law, he explained to them briefly that they were following the dictates of Moses regarding the laws of the holy day. The judge then became furious.

"I've heard of Moses. He was esteemed as the brilliant leader of the Jews. He never would have innovated such nonsensical laws. And besides," he shouted "your parents and relatives are dying in gas chambers and you are hampering our efforts to win this war. How dare you fool around and work at such a slow pace!"

The group of twelve sat quietly and mumbled *Tehillim* nervously as the *natchalnik* went on to accuse them of sabotage. Being accused of such a crime in Russia, especially during wartime, was no laughing matter. The terrified *bachurim* could well be facing a death sentence.

Suddenly a car pulled up to the camp grounds. A delegation of high-ranking Soviet officials stepped out and proceeded to the illuminated hall. The *natchalnik* jumped to attention and hastily arranged seats for the men. The official angrily demanded of the chief director to know why the camp's work force was being kept so late: "How are they to arise at 5:30 in the morning and put in a full day's work if they are being kept up in the evening? Is some kind of theatrical performance going on here?"

The *natchalnik* attempted to calm him. He asked the local commander to repeat the day's episode for the government officials. Once again the story unfolded of the young clerics and their ridiculous antics while clearing the trees. Again the camp prisoners exploded in mirth when the commander mimicked them taking short walks and pausing, carrying tiny pieces of wood on the shoulders of two men.

The government officials themselves also showed signs of amusement as the charade continued. Only one of the officials sat in quiet earnest. This official asked that these twelve students be sent to a small room so that he could further pursue the investigation in private. His prominent rank was evident in the alacrity with which his request was granted.

As soon as the government official entered the chamber in which the terrified students assembled, he opened his remarks with a *"Gut Voch."* The *bachurim* looked up in shocked surprise as he continued to address them in Yiddish.

"I am a Jew like you. No one in the Party is aware of my religious identity. I myself have strayed far from the Jewish path, but before my mother died she made me promise that I would do something good for the Jewish people. But before I fulfill her deathbed request, please explain the cause of your strange actions to me."

The *bachurim*, who were numb with amazement, slowly began to speak. They explained their behavior, interpreted their actions according to Talmudic law, and elucidated on the sanctity of *Shabbos*. They found him a receptive listener.

The Soviet official explained to them that he viewed his presence in the camp as an extraordinary occurence. Several inspectors were traveling through the Siberian camps to check on maintenance and prisoner supervision. Their vehicle had broken down nearby, and upon sighting the lit hall, they came to the camp to ask for assistance. Instead they found the makeshift trial. The Jewish inspector saw Divine intervention in this entire episode.

They re-entered the courtroom and the government official began to question the local commander: "How do these men perform all week?"

"They work wonderfully. Just this past Thursday they had to drag heavy chains. I just don't know what got into them this morning. They acted with no sense."

"They have not lost their minds," the Jewish inspector replied," they have only lost their strength. Their bodies are in a very weakened condition. Increase their rations to eight hundred grams a day to improve their stamina and send them home to bed."

The young students, who had been at death's door that evening, gravely returned to their bunks. Their efforts at sanctifying the *Shabbos*, even after two years of Siberian labor, had shielded them that evening. My father, שליט״א, one of the twelve *bachurim*, told us afterwards that this episode of *hashgacha peratis* warmed them up in the cold Russian winter months ahead.

Aaron Hish

Mechel the Provider

THE CREAKING OF THE WHEELS makes ruin of my sleep every morning. Try as I might to slip back into my twilight zone, the sandpaper rasping of the delivery cart thrusts me into the real world.

As reliable as clockwork, the annoying squeaks never fail to reach me in the stillness of the dawn, for Mechel, the delivery boy, has set out on his appointed rounds with bags of groceries for the sleepy natives of my island paradise — Williamsburg. (Yes, it is an island of calm and cordiality in a harsh and turbulent city.) Stumbling to the window, I catch sight of the delivery cart, really an oversized tricycle supporting an odd tin-enclosed wooden box. The wagon lists to one side, while Mechel is supporting the overloaded end with grunts and muscle strain. Axle squeals, paroxysms, and labored muscle-wheezing are a poor accompaniment to my half-lidded recitation of *Modeh Ani*. But all is forgiven, because Mechel the provider is the source of the cacophony.

Mechel guards his covered wagon jealously. Rain or shine, he inspects the silver-hued exterior for hairline fissures, as if it were his orbital capsule; the thoroughness of this daily ceremony shames the countdown procedures of space-program engineers. After completing his inspection, he drops bags of groceries into its interior as if it were a safe-deposit vault needing no further safeguards. He then climbs aboard, his egg-shaped figure perched on the seat of the tricycle; to watch him pedal his overloaded pyramid away is to marvel at the miracle of the wheel.

As the morning continues, Mechel becomes the star in a scene borrowed from the Pied Piper. Children are attracted to the unnatural sounds emanating from his barrel-chest and are

---

This essay appeared in *The Jewish Observer* of January 1974.

transfixed by his balancing act. His gestures and Atlas-like postures seem to provide endless delight to schoolchildren waiting at their bus stops. When he gleefully raises one of the tots, places him astride the mountain of bags and "blasts off" down the block, a spontaneous chorus of song peals forth from the other children: *Yismechu hashamayim vesagail ha'aretz*, and the crescendo reverberates off the brownstones of my island sanctuary.

Mechel has his own language — a collection of notes of varying pitches — yet everybody seems to understand him. When he distributes candy to the children he knows from grocery visits, the loving glint in his eye needs no words for amplification. When he bends down so that the children may feel his bulging arm muscles (with the tattooed, concentration-camp number prominently showing), and he *ughs* and *ahs* to them, they fully understand. And when they ask him pleadingly, "*Gib mir a ride,*" and he delivers, the smiles on their faces need no expressive words.

His delivery knock on the door strains the hinges, and echoes fusillade-like throughout the house. Yet, housewives don't cringe in fear, but rush to open the door to the overladen courier and offer him a fresh *kichel* or a piece of *haimishe challah*. The beat on the door is totally his own, and no *balleboste* (housewife) hesitates to answer.

Mechel is a mute. He has not said a word for the last forty-three years — since that day in the concentration camp when the *Gauleiter* ordered him to speak up and tell who had "stolen" a bit of food to give life to the starving. Mechel chose not to speak, and after the beatings he sustained, he could not had he wanted to. The adults who knew him from that epoch speak about him in hushed tones of reverence and listen today to his every grunt as if it were wisdom eternal. The new generation, unknowing of the past, intuitively accepts him, admires him, and hails his present feats as if reflecting some past heroism. And Mechel continues bringing food — food for his people ... people who now have new families where he has none ... people who now enjoy economic success and security, while he has his delivery cart.

※ ※ ※

The turning wheels grate away with the dawn, and my initial annoyance never fails to turn into solace: Mechel is still providing for his people, when some others have forgotten too quickly.

V.
Resistance and Rescue

Chaim Shapiro

The Mirrer Yeshivah's Escape From Europe

❧ "The Almighty Has Many Messengers"

OF THE *YESHIVOS* that escaped Nazi destruction, some made it on a grand scale — namely to Japan. Some went to Siberia. Others were dispersed. *Yeshivas Mir* was saved by three people, one Jew and two non-Jews. Thinking back, one becomes amazed at the series of acts, minor and major, the speed of the operation, the efficiency of activities. The puzzle-pieces fall into place, fitting with precision, as though the result of perfect planning. A series of miracles seems to emerge — *nissim gluyim* (revealed miracles).

❧ Miracle Number One: Open Borders

In 1918, when Poland and Lithuania became independent, a bitter dispute erupted between the two countries over the city of Vilna *(Vilnius* in Lithuanian). The Lithuanians claimed the city as their ancient capital, while the Poles also claimed the city. The League of Nations awarded the city to Lithuania. In 1920, the Polish army marched in and annexed the city to Poland. The Lithuanians then declared Kovno *(Kaunas* in their tongue) as the temporary capital, and a state of war lasted between the two countries until 1938.

In September 1939, Poland was divided between Hitler and Stalin, granting the Eastern part of Poland, including Vilna, to the Soviets. They offered the Lithuanians the return of their ancient capital as part of a "mutual defense treaty," which permitted Soviet military bases inside Lithuania. The Lithuanian politicians were on the spot. No Lithuanian could resist regaining the ancient

---

This article appeared in *The Jewish Observer* of May 1973.

capital; on the other hand, they knew the implications of giving the Russian bear a foot in their country. Finally (on October 10, 1939), the Russians forced them to sign the treaty. And so the borders changed and were temporarily opened, and Vilna returned to Lithuania.

This miracle was utilized by all *yeshivos*. Most of the *yeshivos* in Eastern Poland faced a choice between physical destruction by the Germans and spiritual annihilation by the Russians. The Soviets, as sworn enemies of religion, would never permit the existence of *yeshivos*. Until then there was no escape: no one could leave the Soviet Union and there was no other place to go. Suddenly the Soviet-Lithuanian border was opened and Vilna was transferred to Lithuania. All *yeshivos* plus thousands of refugees immediately flooded the city. The Lithuanian authorities ordered all *yeshivos* to move into Lithuania proper, to avoid overcrowding the city. Thus the *Yeshivah* of Mir moved to Kajdani, Kamenitz to Raseinai, Kletsk to Janovo, and so on. Then, just as quickly, the "safety hatch" closed, and the Soviet-Lithuanian border, like any other Soviet border, was sealed for good.

The Lithuanian haven was not meant to last. The Russian bear's paw gained entry — military bases plus a well-financed Communist Party — and before long the bear would swallow the pigeon. So everyone concentrated on emigration, but where to? Palestine's doors were locked by the British, and only a handful of applicants received British entry certificates. The United States was shut tight, while American Jewry naively trusted their "friend" President Roosevelt, and Roosevelt's intimate Jewish friends lulled American Jewry while precious time ran out. Rumors were spread that President Roosevelt promised five thousand visas for rabbis and rabbinical students. We waited for them. And we waited. But they never arrived.

A person must have three items to travel: (a) a passport, without which one does not even exist legally; (b) an entry visa to the country of his ultimate designation; and (c) a transit visa, to pass through other countries en route to the ultimate goal. Most of the *roshei yeshivos* did have passports, for they had traveled abroad on behalf of their *yeshivos*, but the students and the faculty had none. Since Poland was occupied by Germany, the only place one could get a Polish passport was at a Polish Embassy, and because of old enmities, there was no embassy in Lithuania.

Rabbi Avrohom Kalmanowitz, the "father" of the *Mirrer Yeshivah*, had been carrying the *yeshivah* on his shoulders since World War I. As a seasoned world-traveler, he had no difficulty reaching America, from where he dispatched passports for his entire *yeshivah*. It had cost him a fortune, for the Polish embassies tripled the price of passports. And so the *Mirrer Yeshivah* people were equipped with passports, but had no visas.

܀§ Miracle Number Two: Transit Through Russia

No Jew was permitted to travel through Germany. A Jew could only travel through Russia. If one had a visa to America, the route was through the USSR and Japan; if he was headed for Palestine, his itinerary was the USSR and Turkey or Iran. However, Poland was in a state of war with the USSR, so logically no Polish citizen would be permitted transit via the USSR. Yet to everyone's surprise, the Russians did permit Poles to cross their country, and the Soviet consul would stamp his transit visa on a Polish passport. (They had apparently recognized a grand opportunity to dispatch spies all over the world in the flood of refugees.) However, the Soviet consul feared that some "transit passengers" might get stranded inside the USSR, and he insisted on a visa from another country before he would stamp any transit visa.

A secret printing shop began to operate in Vilna, producing British entry certificates to Palestine. It was organized by the Jabotinsky's Zionist Revisionists (later known as the Irgun, later constituting the Heirut Party in Israel — part of Likud). They would supply false British certificates to their party members and to *chalutzim*. There was also another "visa factory" which would falsify any visa for a high price in American dollars, provided one had a passport.

܀§ Miracle Number Three: Japan Comes to Kovno

Most foreign countries maintained their diplomatic and consular offices to the three Baltic republics (Lithuania, Latvia, Estonia) in Riga, Latvia's capital. Travel to Latvia was prohibited, making it impossible to get to the Japanese consul. Suddenly Japan opened a consul in Kovno. Anyone who had a passport and an ultimate visa was issued transit through Japan without difficulty. When presented with a Japanese transit, the Soviet consul gladly gave him transit. The Mirrer students had passports, but no visas, and the rest of us did not even have passports! Then a number of changes took place in the little republic.

On June 14, 1940, the Soviet government accused the Lithuanian government of unfriendly acts against the Red Army bases. It demanded the establishment of a new government "more friendly" to the USSR. The next day an ultimatum was issued to include Communists in the new government. While the government accepted the ultimatum, the Red Army began to take over the country. On June 17, President Smetonas fled by plane to Germany, while Justas Paleckis, a Communist journalist, formed a new government. He immediately ordered new elections fixed to insure a Communist majority. Then on July 21, Lithuania requested admission "to the happy family of Socialist Nations under the guidance of the father of all proletarians, Comrade Stalin." On August 3, the Supreme Soviet of the USSR accepted and approved the request, proclaiming Lithuania as the sixteenth Soviet Republic. (A similar fate befell Latvia and Estonia).

Miracle Number Four: Destination Curacao

Under Soviet rule again, we lost all hope for emigration, for no one leaves the "Socialist heaven." Yet, the Soviets still continued to issue visas; they were no longer "transit visas" but "exit visas." Apparently they had not sent out enough spies, or they had simply wanted to get rid of an undesirable element.

A rumor spread that the consul of the Netherlands was issuing visas to Curacao, a Dutch-governed island in the West Indies. The entire Mirrer group, in possession of passports, received those "Curacao visas." But when they came to get the Japanese transit "en route to Curacao," they found the consulate closed, for when Lithuania became an integral part of the USSR, all diplomatic and consular activities were moved to Moscow. In fact Holland had issued the Curacao visas hours before closing.

Several days later a Mirrer student chanced upon an Oriental. Presuming him to be the Japanese consul, he asked him as a special favor for a transit visa through Japan on his way to Curacao. The Japanese gentleman replied that he had been ordered to close the consulate and had already dismissed his secretary. The student then pleaded, volunteering to serve as his secretary, and to help in filling out the necessary papers. He agreed, and two boys from the Mirrer Yeshivah sat all day stamping visas for whoever presented a passport. (Some claimed later that many visas were stamped upside down, but they were honored anyway.) The Soviets continued to issue exit visas. This spurred the printers of counterfeit visas into more feverish activity than ever, for they could reproduce any visa in Latin letters, but when it came to Japanese, they were at a loss.

The British became suspicious over an increase in entries to Palestine via Syria from Vilna, and they informed the Soviets. They became furious over the prospect of a visa factory operating under their very noses. Furthermore, they themselves had issued visas on fake documents. A search began, but the "Zionist Conspiracy" could not be found. Instead they arrested my roommate from the *Yeshivah* of Kamenitz, Yitzchak Gelbach (Lukover). Yitzchak had illicitly published a ten-year calendar, reasoning that since we were destined to live under a Bolshevik regime, we would need a long-range *luach* to know when the Jewish holidays would occur. He was sentenced to ten years in a Siberian prison camp. [He was freed after the war. A *Breslaver chassid*, he immediately ran to the *kever* (gravesite) of the *Rebbe*. He met the daughter of the only Jewish family there ... He now lives in Jerusalem with children and grandchildren.]

Those from the Mirrer Yeshivah had passports to Curacao with Japanese and Soviet visas, and were ready to leave. When they came to the Intourist office for travel arrangements — the only permissible way to travel through Russia — they were told that first, the price had gone up; second, payment must be made in American dollars. Possessing even one American dollar is illegal in the Soviet Union and one can earn ten years' prison for this crime. The officials of the Intourist "promised" not to prosecute for bringing dollars (a hollow assurance); or, they insisted, "have your relatives in America cable the four hundred dollars per person." And in those days four hundred dollars was a fortune. Mir was desperate!

One *yeshivah* fellow who possessed a German passport with a "J" for "Jude" on it (which means second-class citizenship) mustered the audacity to complain to the German consul who was in the process of closing. The Nazi consul found it amusing to tease the Soviets on behalf of a Jew. He called up: "Don't you accept your own currency?" That Jew was the only individual to travel for rubles; all the others were forced to pay in dollars.

Within three months and with the help of the Vaad Hatzalah, Rabbi Kalmanowitz raised money for the travel expenses. Thus between January and March 1941, the students and faculty were transferred in small groups via the Trans-

Siberian Railroad to Vladivostok, the Siberian port on the Pacific, where they embarked by boat to Kobe-Ku, the port of Japan. Once in Japan, they waited, hoping for entry to the United States But on December 7, 1941, Japan attacked Pearl Harbor, and the United States declared war on Japan. To make matters worse, Poland had also declared war on Japan. Thus, the *Mirrer Yeshivah* people, possessing Polish passports, became enemies of Japan overnight. Japan's only ally was Germany, and they feared that the pathological hatred for the Jews would transfer from Berlin to Tokyo. Remarkably, the Japanese behaved correctly under the circumstances.

Rabbi Kalmanowitz had the delicate task of supplying money to the *yeshivah* in time of war. The anti-Japanese hysteria in America made sending funds to the enemy unthinkable, even for sustaining the *yeshivah* and other refugees. The need was imperative, for while the Japanese were correct and even cordial in their treatment of the Jews, they certainly would not feed them. Rabbi Kalmanowitz managed with the silent approval of the United States government to maintain the *yeshivah* in Japan, and then in Japanese-held Shanghai, by sending funds through Switzerland. After the war, in September of 1946, he finally welcomed the entire *yeshivah* in San Francisco.

➳ Miracle Number Five:

A Ben-Torah in Stockholm, and No Dutchman in Chita

Those of us from the *Yeshivah* of Kamenitz (located then in Raseinai), like all other *yeshivah* students, had given up any hopes for emigration. The Soviets announced a deadline for accepting emigration applications. We could not even apply, for first one needed a passport and a visa, and we had neither. And even if we ever obtained passports, we could no longer get Curacao nor Japanese visas without traveling to Moscow, and who could travel to Moscow? How we envied Mir! And how bitter we were.

Then suddenly, passports arrived from the Polish Embassy in Bern, Switzerland, mailed to us by an American Kamenitz student, with the help of the Vaad Hatzalah. But we were still without visas, and the remaining days of registration were few. We then received letters from Stockholm, Sweden, granting us Curacao visas. We later learned that they were sent by a *ben Torah*, a refugee from Germany, who on the verge of starvation spent his food money on Curacao visas, issued by the Dutch

Embassy in Stockholm. (He is well known today as Rabbi Shlomo Wolbe, until recently *Mashgiach* in Beer Yaakov, Israel, currently in Jerusalem.)

Now that we had "proof" of intention to emigrate, we all registered with the Soviet office, presenting all documents, including the three personal photographs required. To receive the Soviet exit visa, however, we first needed the Japanese transits. So we mailed out visas and passports to the Japanese Embassy in Moscow requesting a transit. They all came back — refused.

We were dismayed. Some attributed the refusal to the form of the Curacao visa, an independent letter, instead of a stamp in our passports. Apparently the Japanese consul in Moscow consulted the Dutch consul who explained the defect to him — all Curacao "visas" were only "annotations" and not legally acceptable, thus the rejection. We reasoned that we would have to find a Japanese consul who could not consult his Dutch counterpart. Someone discovered that in the city of Chita, in the Soviet Far East, there was a Japanese consul. We immediately mailed our passports and Stockholm-Curacao visas to Chita, confident that no Dutchman would be there to "open his eyes." The consul was a gentleman, indeed, immediately mailing back a visa to everyone. Some people who received those Chita visas (thanks to Rabbi Wolbe) had relatives in America who paid Intourist for their transportation, and made it to Japan. Others, myself included, were victims of the slowness of the Soviet mail, and lack of money for Intourist. When we finally were about to receive the Soviet exit visa, they closed the office. We missed the deadline.

✥ Miracle Number Six: Safe in Siberia

Anyone who applies for emigration from the USSR is automatically an enemy of the Soviet regime, for only a fascist will leave the Communist heaven for the capitalistic hell of the outside world. And such a person is treated accordingly: relocation to Siberia, for re-education into Soviet reality. This dreadful prospect of Siberia was hanging over our heads like a nightmare. The nine long cold months of winter, the taiga with average temperatures of twenty below zero, the hard labor, prison life — and what would become of *Shabbos* and *kashrus*? There was no way of escape, for the regime had the addresses and three photographs of each applicant. Little did we realize that this would be the biggest miracle of all. Only one week later, on a

Shabbos and Sunday, June 14 and 15, all visa applicants — *bnei Torah* all — were rounded up, packed into boxcars and shipped to Siberia. Then, the following Sunday morning (June 22) the German Army attacked the Soviet Union. The Nazi war-machine pushed into Russia with full deliberate speed, all the way to Moscow. And with the same speed, only seven days ahead of the Nazi juggernaut, the boxcars with their precious cargo traveled to various prison camps in Siberia, to safety.

As anticipated, the conditions were oppressive and the climate unforgiving especially for *bnei Torah* who were not accustomed to physical labor, the taiga, and starvation. Yet eighty to ninety percent returned safely, saved from Auschwitz.

As I record my memories, whenever I chance across a first or second-generation Mirrer *talmid* or a Siberian alumnus, I am reminded of the *zechus* of Rabbi Kalmanowitz and (יבדל לחיים) Rabbi Wolbe (by grace of his Curacao visas, hundreds escaped the Nazi onslaught, finding refuge in either Siberia or Japan), and the consuls of Japan and Holland in Kovno.

I have attempted to track down these two consuls. I have not succeeded in the case of the Japanese consul, but I have discovered that the Dutchman is Mr. J. Zwartendijk who lives now in retirement in Rotterdam. While serving as temporary consul in Kovno, he once asked permission from Her Majesty's Ambassador to Riga, Dr. I.P.J. de Decker, to issue a visa to Curacao for a friend. When the Japanese and Soviet consul accepted his annotation, he then issued fourteen hundred more, thus saving many Jewish lives. (One visa can cover an entire family of people.) He did this totally on his own, defying orders to close shop, wholly from humane considerations. Mr. Zwartendijk will go down in our history as a noble saver of lives. May G-d bless him with long life, health and joy.

Rabbi Nisson Wolpin

"Never Again" — Who Can Say It?

During World War II, all hopes and thoughts were directed toward "Victory." And when those glorious goals were finally reached — V-E Day (May 8, 1945) and V-J Day (August 14, 1945) — people tended to look ahead, toward personal and national reconstruction, rather than backward, to understand what had happened and why.

Now, two generations later, there is a deep interest in probing, analyzing, and understanding the events surrounding the war and the decimation of European Jewry. Much is clearer because of the great wealth of information now available; but much is distorted — by the assumption that they knew then what we know now, and by viewing distant events through the lens of wishful thinking and personal ideologies.

Representative of some of these fact-distorters is the slogan *"Never Again!"* popularized by the Jewish Defense League. Its message — if not its wording — has gained acceptance in the most staid circles.

✥ The Myth

As is the case with most slogans, *"Never Again!"* inspires mouthing without careful thought. It is our intention to show how the implications of this slogan, when spoken as a cry of defiance rather than as a prayer, are fraught with distortion, deception, and even blasphemy. To do this, we will have to examine whether or not the *Never Again* slogan is compatible with the Torah. But first let us see if the premises on which it is built are factually sound.

This essay appeared in *The Jewish Observer* of May 1975.

The slogan implies that, one way or another, a chain of events took place that victimized Jewry, and this chain shall not recur: *Faced with similar circumstances, the same type of tragedy will not take place again. Next time around we will assert ourselves,* implying that the first time, the victims could have escaped, but ignored the threatening clouds of death. — *Never Again! They should have resisted, but instead disgracefully went to their slaughter like sheep, perhaps even collaborating with their victimizers.* — *Never Again! Last time, Jews who were at a safe distance did not take their brothers' plight to heart, and wrapped themselves in a cocoon of indifference.* — *Never Again! Nations were permitted to close their ears — and their doors — to the terrifying cries of the innocent, while American Jews hesitated to pry open the conscience of national leaders for fear of rocking the boat.* — *Never Again! Fate may have been the cruel master in the past.* — *Never Again! Henceforth we shall be in control of our own destiny.*

It is all very dramatic — and all baseless, even dangerous.

To Prophesy with Hindsight

Historians, political analysts, anthropologists, theologians — all have succeeded in finding root-causes of the holocaust in the events and trends of earlier times. *Why didn't European Jewry read all the obvious sign posts — from declarations of Luther and Nietzsche to Hitler's "Mein Kampf" — that pointed to their ultimate annihilation?...If the destruction of European Jewry was the logical conclusion of the interplay of historic factors and contemporary situations, how could the Jews have ignored them? Didn't they know that anti-Semitism was locked into the bones of the Germans — as well as the French, the Poles, the Hungarians, the Ukranians? Could they so easily forget centuries of pogroms and blood libels? How could they ignore the plans for their own genocide so clearly articulated in Hitler's "Mein kampf?" Could they really pretend that the Great Depression was not forcing the German leadership into finding a convenient scapegoat for the nation's frustrations? Didn't they realize that the only safe haven was home in Palestine?*

The questions press heavily in a retrospective view of the Thirties. But living through events puts them into a different focus. Jews had always been subject to prejudice, persecution, and pogroms; yet, they always survived. While looking backwards from the Forties, one can find many roots to the full flowering of Hitler's genocide program, yet nothing in the Twenties and early Thirties indicated that random events and declarations would prove seminal in ushering in the Final Solution. As sociologist Jacob Katz phrases it in an incisive study "Was the Holocaust Predictable?"*(Commentary, May, 1975)*:

> ... *rather than the past's determining the present, it was the present that made its own connection with the past by adopting figures and trends with which it felt an affinity.*

People still point to the Vladimir Jabotinsky's rally-cries to *aliyah*: "Liquidate the *Galut* or the *Galut* will liquidate you!" Prophets of hindsight use Jabotinsky's stirring calls as indictments of those who perished — weren't they sufficiently warned? Why did they refuse to hearken? But Katz points out that:

> *What Jabotinsky actually had in mind in speaking of a worsening of the Jewish position was the aggravation of economic, social, and political measures against the Jewish Community in Poland itself, not the possible conquest of Poland by the Nazis. Together with many Jewish intellectuals he shared a conviction that Nazi rule was fragile and would crumble through internal difficulties or at the first clash with a foreign power. How unaware he was of even the near future is clearly demonstrated in the very idea of evacuation: he suggested transferring a million-and -a-half Polish Jews to Palestine over the course of the next ten years. Jabotinsky's vision, inspired though it was by a deep passion for the welfare of his people, was as limited as anyone's by the impenetrability of the future.*

Is there any clarity of thought in a contemporary judgment of the Thirties that justifies a cry of *Never Again*?

◆§ The Unopen Gates

Perhaps life in Europe was always hazardous for the Jew. *But, as circumstances did worsen, why did Jews not pack their bags and go to Israel?* This is especially puzzling in regard to the religious Jews who should have been impelled by their special relationship with the Holy Land, who should have been guided by rabbinical mentors to make *aliyah*. *Why did they remain, to be killed?*

To question so is to forget — or to deliberately ignore — that Palestine was under British Mandate from 1922 on and that the British had severely limited immigration. In addition, they had entrusted the Zionist-identified Jewish Agency with management of much of the internal affairs of the land, including control of immigration certificates. The Agency issued these exclusively to Zionists — strongly favoring Labor Zionists over religious Zionists, and simply ignoring requests of members of Agudath Israel and other non-Zionists.

After prolonged discussions with the Mandate, the Agency agreed to issue roughly six to seven percent of the certificates to members of Agudath Israel, although the number of religious Jews eager to emigrate was considerably higher. Thousands of Agudists beleaguered the Agency offices in Warsaw and Berlin, Bucharest and Prague, begging for certificates, but their inability to show a Zionist membership card shut the doors of Eretz Yisrael. For this reason, scores of Agudist training centers were established in Europe where thousands of young people were taught various trades, and farming skills. Yet, even after this preparation, they had to wait years until their turn came under the quota system which limited members of Agudath Israel. This tragic situation continued even after the war broke out, and, of course, many did not live to get their certificates.

— from A History of Agudath Israel, by Joseph Friedenson

The situation was compounded by the British White Paper, issued in 1939, which limited legal immigration to a trickle. There were those who did not try to leave because they did not expect to succeed in their attempts, or because they did not relish submitting to a secular-controlled Agency; there were others who did try, but couldn't get passage on a ship. Did they set such a deplorable example that we must spit a defiant "*Never Again!*" at their conduct?

Yet, there were still others who never thought of emigrating to Palestine, and found justification because of the views of their religious leaders. Yes, the Chofetz Chaim *had* predicted that "a fire would sweep across Europe and the only refuge would be in the Holy Land." True, the Gerrer Rebbe *had* advocated *aliyah*. But there were others of stature who advised against *aliyah*, and those who had hearkened to them perished. *Where was their leaders' dedication to the survival of their followers?*

In offering advice, these men were undoubtedly as conscious of the threat to spiritual survival posed by the secular-fashioned "practical solution to the Jewish Problem," as they were by the nebulous threat to physical survival building up in Europe; but at least survival of each individual did dominate their considerations. By contrast, one must question what was in the minds of the officials of the Jewish Agency who killed a project to transport European Jews to Madagascar, insisting only on passage to Palestine.

Moreover, by what means of prognostication could the religious leaders have divined that the Holy Land would be spared the Nazi onslaught? One must not forget that when General Rommel's Afrika Korps, marching eastward toward Palestine, had reached the banks of Suez in 1943, the Jewish Agency frantically destroyed its secret files housed in Jerusalem, so imminent did the German invasion appear. It was obvious to the religious Jews that only the Hand of G-d could save them — and did save them. But, until then, was the defeat of the Afrika Korps any more predictable than were the consuming flames of Auschwitz' furnaces, that leaders should have banked on the one and avoided the other? In the Thirties, Poland seemed no less safe than Palestine.

✥ The Unhelping Hand

There are many indications that the Zionist Establishment was more intent on settling and developing the Holy Land than on saving lives. The theme "selective immigration" appears recurrently in policy statements and public declarations by such notables as Dr. Chaim Weizmann. As a matter of fact, at a well-attended World Zionist Congress in London in 1937, Dr. Weizmann viewed the impending destruction of European Jewry with fatalistic equanimity. Addressing the 480 Zionist delegates, fifteen hundred visitors, two hundred press correspondents from all corners of the earth, and official representatives from a score of nations, Dr. Weizmann proclaimed:

I told the British Royal Commission that the hopes of Europe's six million Jews were centered on emigration. I was asked, 'Can you bring six million Jews to Palestine?' I replied, 'No. ... The old ones will pass. They will bear their fate or they will not. They were dust, economic and moral dust in a cruel world ... Only a branch shall survive ... They had to accept it ... If they feel and suffer they will find the way — *be'acharit hayamim* — *in the fullness of time ... I pray that we may preserve our national unity, for it is all we have.'*

In the same vein, the Zionist Establishment looked with disfavor at the illegal immigration of Mossad Aliyah Bet. It simply feared rupturing the good relationship with the British which it found so essential for assuring the establishment of the Jewish national homeland after the war. So they avoided defying British immigration restrictions. It was not until the eve of the German invasion of Poland in 1939 that the World Zionist Congress responded to Berel Katznelson's plea that illegal immigration be supported. By then, however, not too much could be done.

Even later, during the war — as Rabbi Michael Ber Weissmandl recorded in his *Min HaMeitzar*, and as was further publicized through the Kastner trial in Israel in 1955, and as Joel Brand recorded in his *Memoirs* — there is evidence that the Jewish Agency (that is, the World Zionist Organization) actually hindered efforts to barter equipment and money for the lives of Hungarian Jews because this would have antagonized the Allied Powers, who were more interested in a swift defeat of Germany than in saving Jewish lives. Allied favor was essential for the postwar goal of making Zion a Jewish home.

In America, Rabbi Stephen Wise, American Zionist leader, had testified before a special Congressional Committee during the war, objecting to the proposal that the American government create a War Refugee Board. On February 23, 1943, Rabbi Wise, as spokesman for the American Jewish Congress, challenged the authenticity of an Irgun-placed ad in *The New York Times*, calling for $350,000 in cash to save 70,000 Rumanian Jews from sure death — killing the effort, even though the cause was just, the need real, and the inevitability of death so certain — as the events of the next few weeks proved. In a similar situation, the "establishment" Joint Distribution Committee refused to respond to a Nazi offer to barter lives for $1,000,000 (an offer which the Orthodox-run Vaad Hatzalah picked up, scraping together the then-astronomical sum). Why *was* this "news" suppressed, why *were* these rescue plans scratched? One can only guess. The strong possibility again looming is that good relations with the British were higher on their priority list than saving lives.

True, those who had placed their highest hopes for survival in the establishment of a national homeland and those who had invested their trust in the dreamers, planners and leaders of that Movement — perhaps *they* should say, "Never Again!" But those who were left behind and perished ... Never Again?

The Distortion

In this age of fruitful activism, when crowds surge spontaneously in public squares, and heads of government quake in reaction, questions are constantly posed: *Why were American Jews so indifferent to the plight of their European brothers? Why didn't they crowd Times Square, picket the German embassy, chain themselves to the White House fence in protest against the inhumane Nazi treatment of Jewry, or at least to bring about changes in restrictive immigration laws?*

Hail to the Chief!

During our era of toppling leaders, it is difficult to envision (or recall) a president who earned the blind faith and trust of almost all his countrymen. But Roosevelt *was* such a man. There was a Yiddish wise crack that *"Yidden gloiben in drei velten"* — Jews believe in three *velten* (literally, worlds): *"die velt"* — this world, *"yennne velt"* — the next world, *"und Roosevelt."* And believe in him they did: as the patrician humanitarian who ignored the wealthy circumstances of his upbringing to redeem the broad masses from a terrifying depression. F.D.R. would do whatever could be done. Arthur D. Morse's book, *While Six Million Died*, documents "the acquiescence of the U.S. government in the murder of the Jews." His book actually fleshes out a secret government memorandum issued in 1944 titled "The Acquiescence," but at the time of this acquiescence there was little public indication that this apathy was the attitude of officialdom, from the top down.

Moreover, the overall mood of the country in the Thirties was inner directed, still staggering with mistrust of foreign entanglements, from memories of the wounds of a world war on a foreign continent — a war then viewed as having had little immediate consequence to an America still attempting to heal its depression-wracked economy. Midwestern "American First"-ers and Southern isolationists were joined in xenophobia by "liberal" labor leaders who feared the influx of jobless foreigners, regardless of the tyranny they were fleeing. Even well-meaning American Jews were uncomfortable with their European brothers who made it to these shores, and "welcoming committees" from Jewish communities that provided refuge for escapees also provided them with rules of decorum that advised against speaking foreign languages in public, or any other such conduct that would make them embarrassingly conspicuous. The national mood was not one of spreading the welcome mat.

One must also bear in mind that the Thirties was a time when Law and Order was a way of life, not a code word for suppression of minority-group activism. Any kind of public protest against American apathy or inaction would have backfired. One need only recall that several years earlier, in 1934, General Douglas MacArthur led *an armed attack* against an encampment of American heroes — veterans of World War I — that had convened in Washington, D.C. to demand consideration for jobs and welfare benefits. Law and Order were to be preserved at all costs. It is unlikely that Jews demanding a more liberal immigration policy for the benefit of foreign nationals would have been treated any more gently.

In addition, public Jewish-pressure tactics would have only added ammunition to the isolationist elements — led by such notables as Charles Lindbergh and Avery Brundage — who were protesting against being dragged into a "Jewish war" in Europe. Any "Jewish" protest against American policies would have confirmed their arguments.

↭ The Unstamped Visa

Thus, in the late Thirties and early Forties, when American immigration policies and bureaucratic red tape made it difficult for penniless refugees to escape Europe and next to impossible for them to gain entry into America, every establishment organization refused to do anything but play it by the book — whether out of fear of officialdom or complicity with British designs. Only a small community of foolhardy and courageous individuals in Europe and America were the exception: men such as Julius Steinfeld, who braved the SS offices in Vienna and demanded, bargained, and pleaded for exit visas for thousands of helpless Jews; and then flew from capital to capital in Europe to raise money to back his pledges and to fulfill his bribes — so involving himself in negotiations with the enemy that he had difficulty, as a suspected German agent, in gaining entry for his family and himself to America!

Or the indefatigable Rabbi Aharon Kotler and Rabbi Reuven Grozovsky, who spearheaded the Vaad Hatzalah efforts to raise funds and save lives.

Or the inimitable Rabbi Avraham Kalmanowitz, who stormed the American countryside, and the world, to save his beloved Mirrer Yeshivah, and joined the Vaad Hatzalah's valiant efforts to save and sustain whomever they could.

Or the resourceful Rabbi Eliezer Silver, who incessantly issued personal checks against funds he was raising for saving lives, maintaining a constant overdraught of $150,000 in his Cincinnati bank account; even leading an unprecedented Rabbis' March on the White House in 1943 to petition Roosevelt's sympathy, resulting in the formation of the War Refugee Board.

Or the unforgettable Reb Elimelech "Mike" Tress, who devoted every fiber of his being to saving lives — shuttling between Washington and New York on any of the seven days of the week, managing the "immigration office" housed in Zeirei Agudath Israel headquarters at 616 Bedford Avenue in Williamsburg, Brooklyn, which ground out employment guarantees and documents for affidavits and emergency visas, saving thousands of Jews from the clutches of death.

Or the entire community of young *roshei yeshivah* and *bnei Torah* who did not hesitate to travel on *Shabbos* to raise funds, who sold personal belongings and private *seforim* collections to rescue lives. And their daring colleagues and counterparts — the Irving Bunims, Chaim Yisroel Eisses, the Sternbuchs and the other unsung heroes who saved lives without the benefit of crews of cameramen recording every drop of perspiration that dotted their brows.

Their means and methods would have horrified the Establishment. But during an era when tens of millions were rendered homeless and stateless by legal decree, and when millions more were to lose their lives by extension of the Nuremberg Laws, legal niceties were all discarded for the sake of a higher calling — that of saving lives. Is their track record so shameful that we must disassociate ourselves from it with a cry of "Never Again"?

⋈ Of Protests, Boycotts, and Parcels

After *Kristalnacht*, when the oppression obviously worsened, some inkling of the desperation of the situation reached American Jewry. Three possible responses were projected from 1935 to 1939: Public protest rallies against the Nazis, sending of parcels to the suffering, and punitive economic boycotts of German goods. *Did American Jewry respond with responsibility?*

The tactic of economic boycott was first begun in retaliation for Germany's all-day boycott of Jewish establishments on April

1, 1933. The American movement, led by the Jewish War Veterans and the American Jewish Congress, picked up its greatest momentum in the late Thirties through 1940.

The Orthodox leadership in America abstained from such acts for fear of antagonizing Hitler and providing him with a pretext for stepping up his anti-Semitic campaigns. This apprehension was echoed by European leaders, as recorded in Rabbi Michael Ber Weissmandel's *Min HaMeitzar*. The Establishment ridiculed this hypersensitive approach, but William Shirer's *Rise and Fall of the Third Reich* reports Hitler's fury at every tightening of the economic screws, and records how he stepped up the genocide process in retaliation.

Efforts to ship relief parcels to Europe had failed to inspire much following in the early Thirties. Suspicious Reform Jews, who were then strongly anti-Zionist, smelled a Palestine trap door under every charity box, even if its label said "European Relief Fund." In 1940, the climate changed and American Jews of all shades began to ship food parcels in volume through their own channels to Jews in German-occupied lands, notably in Poland, but the Red Cross would not guarantee delivery.

Then, because maintaining this life line defied a British wartime boycott against any shipping to Continental Europe — which was by then completely under German control — Dr. Joseph Tennenbaum of the American Jewish Congress used his influence to cut off food shipments to starving, needy Jews. Perhaps this made sense to those who were planning to eventually inherit political control of *Eretz Yisrael* from the British, but not to everyone.

The claim was that the parcels never reached their destination and only enriched the enemy. Orthodoxy, notably the Agudath Israel, had another overriding concern:

> By Mid-July 1941, HIAS and the American Federation of Polish Jews had also ceased sending parcels to Europe. Only the Agudath Israel remained obstinate ... .Tennenbaum responded by picket(ing) the ultra-Orthodox organization. The event was given full coverage in the Yiddish press, and editorial comments fully supported the Council.
> On August 5th, Tennenbaum released a stinging statement against the Agudah:
>> After three weeks of continuous picketing, the Agudath Israel still continues in the sorry role of being the only

organization breaking the British blockade and Jewish solidarity ...

It is to be deplored that the Agudath Israel of America, a sickly weed transplanted from foreign soil to the liberal American environment, should continue to poison the atmosphere without regard for the consequences to the entire Jewish people.

The Agudath Israel stated that it was not convinced that its means of relief violated the British Blockade, and in addition, it questioned the Council's right to act "dictatorially."

— Moshe Gottlieb, "In the Shadow of War," *American Jewish Quarterly Review, December 1972*

One might debate whether this was an honest difference of opinion, or a case of one group (Orthodoxy) putting lives first while the others placed priorities on not alienating British trust so as to be on top when the national homeland was established, in fulfillment of the Balfour Declaration. In either case, the Jewish community was only vaguely informed, and thus was impotent to move events through actions in the public arena, and was challenged and harassed when anyone did attempt to extend humanitarian aid. *Never Again?*

The Slander

The forests of Europe were full of heroic partisans. The cities of France were peopled by valiant underground fighters. *Why did the Jews comply with their murderers? Why didn't they fight back?*

Library shelves full of Holocaust literature render this question an obscenity. Even the simplest outline of a political and military history of World War II will record the fall of Netherlands in three days, of Belgium in seventeen days, the surrender of the well-trained French army, protected by its Maginot line, in fifty-three days. Can one visualize even the best-trained army of Vladimir Jabotinsky's wildest dream withstanding the shock of the Nazi blitzkreig any more effectively than Europe's finest? But that does not answer why the Jews did not resist individually or in small bands against the ever-mounting oppressive measures.

One need only pull out volume after volume from the library shelves to read how the Jews of Europe — forever pursued, forever optimistic — never believed that the Nazi's oppressive measures were aimed at the systematic murder of millions of innocent civilians. Even when they were rounded up and locked into the ghettos, they continued with their richly hued religious and cultural life. (Read Moshe Prager's *Those Who Did Not Yield*, or any accounts of ghetto life.)

Consult Steiner's *Treblinka* or Isaiah Trunk's *Judenrat* or Lucy S. Dawidowicz's *The War Against the Jews: 1933-1945* and find how confused ghetto life was. Read how the Germans deliberately structured a society replete with dead ends and hairpin turns: where security was associated with work assignments, official positions, youth, or physical stamina, and color-keyed identification cards were issued accordingly — only to be called up and re-issued in line with new formulas — with new criteria hinted at, honored, and then defied. Hope and dismay tumbled with one another as limited food supplies, rampaging epidemics, and complete lack of fuel, clothing and medicine took their toll.

When the ghetto denizens were ultimately rounded up in city squares and railroad stations, who was to guess that the destination was a death factory and not a new place of forced labor? Didn't friends and relatives send *"All's well, wish you were here"* postcards from Dachau, Treblinka, and Bergen-Belsen?

◆§ The Defamation

But for rare exceptions, the Jews of Europe did go to their death like *"sheep to the slaughter,"* in fulfillment of the words of the Psalmist. A curse visited on a nation is an experience of shame. *Must one accept the legacy of defamation without a grain of resistance or defiance, without some rallying spirit?*

True, the Jew was never celebrated for his physical might. Yet, no perpetuation of *Toras Yisrael* is possible without a *Klal Yisrael* to live the ideology, to fulfill the destiny. We cannot be a suicide community. Nonetheless — of dominant importance — life must have purpose and meaning that transcends the flesh-and-blood existence.

When searching any era for incidents of inspiration to emulate and pitfalls to avoid, one can be confronted by confusing combinations of shame and pride, exultation and humiliation. What, then, are the salient points around which we heirs of the *Churban* can rally, the heroism of that time that we can perpetuate? Today, there is a prideful focus on ghetto uprisings, such as the Warsaw battle of 1943, and the uprisings in Bialystok and Vilna. Some even go so far as to say that the uprisings, demonstrating Jewish might as they did, proved Jewish ripeness for national independence: as if the ability to fight provided the sense of dignity necessary for self-government. This theme, often underscored during the week that conveniently included *Yom Hashoah* (Holocaust Remembrance Day) with *Yom Haatzmaut* (Israeli Independence Day) at its heels, introduces the non-Jewish element of physical prowess to a claim that by right should only have spiritual substance: *"Reject the culture of the nations ... (and then) I will give you the Land as an inheritance"* (Leviticus 20:23,24). This romanticized focus on the uprisings also ignores the increased bloodshed and the shortening of life the uprisings brought as a result; a painful point, but one that cannot be sidestepped.

True, those who denied the Nazi beast the opportunity to claim sovereignty over Jewish blood did act heroically. Who is to question that? But there were still others who denied the Nazi control over the Jewish soul. And nothing can match that.

This was effectively articulated by Dr. Marek Edelman, one of the leaders of the Warsaw Ghetto uprising, in a recent interview with the French magazine *L'Express:*

"The Warsaw uprising was not a chance to die with glory, but a way of informing the world of the ghetto's existence. Had we any chance to vanquish, to change the course of things? Not the least. The only important thing was to take a gun and shoot. Men have always felt that shooting was an act of heroism...," he said.

Such is not the Polish doctor's idea of heroism. During the war he saw a young boy climb aboard a German truck headed for the gas chambers — to be with his mother, to console her in her last moments."There is an act of heroism far superior to using a firearm."

— quoted by Edwin Eytan
in the *Jersey City Jewish Standard*

True, "madmen" escaped and told tales no sane person would believe (and remain sane). But rejecting the old "all-will-be-well" frame of mind meant assuming a new one. And this new one required a whole new set of responses that were virtually impossible. Are they to be faulted for tending to believe what they could deal with?

As for joining partisan groups — remember that not even two percent of the French, Polish, or Hungarian populace was active in underground activity. Of course, Jews had more at stake, but many Polish and Ukranian partisans would as soon shoot a Jew as let him join their group. Further, German treatment of Jewish resistance fighters was unbearably harsh, as reported by Michael Elkins in *Forged in Fury*:

> The Germans decreed death by shooting or hanging as the legal punishment for an act of resistance.
>
> If one thinks carefully and personally about the fortitude required to accept the law and to live by it, the result is likely to be humbling.
>
> The resisting non-Jew braved swift death. Sometimes the death was slowed and rendered more painful by a local German commander with a taste for brutality, but ... regulations ... specified the noose or the bullet as ... maximum ... For the Jew, this punishment was minimal and merciful, and rare. The regulations specified that a resistant Jew might be killed "in any manner considered most conducive to discipline and deterrence of further resistance. In the province of Lublin ... SS Lieutenant General Globochnik (decreed) the Jew caught with a gun or in an act of sabotage (be) hung ... on a hook .... In Minsk, SS Lieutenant General Herff ... blinded captives with hot irons .... Arthur Greiser, gauleiter of Warthegau, burned Jewish resistance fighters at the stake .... Baron Gustav von Waechter favored the thumbscrew and the iron boot during his month's rule at Krakow .... SS Major General Fritz Katzman ... fed captured Jewish resistants spasmodic poison so they could die in agony for the edification of his dinner guests in east Galicia .... Bernard Bender put his captives into pits with starving wolfhounds .... Leopold Gleim reconstructed the rack of the Spanish Inquisition and used that to tear them apart.

Once the cattle-cars reached their destinations — after endless days of travel — and disgorged those passengers who survived the dark, filthy, crowded trip, the environment was a confusing mixture of the terrifying and the disarming: Franz Stangl designed *Treblinka* — its musical name, flower gardens, station-clock with hands painted permanently at 2:30, and its ten-car platform length — to disarm the light-blinded passengers, and to facilitate their swift disembarkment to make room for the next train scheduled for 70 minutes later. On the side, booted camp guards carried bull whips and rifles, glaring unspoken warnings against one misstep, one wrong gesture ... So the starving, disease-ridden, fatigued, heavily guarded ghetto-residents-cum-concentration-camp-victims never rose in rebellion.

We can —and must — pray that this shall not be our lot. But was their conduct guilty in a way that we have the *right* —never mind the duty — to cry "Never Again"?

Joseph Friedenson (editor of *Dos Yiddishe Vort*), a survivor of four concentration camps including Buchenwald and Auschwitz, wrote of a selfless Reb Binyamin in his essay in this book, "Why Didn't They Fight Back?"

Is the heroism of Reb Binyamin, and the millions like him, to be erased with a defamatory *"Never Again"*?

... The circumstances of Reb Elchonon Wasserman's demise are recorded in the introduction (by his son, Reb Simcha) to his *Koveitz He'aros:* Reb Elchonon had just returned from a trip to America. He was begged to stay on, but refused. His children — his students in the *yeshivah* at Baranovich — needed him during this frightful period. So he returned, but found them scattered — in flight for their lives. He was united with some of them in a ghetto roundup, and — as death hovered as an imminent certainty — he taught his disciples a lesson in the triumph of Jewish might. First he lectured on the Talmudic theme of *Kiddush Hashem*. Then he exhorted them:

> "It seems that we have been chosen to atone for our brethren. If so, we must repent, sincerely and fully. We must realize that our sacrifice will be a more perfect one if we sanctify ourselves. — In that way we will save the lives of our brothers in America."

I suppose Hannah Arendt (author of *Eichmann in Jerusalem*) would say that Reb Elchonon went sheep-like to his slaughter. We pray that the blood of "Reb Elchonons" never again be allowed to flow. But should it flow, do we reject Reb Elchonon's martyrdom with an arrogant *"Never Again"*?

The Blasphemy

Underlying the entire *"Never Again!"* assessment of the destruction of European Jewry is the theme: "Last time we were manipulated. Next time we'll be in control of events."

Until now we have dealt with facts, seeking to determine whether they impose a burden of guilt for cowardice or indifference upon the Jewry of World War II.

Actually, this is not the relevant discussion. The more basic question is if man is actually capable of altering the course of events, promising himself *"Never Again!"*

Throughout his life, a Jew is taught to acknowledge G-d as the source of all that befalls him: the *Shehecheyanu* blessing is directed toward Him "Who has sustained us" when a Jew bites into the first nectarine of the season, dons a brand-new suit of clothes, rejoices for the birth of a daughter. And the Jew recites *"Dayan haemes"* — proclaiming Him a truthful judge when a close relative dies.

If a Jew is not guilty of personal neglect, he blames no one for the loss he suffers, for the tragedy he witnesses. The circumstances may be puzzling: death of an innocent babe, or of a beguiling child; sudden demise of a young man in the promise of life, of a mother who is the hub of her family; the unexpected departure of a shy scholar, or the brutal murder of an elderly man — all can be perplexing or painful. But the Jew must accept his fate unquestioningly: *"HaTzur tomim poalo — G-d is perfect in all His acts."*

When the murder of these six or seven is multiplied million-fold, the pain becomes traumatic, but no less the act of G-d. More: the staggering dimensions of the catastrophe of the Six Million makes its divine source all the more apparent. Yes, the bankruptcy of Western civilization was also apparent in the fruition of Hitler's mad plans, without condemnation by others. But this does not place them in charge of events. Even the policies dictated from the very top of the decision-making hierarchy are not really man's alone, for "the hearts of kings and princes are in the hands of G-d."

To be sure, *hishtadlus* — human effort — has its place in the range of actions a person is expected to pursue to protect himself. And one must examine the past to determine which mode of conduct is effective and which is not. But the *ma'amin* — the believing Jew — knows that the outcome of events is influenced by his own spiritual station, and his major efforts are always directed toward perfecting his spiritual strategy rather than toward improving his political or military moves. All — absolutely all — is in G-d's Hands, and *teshuvah, tefillah,* and *tzedakah* — repentance, prayer, and charity — are the measures by which He allows Himself to be influenced.

In such a cosmic view, how can insignificant man, absolutely dwarfed by the enormity of this shattering act of G-d, raise a puny fist in defiance, brandishing all the hollow glory of "My might and the strength of my arm," and say *"Never Again"*? How can the Israeli counterpart fly a banner, with the clenched fist emblazened with the defiant words: *"Rak Kach!* Only this way!" — denying any and every other approach, investing solely in his muscular vanity?

⋅§ The Misapplied Lesson

"Never Again" is of course, an implied judgment of the past. But as the expression indicates, it is primarily the basis for a plan of action for attacking current and future problems.

It draws on the past in its own way to declare that compromise and retreat are the bywords of defeat, and that survival for the beleaguered Jew is only possible when he is not afraid to assert himself with physical prowess and political clout.

This generalization has then been applied uniformly to any and all problems that face individual Jews and Jewry at large: *Are territorial concessions demanded of the State of Israel? Are Soviet Jews suffering persecution? Is a prominent anti-Semite given red-carpet treatment in the U.N. or at a college-campus symposium? Are the Jewish poor being ignored?* The "Never Again" response invariably has been to slug it out. Regardless of the complexities of international intrigue and diplomacy, in spite of the "hostage" status of Jews in enemy lands, forgetting gains made through low-profile approaches, ignoring the possibilities of loss of life in pursuit of extreme policies, and — most hazardous of all — completely losing sight of the decisive role of G-d's providence in the destiny of Jewry, the "let our right be proven with our might" approach is simplistically applied to every and all situations, even guiding young children in making life and death decisions on the basis of elemental gut reactions.

The dangers of pursuing such a single-minded approach are self evident. By the same token, rejecting a one-dimensional *Never Again* approach does not mean an unbending commitment to passivity. There is always the *hishtadlus* factor of action on the human level which at times calls for resorting to arms or forceful action in one form or another. Each problem must be examined for its own array of possible solutions, and the correct one must be selected for the particular situation — coupled with a prayer that we be guided in our choice and that, most important, we be worthy of redemption.

※ ※ ※

An exhaustive discussion would be required to do justice to each of these problem areas mentioned, but the main focus of this article has been the historical background from which the *Never Again* slogan draws its assumed justification, calling, as it does, for its own brand of preventive steps and healing of wounds. Having spoken of this background, we must devote a few lines to the Reconstruction in contrast to the one the *Never Again* philosophy inspires.

The Reconstruction

Everybody carries his own set of mental images of striking contrasts: destruction and rebuilding, agony and glory. Those whose cradle of Jewish consciousness was rocked by the hands of Leon Uris and Otto Preminger in *Exodus* has his set of scenes: *the ghettos where bodies were swept away with the morning trash (cut —); the blue-and-white flag fluttering in the breeze against the azure sky of the Holy Land.*

I, personally, harbor a different set of images.

I flinch whenever I envision the photograph of the grinning Nazi shaving off the beard and *peyos* of a stoic Polish Jew, yet marvel at the barbarian congratulating himself for his Aryan superiority, deluding himself that he is victorious over *Netzach Yisrael* — the faith of eternity. Then the mental image switches and I am in the crowded synagogue in the Far West of my youth in 1950. The Ponevezher Rav is on the pulpit reporting on his findings during a tour of the European continent, reciting the geography of Eastern Europe, to the tearful accompaniment of congregants: *Ponevezh ... Bialystok ... Vilna ... Kamenitz — rubble ... trash heaps ... empty shells ... ashes.* "But we shall build on a hilltop in Bnei Brak a new Kamenitz, a new Ponevezh, a new Vilna." And he did (or, rather *they* did, contributing fully ten times the maximum amount they had ever before contributed to any *yeshivah*).

Or the Bluzhever Rebbe, arriving in New York totally crushed by his personal losses from the destruction of the war, suddenly too involved in guiding, counseling, helping others in reconstructing their lives to give thought to his own suffering.

Or the young fellow — who had spent four years in a barn of a Polish farm, only venturing out on moonless nights — sitting in front of me in a Torah Vodaath classroom, swaying over a page of *Gemara* and *Tosafos*.

Or the *Chag Hasmichah* in the Bobover *Beis Hamidrash* in

Boro Park in Spring of 1974, when the venerable Rebbe recounts how thirty years earlier the town square of Bobov was crowded with Jews being rounded up, and a question mark hung in the air — *The dayanim, the rabbis, will all be gone. Who will answer questions in the future? Who will ask questions in the future?* And here — *dayanim, rabbonim* — leaders and followers — here is the answer!

Or the *shmura matzos* being gingerly rolled flat in the brick oven, the long wooden rod wielded by an arm tatooed in Auschwitz.

There was a destruction, and now a reconstruction. Were there people then who were seized by paralytic grief thirty years ago — or besieged by despair? *Never Again!*

Yisroel Saperstein

" — Like Sheep"?

✑ "Resistance Would Be Folly"

ROOTS ARE ALWAYS important, especially in times of shifting values. So people ask, "What was it like before I was born? How did my predecessors live? How did they die?"

Some young Jews find their past a stumbling block to defining their personal identity, for how can they be proud to be descendants of a people who, like sheep, submitted *en masse* to slaughter at the hands of the Nazis?

This stigma has been placed on our nation because it is believed that Jews behaved in a cowardly fashion during World War II — a reaction that was uniquely Jewish.

Nothing dispels myths as well as facts. Let us listen to the sounds of history and the facts will emerge:

> *We have yielded to force. Since we are not prepared even in this terrible hour to shed blood, we have decided to offer no resistance.*

This sounds like the voice of a miserable ghetto Jew, without backbone, or dignity — for who but an Eastern European, *galus*-complexed Jew could be so cowardly?

But listen again. It is the voice of the Chancellor of Austria, Dr. Schuschnig, broadcasting his country's surrender to Germany on Friday evening, March 11, 1938.

Another voice rings out from the past:

> *"We were abandoned, we stand alone,"* he declared, explaining his lack of resistance to German seizure.

This essay appeared in *The Jewish Observer* of June 1976.

Is it a typical apologist attempting to rationalize the behavior of his shameful Jewish ancestors?

Listen more closely. It is the broadcast of General Sirovy, Premier of Czechoslovakia, explaining Czech surrender of the Sudetenland to Germany at 5 P.M., September 30, 1938. This surrender doomed close to one million Czech citizens to being uprooted from their homes and deprived of all personal possessions. Yet this country, with its fully prepared armed forces, declared that she was abandoned and therefore could offer no resistance. She was surrendering.

Czechoslovakia surrendering? How could an independent country that had the most formidable defense fortifications in Europe next to the Maginot line in France, a nation that had a well-equipped, well-trained, modern army of thirty-five divisions — how could it surrender the Sudetanland, the key to its entire defense structure, without any resistance?

After the Czechs yielded, the Nazis inspected their fortifications. They had this to say: "The Czech border fortifications caused general astonishment ... A test bombardment showed that our weapons would not have prevailed against them." Even the usually arrogant Hitler was impressed and admitted that taking them through battle would have been very difficult. (From the memoirs of the Nazi Minister of Armaments, Albert Speer, *Inside the Third Reich*, p. 111.)

"The position is quite clear, resistance would be folly." A quote from another of those cringing, shuffling, old-time ghetto Jews — right?

Wrong. Those words were spoken by Dr. Hachu, President of Czechoslovakia on 2 A.M. on Monday, March 15, 1939, as he surrendered what remained of Czechoslovakia to Hitler.

⊷§ "Hard to Believe One's Eyes"

History is more than sounds. It is also scenes to be viewed and analyzed.

So watch as one-and-a-half million humans are driven eastward across the Vistula River, after having been dragged out of their homes. The temperature is -40° F, and freezing to death is a common phenomenon. *How does this great mass of humanity permit itself to be driven? Why are Jews so cowardly?*

A closer look reveals that 1,200,000 of these people are Poles. Only the remaining one-fifth are Jews. Did anybody ever wonder why Poles permitted themselves to be driven, to freeze to death?

Somehow I have never heard the question asked.

But there is more to be seen: It is hard to believe one's eyes, watching 5,750,000 military men — men trained in the art of warfare — being marched by the Nazis to certain death by starvation and exposure to freezing conditions. These men were brave Russian soldiers, now Nazi prisoners. *Were these, too, "cowardly men" who could not think for themselves, unable to form a plot, too defeated in spirit to unite to rebel?*

There is yet one more scene:

They were led barefoot to the quarry ... At the bottom of the landing the guards loaded stones onto their backs to carry to the top of the steps. On the first trip up, the stones they handled weighed some sixty pounds each, and they were encouraged with generous blows ... The second trip up the stones were heavier, and whenever these men sank under their burden, they were kicked and bludgeoned. By evening half were dead, the rest holding out till morning, when they too died.

Why didn't these men throw their stones at their tormentors? Didn't they clearly see that they were being worked rapidly to death? Why was none of them courageous enough to take some Nazis with them? But what can one expect from cowardly Jews? Oh? — These are not Jews? They are United States Air Force officers? Oh.

It would seem obvious that when men — or nations — are faced with the threat of a more powerful force, they endeavor to preserve their lives for as long as possible. As one historian points out: "*How could a group, even a large group, rise in revolt against the marching guns, flame throwers, and tanks of the SS?*"

When one sees *in print* such an obvious explanation for the total absence of any wide-spread revolt against the Nazis, it seems almost *too* self evident; but at least it clears the air of the malicious canard hurled at the previous generation.

Except that the writer quoted is *not* explaining Jewish behavior. He is discussing the conduct of *another* nation.

➳ Time to Speak for Ourselves — to Ourselves

Apparently, then, it is time for us to speak for ourselves — to ourselves ...

When Aleksendr Solzhenitsyn can declare in an interview published in thirteen languages that the men with whom he was imprisoned in Communist Russia are giants, it is time to examine the true greatness of *our* imprisoned. Reading *One Day in the Life of Ivan Desinovich*, which describes one of the camps where these "giants" dwell, one finds very little to justify the title "giant" (except, perhaps, for one fellow who eats with his back straight instead of hunched). Not only is there a complete absence of any bravery in the popular cowboy-and-Indian style, but there is not even mention of one act of moral courage! *Did anyone give up a portion of food for someone else? Did any groups convene to read books of democratic ideals, to declare that they are ready to die for their ideal?*

It is time, then, to appreciate the idealism of the Jewish people. From the time the first Jew was thrown into the ovens — that is the first Jew, *Avraham Avinu* — the Jewish nation time and again has placed its ideals above life itself.

During this past thousand years of *galus* in Christian lands — where restrictions on every facet of life abounded, where pogroms, imprisonment, and decrees of expulsion were never rare — every individual Jew knew that if he wanted to live safely, securely, and comfortably, all he had to do was enter the nearest church and say one word: *Yes*. Not only would the restrictions suffered for being a Jew be removed, not only would he receive vast honors and recognition from the Church for his act; but, often, as a seasoned merchant he would find countless new opportunities open to him and he would grow in both riches and power. Yet the persecuted Jews remained Jews, true to their ideals and faithful to their traditions.

The fires of *mesiras nefesh* continued to burn in the breasts of our people, even in the most terrifying of circumstances. Jews who smuggled *tefillin*, *Chumashim*, *shofros*, and even *Sifrei Torah* into the concentration campes, instead of an extra morsel of food, or their jewels, or money ... Jews who lit Chanukah candles in the dark depths of Auschwitz and Buchenwald — where they had a *minyan* ... Jews who, after a whole night of body-breaking labor, went with their last ounce of strength to the back of their barracks to put on a pair of *tefillin* ... The queues for putting on *tefillin* were so long in Buna-Auschwitz that a *gabbai* was appointed to make certain that nobody kept on the *tefillin* for longer than a brief moment. In Tirnau, Jews lined up in the dead of night, from 3 A.M. to 5:30, for a turn to put on the *tefillin* ... Jews who baked *matzos* in the Kluga Death Camp in Estonia, where there was a regular *minyan* complete with *tallis* and *tefillin*

... Jews whose *v'ahavta l're'acha kamocha* (love for one's fellow) was so strong that slave laborers who were allocated less than survival rations left over some of their own precious portions of food for others in a nearby concentration camp, who would sneak over at night for a little sustenance. It was our Jews who, even after having been forced to surrender their bodies as other nations had surrendered theirs, still remained in command of their own spirit.

It is time for us to proclaim our heroes, if not to those who read thirteen languages, then at least among ourselves and our children.

Gershon Kranzler

Setting the Record Straight

THERE IS MUCH TALK about no one having cared; no one having done anything; about the leaders of American Jewry having sat by idly while millions of our best died in the Holocaust. Much, unfortunately, is true — sadly so — as concerns those who had the power, the means, the big organizational machines, and the access to the mighty to do something. The silence, the soft treading, was too loud, and the gestures too light and tokenish to dislocate the business-as-usual attitude of the broader masses, when so much should and could have been done. Let's face it.

But for the sake of truth, and for the sake of the overwhelming *ahavas Yisrael* of one great Jew, and of the men around him — the masses of young and middle-aged *chaveirim* (colleagues) whom he roused to action — we must not remain silent. Make no mistake; Reb Elimelech Gavriel ("Mike") Tress and Zeirei and Agudath Israel were not the only ones who wrought miracles with their limited means. There were such giants of rescue work as Dr. Griffel, Rabbi Eliezer Silver, the Sternbuchs, the Vaad Hatzalah, and many others ... Yet, whatever we did attempt to do was so little, considering the magnitude of the catastrophe, the monstrousness of the crimes, and the gigantic challenges that were not met. Yet, our children need not be ashamed when the cry is raised: "*Where was your ahavas Yisrael?* What did you do when your brothers died by the thousands, day in, day out?"

It would be easy to quote facts, statistics impressive enough considering the handful of people who compiled an unparalleled

---

This appreciation appeared in *The Jewish Observer* of November 1971.

record of achievement by ceaseless work, self-sacrifice, and sheer foolhardiness. For, they rushed in where others dared not tread; they broke every rule in the book, in frustration and despair, when red tape and legalities blocked move after move. Yet, history requires more than dry facts. The emotional impact and the human expenditures were too great. The insurmountable obstacles, the daily tension, the suffering, were too forbidding to be hidden from the young and those who seek the truth.

≈§ The Overwhelming Flow of Memories

Once tapped, the flow of memories is overwhelming. It rips aside the veils of hazy remembrance of time, of human frailty, ingratitude, and forgetfulness.

I would call on you *chaveirim* of Zeirei and Agudath Israel to come forward and line up your memories alongside mine, though modesty and the pain that grows from what remained undone does not permit a full assessment of what was indeed accomplished. Yet our children are entitled to some perspective on what was done in those years, from the beginning and even before World War II. Let the Jewish world know that there was an American-born young Jew who died much too young because he sacrificed himself for the *Klal*. He gave all of himself and inspired others to do the same so that hundreds and thousands — who now crowd Williamsburg, Boro Park, Queens, Monsey, Bnei Brak, and Jerusalem, the thriving centers of living Judaism — were saved, found jobs, and got a start on building life over again.

Stand up, my *chaveirim!* Say testimony to the Jewish world that Mike — and we all — cared. Join me once more in that dusty, dingy, but grand old building at 616 Bedford Avenue, in the heart of Williamsburg, where we struggled, worked so feverishly, devotedly, wholeheartedly; where we fought and outthought the high and the mighty to save Jewish lives; where we even were *mechalel Shabbos*, when the occasion demanded it — when Reb Aharon Kotler asked us to: for example, when our revered *chaver* Rabbi Gedalyah Schorr flew to Washington on a Friday night! When we did not go to sleep for nights on end to mass-produce documents for affidavits, emergency-visas — legally and not so legally. When we battered at locked doors and once in a while succeeded in opening some to bring a ray of light and hope to brothers in suffering. When there was no money to pay the glorious weekly salaries of eight, ten, or twelve dollars for the secretaries we began to hire, until we had a staff of almost fifty workers in those crowded rooms at 616 Bedford Avenue. When we borrowed and *schnorred* for postage for the thousands of airmail letters and cables we sent across the oceans and continents. When Mike Tress spent his personal money, sold block after block of valuable stocks, to keep the machine running after he had set it up with his own desk and typewriter, in the little room on the ground floor, leaving behind a promising career with one of the big industrial companies of the country. When he, and all of us with him, took the most desperate chances, trying again and again, against all odds, in hope that perhaps one more life, one more Jewish child might be plucked from the living fire.

Gavriel Beer, you recalled the fever of those days when we met at the *Kotel* on a Friday evening last summer. You, too, Manny, also brought back the frenzy, when you told me: "I recall when you took your parents' rent money, plus the $29.00 you had saved up, to give to a poor refugee, starting from scratch." Of course I did. We all did it — not once, but many and any time another emergency arose. The landlords could wait; the personal careers, bank accounts, aspirations had to wait for Jewish lives were at stake.

⋰ Galvanized Into Action

The kids today say nothing was done; no one cared. They are wrong, Mike. Perhaps they don't know how you galvanized all of us into action, setting an example and teaching us to forget our private lives. For you had a heart big enough, the sensitivity, and the courage to perceive and harken to the call of Jewish destiny — to the calls for help. And they all called *you*, called on *you*, calling you Reb Elimelech, Michael, or just plain Mike — the rabbis and Rebbes who loved and revered you, like the thousands of kids whom you organized into groups and workers for *Yiddishkeit* and Torah causes. They all called on you because you had no office hours; you did not know the word "no", you never said, like the others, "Sorry, not a chance to help your parents — your children — husband — wife ... "

※ ※ ※

Mrs. K., you will be happy to attest to the fact: You and so many hundreds like you, who came crying to our office when all the official organizations, Jewish and non-Jewish, gave up hope in the face of what seemed like unsurmountable obstacles. You could tell what you reminded us of so many times in subsequent years, whenever we met. The Red Cross, HIAS, and all the others had told you that nothing could be done for your husband who was caught in Finland, at the very beginning of the war. Your bitter tears inspired us to send a cable to the King of Sweden, who dispatched a personal representative to Helsinki to bring your husband to Stockholm. From there we got him to the United States with an affidavit. Now you have a wonderful Jewish family, *talmidei chachomim*, and grandchildren, because Mike cared and did not give up when others did.

A Glimpse at the Files

Recently I had the opportunity to go through a few of the once-secret files of the State Department that are now available for research at the Library of Congress in Washington. I saw the files of voluminous correspondence in response to our letters, cables and petitions, and the internal warfare between those who helped us (Henry Morgenthau at their head, and including Sumner Welles and Cordell Hull among them) over the protest of minor officials, who tried every trick under the sun to prevent what they called violations of neutrality, international laws, and the dangers of creating precedents. Only then did I realize how much we had initiated with our desperate, amateurish efforts. I saw the appeals that produced millions of dollars to be sent to the camps in Europe and the Far East. I saw duplicates and triplicates of orders sent through Spain and Switzerland — through the diplomatic channels, pouches, and cover-up outposts — to open doors, bribe officials, purchase life, or at least a chance of survival in France, Poland, or Portugal.

It Started With Reb Elchonon

It had already started before the War, when Reb Elchonon Wasserman came to our pre-616 branch in Williamsburg, at the Stoliner Rebbe's home. He started us off, encouraged us and when we accompanied him to the ship for the journey back to his yeshivah from which he never returned, remember, Reb Moishe, how he comforted us and told us of the challenges ahead? — How he blessed us and told Mike that the fate of the Torah world was in his hands? Mike never stopped working for it, until his last breath.

❀ ❀ ❀

At the very beginning, more than three decades ago, we did not wait to learn to "walk" in our rescue work. There was no time! We watched our mentors and went to work feverishly — trying to outdistance the shadows of terror — lest we be too late. But it was our *chaveirim* who made it possible. The S brothers, fledging lawyers; Louis, Sol, and their brothers beginning their flourishing accounting practice; Reb Dovid, who had done so much admirable pioneer work in England and in this country, helped us organize our work ... all the other *chaveirim* from the Bronx, Brownsville, and the East Side who gave us days, and weeks, around the clock, guiding us, giving us technical advice ... worked with, went along with Mike, as he struck out for new avenues of aid, new daring schemes and large-scale organizational campaigns, because his and their *ahavas Yisroel* did not let them rest in the face of the growing catastrophe.

There were also the then-young *chaveirim* of our older Pirchei groups, from our Nathan Birnbaum Group. They can tell the children of today how they canvassed congregations, learning to become public speakers, legal experts on affidavits, on international diplomatic regulations, using the skills Mike had taught them, to canvass communities for help, for affidavits, for potential yeshiva *bachurim* and other causes. Most were barely seventeen or eighteen at the time, but they had been touched by the spark of Mike's *ahavas Yisroel*, and they cared!

✦§ Rabbi Schorr's Hot Tears

There was Rabbi Gedalyah Schorr, our foremost teacher and leader in those years. He had just returned from Kletzk at the outbreak of the war, and was inspiration and conscience to Mike and all of us. He overcame his reticence to tell his thousands of *talmidim* of our open and secret activities, of his work for and with Rabbi Aharon Kotler, Rabbi Reuven Grozovsky, and with Rabbi Avraham Kalmanowitz, whose historic genius at mobilizing hearts and hands to help was even effective among the most hard boiled of Washington's officials. He never told about the famous Hungarian campaign that failed at the last minute, like so many other ploys and schemes we young Agudists attempted alone; or about those in which we participated with the larger organizations because they had better chances of success in saving Jewish lives.

Remember that first speech Rav Schorr made on *Shabbos*, at the Zeirei Agudath Israel *minyan* at 616! A cable had arrived just before nightfall when we had gathered for *Kabbolas Shabbos*. The next morning, before *Kriyas haTorah*, he stepped in front of the *bimah*, beating his fist on the table. With tears streaming down his face — and our own faces — he screamed: How dare we follow our own personal pursuits at a time like this? Where is your conscience? Jewish lives can be bought for money, and you think of jobs, careers? You have the heart to sit and learn when each moment may be too late?

That was all we needed. At his and Mike's appeal, *yeshivos* and day schools for boys and girls everywhere were closed. Some of us manned the telephones for 72 hours. Others organized hundreds of teams of boys and girls who searched the streets for money with spread tablecloths, not mere *pushkes*. The subways, apartment houses, and housing projects resounded with the music of the appeals our boys made everywhere. They attended every meeting of any Jewish organization, from the tip of the Lower East Side to Washington Heights and the Bronx, each team vying with the other to raise more and more money. Never was there greater inspiration, more genuine learning of what Torah and *ahavas Yisrael* really means, than in those days when no one had time to eat or to sleep, to attend to business, studies, or work.

✥ Care After the Rescue

When our rescue efforts succeeded, Mike did not stop caring. To this I can testify, and so can many others.

So come forth, Mr. Josef Rosenberg — thanks to whose *mesiras nefesh* we can proudly display the Non-*Shatnes* labels in our garments. You rescued a *mitzvah* from being "stepped on," as you said so often. Come forth and testify, for you were among the first when we established the Refugee Home at 616, where you began your work for the *Klal* "with microscope and inspiration," with your insuppressible idealism. Tell today's generation that Mike and the *chaveirim* of Zeirei Agudath Israel cared. Tell them how we *schnorred* or borrowed furniture, linens, pots and pans; how we all dug into our pockets to provide food, clothes, and medicine.

You too, Reb ..., the great scholar and teacher of new generations of *talmidei chachomim*. You remember the work we did, for you were among the first youngsters we took in, before your brother and sister came over from the other side. Tell your *talmidim* what happened when you were ill, you or the other youngsters that flocked to us; tell them how Mike cooked; how our mothers brought food and medicine to nurse you back to health.

You, too — the two brothers from Frankfurt — tell the jury of Jewish history how Mike sent you to *yeshivah* and later set you up in business; tell them how there were sometimes as many as ten or more eating in Mike's newly established home, when he was blessed with a life partner who shared his boundless *ahavas Yisrael*.

Come forth — you, the successful precious-metal dealer from Long Island. Tell about your work in the early years of the war, when you came — the only one saved from your family — how Mike started a new department to set you and your friends up in business. Tell them how we bought you that first rickety panel-truck. Tell them what Mike did for your friend, now a textile tycoon, and for his little sister, for whom he found a warm family that sent her through school, gave her love and care, until she married, and who now has a wonderful family of her own.

Tell how Mike and our *chaveirim* found jobs, schools, and homes for all who came to 616 Bedford Avenue, weeks or even days after they arrived. Mr. S., of blessed memory, from your place on high, testify through your wife and children. Surely you must have told them how Mike sat with you, as with the scores of others, when you arrived despondent, looking with you at the picture of your family left behind in that small German town. Mike got you your first job and kept his promise: he brought them all to the U.S. — each of your wonderful daughters now married to a *talmid chacham*, your wife the matron of a dynasty of children and grandchildren all *bnei Torah*.

Remember your mission to Kobe, Japan, Frank N.? Remember how Mike enlisted your help? You were the only one who could travel to the Far East, get visas, and arrange transportation for Reb Aharon and hundreds of the most famous talmudic scholars of the Lithuanian and Polish *yeshivos*.

And you, Rabbi P. from Jamaica, N.Y. — remember what you said when we met recently, decades later: "Mike Tress and the Agudah office at 616 Bedford Avenue did the work; others made a lot of noise and got the credit." You ought to know, you were among the numerous rabbis who helped us compile lists of famous and unknown scholars to be submitted to the State Department or to diplomats from

Latin American countries from whom we tried to purchase visas or emergency stays.

Reb Mordechai Schwab, remember the evening you and a group of your *chaveirim*, each one a *gadol baTorah*, arrived in the United States? You came to our downtown office, into the midst of an executive meeting, threw down your raincoat, and ran over to the smiling young man pointed out to you as Mike Tress. You embraced him and each one of us — tears in your gentle eyes ... The brief speech you made then on behalf of the hundreds of your *chaveirim*, about the *ahavas Yisrael* and *chessed* of the group of young men, Mike at their head!

※ ※ ※

Of course, it was not Mike alone. It was all of the *chaveirim* of Zeirei and Agudath Israel who raised funds, ran emergency campaigns, cajoled business associates, customers, and suppliers to give ads, provide training, clothes, affidavits, or whatever else was needed. So many of you helped set up so many others in business ... You opened your homes and hearts to us when we arrived — strangers in a new, hostile world — hurt, lonely, full of traumas that no psychiatrist could cure. When all of you, Mike at your head, put your arms around me, took us into the circle of the *Yom Tov rikkudim* (dances), it was worth more than any medicine or treatment.

As the Circle Widened

At first it was only our *chaveirim*. Gradually Mike broadened and widened the circle of those who worked with him, called on him for help, and became his close associates, friends, admirers. They were your *chassidim*, Reb Elimelech, though no one showed more deference and reverence for them than you: the sainted *Rebbeim* of Boyan, Kapitshenitz, Novominsk, Modzitz and Stropkov, those who had been in the U.S. before, and those who joined the ranks of the *Admorim* during and after the war, from the least known to the most famous. The Satmar Rav and Lubavitcher Rebbe worked with you and treated you with the kind of respect reserved for very few *Amerikaner*. Soon your Yiddish became as eloquent as your flawless English, and you were able to cast the magic of your wholehearted call for help over huge audiences that ranged from Hungarian *chassidim* to the most-assimilated American Jews.

But not only the chassidic world; some of the greatest names of the past and present world of *gedolei haTorah* were among Mike's guides, co-workers, and admirers. There was Rabbi Eliezer Silver who commuted by plane (at a time when even travel by train was severely restricted) from one part of the country to the other, and from one corner of the world to the next to help organize our rescue work ... Rabbi Feivel Mendelowitz, the great mentor and molder of generations of Torah scholars, was among our greatest supporters; he opened the doors for us to outstanding community leaders who were his personal *chassidim* ... The legendary Reb Michael Ber Weissmandl, superb scholar and Kabbalist, who singlehandedly fought the SS extermination machine, jumped from trains destined for concentration camps, organized resistance — he, too, was one of Mike's great admirers and guides in our growing work — from his arrival in this country at the close of the war until his untimely death. The most famous names of the *yeshivah* world were the most intimate co-workers, Rabbi Aharon Kotler, Rabbi Reuven Grozovsky, Rabbi Elye Meir Bloch, Rabbi Motel Katz, Rabbi Avraham Kalmanowitz — giants of the Jewish spiritual world, who built new fortresses of Torah scholarship in America ... It was Mike Tress and our officers of Zeirei and Agudath Israel that were privileged to work with them, as they changed the intellectual climate of Jewish America in the decades after their arrival; as they produced the miraculous renaissance of a high-level Torah *chinuch* in the United States from the remnants and embers of the great East European Jewish centers of Poland, Lithuania, and Hungary.

◈§ Mike Went on

Most of us dropped out eventually, each one continuing to nurse the spark of inspiration which Mike Tress had ignited in us, each in his own way, in different realms of work for the *Klal.* But Mike's work and the work of his close associates went on, growing in pace and with broadened scope, in the years of post-war emergencies — in Europe, in Israel, in the Far East — on a global scale. One could go on endlessly, pouring forth memory upon memory, fact and experiences that are buried, lost, because Mike and all those who worked with him shunned publicity.

◈§ When All the Files are Opened

Some day the open and secret files of the government offices in Washington, in the embassies of Europe, the Near and Far East, will be searched to compile official records. Some day concerned scholars will scour the old file cabinets and cellars stacked with boxes of faded correspondence that began to flow from and to our modest office at 616 Bedford Avenue before Mike Tress and the office moved to Manhattan, to a more highly professional level. They will uncover the work above and underground. They will see Mike in and out of uniform, in the camps after the war, in Poland, Hungary, Germany and France. They will find the voluminous, multibranched international activities that he and his associates organized with modest means. They may even be able to unscramble the warp and woof of unstructured and structured *mesiras nefesh* of Zeirei and Agudath Israel during the years when groups of Pirchim and Zeirim tried to fill the gap left wide open by those who could have done so much more.

To those who had been touched by the challenge of the time, and who had been inspired by the greatness of one dynamic, wholehearted *chaver*, the full dimensions of our work for *hatzalah* will never be fathomed, gauged, or recorded. They are part of the eternal stream of *Mesoras Avoseinu Beyodeinu*, the tradition of boundless faith, self-sacrifice, and idealism that spans the ages, binds the past to the present, and flows on into the future of our children, the generation after us.

※ ※ ※

A last fleeting reminiscence: When we printed our first modest stationery, Mike chose the famous quote to be placed at the bottom: "He who saves a soul in Israel saves an entire world!" It was to guide him and direct our work as the beacon of light that he had held up for all of us to follow. History books may never record it. But to the thousands to whom it brought hope and a chance to rebuild life anew, it is emblazoned into the very fabric of their hearts and souls. May it serve as an inspiration and obligation for our children to perpetuate a record of modest, yet vital, achievement far beyond the keenest expectations, simply because there were those who cared.

Lewis Brenner

Why Auschwitz Was Never Bombed

IT TOOK over thirty years for the truth to surface. And now that it has, Professor David S. Wyman's article, "Why Auschwitz Was Never Bombed" (in the May 1978 *Commentary Magazine*) should be required reading. After sifting through the primary sources, including many documents that have only recently become declassified, Prof. Wyman has underscored what Orthodoxy has known and believed for many years. In brief, the American government and the world at large had been alerted to the massive annihilation of Jews taking place under the Germans. Among the very few who took the situation to heart were a number of Orthodox Jews, who applied their untiring efforts to saving the remnants of their brethren from extermination.* They, and they alone, persistently attempted to agitate the United States government to destroy the death machinery of Auschwitz by bombing it, but they did not succeed in their attempt. The details, as recorded by Wyman, are worthy of study. What follows is a summary of some of the points that he presents.

The time was April 1944. The Nazis were concentrating the 760,000 Jews of Hungary for deportation to the killing center at Auschwitz. Two young Slovak Jews who had escaped from Auschwitz to a Jewish underground facility dictated a thirty-six page report on the 1,750,000 already killed in Auschwitz, with a precise description and geographic layout of the entire extermination facilities. A copy of their statement reached Jewish

---

* Since corroborated by the Goldberg Commission in Spring, 1984.

This essay appeared in *The Jewish Observer* of May 1978

leaders in Budapest by early May. To whom was this message sent?

[All quotations from the article are in the type style used for this sentence. — Ed.]

✒ A Letter to Sternbuch

> By mid-June, the Slovak underground had smuggled the report to Switzerland, where it was passed to the American legation and found to be consistent with earlier trustworthy but fragmentary information that had filtered out concerning the Auschwitz death camp. During June, this information spread to the Allied governments and began to appear in the Swiss, British, and American press. By late June, then, the truth about Auschwitz, along with descriptions of its geographical location and layout, was known to the outside world. In mid-May, as deportation from the eastern provinces of Hungary started (under the direct supervision of Adolf Eichmann), Jewish leaders in Budapest sent out a plea for the bombing of keypoints on the rail route to Poland. Dispatched via the Jewish underground in Bratislava, Slovakia, the request was telegraphed in code to Isaac Sternbuch, representative in Switzerland of the American Orthodox Jewish rescue committee (Vaad Hatzalah). It reached him about May 17.

This is the very same Isaac Sternbuch who was in constant touch with Michael G. Tress, leader of Zeirei Agudath Israel of America, and director of its emergency rescue efforts, many of which could not be revealed due to the opposition of the Roosevelt administration. These activities were thus not yet subject for the *Commentary* article.

Prof. Wyman continues to tell us:

> Sternbuch immediately rewrote the telegram for transmission to the headquarters of the Union of Orthodox Rabbis in New York and submitted it to the military attache of the U.S. legation in Bern, requesting that it be telegraphed to the United States through diplomatic lines. Three days later, a similar but more urgent telegram arrived from Bratislava. That appeal also went to the U.S. military attache for delivery to New York. The pleas kept coming every two or three days for the next month, and Sternbuch continued to relay them to the military attache. Yet by June 22, Sternbuch had received neither reply nor acknowledgment from New York. For unknown reasons, the messages had been blocked, either in Bern or in Washington.

Why Auschwitz Was Never Bombed / 253

❧ Outcry From Reb Michael Ber

At the same time, the most gripping appeal for help came from that great *tzaddik*,

Rabbi Michael Ber Weissmandl, and [from] Mrs. Gisi Fleischmann, both leaders of the Slovak Jewish underground, [who] wrote a long letter pleading with the outside world for help. They described the first deportations from Hungary and stressed the fate awaiting the deportees on arrival at Auschwitz. Their stark account revealed that four forty-five-car trains were leaving daily, each train carrying about three thousand people. During the two to three day trip to Auschwitz, the victims were pressed together, standing, in closed freight cars without food, water, or sanitary facilities. Many died on the way. After describing the plight of these Hungarian Jews, Rabbi Weissmandl and Mrs. Fleischmann appealed strenuously for immediate bombing of the main deportation routes, especially the Kosice-Presov railway. They also cried to the outside world to "bombard the death halls in Auschwitz." Writing in anguish, the two asked: "And you, our brothers in all free countries; and you, governments of all free lands, where are you? What are you doing to hinder the carnage that is now going on?" Smuggled out of Slovakia, the plea, accompanied by copies of the Auschwitz escapees' reports, reached Switzerland, but not until late June ... Mrs. Fleischmann and Rabbi Weissmandl were deported to Auschwitz, at different times, during the fall of 1944. She was gassed there; he escaped from the train and survived the war.

Rabbi Weissmandl later made his way to America. Settling in the Williamsburg section of Brooklyn, he would go from *shul* to *shul* crying out in his anguish over the failure of United States Jewry to do anything to save its brethren from extermination. While he continued to bewail the misfortune, he involved himself in the re-establishment of the great *Nitra Yeshivah* in the Mount Kisco (New York) farm settlement. This Orthodox leader left a book entitled *"Min HaMeitzar* — From the Depths" — a scathing indictment of those who refused to place rescue work as the top priority in Jewish activity.

❧ The Rosenheim Appeal

The role of the World (office of) Agudath Israel in these efforts is highlighted by the activities of its president, Reb Yaakov Rosenheim. Prof. Wyman records that:

Rosenheim's appeals to Washington were first relayed to the War Refugee Board (WRB), an agency that President Roosevelt had established by executive order five months earlier, on January 22, 1944. The President had charged the board with carrying out all measures within its [the government's] power to rescue the victims of enemy oppression who are in imminent danger of death.

We are told that although Roosevelt named the Secretaries of State, Treasury and War as equal members of the War Refugee Board, in actuality Henry Morgenthau (Treasury) was the real boss. Imagine the opportunity this "could-have-been-modern-day-Mordechai" was given to save his people! Yet, through John W. Pehle, his delegated head of the War Refugee Board, Morgenthau refused to take action upon Reb Yaakov Rosenheim's recommendations to bomb, on the grounds that it was impracticable: the targets were too far from the Allied air bases; or this would deflect material from the major purpose of fighting the war. In the WRB's words,

"We must constantly bear in mind ... that the most effective relief which can be given victims of enemy persecution is to insure the speedy defeat of the Axis."

In concrete terms, this position meant that the military had decided to concentrate strictly on the war and avoid the diversion of resources into rescue or relief activities.

Prof. Wyman documents that the policy was conceived out of thin air, not as the result of any investigative study. And actually, not only was such a bombing practical, oil installations only five miles away from Auschwitz were being bombed on a regular basis.

An Emergency Committee to Save the Jewish People of Europe pressured for the bombing of Auschwitz. A more dramatic proposal was made by the World Jewish Congress to the War Department directly calling for the bombing of the crematoria, but not all Jewish leaders concurred in this view. In fact, the United States section of the World Jewish Congress, reports Wyman, opposed bombing the death installations because Jews in the camps would be killed. Others in America disagreed.

☙ Night Call from Rabbi Kalmanowitz

At the beginning of September, pressure built once more on the War Refugee Board for bombing rail lines, this time the lines between Auschwitz and Budapest, where the last large enclave of

Hungarian Jews was threatened with deportation. These entreaties came from the Orthodox rescue committee in New York. Rabbi Abraham Kalmanowitz, anxious for the appeal to reach the WRB as soon as possible, placed a night phone call to Benjamin Akzin, who relayed the plea to Pehle the next day. Akzin took advantage of the opportunity to spell out to Pehle, in polite terms, his dissatisfaction with the inaction of the War Department regarding the bombing requests ... But the Board did not move on the appeal.

Note that this insistent campaign emanated from the Orthodox community, which acted on the basis of Torah law and its stringent requirements for the preservation of human life, even at the expense of the desecration of the Sabbath. The leadership of the Orthodox rescue committee in New York — which included Rabbi Reuven Grozovsky, Rabbi Aharon Kotler, and Rabbi Eliezer Silver — put aside all personal needs to do everything possible to save their brethren. Earlier accomplishments — the rescue of the entire *Mirrer Yeshivah*, among many others — were dwarfed in their eyes by the mounting tragedy, and they continued to plead and beg for the saving of more and more of their brethren.

To the United States government, however, the terrible plight of the Jews apparently did not merit any active response. This, concludes Wyman, *"remains a source of wonder, and a lesson, even today."*

↩ More Than the Record of a Struggle

Professor Wyman's account signifies more than just a day-to-day account of the struggle to save European Jewry. It highlights a fact too often ignored by serious students of Jewish history: only those who are totally guided by Torah, and those under their tutelage, can size up a situation and its true needs properly, because their Torah perspective frees them from the shades of self-seeking motives or the influence of shallow thinking, sloganeering, and popular pressure. Men of this calibre were able to grasp the full dimension of a problem and discern the true implications of a situation. When others were content with press releases, large newspaper ads, and official protests, the Sternbuchs, Weissmandls, Rosenheims, and Kalmanowitzes were *moser nefesh* for the cause of *hatzalas nefashos*, rescuing lives. It is no wonder that their names appear so prominently in the official record of the efforts to bomb the rail lines to Auschwitz.

In retrospect, the gravity of the situation may now appear

obvious, but during the middle of the war people greeted with skepticism the reports that the Nazis were bent upon the total annihilation of the Jews. They may not have noted how Hitler was neglecting the military war in order to pursue his war against the Jews; that the railway system and the rolling stock, which were so strategically necessary for supplying the armies, were being diverted for transporting Jews from all over Europe to the gas chambers. Those pleading for the bombing had hoped that if the extermination process could not be stopped, at least it could be delayed. Professor Wyman points out that hundreds of thousands of Jews (including Anne Frank) were on those last trains being shipped out of Holland, France, Italy, and Hungary in the concluding months of the war. From Hungary alone 500,000 victims were gathered in the spring of 1944 and shipped by Eichmann on *top priority trains* along vital railroad lines to Auschwitz.

The legacy of the war is the near-total destruction of European Jewry. The footnote to this tragic chapter is the dominant role the Orthodox leadership played in attempting to stop the destruction. Perhaps this article will encourage some serious scholar to delve further into recently opened archives and compile a complete account of Orthodoxy's role in the rescue efforts. And, more important, people will realize that life-and-death decisions for our people should be made by those who are above petty political considerations.

Rabbi Joseph Elias

Heroic Efforts, Fatal Failings

THE DESTRUCTION OF EUROPEAN Jewry continues to spawn books of all types, ranging from autobiographical accounts[1] and photographic reportage[2], to anthologies and collections of source material designed to tell the reader "how it happened — what it means," to use the words of one such book, *The Holocaust Years*.[3] Some of the books make, at most, a very minor contribution to our knowledge and understanding of the Holocaust, while others may actually mislead the reader by omission or commission. Thus, *The Holocaust Years* contains some excellent selections of sources, but presents instances of governmental persecution and discrimination, thereby in effect totally negating any specific Jewish aspect (shades of Hannah Arendt's thesis that the Holocaust was a crime against humanity rather than against the Jewish people).

On the other hand, however, some new and highly significant books have recently been published, as sealed archives have been opened and secret documents have become available. An increasing number of works throws a very clear light on some basic aspects of the destruction of European Jewry that were hitherto shrouded in an acrimony of confusion. While the details of how the Nazis' extermination process worked were clarified

---

This review appeared in *The Jewish Observer* of March 1985.

1. *Soldiers from the Ghetto*, by Shalom Cholawski (A.S. Barnes, N.Y. 1980), which provides an insight into the world of the partisans.

2. *The Warsaw Ghetto in Photographs*, by Ulrich Keller (Dover Publications, N.Y., 1984).

3. *The Holocaust Years: Society on Trial*, by R. Chantok and J. Spencer, in cooperation with the Anti-Defamation League (Bantam Books, N.Y., 1978).

long ago, this has not been the case with the role played by their adversaries. What could, and did, the victims do to resist? More important, what could and did the free nations do to save them? Finally, in particular, what did their Jewish brethren in the outside world do?

◆§ What Did the Rest of the World Do?

The two outstanding books on these subjects, both characterized by their careful use of archives and of interviews with actors in the great tragedy, are Monty Noam Penkower's *The Jews Were Expendable: Free World Diplomacy and the Holocaust* (University of Illinois Press, Urbana, 1983), and David S. Wyman's *Abandonment of the Jews, America and the Holocaust 1941-45* (Pantheon Books, New York, 1984). Both books demonstrate, in a manner and detail not done before, the way in which the free nations, notably the United States and England, "abdicated their moral responsibility and thus became accomplices to Hitler's crimes" (Penkower) — not only by passively standing still and watching the murder of the Jews, but by actively frustrating rescue possibilities, out of fear that they may be swamped with "these useless people" (in the words of one official). Penkower's book is a study in depth of nine issues that arose during the Holocaust, from the question of a Jewish army to that of bombing Auschwitz; Wyman's work is a chronological study of the entire period. Their conclusions on the duplicity of the Allies are the same, and they uncover much evidence heretofore buried in the files. For instance, the refusal to bomb Auschwitz and the rail lines leading to it, as first called for by Rabbi Michael Ber Weissmandl, is traced here in detail and this refusal by the Allies is shown not to be based on any legitimate grounds of impracticality or interference with the war effort.

◆§ A Finely Drawn Picture of Failure

Likewise, the two authors present us with the finely drawn and clearly documented picture of the failure of the Jewish establishment and its major organizations to respond adequately to the crisis, even though there were individuals who labored heroically for *Hatzalah*. There were three factors at work: genuine fear of any action that might be "illegal" hobbled the Joint Distribution Committee's work when crucial major possibilities of rescue arose; there was the patriotic desire not to disregard Roosevelt's wishes, and the fear of stirring up anti-

Semitism; and finally there was the commitment of the Zionist movement to put the attainment of a Jewish State before the pursuit of rescue possibilities. These factors vitiated the rescue efforts, divided the organizations when unity of purpose was necessary above all, and actually led to numerous tragic instances where imminent rescue possibilities were hindered and sabotaged: the picketing of the Agudath Israel offices by the American Jewish Congress and other groups when Agudath Israel insisted on shipping food packages to Poland at the beginning of the war; Stephen Wise's characterization of the Sternbuchs' reports as "atrocity tables," at the very time that he himself had the same terrible information and kept it secret;[4] the discrimination against the Orthodox and non-Zionists in the work of *Aliyah Bet*;[5] the opposition of Wise and his associates to the congressional rescue resolution which, in the end, brought about the creation of the War Refugee Board; the Zionist opposition to the proposed congressional resolution to open refugee shelters in Palestine which led to its defeat; all these are just some of the instances documented in these books. At the same time, the two authors highlight the work of the *Vaad Hatzalah* and Agudath Israel as uniquely single-minded and effective in its emphasis on rescue by any means.

⇜§ Different Approaches ...

Yet there are differences in their approach to a number of issues. Wyman, who focuses on the United States' role, apparently never took a firsthand look at the work of Rabbi

---

4. See the comments of Rabbi Sherer (at the end of the essay) for the central role played in all matters of Jewish concern by Stephen Wise, leading Reform Rabbi and accepted as the spokesman for American Jewry at large, both by American Jews and by governmental and political circles.

The role of the Sternbuchs during World War II is described in full in *Heroine of Rescue, The Incredible Story of Recha Sternbuch*, by Joseph Friedenson and David Kranzler, which was reviewed in *The Jewish Observer*, April 84. The Sternbuchs obtained, and forwarded to Yaakov Rosenheim in New York, full reports on the extermination of European Jewry, hitherto not known to the public. Stephen Wise belittled these reports and prevented action on them even though he had also received the information, because he had promised the State Department to keep it secret for the time being.

5. Aliyah Bet was the illegal Aliyah organized, under the aegis of the Jewish Agency's Vaad Hahatzalah (not to be confused with the Orthodox Vaad Hatzalah in New York). It involved bringing illegal immigrants via the Black Sea to Palestine. The organizers of the transports insisted that Orthodox Jewish refugees could only compose six percent of the transports, even though they comprised a much larger part of the fleeing Jews, with some of the organizers boasting of not admitting any Orthodox Jews (Penkower, pp. 169-170 on this topic).

Michael Ber Weissmandl's Working Group,[6] and has only limited acquaintance with the efforts of the Sternbuchs (his inability to use Hebrew materials must also have been a handicap). As a result, he not only plays down the significance of their work in those instances where he takes note of it at all, but casts Saly Mayer in a heroic role and likewise bestows inordinate praise upon McClelland (for an accurate and documented assessment of his role see David Kranzler in Appendix 4 of the Goldberg Report, p.17). He tries to defend Wise's silence on the first extermination reports, apparently unaware of Wise's attacks on Yaakov Rosenheim in this matter; and he also discusses the efforts to save Jews by means of Latin American passports without any awareness of how these efforts were initiated and how comprehensive they were. Penkower, in contrast, gives the fullest recognition to the imaginative and daring work of the Orthodox activists. On a different issue, Wyman dramatically contradicts Penkower's positive evaluation of the Fort Oswego episode; perhaps Wyman was better able to gauge the real feelings of the town's people.

... Different Conclusions

More important are the differences in their conclusions. Penkower, despite his admiration for Rabbi M.B. Weissmandl, stresses that "Sternbuch's attacks on Mayer and Kastner and Weissmandl's bitter recriminations against free-world Jewry in general ... reflected a failure to grasp the fundamental powerlessness of a people abandoned to its fate" (p. 215). Quite apart from the fact that the saving of even one life is a supreme goal for us, and therefore the criticism that nothing major could have been achieved totally misses the point, it is by no means clear that Penkower's assessment is correct; Wyman's list of missed possibilities very definitely suggests the opposite conclusion. Many of these possibilities depended on cooperation by governments, but not all; and the achievements of the activists

---

6. The Working Group was an underground group of Hungarian Jewish leaders, representing varied backgrounds, dominated by the personality of Rabbi Michael Ber Weissmandl. Working with the Sternbuchs in Switzerland, he inspired and set into motion a large number of efforts to inform the free world of the "Final Solution," and to develop rescue plans based on the fact that during the latter part of the war Nazi officials became more open to bribery. The most ambitious of these plans, the "Europa Plan," involved the "purchase" of one million Jews. Owing to the refusal of the Joint and the other major Jewish groups to provide the necessary finances, the plan failed. Key figures in obstructing these plans were Saly Mayer and Roswell McClelland, the representatives in Switzerland of the Joint and the War Refugee Board: McClelland derisively dubbed Rabbi Weissmandl "the holy man."

proved that even impossible things could be done by desperate people. Wyman, who describes himself as a Gentile Zionist, is deeply critical of Jewish leadership in general and Zionist leaders in particular, even though he stresses that they should not be condemned, since they meant well.

✑ The Goldberg Report

Against the background of these two books, it is interesting to read Seymour Finger's *American Jewry During the Holocaust* (March, 1984), the headline-making report by the research director of the American Jewish Commission on the Holocaust — popularly known a the Goldberg Commission — which was established to determine (a) whether American Jewish leaders knew, and (b) whether they could have done more about the Holocaust. The report, albeit coached in very careful terms, does show that they knew and that more could have been done. The Report deals gently with the leadership in general, and personalities like Wise and Mayer in particular (oddly enough, Wise is even credited with helping bring about the creation of the War Refugee Board, even though he impeded it by all means fair and foul); but it does stress that the Orthodox efforts, although based on the activities of a small group of men, achieved far more than those of the secular groups.

Throughout the report, as in the other books discussed, there can be felt the influence of Professor Yehudah Bauer, who has been aptly called an apologist for the Zionists' wartime leadership. He has persistently argued that Jewry was really impotent, and has rather consistently belittled the rescue schemes of the Sternbuchs, Rabbi Michael Ber Weissmandl, and others. The articles by David Kranzler, "Orthodox Goals, Unorthodox Means," and Samuel Merlin, on "The Europa Plan," which are in the appendix to the report, are a helpful corrective. So is a new volume, *The Holocaust Studies Annual*, vol. 1, (Penkevill Publishers, Greenwood, 1984) which contains, among other articles, a study of Jewish disunity during the war, which concludes that the stress on "the pre-eminence of the Zionist program in relation to the refugee question" (Nachum Goldmann) profoundly weakened American Jewish rescue efforts. Other articles indicate that individuals and their efforts made a difference, by reference to Varian Frey's efforts in Vichy France, and the successful sheltering of refugees in the Panama Canal Zone.

~§ Unexpected Rescue, From Unlikely Places

The fact that opportunities for rescue could unexpectedly appear in unlikely places, and thanks to unexpected helpers, is illustrated by Rabbi Chaim Uri Lipschitz's *Franco Spain, the Jews and the Holocaust* (Ktav, New York, 1984). The author makes a well-documented case that Franco saved more than forty-five thousand Jews, either by letting them find refuge in Spain or by extending his protection to them (specifically the Sephardic Jews, who claimed to be of Spanish origin). Franco was by no means consistent in his policies, but he did more than anybody could have expected from a Fascist ruler closely linked to Hitler. Moreover, his motives were not crudely self-serving; he could, for instance, expect no practical returns from his efforts, long after the war, to aid Egypt's Jews. And Rabbi Lipschitz tantalizingly touches on a plan of Franco's to be of help to Russia's Jews. In all, this is an intriguing work.

~§ From The Heart of Rosenheim ...

In the writings of Penkower, Wyman and Finger, the significant role that Yaakov Rosenheim and Rabbi Michael Ber Weissmandl played in the tragedy of the Holocaust clearly emerges, but not enough about these two men themselves. Two recent books help us gain a better understanding of these outstanding personalities, as they contended with the war and its challenges.

Moreinu Yaakov Rosenheim's place in modern Jewish history is secured by his key role in the founding of the Agudath Israel World Organization, and his service as its president until his passing in 1965. Agudath Israel was not meant to be a political party, like others, and Yaakov Rosenheim was not a political leader in the usual sense of the word. Torah personality and profound thinker as well as a dynamic leader of men, he chose as his aim to guide the life of *Klal Yisroel*, and to solve its problems, in the spirit of the Torah. The ultimate challenge to the attainment of this goal was represented by the events from 1933 to 1948, from the rise of Hitler, through the Holocaust, to the emergence of a Jewish State. *Comfort, Comfort My People, A Collection of Essays and Speeches by Moreinu Jacob Rosenheim*, edited by Dr. Isaac Levin (Research Institute of Religious Jewry, New York, 1984) brings within the covers of one book the thinking of this extraordinary personality about the earthshaking events of the time in which he himself was called to act.

Many of the articles and their practical conclusions are no longer directly relevant but the original thoughts and imaginative approaches contain many lessons for us. It is obvious from these writings how clearly Rosenheim saw the needs of the time. He cried out against political efforts to block rescue efforts in favor of seeking statehood. He saw the need and launched the struggle to save the souls of the children that had been rescued from the Holocaust and represented the future of the Jewish people. Of particular interest is his exchange with Dr. Isaac Breuer over the creation of a Torah State in *Eretz Yisrael*, and the form that it should take. The value of this work is enhanced by the historical photographs included.

... and the Cries of Reb Michael Ber

Rabbi Michael Ber Weissmandl is the subject of a biography by Abraham Fuchs, *The Unheeded Cry* (Mesorah Publications, New York, 1984). It is a fascinating volume and introduces the reader to the many facets of Rabbi Weissmandl's life — as *talmid chacham* and scholarly researcher, as *Rosh Yeshivah* and educator, and in between as an utterly indefatigable leader in the searing struggle to save Jewish lives. This book, which is thoroughly documented and illustrated by many historical photographs, seeks to correct the mistakes and injustices from which he has suffered at the hands of so many of the Holocaust historians, and to establish firmly his place as a brilliant strategist and totally unselfish fighter against the Nazi's Final Solution.

A recent writer on the Holocaust expressed surprise at the fact that it was left to an "ultra-Orthodox" rabbi from Hungary to propose the bombing of rail lines to Auschwitz. Such surprise is, of course, quite out of place — it flows from the fatuous sense of superiority with which the "moderns" tend to view the Torah Jew, and to belittle his wisdom and insight. The expression of surprise is doubly ludicrous when it relates to a man of such towering stature as Rabbi Weissmandl. Abraham Fuchs excellently delineates the guiding principles of his policies: never to give up, never consider his own safety, to respect no laws when it came to saving lives, and to play on the enemy's conviction of Jewish international power. As David Kranzler showed in his work on the refugees under Japanese control, the Japanese protected the refugees because they mistakenly believed that the Jews controlled the United States and this country would be influenced by their treatment of the refugees. In the same way, the Germans in time became victims of their own propaganda about the power of international Jewry, as Penkower's book shows in detail, and Rabbi Weissmandl, perceiving this weakness, exploited it by dangling all sorts of promises before them. Fuchs perceptively presents Rabbi Weissmandl's ideas (though he does not correctly explain his opposition to Zionism, p. 352); his work will undoubtedly become an indispensable aid to the understanding of this era.

~§ Religious Responses

While the books discussed are primarily concerned with the actions of the leaders, other works deal with the responses of the Jewish masses to the fate that threatened them. Isaiah Trunk's *Jewish Responses to Nazi Persecution* (Stein & Day, N.Y., 1979) explores "collective and individual behavior *in extremis*." The first part of this volume analyzes the different kinds of responses that could be found, and the author's observations on the way religious Jews reacted (pp. 21-25). It is particularly interesting in the context of the economic difficulties of maintaining one's integrity and moral standards under ghetto and camp conditions. The second part of the book presents extracts from sixty-two eyewitness testimonials — chilling and horrifying insights into the realities of life and death under the Nazis.

That Jews could and did preserve their spirit even under these conditions is, of course, the point of *Sparks of Glory*, the classic work of Moshe Prager, translated by Mordecai Schreiber, and now available in a new edition, as part of the Artscroll History Series (Mesorah Publications, New York, 1985). Prager's central point is that Nazi hatred of the Jews was directed, in the first place, at what the Jews stood for — their spiritual legacy which they had preserved throughout their history. Therein lay the particular importance of spiritual resistance, of the defiance that Jews, who were unable to fight back, demonstrated by remaining Jews and preserving their faith even at the gates of death.

Forty years after the collapse of the Nazi empire, we are still struggling to come to grips with events that we are not really able to understand. Yet it is important for us to be aware of the heroism and wisdom shown by personalities like the Sternbuchs and Rabbi Weissmandl, as well as the faith and grandeur of all those unsung victims who died with the *Shema* on their lips — a lesson to us of the greatness that can be attained through Torah if we but strive for it.

Excerpts from Rabbi Moshe Sherer's Comments Appended to the Report of the American Jewish Commission on the Holocaust

This report seeks to achieve mutually exclusive goals: to be both painstakingly candid about the guilt of the American Jewish leaders during the years under consideration, and at the same time be graciously protective of Jewish leaders whose heartless obsession with legalisms prevented the rescue of large numbers.

Professor Finger's attempts at even-handedness simply do not work. On the one hand he deserves plaudits for courageously exposing the grievous faults of the secular Jewish leadership. On the other hand the excuses he offers to justify their actions, attributing them to "serious misconceptions," do not hold water.

Professor Finger is to be commended for his vivid portrayal of the callousness of the Allied Governments to the plight of the Jews. It is vital that his report about the inaction of American Jewish leaders should not be misconstrued as a diminution of the thousandfold greater guilt of the governments of the free world, who ignored the plight of human beings whose only "sin" was that they were born Jews.

Within that smaller framework, the Finger Report does set the record straight, even at the cost of opening old wounds. For instance, Dr. Stephen Wise, who served simultaneously as president of three well-known organizations — the Zionist Organization of America, the World Jewish Congress and the American Jewish Congress — was the chief architect of an American Jewish policy, which resulted in the loss of many thousands of Europe's Jews who could have been saved. He and his policy must stand in judgment before the tribunal of history. The course he and his colleagues charted was surely based on what they thought was best for the Jews: not to rock the boat by antagonizing the Roosevelt administration, not to disturb the general war effort by aggressively pushing for special methods to save Jews, and not to risk creating more anti-Semitism by being conspicuous. But it was also a tragic disaster.

History will also point a finger of guilt at these same leaders for their fear of resorting to methods that violate government regulations to save Jews, simply refusing to "dirty their hands," even though the alternative for the victims was an unmarked grave or ending up as a piece of soap.

This policy of inaction also was influenced by the general philosophy of Zionist groups that rescue opportunities were secondary to concentrating on building a Jewish homeland in Palestine after the war was over. Alas, they did not perceive how utterly ridiculous and heartless it was for Jewish leaders to concentrate on a postwar homeland, when the people for whom they were seeking this home were being slaughtered like sheep.

Professor Finger is to be commended, on the other hand, for helping document the fact that the Orthodox Jewish community, through Agudath Israel and the *Vaad Hatzalah*, "saved significant numbers of European Jews." Justice Arthur Goldberg's Commission, by focusing public attention on the uniqueness of the Orthodox Jewish rescue activity, has made an important contribution to the history of that era.

Of course, one dare not say that the Orthodox Jews and other activists did enough to rescue Jewish lives. For every peaceful breakfast that we ate when Jews were being gassed and burned, none of us can have a clear conscience. The historic fact remains, however, that Orthodox Jews were the only element (together with the Peter Bergson-Shmuel Merlin group and possibly the Jewish Labor Committee) for whom there was no other issue during those years except the rescue of Jews.

Beyond the facts lies a deep lesson to be learned: when one views events from a Torah perspective, the perception is diametrically different from the experience of seeing the same object through secular eyes. The Torah Jew is inculcated from early childhood with a special sense of *areivus* (responsibility) of one Jew for the other and for all mankind. When one's heart is overflowing with love for G-d, then that love naturally flows over to man who was created in the image of G-d. The tighter one clings to his roots as a Jew, the more profoundly one thinks and acts as a Jew.

It is my hope that these revelations will help to inspire Jews to think more Jewishly and to act more Jewishly.

VI.
A Guide to Remembering

When Remembering is a Mitzvah: A Symposium

⇜ The Focus of Remembering

REMEMBERING THE SUFFERING of World War II has many purposes. It provides a much-needed catharsis for the survivors. It provides us with the *"mas'chil bignus* — the opening with degradation" that helps us better appreciate G-d's mercy in granting us relief and the strength to rebuild.

But we must exercise caution in regard to our focus. Recounting the details of violence enacted against Jews can breed more violence. After performing the *mitzvah* of destroying an *ir hanidachas,* an incorrigibly depraved city, the Torah says, "... and G-d will grant you mercy." A special Divine intervention is necessary to counteract the effects of involvement in a brutal act, otherwise one act of brutality prompts another.

Before the destruction of the Second *Beis Hamikdash,* the *Sanhedrin* stopped judging capital cases when the incidence of murder increased, because executing murderers had a numbing effect on society, promoting callousness more than it inspired fear in the hearts of would-be murderers. How much more so can anti-Semitic groups take inspiration from detailed accounts of atrocities the Nazis committed against the Jews!

⇜ We Should Not Commemorate ...

We should not commemorate *Churban* Europe in the manner of the secularists. Monuments are not our medium, for even granite is ephemeral when compared to the eternity of the spirit.

This symposium appeared in *The Jewish Observer* of March 1985.

We cannot join them on the designated *Yom Hashoah*, for convening a day of mourning in the month of Nissan is almost as objectionable as throwing a party on *Tishah B'Av*. Both represent total apathy toward the Jewish calendar.

Putting an accent on physical heroism instead of *Kiddush Hashem* is not our approach to commemorating the *Churban*.

An event of such enormous scope should be a constant presence in the Jewish consciousness — remembrance instead of commemoration. A once-a-year commemoration risks the Mother's Day Syndrome, wherein one day of attention soothes the conscience of those guilty of three hundred and sixty-four days of neglect.

To be capable of convening a day for remembering requires *ruach hakodesh* (Divine inspiration), much as that possessed by the men who convened Chanukah a year after the miracle of the oil, men who were capable of sensing if the anniversary has the same "feel" or vibrations to it as the original day did.

We are a community of limited resources and we must select our tools for remembering and transmitting our experiences with care. Oral histories, for example, are an invaluable tool for transporting American children to other times and places. The spiritual beauty of prewar Europe, for example, should be high on the list, as well as spiritual heroism during the war. The Torah community provides an ideal source for these insights. On the other hand, accounts of personal suffering will merely duplicate some of the harrowing diaries of torture and death that already have been published. We must endeavor to do that which no one else can accomplish.

— *Rabbi Dovid Cohen*

◆§ Forgetting: Comfort or Betrayal?

The Midrash relates that Adam and Chavah wept for their murdered son, Hevel, and could find no source of comfort in face of his dead body lying in their presence. Their attention was caught by a raven, which appeared with a dead fledgling at his feet. With his beak, the raven dug a shallow grave, shoved the body of its child into the hole, covered it with earth, and left. The bereaved parents of Hevel followed the raven's example, and found consolation in their ability to forget their buried son.

One might wonder why, of all creatures, the raven, the symbol of brutality, was selected to teach human parents how to deal with grief, unless we understand that it was not mercy that prompted the raven to cover his offspring from his view, but callousness in wishing to forget its own grief.

Yes, there is need to bury the dead, but permitting oneself to forget the dead lacks in humanity.

— Rabbi Shmuel Unsdorfer

✍ The Formula for Understanding Events

Some people tend to seek out joyful occasions and truimphant events for understanding the Jewish experience, passing over the painful and the tragic. Others find "too many unanswered questions" in the unhappy chapters of Jewish history, and only find positive experiences meaningful. We must understand that everything that befalls Jewry is the expression of G-d's will. We are described as both "a nation sated with pleasure," and "a nation that survived the sword." Whether pleasure filled or sword threatened, we are G-d's people, each condition is merely one side of a two-sided coin. Concentrating on one while ignoring the other is only dealing with part of the whole.

— Rabbi Chaim Segal

✍ Why Remember?

To be sure, we must remember the suffering of the war years, if for no other reason than to respond to the urging of the scribbles that greeted us on walls in Auschwitz, Birkenau, and Dachau, inscriptions written by Jews on their way to the gas chambers:

"I was here. Shlomo ben Yehudah."

"I was here. Yosef ben Shimshon."

or simply:

„זָכוֹר ... לֹא תִשְׁכָּח."

But toward what end should we remember?

— To inspire us to improve ourselves culturally? Let us not forget that this terrible destruction emanated from the land of *dichter und denker*, poets and philosophers! The six German governors of the six sections of occupied Poland were all possessors of Ph.D.'s. And Hermann Goebbels had three doctoral degrees!

— To strengthen our commitment to democracy? But Hitler did not overthrow the previous regime. He was elected democratically. And here in America, the Democratic Party could not manage to pass a resolution to condemn anti-Semitism.

— To bellow "Never Again!"? That casts aspersion on the *Kedoshim*, as if they were guilty of complicity in their slaughter, and we who are so much wiser would not fall into the same trap. For "Never Again," we must pray.

Remembering must be aimed at something nobler: to reflect on the way of life of prewar Europe, and the spiritual heroism during the war, so they may serve as examples to us, the survivors, and their children.

— *Joseph Friedenson*

Rabbi Nisson Wolpin

Heroes: Remembering and Understanding

I WAS ADDRESSING my words to Oizer Becher, a thoughtful friend, survivor of two ghettos and a labor camp, who manages to be dispassionate yet understanding at the same time:

Remembering the destruction of World War II is important, but it ends up as an unrelieved study of martydom and becomes depressing. So we look for heroes to admire ... Are the only heroes those who fought physically? We know that there were so few who succeeded in joining resistance groups. Furthermore, one questions the way in which their course of action is used for staging responses to contemporary situations. Why highlight examples of heroism that serve to set up models not always meant to be emulated? The attention focused on ghetto uprisings is a case in point.

The Warsaw Ghetto uprising has always been a highly emotional focal point for our feelings regarding World War II. Pity, horror, valor and brutality — all peak in remembering the events that transpired there. The Warsaw Ghetto was the largest and most crowded of those cramped city quarters into which Jews were forced. The ghetto inhabitants made valiant attempts at assuring that "life as usual" continue within its suffocating confines. Torah study, *mitzvah* performance, and a sense of responsibility and concern for one's fellow Jews were maintained under the most harrowing conditions. And, then, there was the uprising, with all that it signified.

Every year, the anniversary of the Warsaw Ghetto uprising is marked with a grandiose memorial assembly in New York's

---

These conversations appeared in *The Jewish Observer* of September 1979.

Temple Emanuel, as well as a number of smaller regional gatherings. Again, the mixed emotions churn. Many people seek a legitimate format for remembering but are offended by the choice of the cathedral-like setting of a Reform temple — especially for honoring the memory of those who were so loyal to Torah Judaism. ... Sure, they want to remember and cry, but not during the month of Nissan when expressions of mourning are proscribed by *halachah* ... They are proud that some denizens of the ghetto were capable of rising above the oppressive Nazi rule and taking their fate into their own hands. Yet, those who maintained their Jewish identity of *emunah* and *bitachon* in the face of death were equally brave, if not more so.

Some use the anniversary to argue that the uprising was a historical turning-point in the fortunes of the Jewish People, for with the bold shots fired at the German soldiers, the brave battlers of Warsaw demonstrated that the role of passive victim was giving way to that of active determinant of one's fate. This, too, is discomfitting, for obviously our destiny as a people is not determined by a show of force. Not through our physical might or our military prowess did we survive nineteen centuries of *galus*. A *"Shema Yisrael"* shouted defiantly in the "showers" of Auschwitz or *matzos* baked under the shadow of death in Bergen-Belsen could well be selected as more viable symbols of Jewish perseverance and eternity.

One can debate these points without wincing. After all, emotions should be examined without compunction. One has every right to go beyond feelings of respect or reverence or grief to justify participation in one particular gathering or another.

◆§ To Avoid Indelicate Discussion?

One specific point is far more sensitive and one tends to gloss over it to avoid indelicate discussion. Once it has become part of the public domain, however, its status is different. Thus we permit ourselves to discuss it: there is a possibility that more lives were lost as a result of the uprising than had the Jews of the Warsaw Ghetto remained passive. When death was a certainty in either case, some questioned whether it might not be worthwhile sacrificing hours or even weeks of life to drag the enemy down with them — echoing Samson's "Let my life expire with the Philistines!" The question is a difficult one, and indeed, halachic authorities reputedly had lent their guidance in making the grave decisions regarding "to fight or not to fight."

But what about the feeling of "going down like a man" as a justification for loss of life? How does that fit into this perspective? This, for sure, is a sentiment foreign to Jewish values, and should not find its way into the heroic aspects of our tearful remembrances.

Yet, Dan Kurzman in his book *The Bravest Battle* injects this attitude in his description of a key incident prior to the uprising:

> It was on January 18, 1943, that Mordechai [Anczielewicz] finally made the people listen. The Germans, without warning, swooped down once again on the Jews. Mordechai and nine comrades, each armed with a pistol or a grenade, joined a terrified procession of Jews being led to Umschlagplatz. Suddenly one fighter hurled a grenade at the German guards, and a firefight broke out. Mordechai emptied his pistol at the Nazis, then snatched one from a German and continued firing until a comrade pulled him into a courtyard. Mordechai emerged from the battle as the sole survivor.
>
> But this show of resistance, together with other spontaneous actions and the threat of a simultaneous Polish uprising, forced the Germans to end the *Aktion* after four days. And the surviving Jews, euphoric over the revolt, realized at last that if they had to die, it was best to fall proudly in battle. Besides, many thought now, why give up so easily when German defeats at Stalingrad and in the Middle East signaled an early end to the war? (pp.37-38).

The possibility of their foray bringing the *Aktion* to an early end was an honest consideration, not to be dismissed. But why — at least according to Kurzman's account — did Anczielewicz not have any doubts about leading nine other men to their death? Why is "it best to fall proudly in battle"? As this story is being preserved and retold, the heroic image of the "macho" Jew truly is flaunted as the one worth commemorating — but is it?

I eyed Oizer Becher's thoughtful countenance, and awaited his comment.

✦ A Different Evaluation

"I don't accept Kurzman's evaluation of the good life or the noble death," Reb Oizer offered. "But in some ways, the death of the nine at that particular time and in those particular circumstances was a source of life support to the rest of us — a martyrdom of *hatzalas nefashos* (saving souls). I do not offer a halachic opinion on the matter. That is beyond me. But I will tell you how such defiant acts, which today we might view as gestures of futility, were the source of life to others."

Reb Oizer paused a moment, stroked his graying beard, and shuddered. "If you would have seen Yiddel Streicher before the war — or if you could see him now, in Bnei Brak — you could never picture him without his confident smile, his *gut vort*. We were in the Aschlog Labor Camp together. We had just broken ranks after a line-up. A visiting colonel with a penchant for dachshunds had just completed an inspection. He was walking away, jauntily swinging his riding crop, with two puppies yapping at his heels.

" 'How I envy him,' Yiddel sighed.

" 'You envy that murderer?' I asked, astonished.

" 'No, no,' said Yiddel. 'The little dog — his liveliness, his energy, his freedom to go where he wishes.'

"You see," said Reb Oizer, "Yiddel Streicher, one of the proudest Jews I know, a man who inspired others with his *bitachon*, his trust in G-d, and consideration of others — at times felt lower than the dachshund at a Nazi colonel's heels. I would have done anything to pick up his spirits, but I was at a loss. Yiddel had hit bottom. In such a setting, what could be dismissed today as a hollow gesture of defiance was a lifegiving act of encouragement. The death of the nine, at that time and in that place, raised us to at least one notch above the bottom."

So we can appreciate the need for heroes of physical prowess under those crushing circumstances, in the ghettos and camps. We needed heroes larger than life to simply feel alive and of the least value. And I've heard of the hero of spirit that rose even higher. But where does that leave everybody else?

∙§ Where Does That Leave Everybody Else?

My attention turned to Joseph Friedenson, whose qualifications to speak on this topic include, in his own words, "seven diplomas from seven German universities of murder and atrocity."

"I cannot speak for others," he said. "But as for me, I have countless people who inspired me: some who taught me how to die — if need be; and others who taught me much to apply as we continue to live, with G-d's help. For instance, there was a fifteen-year-old girl from Chust.

"Aviezer, a colleague of mine from the *yeshivah* in Lublin, and I had been assigned the unsavory task of transporting the refuse. We lugged an empty wagon to the various depositories — outside the kitchens, the latrine, and so on — filled the wagon, and emptied it into the dump. No one would call the job a pleasant one, but it was considered the best in the camp. I got it through pull — I was recommended by Reb Yosele Perlow (the then young Novominsker Rebbe, of Warsaw). Its value? This job kept us alive, for morsels of food could be found in the kitchen scraps, and our appointed rounds gave us a certain freedom to roam the camp at will. We were once pushing our malodorous cart past the ditch that separated us from the women's compound when we caught sight of a young girl, waving frantically at us.

" 'What's the matter?' Aviezer asked. 'Is something wrong?'

"A strong wind was blowing toward her, and her voice did not carry well. She held her arms together, and shivering called out, 'Kent yir mir kriggen a ... vetter?'

"Aviezer looked at me for an explanation. 'It's cold. I think she wants a sweater,' I offered.

"His first reaction was a shrug of the shoulders: 'Where does one get a sweater in Birkenau!'

"Several days later, we passed a warehouse that stored the clothing and personal effects of the *korbanos* of the gas chambers. Aviezer slipped through the door and emerged a few minutes later looking no different. As he took his place next to me, pushing our cart, he said, 'I put on a warm woolen sweater under my prison tunic.' In his emaciated condition one could not detect the difference.

"Next day, we passed the women's compound again. The girl was standing at the same spot, as if waiting for us. Aviezer took off his jacket, removed the sweater and hurled it over the barrier. She picked it up, shook it out and looked at it quizzically.

" 'What's this?' she shouted (the wind was on her side).

" 'A sweater,' he replied. 'You said you need one.'

" 'Sweater? No!' she cried out. 'I want a *Siddur*! Next week is Rosh Hashanah!'

"We looked at each other sheepishly. We were so occupied with mere physical survival, it never dawned on us that such a young girl had wanted a *Siddur* to warm her soul. The next time we passed the storage areas, Aviezer made sure to sneak in and smuggle out a *Siddur*, which eventually found its way into the girl's hands.

"Later Aviezer and I attempted to evaluate why we did not

daven during the day. The main impediment was the load that wafted its offensive message our way, as we pushed the refuse cart from station to station. Finally we hit upon a solution: We would pull the cart rather than push it, putting our putrid load out of sight and (when facing a head wind) out of mind.

"Aviezer and I would start from the beginning of *davening* — *Ma Tovu, Berachos,* and so on — helping each other when memory didn't work, picking up a cue from the girl from Chust, who was cold without a *Siddur*."

Rabbi Nisson Wolpin

Focus of Remembering

I HAVE NO TROUBLE explaining to myself why I should overcome instinctive emotional impulse, and stay away from *Yom Hashoah* assemblies. I mourn the losses of World War II, and I do seek a legitimate format for expressing my grief. Yet I cannot participate in these public gatherings and I find my reasons compelling.

But every so often I meet people who are genuinely disturbed — survivors, children of survivors, men and women of conscience, compassion, and concern — and somehow my reasons do not satisfy them: "Why don't you join us in communal mourning? Occasions such as this must cut across denominational differences. We were all equal as victims, and we should all be together as rememberers!" Now I believe I can answer them, thanks to Elie Wiesel.

◆§ Inadequate to the Task

My reasons are simple enough. The day selected for *Yom Hashoah* is the twenty-ninth of Nissan, and *halachah* forbids us to express mourning publicly during the month of Nissan. Even when a person dies during this month, eulogies and tearful commemoratives are postponed. We dwell within the time frame of our calendar, and it does not tolerate tears during the month of redemption.

"How about another day, another month?" The question was posed to the revered Chazon Ish, and he answered very simply: "We in our time are not of great enough stature to establish national days of celebration or mourning." If the Chazon Ish — speaking for the generation of Rabbi Isser Zalman

---

This essay appeared in *The Jewish Observer* of April 1980.

Meltzer, the Gerrer Rebbe, the Belzer Rebbe, the Chebiner Rav, the Brisker Rav — felt inadequate to the task, what are we to say?

So we must make use of the days we already have: Those who know when their town of origin was destroyed can use that date. Telshe, for example, "remembers" on the twentieth day of Tammuz. The rest of us rely on *Tishah B'Av*, the day of national mourning, for our remembering and our grief.

~§ Trading Martyrs For Mediniut

More, there are ideological reasons why I cannot accept the *Yom Hashoah* date. It is not mere happenstance that placed this commemoration just a few days prior to *Yom Haatzmaut*, selecting the day marking the end of the Warsaw Ghetto uprising. The choice of date is a political statement by an Israeli Knesset subcommittee, and I do not subscribe to that statement. For a clearer understanding of the reasoning behind it, take note of its complete name: "*Yom Hashoah Vehagevurah* — Holocaust and Heroism Day," and the message of this juxtaposition is more than implicit. Besides, it has been clearly stated many times: "Until now we Jews suffered a *galus* mentality, and accepted our fate like sheep. We were not worthy of nationhood. With this military action of the Warsaw Ghetto Uprising, however, we've proven our worth. We can fight. And we will again. The long centuries of suffering were closed with this expression of armed might, which in turn ushers in a new era of statehood and dignified nationhood."

How can I accept this without denying the dignity of those of the Six Million that had no recourse to arms, and yet had the courage to preserve their Judaism, and their basic humanity, in the presence of their murderers? Are the men of spiritual might less heroic than the men of the daring Molotov cocktail? Wouldn't I be identifying myself with those who believe in "the might of my arm" if I focus my memorial for the six million martyrs exclusively on those who bore arms to fight? This I refuse to do.

There is more: can I join this memorial celebration without denying nineteen hundred years of stateless nationhood? Was there no Jewish People prior to 1948? It seems that the exponents of *Mediniut* stop at nothing to promote their ideology, and do not even hesitate to exploit the memory of the Six Million, if necessary, to sell their particular brand of heroism, their concept of peoplehood. I, for one, cannot be a party to their designs.

◦§ Where Martyrs Deign to Tread

Then there is a matter of location. The big Memorial Assembly that attracted national attention was held in New York's Temple Emanuel, a place that *halachah* enjoins one not to enter, a place where most of the Warsaw Ghetto martyrs would not only feel like "strangers in an alien place," but would likely cross the avenue to avoid passing in the shadow of its imposing facade. A service in this house of worship is less a tribute than an insult to their memory.

But when welled-up emotions cry out for release, and along comes this widely publicized gathering, arguments spoken from my head do not always sway the hearts of the listeners. So, in the past, my explanations for staying home were not accepted by all *Yom Hashoah* mourners, who asked: "And why weren't *you* there?"

This year, however, my lot was made much easier, thanks to Elie Wiesel, poet of the Holocaust. His words gave *me* words of explanation that others must accept. I quote from the *New York Times*:

> There was a hush as Elie Wiesel, the writer, told of the *shammos*, or beadle, of a small Eastern Europe synagogue who, after each massacre of Jewish townspeople, would say to G-d, "You see, we are still here."
>
> Finally, no one was left but the beadle himself. He ascended the synagogue pulpit and said in a whisper, "You see, I am still here."
>
> "But," he added, "You, G-d of Abraham and Isaac and Jacob, where are You?"

This monologue, of course, is a lie. The *shammos* who survived, no less than the congregants who didn't, had "*Shema Yisrael*" on his lips to the very end. If Mr. Wiesel, in his time of suffering, did not, who are we to judge him? But for his denying the G-d of Avraham, Yitzchok, and Yaakov in the hour of remembering, we do not accept him. We only use his words as corroborating testimony to that which we knew all along: "But alas, there is no fear of G-d in this place" (Avraham to the king of the Philistines).

No less than the *neshamos* of the *kedoshim*, I too cannot enter the portals of a place devoid of fear of G-d. Neither, for that matter, should my colleagues — unless they thoughtlessly follow in the footfalls of Wiesel, like sheep.

Joseph Friedenson

Heroics and "Remembrance" — a New Jewish Religion?

ONE SHOULD NOT wonder why Orthodox Jews do not actively participate *en masse* in the commemoration activities of the Holocaust. Although we all agree that the Holocaust should not be forgotten, we are not in full agreement with "what" and "how" to remember, and what lessons to draw from the Holocaust.

We find it somewhat blasphemous when most remembrance gatherings are focused on the Warsaw Ghetto uprising, or that this uprising is foisted as the central symbol of Jewish martyrdom and heroism during the Holocaust years. While we too certainly honor those who gave their lives in defense of the Jews of the Ghetto, we cannot accept the implied defamation of the honor and dignity of millions of others whose militancy did not express itself in the handling of a rifle. My late father, Reb Eliezer Gershon Friedenson, who gave away his last morsel of bread to the weeping children of the ghetto (see "My Father's Survival in the Warsaw Ghetto"), was no less a hero for not having ever shot a gun. Nor was Rebbetzin Cyly S., who greeted me on my second day at Birkenau:

> As I took my place in the food line and watched the orderly ladle out a portion of soup, I hungrily picked up the bowl — I was literally starving — yet, instinctively I held it at

---

This essay appeared in *The Jewish Observer* of May/June 1983.

a distance. Never had treifah food touched my lips; and hungry as I was, I could not bring myself to taste the soup. Cyly slipped behind me and whispered, "Eat it! Eat it! It's a mitzvah to survive — a mitzvah!" With those words of encouragement, I forced myself to eat, for she was right.

It was not until after the liberation that I learned that she herself never ate treifah food during her entire internment in the camps. Was she less a hero than Mordechai Anczielewicz?

And what of the thousands of young men and women who did not part with their elderly fathers or mothers, although they could have saved themselves, and accompanied them right into the gas-chambers? And those who sacrificed themselves in order that others should live? They were all heroes. Yes, we find this new segregation of heroism at the commemoration reprehensible to our whole *hashkafah* on the Holocaust.

ও§ Completing the Task of the Nazis

Some of us among the Orthodox *She'eiris Hapleitah* find it difficult to commemorate the Holocaust with those for whom "Remembering" has become the new Jewish religion; those who created a "Holocaust Judaism" to substitute for all other tenets of Judaism. Someone who declares that he remembers the Holocaust, but does not bring up his children as Jews, or does not give his children a Jewish education, does not *really* remember the Holocaust. Worse, he finishes that which its designers had set out to accomplish — he carries on the work of the archenemies of our people; he is guilty of complicity with the Nazis who had plotted our disappearance, for a Jew who does not live Jewishly and who makes no effort to perpetuate Judaism is completing Hitler's work in a spiritual sphere. Crying and shouting "Remember!" — remembering just for the sake of remembering — does not impress me.

When others urge us to remember, I must ask: for what purpose? If their purpose is to remind the world of what had happened, then, to be sure, I can go along with them and participate in any Holocaust gathering. But if remembering should also have an inner Jewish purpose, then I must exempt myself from participating, for I find it impossible to go along with a Holocaust remembrance program that leaves out this most vital call for Jewish eternity.

✎ Looking Back ... and Ahead

Looking back at the terrible suffering and destruction, we are saddened beyond words, yet we can draw inspiration from the spiritual heroism of so many. Even while mourning, our sights are invariably set on the future. A Jewish agenda is rich, multifaceted, and does not permit one to be immersed in despair for too long. Even *Tishah B'Av* is followed by *Shabbos Nachamu*, which is the symbol of the indestructability of our people, guaranteed by Divine promise. Our sense of Jewishness does not feed exclusively on the commonality of the shared suffering of the Holocaust. Unfortunately, there are such Jews who do not participate in "the *Yom Tov* cycle," and do not know the joy of *mitzvah* performance, the stimulation of Torah study, inner struggles for improvement, a *drashah*, a *tisch* — these do not exist for them. If all the Jewishness they have is the Holocaust, far be it from me to deny them their sole means of Jewish identity. But to me this black chapter is but part of something much larger, part of something all-encompassing.

I am told that one of the purposes of the Holocaust memorials is to strengthen the link of the Jewish masses to *Eretz Yisrael*. The love for the Land may have a basis for enriching every aspect of Jewishness, but it can never replace Judaism, as the authors of Zionism would have us believe. Those whose Jewish identity consists only of Zionism also have my sympathy, but not my apologies. I have no intention of selling short my full-bodied Jewish identity for something so limited, limited and therefore false.

✎ Our Obligation Remains

But the fact that we cannot always fully participate in the Holocaust memorials organized by secular Jews does not relieve me or my fellow survivors of our obligation to pass on our legacy to future generations — to let them share in the riches of our childhood and witness the destruction of our youth. In 1975, I and several colleagues presented a problem before the *Moetzes Gedolei HaTorah* (Council of Torah Sages) of Agudath Israel of America, as to how the Holocaust should be commemorated.

The meeting was attended by: Rabbi Yitzchok Hutner, Rabbi Nachum Perlow (the late Novominsker Rebbe) and, יבדלו לחיים, Rabbi Moshe Feinstein, Rabbi Yaakov Kamenetzky and Rabbi Yisroel Spira (the Bluzhever Rebbe).

Among other things, the *Moetzes Gedolei HaTorah* placed a *chiyuv*, an obligation, on all *mechanchim* to teach their children about the events of the horrible years of World War II, with special emphasis on the stories of *kiddush Hashem* and *mesiras nefesh* during that period. Educators were also instructed to inform their students about the seventh *Siyum HaShas* of *Daf Yomi* (then about to be convened), which was set aside *l'illuy nishmasam* of the *kedoshim* (in honor of the memory of those martyed).

This decision was proclaimed, but we never fully responded to the responsibility it places upon us. This obligation, still unfulfilled, weighs heavily on our shoulders.

Dr. Bernard Fryshman

Straw Hat in a Sea of Black

SEVERAL CHAPTERS HERE find fault with secular-sponsored memorial gatherings dedicated to the Six Million martyrs of *Churban Europa*. While the lack of gatherings with a Torah basis has yet to be corrected on a broad scale, some do take place — like the one I participated in Williamsburg.

This time it was to be a trip to Portland; as usual I was bedecked in my summer "going-to-meeting" outfit: light suit, sedate tie, and light — almost white — straw hat. I entered the Pupa Beis Midrash at 5:10 a.m., and forty-five minutes later I was on the way out, to my car.

It dawned upon me that even in Williamsburg, 6 a.m. is a little early for everybody to be in *Shul*. From all directions men streamed into the doors I had just left. Curious, I followed them back inside and found myself among a huge crowd of *chassidim* waiting to begin the *Selichos* of the twentieth of Sivan. The person next to me moved his *Selichos* book over, and soon after, there were hundreds of black-hatted Pupa *chassidim*, and one light-beige-straw-hatted Jew, saying *Selichos*.

By 6:30 a.m., I was counting the number of Pizmonim left; by 6:40 I was seeking a way to leave unobtrusively; by 6:44, I was thinking up excuses to offer my fellow commissioners.

At 6:45 a.m., the late Pupa Rav himself — in spite of advanced age and infirm health — went to the *Amud* to say the special *Kail Molay Rachamim* (memorial prayer) relating to the *gezeiros* (decrees) of *Tach v'Tat* and to the *Churban*. With every word, with every *krechtz* (sigh), I could sense the *Rav* reliving for

---

This essay appeared in The Jewish Observer of January 1984.

his *Kehillah* what had taken place. With every *pasuk*, he took those of us who had not lived through the horrors along with him as he surveyed the *Churban* that befell the Jews of Europe.

I have, of course, seen the displays, the visual evidence; I have read the books and heard the stories of what happened to the Jews between 1939 and 1945. I consider myself somewhat unemotional in my outlook, yet I did not dare look at my watch for fear that the blurring of the dial would betray — to me — that there were tears in my eyes.

> *There is no point in going into detail about my subsequent hair-raising car ride. Suffice it to say, the fact that I arrived at the airport safely and on time, is attributable to factors outside my control and understanding.*

There are no "Holocaust" buildings, exhibits, monuments, or archives in Williamsburg. Pupa shows no films, holds no speeches, convenes no conferences. Yet months later, the memory of how this Torah community commemorated the *zeicher* of its *Kedoshim* persists and tugs.

VII.
Through the Eyes of the Media

Rabbi Nosson Scherman

The Real Elie Wiesel

ELIE WIESEL was paying a visit to the *Vizhnitzer Rebbe.*
Twenty years had gone by since he had last visited the *Rebbe.* It had been in Hungary, and he had been brought by his mother to receive the *Rebbe's* blessing. In the intervening years of Holocaust and horror, Hungary's Jews were swept away. A way of life went up to its Maker through the chimneys of Auschwitz. Mankind was given the opportunity to face, if it dared, its potential for bestiality. Elie Wiesel was no longer a *chassid* when he faced his former *Rebbe* and told him that he was writing stories about things that had happened or could have happened.

The Rebbe leaned forward as if to measure me up and said with more sorrow than anger: "That means you are writing lies!"

"Things are not that simple, Rebbe. Some events do take place, but are not true: others are, although they never occurred."

These simply stated words are, indeed, not simple. They are the creed of the novelist, and if he can capture the truth in things that never occurred, then he is truly a creator, rather than a mere spinner of yarns. That Wiesel is a seeker of truth cannot be denied. He seeks meaning in the Holocaust and in what has become of his people. His search is made with agonizing intensity and, if any human being can make his pen an instrument of torture, it is Elie Wiesel. But while he is obviously in search of meanings, he presents himself as a witness whose mission is to testify. And an objective witness he is not.

This examination of some of the writings of the "dean" of Holocaust literature appeared in *The Jewish Observer* of March 1971.

☙ "Making It" on the Literary Scene

With his *Beggar in Jerusalem*, which appeared in English in 1970, Wiesel finally "made it" as a novelist, known and respected by the general public. After seven books that were admired by critics, but little noted by the masses, his name began appearing regularly on the barometer of literary distinction, the *New York Times'* Best Seller List, and public libraries accorded him the honor of placing his *Beggar* on their Rental Collection shelves. Wiesel, too honest to court popularity at the price of compromising his agony, had stumbled upon a sure-fire formula by letting his search take him to the *Kotel* and the Six-Day War. Small wonder that the public was willing to pay a nickel a day to rent *Beggar in Jerusalem* from libraries that carried none of his earlier books. And small wonder that Wiesel found his name in the pantheon of popular Jewish writers, alongside Bellow, Malamud, and Roth.

Yet, in the hopes of the Torah Jew, Wiesel should have far transcended the others. The Torah Jew looked on in horror — or simply looked the other way — while the American Jewish literary establishment became the object of adoration as never before. Its creations — confused, self-hating, assimilated protagonists with meager Yiddish vocabularies of profanities and high-calorie foods — became a new kind of urban-American-culture hero. In the wake of the anti-heroes of these novels, non-Jewish intellectuals found their own image — brooding, alienated, complex, estranged outsiders. Even as WASP-ish a writer as John Updike felt compelled to appropriate a Jewish hero into his novel, *Bech*. The distinguished critic Alfred Kazin says, "I don't think that there has been anywhere in the history of the Jewish people anything quite like the influence that Jewish intellectuals have exerted on American culture."

Perhaps the adventures of the *Herzogs* and the *Portnoys* are real, whether or not they ever occurred. For many to whom Jewishness is an unchosen, uncomfortable accident of birth, they probably *are* real, but the rest of us can ignore them at little peril. Problems the Orthodox Jew certainly has, but among them is not that he is "an American who happens to be a Jew," wondering why it had to happen to him.

Elie Wiesel is another matter. We cannot fail to notice him. The *Vizhnitzer Rebbe* remembered him as "the grandson of Dodye Feig," one of his leading prewar *chassidim*. He entered the sealed boxcar to Auschwitz as "Dodye Feig's grandson," and emerged from hell emaciated in body and spirit, hunted and haunted by memories, questions, and doubts. For all his shocking blasphemies and heresies, he was still Dodye Feig's grandson. His life would be easier if he could forget that, and turn his Torah past into a money-making tool in the service of his immense literary talent; purveyors of Jewish nostalgia live well nowadays. But Elie Wiesel apparently does not know how to take the easy way out. He has much to say, much that we would want to accept and, yet, much that we must reject. But it is most difficult to ignore him especially since he has become the rage in so many religious circles as well as among the literati.

ৰ্ব্ The Man

Elie Wiesel was born in the Transylvanian town of Sighet in 1928. Jews comprised forty per cent of its population of twenty-five thousand, but they were its brain and soul if not its body; they *were* Sighet. Wiesel grew up in *yeshivos* and *batei midrashim*, becoming an accomplished Talmudic scholar and an aspiring student of *Kabbalah.* In 1944, the German army occupied the soil of its Hungarian ally and, soon afterwards, the deportations of Jews began. Together with his parents and his sisters, Wiesel rode the one-way railroad to Auschwitz. From Auschwitz, he was transferred to Buchenwald, where he hung on to life until the liberation. Along the way, Wiesel was separated from his mother and sisters, and he watched his adored father die a slow death from starvation.

The Allies wanted to send him back to Sighet when the sun began to shine again, but Elie, then seventeen years old, refused to go. American G.I.'s, weaned on patriotism and love of country (this was 1945, not 1971), could not understand how someone could resist the urge to "go home." But Wiesel *had* no home. Sighet was no more.

Any doubts he may have acquired about his reluctance to return were dispelled years later when he returned to Sighet as a tourist. The story appears in fragments in his writings — in his novels as he imagined it and in his memoirs as he experienced it. (It is often hard to separate Wiesel-the-novelist from Wiesel-the-autobiographer. In his work, truth and fiction fuse, because to him, fiction *is* truth; he is interested only in his vision of truth, whether or not it actually occurred.) Sighet was gone and Hungary was no longer his country. He had seen city and country cast out its Jews not because the Nazis forced them to, but because the Nazis supplied them with an initiative they had always hoped for, but could never muster up on their own. Thousands of Jews were herded into the town square and marched to the boxcars while erstwhile friends and neighbors looked on in indifference or in glee, pausing for a time, only to return to their daily routines or to loot the homes and businesses of those who had always been unwelcome exiles, despite their delusions.

The seventeen-year-old survivor was all alone, without family, country or even language because he made up his mind not to use the tongue of the nation that could not even manage a modicum of compassion for the loss of a slice of life itself. Did he still have his faith? His G-d? He did not know. He had hoped to find them again, but he was not certain.

So he went to Paris. In snatches from the foggy truth-fiction world of his novels, we find him walking through the streets, getting an education, scrounging from Jewish welfare organizations, starving himself to the point of physical collapse, haunted by memories, becoming first a successful journalist and then a novelist in French, his adopted language and the one in which he still writes.

The Writer

The world's apathy while six million died is, in its own way, as great a crime as the massacres themselves. The current attitude is to divorce the "Final Solution to the Jewish Problem" from its roots in anti-Semitism and to homogenize it into the shameful history of man's inhumanity to man.

The Allies had their Dresden: they cold-bloodedly devastated a German city of beauty and culture, a city with no military significance, as an act of reprisal during World War II.

The Americans had Hiroshima. And now there is My Lai.

The gypsies, too, were victims of Hitler.

Nowadays, it is unfashionable to single out the fate of the Jews and hurl it at the sensibilities of the world. But with horror and disillusion Wiesel recoils from the charge that Jews are exaggerating their victim status of the 1939-45 years in order to gain license to twist the arms of world leaders at the expense of today's persecuted peoples, the Third World.

"What was so unique about your experience?" people ask. "Others died as well!" If others died, if man is naturally aggressive, if no one has clean hands, if even the Jews can be tarred with the brush of their murderers, then those who killed and those who refused to take notice can hold their heads high again. They can rail at the temerity of the victim who dares remind them of their guilt. Small wonder that "good" Germans have made a best seller of the works of the Frenchman, Paul Rassinier, whose three books insist that the "death camp" stories are gross exaggerations concocted by Jews for political purposes, and substantiated by the victorious Allies to justify their own criminal excesses during wartime and occupation. Small wonder that critics and reviewers cannot quite decide what to do with Elie Wiesel.

On the one hand he is acclaimed as *"this generation's only prophet"* (Andre Schwartzbart); as an author *"whose work justified a whole literature" (Book World);* as one next to whom *"other literature seems meaningless" (The Saturday Review),* and as *"a writer on a plane almost entirely uninhabited except by him"* (S. N. Behrman). As the creator of a *"mythology whose truth is searing and undeniable,"* Wiesel is one of the few authors who have become so "in" that they are above even legitimate literary criticism. That is, as long as he inhabits his shadow world of truth-fiction, and does not venture into the arena of the here and now.

But Wiesel also commits the sin of telling the world that its crime of apathy during the Holocaust imposes upon it the obligation of atonement; that its continued apathy gives Jews the right to live in their country, to have their Wall, even their war. Here, the followers part company with the "Prophet." Let him preach about the Dark Age of 1933-1945, but how dare he suggest that his sermons can apply to terrorism against British soldiers in the Palestine of the Forties or against the poor, oppressed Palestinians in the Seventies! Prophets may expect honor in cathedrals, not in the market place.

✥ The Testimony

The world would like to forget its sins, but Wiesel will not let it. He is a *witness*. This is a theme that appears throughout his writing. Someone must remember what once was, and how cruelly it was snuffed out. Jews in the camps risked their lives to salvage scraps of evidence, to sear every honor into their memories. Wiesel tells how as a youngster he was prophetically told by a *Rebbe* that he would see things beyond belief and he would somehow have to make people believe them. He used to think that the knowledge of what the human being can do when he becomes a human beast would shock people into change. He is saddened now by the realization that he is accepted as a mythologist, but not as a therapist; his tales are worth notice — even at the cost of a nickel a day — as long as they do not become uncomfortably close to real life.

Still, witness he must be, and most of all, witness to the crime of the onlooker. In perhaps his most powerful novel, *The Town Beyond The Wall*, Michael, the hero, returns illegally to Szerencsevaros, his home town. There he is arrested, tortured, and imprisoned by the Communist police. Why has he returned? To find the owner of a face that symbolized all those who watched, without emotion, as Jews became "objects and carefully numbered victims." He found these spectators incomprehensible. He could understand the executioners, the haters, the victims, but he could not understand the indifferent.

It happened on a Shabbos. Jews were being herded in the courtyard to await deportation. Without food or water, they endured beatings, hunger, and exhaustion, waiting for the train to hell. The misery is symbolized by Michal — Wiesel's eight-year-old little sister pleading for water that no one could give her.

A few passers-by; they averted their faces; the more sensitive bowed their heads.

It was then that I saw him. A face in the window across the way ... It was gazing out, reflecting no pity, no pleasure, no shock, not even anger or interest ... What? Men are going to die? That's not my fault, is it now? I didn't make the decision. For seven days ... he, standing behind the curtains, watched. The police beat women and children, he did not stir. It was no concern of his. He was neither victim nor executioner. A spectator, that's what he was. He wanted to live in peace and quiet.

For the onlooker Wiesel has only contempt — not hatred, just contempt! "Your duty was clear: you had to choose. To fight us or to help. In the first case, I would have hated you; in the second, loved. You never left your window: I have only contempt for you."

The very fact of their survival proves the guilt of the onlookers and earns them contempt. Those under the Nazis would have gone to the death camps as well had they earned sainthood by rising to the challenge. Those in the free world might have had the Auschwitz rail-line bombed — or given Joel Brand money to buy lives — or convinced Pope Pius XII that some sins were greater than lending comfort to Communists or jeopardizing the Church's diplomatic position. Or they might have become very unpopular in at least making the attempt. But they didn't and the survival of some of the victims is a discomfiting reminder of what happened to the less fortunate.

◆§ The Blasphemies

One cannot blame the Gentile world for wishing the memory of 1939-45 would go away like a bad dream. The memory is an indictment of Western civilization as a whole because the bulk of the exterminations was not carried out by evil madmen, but by very "ordinary, respectable technicians" like Adolph Eichmann. The real story of what happened becomes all the more shocking because it must make all cultured, loving family-men wonder whether they would have reacted any differently had the Six Million lives been placed in their laps, or what they would have done had the face in the window been theirs. What would have dominated: indifference? humanitarianism? anti-Semitism?

So the world needs eloquent, insistent, persuasive witnesses. As a witness Wiesel performs a necessary task. But he does not stop there. He goes beyond describing what happened and "how it felt" and enters the jury box, and dons the judge's robes. He dares to say that because he can find no purpose in the Holocaust, then there *was* no purpose; because he cannot see how the Hand of G-d could strike down the innocent, then either G-d stands condemned or does not exist.

The "onlooker" is not only the human face in the window. Not content with bearing witness against humanity, Wiesel stands in the court of his conscience also to condemn the Creator for looking on and allowing it to happen. But this he does not do with the pleading entreaties of a Reb Levi Yitzchak of Berditchev. Instead: "A Messiah who is able to come, and yet at Auschwitz failed to come, is not to be conceived."

There are others who have preached heresies that grow from the Auschwitz experience. We, as Torah Jews, need not respond to them any more than we need respond to the peddlers of alienation, assimilation, and Jewish self-hate merely because they are Jewish and purport to speak for Jews. Negating the Deity or exchanging Him for an idol — more indulgent, understanding, and pliable — is an old tactic. Our Sages told us long ago, "The Jews worshiped idols only to permit themselves to satisfy their lust for adultery" *(Sanhedrin* 63b). Deniers of G-d have always been dignifying desire under the guide of a philosophy or theology; so what else is new?

Wiesel is different. When he associates an end to his belief with a hanging on a gallows in *Night,* we must be doubly shocked, because this is Dodye Feig's grandson talking; because if there had been no war, we could picture him today as a distinguished rabbi, *rosh yeshivah,* or community leader, or as a great writer leading the way in bridging the communications gap with our young and old alike, who are living in a world awash with messages and stimuli so foreign to the very essence of a Torah life. So we experience a severe jolt at hearing Dodye Feig's offspring replace "Blessed ... (is) the true Judge" with words of doubt and expressions of an unconsummated search.

The shock is then compounded by a deep disappointment. Not only does Wiesel fail to give new expression to hallowed values, he even fails to be the eloquent witness we so desperately need. For by attempting to be more — the interpreter and judge and jury, as well — he is less. The destruction is still without its articulate witness, and we must continue to bear the suffering of the Holocaust, and to carry on our attempt to miraculously rise from its ashes without the help of his genius.

No Right to Condemn

In a very real sense, Wiesel is as much a casualty of the camps as any of the Six Million. It would be very easy — and very dishonest — to dismiss him as a spiritual deviant and focus on the less troubled. His problem, however, is not his alone. He broods more, he remembers more, he articulates more, but he is not alone in looking for a purpose in a mind-boggling monstrosity. Others gave up the search and cast away their faith with it. He admits that he *may* have lost his faith, but he wants to get it back. He once hoped for the coming of *Moshiach,* he says, while now he hopes to regain that faith again.

Surely we have no right to condemn so troubled a soul. After all, we Americans were *here.* We were unborn, or children, or concerned with ration stamps and victory. We did not know, or could not believe, or were too busy to comprehend. A few of us were earning the gratitude of eternity by being in the front lines of relief work — battling government, the establishment, and apathy. But we were still *here* and it is all too easy for us to find meanings and purpose in someone *else's* suffering.

This argument is legitimate, but it is often carried a step further: "Because we were not victims of the Holocaust we do not have the right to find abstract meaning in it; nor do we have the right to criticize one who did suffer, who lost everything he had — even his belief, one who saw G-d staring indifferently through the window and later saw not at all."

But we *are* victims of the Holocaust. Whatever its purpose and meaning, it was a message to the entire Jewish people. The ways of G-d may be mysterious, but it is for us to decipher His message, even if it is more than we can bear. To criticize the Wiesels of the world is not to say that we would have been more virtuous had we been in Auschwitz instead of America. The Talmud *(Kesubos* 33a) says that if Channanyah, Mishael and Azaryah — who were willing to submit themselves to a fiery death in Nevuchadnezzar's furnaces — had been tortured instead of being condemned to a relatively quick death, they would have chosen to bow to the king's statue. If that had happened, however we might feel compassion for three great men whose resistance was broken, their weakness would not have legitimized their act. Nor would it mean that men should or must break on the rack.

Wiesel's outcry is a gut reaction; one who denies it courts vilification as a speaker of cheap talk, a philosopher from afar. At the same time gut reactions are usually violent and often wrong. Would the world have even a fragile peace today if every provocation produced a violent reaction?

৵ Those Who Do Testify

Unquestionably, the calamity of Europe demands interpretation, but we must relegate the search for its meaning to only the greatest. The surviving few bore the awesome responsibility of rebuilding the ramparts of Torah life and education in America and Israel. Those rebuilders of Jewish life responded to the Holocaust as eloquently as Wiesel. They too are "prophets." They too are "on a plane inhabited by few." Beside their accomplishments, too, does "all other literature seem meaningless."

Their prophecy is not an elegant articulation compressed between the covers of a book. It is, therefore, a lesser source of immediate satisfaction because one cannot read their message, put it down, and contemplate on its call to hope or hopelessness, life or death, longing or dismissal. They are not distilling life into words; they are creating new life in the form of new generations. They are conceiving great-grandchildren for the Dodye Feigs, worthy of their stilled aspirations. So their story is still unfinished, still imperfect, still developing because they are grafting Torah onto new conditions, new lives, new countries. They have laid the foundation for a revival of Torah life in countries and under conditions that were as unconducive to the task as could be imagined. But they are succeeding where the literary creator has failed.

Wiesel seeks a rational philosophical understanding of *Churban* Europe. In "The Loss of Europe's Torah Centers" (elsewhere in this volume), Rabbi Eliyahu Dessler deals with aspects of such an attempt at determining its meaning. But the work of *yeshivos* and *kehillos* are an unverbalized expression of this understanding. They are a response. To expire in a bed of hopelessness would be to complete Hitler's work by adding our spiritual suicide to his physical genocide. In his later works, Wiesel finally does find some hope and inspiration in the drama of soldiers trading their lives for the Wall, and in throngs of Russian young people defying Red darkness with improvised torches and a cry resounding across centuries, the cry of "*Am Yisrael Chai!* — The Nation of Israel lives!"

Israel will indeed live. But a life needs more than moments of high drama. Those who are truly restoring the losses of the Holocaust are succeeding with little fanfare and much quiet heroism. Yet, in spite of his wavering convictions, Wiesel has captured much of the same quiet heroism, the kind that is so natural and unassuming that it takes a man of Wiesel's sensitivity to see how profound it truly is.

— Rosh Hashanah and Yom Kippur in Auschwitz, with Jews pouring out their hearts in prayer, and wishing each other "*Gut Yor! Gut Yor!*"

— A "madman" keeping up the spirits of his cellmates by trying to convince them he is *Moshiach*, and trying to save others by confessing to a crime he did not commit.

— A former *rosh yeshivah* and a former *yeshivah* student digging side by side in Buchenwald while maintaining their belief and sanity by learning a *blatt Gemara* together, by heart.

— A *shtiebel* on Manhattan's West Side performing the "miracle of keeping the tradition alive" and, with their warmth, love, and brotherhood, forcing free the tears that had been imprisoned within the Auschwitz survivor for a generation after.

※ ※ ※

In *The Town Beyond the Wall*, unfortunate Michael, rotting in his cell, finds meaning in life by trying to revive in a tragic mute the will to live. He is speaking to us; let us listen. Perhaps Eliezer Wiesel, his creator, will listen, too:

"To flee to some sort of Nirvana — whether through a considered indifference or through a sick apathy — is to oppose humanity in the most absurd, useless, and comfortable manner possible. A man is a man only when he is among men. It's harder to remain human than to try to leap beyond humanity.

"Jump onto the stage, mingle with the actors, and perform — you, too. Don't stay at the window ...

"One day the ice will break and you'll begin to smile. Then you'll shake yourself and the shadows will fall away from you as the fever leaves a sick man: You'll open your eyes and you'll say to yourself, 'I feel better, the sickness is gone. I'm different.' And that will be proof that man survives. That he passes himself along."

Michael had come to the end of his strength. Before him the night was receding, as on a mountain, before dawn.

The other bore the Biblical name of Eliezer, which means, "G-d has granted my prayer."

Rabbi Joseph Elias

Dealing with "Churban Europa"

THE LAST YEARS HAVE seen an ever-growing flood of publications centering on the Nazi era and the destruction of European Jewry; autobiographical accounts by survivors,[1] learned studies and surveys of the period,[2] monographs dealing with particular localities and episodes,[3] or specific aspects of what has come to be known as the Holocaust.[4] If we also think of the proliferation of courses and chairs in Holocaust studies, research

---

This review article appeared in *The Jewish Observer* of October 1977.

1. G. Korman (ed.), *Hunter and Hunted* (Viking, 1973), is an anthology of autobiographical accounts of various phases of the Holocaust;

    S.B. Unsdorfer, *Stories of Simcha* (S.Z. Hoff, 1975); the first half of this book contains recollections and stories of the Holocaust largely drawn from the author's own experiences (one of his previous works was *The Yellow Star);*

    B. Bar Oni, *The Vapor* (Visual Impact Inc., 1976), recounts the struggle for survival of a Polish girl, first in the ghetto and then among the partisans;

    R. Klueger — P. Mann, *The Last Escape* (Doubleday, 1973), describes the efforts to rescue Roumanian Jews through illegal emigration to Palestine.

2. L.S. Dawidowicz, *The War Against the Jews* (Holt, Rinehart Winston, 1975), represents a comprehensive survey of "The Final Solution" and how it was put into effect;

    R. Hilberg, *The Destruction of European Jewry*, is a scientific study of the Nazi machinery for destroying the Jewish people;

    L.L. Synder, *Encyclopedia of the Third Reich* (McGraw Hill, 1976), is a useful reference work, though much of its material is inconsequential.

3. D. Kranzler, *Japanese, Nazis, and Jews* (Yeshiva University Press, 1976), deals with the Jewish refugee community of Shanghai;

    G. Thomas and M.M. Witts, *Voyage of the Damned* (Fawcett, 1974) is the story of the refugee boat St. Louis;

    M. Dank, *The French Against the French* (Lippincott, 1974), deals with the battle between the French underground and the French collaborators, only touches incidentally on Jewish aspects;

    J. Garlinski, *Fighting Auschwitz* (Fawcett, 1975), is the story of the resistance movement in Auschwitz ;

    E. Papanek, *Out of the Fire* (William Morrow, 1975), tells of the rescue of refugee children from France to the United States.

4. Dr. H.J. Zimmels, *The Echoes of the Nazi Holocaust in Rabbinic literature* (Ktav, 1975);

    M. Prager, *Sparks of Glory* (Mesorah, 1985) and M.D. Weinstock, *Light in the*

centers and archives, it becomes quite clear that — forty years after the event — there is a renewed concern with the Holocaust.

There are a number of reasons for this phenomenon, some of them not very laudable. Holocaust studies represent an academic "growth area," and opportunists have quickly grasped what this implies in prestige, status, and academic opportunities. There is an element of political expediency (as pointed out by Rabbi Hutner) in some of the harping on the events of 1939-1945, and also an obvious effort on the part of some to exploit them ideologically.

At the same time it is surely true that the terrible wounds of the Nazi era have not yet healed. (If any proof is needed, a recent study about the effect of the Holocaust survivors' trauma on their children amply provides it.) There is a need to come to grips with what happened, and some time had to pass after the event before efforts could really be made in this direction. Perhaps there applies on our level, too, what our Sages told about Rabbi Yehudah HaNasi and Rabbi Yochanan: Rabbi Yochanan explained a certain verse in *Eichah* in sixty ways, whilst Rabbi Yehudah HaNasi only had twenty-four interpretations — not because he, who lived much closer to the destruction of the Temple, had less to say, but because he remembered more and therefore was silenced by the intensity of his grief *(Yerushalmi, Taanis* 4).

However, if we have really reached the point where the *Churban Europa* can be discussed meaningfully, and we must be grateful to those sincerely trying to do so, we must admit that a vast part of what has been written falls woefully short of this objective. In his essay Rabbi Yaakov Weinberg pointed out that the Holocaust was unique in that it was the first overwhelming catastrophe in Jewish history where Jews asked, "Why did G-d do this to us?," rather than "What did G-d want us to learn from

---

Darkness (Horizon Publ., 1972), contain stories of *Kiddush Hashem* during the Holocaust;

A.D. Morse, *While Six Million Died* (Discovery Press, 1967), details the procrastination of the American government and its resistance to the rescue of Jews;

M. Shonfeld, *The Holocaust Victims Accuse* (Bnei Yeshivos Publications, New York City, 1977), deals with the guilt of the secular Jewish and Zionist leadership in the destruction of European Jewry; incidentally, the English translation of the book has been enlarged with some questionable additions, and the language used by the translator takes away somewhat from the impact of the material.

G. Sereny, *Into that Darkness — From Mercy Killing to Mass Murder* (McGraw Hill, 1974), is the story of the creation of the Nazi murder machine;

I. Trunk, *Judenrat* (MacMillan, 1972), is the definitive study of the Jewish councils established — and exploited — by the Nazis;

T. Des Pres, *The Survivors*, an anatomy of life in the Death Camps (Pocket Books, 1977), seeks to determine how some survived the camps.

this experience?" Challenging G-d, and sitting in judgment on Divine Justice, comes naturally to modern man who considers himself the measure of all things; but it is not only terribly wrong — it is an exercise in futility, and blinds man to the true meaning of what happened.

The Inadequacy of Human Interpretation

It is obviously a futile effort, for man can never plumb the depths of Divine counsel. "Where were you when I founded this earth?" G-d asks of Job, driving home to him the limitations of human insight *(Job 38:4)*. In truth, the Jew — conscious of the infinite wisdom of the Creator — always accepted His judgment. He was sure in his conviction of the ultimate meaningfulness of all that happened, and therefore could concentrate on squeezing out of it whatever meaning he could discern in it. In contrast, secular man, approaching the Holocaust with an anthropocentric perspective, is unable to cope with it. The political, social, and psychological concepts, which are the sum total of his intellectual equipment, are insufficient to deal with what happened; and if he is clear sighted enough to perceive this, he must confess that the Holocaust is totally and uniquely unintelligible to him, since he cannot view it in the context of a Divinely guided history, and he will even assert that it has no meaning at all.[5]

Thus, it is not surprising that in most of the books that have appeared in recent years, data are accumulated, experiences are recorded, theories are put forward, but there remains not only the unspeakable pain but the inability to penetrate below the surface of what happened. We are left with a riddle which challenges man's very inability to function (this is particularly noticeable in the studies of the survivors and the books written by them).[6] Yet, there are some works, written from a Torah perspective, that

---

5. Wiesel's words (in *Legends of Our Time*) give expression to this: "What Auschwitz embodied has [no meaning]. The executioner killed for nothing, the victim died for nothing. No G-d ordered the one to prepare the stake, nor the other to mount it ... At Auschwitz the sacrifices were without point, without faith, without divine inspiration."

6. D. Rabinowitz, *New Lives* (Knopf, 1976), a study of survivors of the Holocaust living in America, reflects the multiplicity of feelings and the uncertainty and confusion of goals which characterize so many who have managed to survive and who have had no roots in Jewish tradition (the same impression emerges from G. Sereny's *Into That Darkness*, and from one of the abovementioned studies, reported in an article in the New York Times Magazine of June 19, 1977; *Heirs of the Holocaust* by Helen Epstein).

In contrast, anybody familiar with the Orthodox communities created by Holocaust survivors in this country will readily agree that, however traumatic their war experiences were, they do not suffer from the same lack of purpose or uncertainty about the meaningfulness of their life.

throw a penetrating light on the era of the Holocaust and, even more interesting, when we dig deeper into the mass of the Holocaust literature, we find sparks of the truth in almost every place, which help us toward an understanding of what this era may have been meant to teach us.

To be sure, we are not able to say that the *Churban Europa* happened for this or that reason; just as in the case of individual bereavement we must silently bend our head, so too when it is multiplied not a thousandfold but six-millionfold. All we can affirm is that death — or suffering — is not meaningless, but finds its fulfillment in that world for which our life is only a preparation. Yet, having made this clear, we can and must not only remember what happened, but seek to learn from it what we can.

In searching for a clue to the meaning of events, *Gedolei Torah* have pointed to the coincidence between — on one hand — the rise of alien ideologies within the Jewish people and — on the other hand — the murderous hostility of the Nazis and the indifference of the other nations. Some have pointed to the fact that the *Churban Europa* began in Berlin, the birthplace of the *Haskalah* and assimilation, and have seen in the Nazi rejection of the Jew the answer to the dream of being like our gentile neighbors. Others have stressed the emergence of Jewish secular nationalism; when there arose the idea that Jews are a nation like all others, denying their Divine role, the other nations could rise against it with impunity.[7] These interpretations seek to provide some key to the disaster that befell us. When we now turn to the books that have appeared, we find evidence that the actual course of this disaster constantly manifested the factors we pointed to: the failure of secular Jewish leadership, whether assimilationist or nationalist, and the unrelenting hostility of the nations. We will try to illustrate this pattern by reference to the attitude of the non-Jewish world, the policies of the Jewish leadership in the free world, and the situation under the Nazis.

✑ The Attitude of the Non-Jewish World

While Six Million Died by Arthur Morse has become the standard text on the perfidy of the American government in professing sympathy and solidarity with the cause of saving Europe's Jews while at the same time doing everything possible to

---

7. See Rabbi A. Wolf, *Hatekufah Ubayosayha*, pp. 68-77, for a summary of different intepretations, as well as Rabbi N. Scherman's article based on it, in this volume.

play down and cover up the tragedy and block any effective rescue work. The author notes that over one million places on the United States immigration quota were left unfilled in the years 1933 to 1945, and the role of Cordell Hull and his henchmen is fully aired. (Their attitude to rescue is also highlighted in *The Voyage of the Damned,* by Thomas and Witts, the tragic account of the odyssey of the St. Louis whose passengers were refused admission to Cuba and — refused a haven in the United States of America — finally found refuge in European countries where most of them were later seized by the Nazis.) Roosevelt's personal role is not adequately explored, however, and Stephen Wise and the Jewish establishment are portrayed as working loyally for the rescue of the European Jews, as we shall see, a picture far from the truth.

Into that Darkness by G. Sereny is an extremely important book, both on account of its main theme, the creation of the extermination apparatus, and because of the various related topics explored by the author. Mrs. Sereny traces the life history of Franz Stangl and his rise from participation in the early Nazi-euthanasia program to the command of the Treblinka extermination camp. She shows how the euthanasia project of the Thirties served as a preparation for the later elaborate programs to destroy vast numbers of lives, and she shows how the Vatican's tolerance of Nazi "mercy killing" opened the door to the full horror of Nazi murder. Incidentally, she confirms what has widely been suspected, that the much ballyhooed, official Vatican series of documents on the war, presently being published, deliberately omits documents incriminating the Pope and establishing his early knowledge of the "Final Solution"; the author herself saw these documents in Polish diplomatic archives. At the same time she throws light on the help given to fleeing Nazi war criminals in Rome after the war.

A point frequently made by Sereny — that the non-Jewish population in Eastern Europe constantly betrayed Jews to the Nazis — also emerges from many of the autobiographical accounts of survivors, such as Bryna Bar Oni's moving story, *The Vapor,* of her effort to survive in hiding, threatened not only by the Nazis but also by her Polish neighbors and even by many partisan units. (She became one of twenty-three survivors, out of three hundred and seventy who had fled the ghetto of her hometown.) But this was not only a problem in Eastern Europe. In France extraordinary efforts were made by many Frenchmen, and particularly the *Maquis* (underground), to aid the Jews, as shown for instance in J. Joffo's account, *A Bag of Marbles*. Yet, at the same time — as shown in M. Dank's *The French Against the French* — there were sizeable elements that collaborated with the Nazis, especially the French police. This is particularly understandable if we remember that Petain obtained the consent of the Pope to the anti-Jewish legislation which he adopted and which formed the basis for the persecution of the Jews in France.

If the war years saw so much gentile callousness toward the "Final Solution," we should not be surprised about the postwar tolerance for Nazi criminals and neo-Nazis evident not only in Germany but also in the United States and other countries. Beate Klarsfeld's *Whoever They May Be* is the autobiography of a German who turned Nazi-hunter; from its pages there emerges a sense of futility which forces us to face the fact that neither the preaching of humanitarianism and enlightenment nor the fight against Jew-haters will solve the problem of the Jew. The fact that the wave of revulsions over Nazi crimes, which rose at the end of the war, spent itself so quickly, underlines the deeper significance of the perennial tension between the Jew and the nations; we are meant to recognize that we are different, and must shoulder the burden of our sacred mission. We must see the attitude of the nations as rooted in the depths of historical destiny — *"It is a law that Eisav hates Yaakov"* — and serves as a scourging rod, to recall Yaakov to a sense of his unique and lonely task as G-d's messenger. Not only the Nazi crimes, which are beyond all human understanding, but the betrayal of the Jews by most of the free nations can only be explained in this way.

⇨ The Role of the Jewish Establishment

It is easier to be enraged by the failure of the nations and churches than it is to face the facts about the Jewish role in the Holocaust. Ben Hecht's *Perfidy* shook the Jewish world when it appeared; yet it was a toned-down version of the original. "If this had been published, the world would have learned that the leaders of the Jewish people — the best-known, most respected leaders of Zionism — were actually criminals," said Ben Hecht. "One who fought with all his might against our rescue and publicity campaigns was Rabbi Stephen Wise, president of the various Jewish congresses." Since Elie Weisel recorded this interview in 1959, so much material has come to light that it is almost unbelievable that Stephen Wise's name is remembered anywhere with anything but shame. (G. Korman's introduction to *Hunter and Hunted*, whose publication was sponsored by the Bnai Brith Commission on Jewish Adult Education, still presents him as the champion of rescue efforts.)

The failure of the Jewish establishment is well documented not only by Moshe Shonfeld but also by others. It was due partly to the love of its leaders for publicity and pronouncements, while, at the same time, showing incredible pettiness and lack of imagination or sensitivity in dealing with the immensely urgent demands of rescue. The handling of the St. Louis is one instance; and another is the failure to help Ernst Papanek to rescue most of his orphans from Europe — the picture of the American organizations and their attitudes, drawn in *Out of the Fire*, is truly devastating.

More fundamental, however, were two basic premises to which the secular establishment was firmly committed: (1) the only way to aid the Jews of Europe is to help the Allies win the war, and (2) nothing may be done for rescue which might in any way interfere with the efforts for a Jewish state in Palestine (Shonfeld, from whom the passages quoted in the next few paragraphs are taken).

The first premise quoted was based on quasi-patriotic considerations, and (as explicit in the statements of Saly Mayer in Switzerland and Chief Rabbi Ehrenpreisz in Sweden) on the fears of assimilated leaders that a wave of uncouth, backward Eastern European immigrants would sweep into the Western World and endanger the status of the acculturated modern Jews. These leaders resolutely closed their eyes to the fact that by the time an Allied victory occurred practically no Jews would be left to be saved. Stephen Wise in 1943 effectively blocked a promising chance to save seventy thousand Roumanian Jews. In 1944, when public pressure built up for the creation of a special War Refugee Board, he testified before Congress against this proposal, and when four hundred Rabbis, led by Rabbi Eliezer Silver and Rabbi Avrohom Kalmanowitz, marched on Washington in support of the idea, it was Stephen Wise and his associates who persuaded Roosevelt against receiving the Rabbis.

In his fine study of the Jewish community in Shanghai, D. Kranzler points out that the only place on earth where German Jews could go without a visa in the Nineteen Thirties was Shanghai — until the American government, with the active support of the Jewish organizations, asked the Nazi government in 1939 to stop emigration to Shanghai. Saly Mayer, representative of the Joint and the Zionist Organization in Switzerland, blocked efforts for admission of additional Jews to Switzerland, and Ehrenpreisz did the same in Sweden.

The second premise governing the policies of Jewish leaders was eloquently defined in 1943 by Yitzchak Greenbaum, member of the Jewish Agency and, curiously enough, chairman of its Rescue Committee in Jerusalem: "When they asked me, couldn't you give money out of the United Jewish Appeal funds for the rescue of Jews in Europe, I said, 'No!,' and I say again, 'No!' ... one must resist this wave which pushes the Zionist activities to secondary importance." But it was not only a question of finances; in the words of Chaim Weizmann, in 1937, "The hopes of Europe's six million Jews are centered on emigration. I was asked, 'Can you bring six million Jews to Palestine?' I replied, 'No ... From the depths of the tragedy I want to save two million young people ... the old ones will pass ... They were dust, economic and moral dust in a cruel world ... Only the young shall survive.' "

There was enunciated the fateful policy of selective rescue which, for instance, led Henry Montor, executive director of the UJA to refuse to support Revisionist efforts to bring any and all escapees to *Eretz Yisrael:* "Palestine cannot be flooded with ... old people or with undesirables." (We shall touch further on upon some of the consequences of this policy in Nazi-occupied Europe; here it only remains to point out that this policy, which also governed the partisan distribution of certificates before the war, was the major factor in limiting Orthodox *aliyah*, rather than Rabbinic opposition.)

The abandonment of the Diaspora, and the writing off of those considered useless to the future state, led to the actual rejection of rescue possibilities which might have lessened the pressure for the opening of the gates of Palestine. Rescue work suffered further from conflicts over how to react to the closing of the doors of Palestine by the British (Ruth Klueger in *The Last Escape* describes her conflicts within the Zionist movement on whether legal rescue work should be undertaken), and the American prohibition on transfers of funds to enemy territory (Kranzler and Trunk record the hesitation of the Joint to circumvent this law, in contrast to the *Vaad Hatzalah* which found ways of transferring needed funds even before the United States government officially approved). The sabotage of Joel

Brand's rescue mission in deference to British wishes is of course the most extreme instance of sacrificing Jewish lives to political considerations.

It is extremely painful to peruse a book like Moshe Shonfeld's *The Holocaust Victims Accuse*, which chronicles these and other instances of the failure of the Jewish establishment.[8] Yet it is most imperative than the true picture of what happened be faced up to, not only to keep the historical record straight but much more importantly, because there are profound implications for the present and the future. With the exception of a few very rare individuals — such as Dr. Griffel in Turkey, Elimelech Tress and Julius Steinfeld in the United States of America and the organizations that they succeeded in inspiring — nobody did enough for *Hatzalah*, and therein lies a terrible lesson for us. At the same time, it is frightening to look back upon the failure of the big Jewish organizations, in their flawed approach towards rescue work which so clearly emerges from our sources. If, as we said at the beginning, the Holocaust was to serve as a warning against our loss of Torah values in the process of assimilation, the failure to do adequate rescue work doubly and triply underlines this warning. We must do our utmost not to permit alien ideologies to dominate Jewish life — whether we think of American issues, the needs of Russian Jewry, or *Eretz Yisrael*.

৺§ Under the Nazi Rule

Lastly, we must also face up to the fact that the inroads of such ideologies — whether assimilationist or nationalist — may not only have prepared the ground for the *Churban Europa*, but

---

8. In *Blaming the Jews: The Charge of Perfidy* (in *The Jewish Presence*, a collection of essays on identity and history, 1977), L. Dawidowicz tries to clear the Jewish leadership of such charges. She argues that Kastner, the Zionist leader in Hungary, was not a traitor but "a self-deluded egotist, obsessed with the sense of his historic mission to save *some* Jews" (emphasis mine); and she claims that "timidity, miscalculation, and misjudgment" on the part of the leadership is not the same as betrayal — people merely realized too late what was happening. Faint as her defense is, it is still too kind to these leaders. Stephen Wise and others knew relatively early what was going on and acceded to a cover-up; they failed to put public pressure on the governments, tried to silence those who did, and at crucial moments actually opposed rescue projects. It is strange for a historian, in belittling the work of the Irgunists, to write that "its one accomplishment ... was that it ... brought about the creation of the War Refugee Board," as if this had been a small thing. She stresses that "Saly Mayer was authorized to keep negotiating" with the Germans after Brand had been sidetracked; yet she must know that Saly Mayer actually opposed removing Jews from Nazi-held territories. She mentions that in 1944, Weizmann proposed the bombing of Auschwitz — ignoring the fact that this was urged much earlier by Rabbi M.B. Weismandl, whom — unbelievable! — she totally ignores in all her writings — and that England, possibly on Russian instigation, refused; yet there is on record an English denial that such a proposal was ever made.

were also manifested in the way in which European Jewry faced its hour of tragedy.

D. Rabinowitz in *New Lives* tells the story of the survivor who looked at the pictures of the Warsaw Ghetto uprising displayed in the office of a Jewish organization to illustrate death with honor, and mused, "I thought that everyone who died, died with honor." Most of the books concerned with the Holocaust at one point or another come to grips with the question of resistance: did the Six Million go like sheep to slaughter? The point is made by R. Hilberg and L. Dawidowicz, among others, that Jews historically have become conditioned to violence. Be that as it may, in Nazi Europe mass resistance was out of the question.[9] Foot quotes De Gaulle as calling resistance "a bluff that worked," and even that only under the very special conditions that existed in France. A limited amount of sabotage and underground work was possible in Eastern Europe, and was indeed done; but on a mass scale, resistance — except just prior to liberation — could at most be a heroic but suicidal gesture of defiance and revenge.

Moreover, J. Garlinski, in his meticulous account of underground work in Auschwitz, *Fighting Auschwitz*, stresses that it took months to set up any organization, and therefore Jews, unlike other prisoners, were unable to do so: they were destined for the crematoria and had an average life expectancy of three months. They did not even have the time to make those basic adjustments to the surrealistic and horror-laden underworld of Auschwitz (another planet) which alone held out a hope of survival (Des Pres). Sereny points out that the Nazis fiendishly provided entirely different receptions in Auschwitz for Jews from Eastern and Western Europe, playing on their different world outlook in order to mentally disorganize and overwhelm them. In the same way, the Nazis turned the treatment of the Jews in the ghettos into a devilish art, alternating murder with promises of a respite, deliberately creating confusion and uncertainty, and after every *Aktion* fanning hopes of survival for those that remained.

And yet, as we read the accounts of those terrible days, we are made to realize by all writers that there was a possibility of resistance of a different nature than is usually envisioned. The Nazis did not want only to destroy the Jew; they aimed to destroy his spirit and everything he stood for. In this they glaringly failed and, while there were many, from the most diverse backgrounds,

---

9. Cf. Dawidowicz, in *The Jewish Presence*.

who gave strength to others by their own fortitude, there is one note that is struck again and again in the accounts of the time, by secular writers as well as religious ones:

> Suddenly we saw a group of men. At their head was an old rav, wrapped in his tallis and holding in his hand an open siddur. He passed before us as a figure from out of this world, and called aloud: "Be comforted, be comforted, my people" (Chaim Lazar, quoted by Shonfeld).

> Pain and ... fear ... kept us awake ... The moon shone through the window ... and gave the pale, wasted faces of the prisoners a ghostly appearance. It was as if all the life had ebbed out of them. I shuddered with dread, for it suddenly occurred to me that I was the only living man among corpses.
>
> All at once the oppressive silence was broken by a mournful tune. It was the plaintive tones of the ancient Kol Nidre prayer. I raised myself up to see whence it came. There, close to the wall, the moonlight caught the uplifted face of an old man who, in self-forgetful, pious absorption, was singing softly to himself ... This prayer brought the ghostly group of seemingly insensible human beings back to life ...
>
> We sat up very quietly, so as not to disturb the old man, and he did not notice that we were listening ... When at last he was silent, there was exaltation among us, an exaltation which men can experience when they have fallen as low as we had fallen and then, through the mystic power of a deathless prayer, have awakened once more to the world of the spirit (Szalet, quoted by Des Pres).

Des Pres, to be sure, at bottom, does not know how to evaluate such phenomena. He recognizes that survival in the camps was tied up with a man's essential humanity, the ability for caring and sharing; yet he sees this as merely an expression of innate and instinctive biological forms of basic behavior. Dawidowicz, too, stresses the role of the spirit. She writes:

> Morale was sustained by rabbis and pious Jews who, by their own resolute and exalted stance, provided a model of how Jews should encounter death.

She points out that, while many gave up their loyalty to tradition, there was a mass sacrificial endeavor on the part of religious Jewry to cling to Torah observance, even though it was in effect made illegal by the Nazis. The faith and pride in one's

Jewishness, despite everything, is reflected in the story of the child in the ghetto school who heard the story of Yaakov and Eisav and exclaimed: "Teacher, we are Yaakov's descendants, and they are Eisav's, right? It's good that way. I want to belong to Yaakov and not to Eisav." Yet Dawidowicz adds that "for believing Jews the conviction that their sacrifice was required as a testimony to Almighty G-d was more comforting than the supposition that He had abandoned them altogether." This statement hardly does justice to the genuine faith in G-d's closeness of the true believer, and rather makes it appear to be a convenient psychological device.

In contrast, M. Prager, M.D. Weinstock, S.B. Unsdorfer in their books — and Shonfeld, in some of his vignettes — heart-rendingly capture on paper the true spiritual greatness and all-pervading humanity of so many simple people whom the awesome challenge turned into heroes. However, the light of Torah does not only shine through such people. Compare the following lines by Ernst Papanek, Austrian socialist educator and self-confessed total ignoramus in Jewish matters:

> *It was pure arrogance on our part to think that we could decide whether the Orthodox orphans would get kosher food or not. [These forty children, between eleven and thirteen years of age,] were tied together by the most powerful common background we ever saw ... Despite everything, the Orthodox children were always the most confident of their ultimate triumph and the least scared by their persecution. They knew who they were, and what they were persecuted for. They did feel different, they did feel special, they did feel that they had been chosen by G-d to fulfill some Almighty purpose. In one sense they didn't have to win over anybody or anything. They won by being.*

The enormous strength of Torah, both in assuring the loyalty of its faithful followers and in giving them endurance and vitality, is shown in the Rabbinic responsa of the time, many of which are collected by Dr. H.J. Zimmels[10] in *The Echoes of the Nazi Holocaust in Rabbinic Literature.* Despite some ineptitude on the part of those who edited the volume, it is a remarkable and

---

10. Trunk and Dawidowicz have stressed what they saw as a conflict between Rabbis over the permissibility of preparing lists for deportation. The Kovner Rav, when asked by the Judenrat to rule on this question, collapsed; when he had recovered, he replied, after careful consideration, that a list could be prepared. This ruling seems in conflict with that of all other Rabbis and the view of the Rambam; Zimmels, however, explains that the question in Kovno was different from the case in other localities.

deeply upsetting work, reflecting the greatness of the Jew whose longing — even in the valley of death — was to do the will of his Father in heaven. The Torah Jew put himself in mortal danger by the *peyos* (sidecurls) he wore, or by his attendance at a *minyan*; yet he acquired an inner strength that protected him from a fate worse than death, becoming a lackey or imitator of his oppressors.

In contrast, among those estranged from Torah, there was the possibility of some men emerging who chose such a life of shame. Shonfeld quotes Efroiken, a standard-bearer of secularism, whom the Holocaust brought to the gates of repentance.

> *From where did the thousands of Jewish police (Kapos), who served the Germans in the concentration camps and the ghettos, come? The survivors of the Holocaust all concur that they originated from the underworld and from the Maskilim, the very people who denounced their "unenlightened" brethren for their more traditional garb. Did not these Maskilim harbor the same feelings of scorn and even hatred as their masters, the Nazis? ... Here one must record the blatant fact ... that Torah-true Jewry — Jews wearing traditional Rabbinical or chassidic garb — never held positions in the Jewish police force which administered ghetto Jewry, and never served as Kapos.*

Actually, there were some isolated cases of Kapos emerging from among the religious ranks, but they were a rarity indeed.

It is important to note that Trunk indeed points out that the *Judenrats* and ghetto administrations were largely dominated by assimilationists (the Jewish police in Warsaw was commanded by a *meshumad* [apostate], and the Vilna Ghetto by Jacob Gens whose wife was a Lithuanian Christian) or Zionists (Merin, the "ruler" of Sosnowitz, for instance, was a Revisionist, and Rumkowsky, "the king of Lodz," a General Zionist). From the various studies there emerge many reasons why they played such a dominant role in the ghettos and later as Kapos in the camps. They had a better secular education, often were professionals, and knew German; not just those who only realized their Jewish identity when the Nazis took over, but a good many secularized Jews who had played a role in Jewish life, in a way felt closer to their new masters than to the poor, ragged, old-fashioned Jewish masses; their ambition and power-seeking were not restrained by Torah considerations; and they felt confidence in their own ability to decide what was right and wrong.

In the beginning, most Judenrat members meant well; but as the Jewish councils emerged more and more as impotent tools of Nazi persecution, their more realistic members sought to get out or resisted the Nazis and were killed. With some notable exceptions, those who remained deluded themselves that they were doing a good thing. By preparing the lists of Jews who were sent to their deaths, they thought that they were saving other Jews, but in reality they merely stoked the crematoria.

It is noteworthy that in connection with their work — as for instance in the case of Abba Kovner, head of the *Hashomer Hatzair* in Vilna — there appears again the infamous policy of "selective rescue." Dessler, the Vilna Jewish police head, wrote in his diary (quoted by Shonfeld): "Those who were deported were chosen by my Jewish police for I wanted to save the young and the intelligentsia."

But when the time came for a breakout to the forest,

> *Kovner promised exit to fifty of his friends from the organization exclusively ... Tens of young, healthy, strong people gather in the courtyard and plead before Kovner that he permit them to join those leaving, but he threatens them with his revolver and chases them away* (Lazar, quoted by Shonfeld).

What a contrast to the role played by the Rabbis, as outlined by Trunk and others!

In Sosnowitz, Moshe Merin, mentioned above, wanted the Jewish Council to make up a list of a thousand Jews to be handed over for deportation. When the *rav* of the community, Rabbi Yeshaya Englard, blocked him in this, Merin made up the list himself and, in revenge, put Rabbi Englard and his family on it. At the last moment, he apparently reconsidered and offered to take Rabbi Englard off the train. But the *rav* asked whether he would substitute others in his place and, upon receiving a positive reply, insisted on going to his death. Or take the contrast, in Auschwitz, between Eliezer Greenbaum — son of Yitzchak Greenbaum, whom we mentioned before — an all-powerful Kapo who, according to K. Tzetnik's testimony, delighted in murdering religious Jews (he was later killed by Jews in *Eretz Yisrael*, according to Shonfeld) and Rabbi Meisels who took his life into his hands to fulfill the last request of a few hundred boys marked for extermination, and blew *shofar* for them on Rosh Hashanah.

Of course, the Merins, Kovners, Greenbaums, *et al*, were a

relatively small number, and it has been argued that they, too, were victims of a situation too immense for them, but the fact that such figures could appear is a tragic demonstration of how low it is possible to fall when Torah is forsaken. Just as the drift away from Torah deeply affected the rescue efforts of Jewry in the free world, so it cruelly affected the Jews under the Nazi heel. Again, assimilation to a non-Jewish world and its values not only helped prepare for the disaster, but accompanied and worsened it.

Therein lies the particular importance of remembering the *Churban Europa* in all its aspects. We must not only seek to feel some echo of the pain and horror of those days; we must also learn from the *mesiras nefesh* of the ordinary Jew who, going to his death, would not have changed places with his murderers, and of his leaders who inspired him; also, however hurtful this is, we must be aware of the danger to *Klal Yisrael* which results from the forgetting of Torah and the emergence of leaders estranged from it; and finally, we must remember that we must go our way without expecting anything from the world around us.

Jewish Historiography

Measured by these objectives of our study of the period, most of the books here touched upon must be judged superficial in their interpretation and understanding of the events — and in some cases outright misleading — even though a good many of the data they offer have proven most revealing to us.[11] The efforts by Shonfeld to set the record straight are of course of great value; so are the accounts given by Prager, Unsdorfer, or Weinstock, among others, and such specialized works as Zimmels's. I would,

---

11. Attention should also drawn to the fact that a great deal of material is presently published for school children and their teachers; here the absence of a Torah orientation is particularly dangerous. The Board of Jewish Education of New York has published *Program Materials for the Holocaust*, a kit stressing the observance of the "Day of the Holocaust" and defining the educational objective as "identification with the Six Million, and the immortality of Israel (נצח ישראל)," the rise of the State of Israel is presented as the fulfillment of the *Ani Maamin* sung in the ghettos, and the historical material included (particularly an extract from Abba Eban's *My People*) is crudely misinformed in its account of Jewish rescue efforts and its secularistic approach.

An article by Abraham I. Katsh recommends that the Holocaust should be included in the daily prayers just like the Exodus from Egypt, a *Zachor* sign be hung in every succah, and a resistance story be added to the reading of *Megillas* Esther!

B. Stadtler, *The Holocaust* (1973, Anti Defamation League), is meant as a history book for children but fails totally to convey the values of *Kiddush Hashem* with which we are concerned; there are many cliches — and a blunt statement that "Rabbis and community leaders were no more or less human than other people." More useful, because offered without interpretations, is a set of twenty posters for display purposes, published by the Anti Defamation League; when exhibiting them, we should, however, add pictures reflecting our particular concerns (Gedolei Yisroel, etc.).

however, like to single out Kranzler's work on Shanghai as an example of what a Jewish historical monograph should be like.

Japanese, Nazis and Jews is a thoroughly researched volume, complete with documentation, source references and bibliography. Unlike Trunk's volume, for instance, it deals thoroughly also with aspects of the themes that relate to Torah Jewry. Above all, however, it seeks to lead the reader to look deeper, behind the facts.

Only *neviim* (prophets) can uncover the hidden pathways of historic cause-and-effect relationships. But we can — and should — try to perceive history as an expression of Divine Providence. Thus, Dr. Kranzler points out how Jacob Schiff, the American financier, in 1905 helped the Japanese against Russia because of Russia's persecution of the Jews, and thereby he prepared a haven of refuge a generation later. The Japanese not only remained grateful; they became so convinced of the world power of Jewish financiers (an idea usually conducive to Jew-hatred) that they decided to treat their Jewish refugees well, thereby hoping to gain sympathy from the Jewish-dominated world.

It is interesting in this connection that the Japanese repeatedly tried to enlist "their" Jews in establishing a better understanding of Japanese problems in America. It was crucial for the well-being of the Jews in China and Japan that they should not be rudely rebuffed, yet Stephen Wise once again played the patriotic statesman at the expense of the local Jews, providing a maximum of irritating words and a minimum of help. He expressed his hostility to the Japanese and gratuitously wrote that "Japan is bound to take an anti-Semitic attitude, and indeed has already done so" (November 22, 1938). Fortunately for the Jews of Shanghai, this statement never reached the Japanese. In contrast, the role of the *Vaad Hatzalah* and in particular, of Rabbi Kalmanowitz, the Mirrer *Rosh Yeshivah*, shines brightly — yet another illustration of the thesis we have tried to develop in this review article.

Rabbi Nisson Wolpin

"Holocaust"

— At Least They Know

IT IS DIFFICULT to imagine someone not aware of "Holocaust," the nine-and-a-half-hour telecast first aired on NBC-TV the week preceding Pesach in 1978. If one could avoid *TV Guide* or newspaper advertisements and discussions announcing its advent, then one would have discovered its existence by having most telephone calls placed during critical evening hours greeted with a busy signal, or a hasty: "Call back after 11:00 (click)."

It is equally difficult to imagine anyone not aware of the tragic destinies of the fictional families Dorf and Weiss, who represented the fate of the persecutor and the victim in microcosm. Even non-TV-owners who did not borrow viewing space in front of a neighbor's set knew the vicissitudes of the various members of these families, thanks to morning-after recaps on buses, elevators, and in newspaper columns.

And no Jew *should* be unaware of a phenomenon that focused the attention of millions of Americans on some aspect of Jewish suffering during World War II; and indeed, according to media experts, more than half the country's population watched at least some part of this "docu-drama."

৵ A Media Event

Judging by comments in newspapers and magazines, the program was more than the record of an event; it was an event in itself, bringing in its wake study guides, a best-selling book based

---

This review appeared in *The Jewish Observer* of May 1978.

on the TV script, specially convened discussion groups, and ripples of discussion and controversy.

The most superficial level of this "Holocaust" analysis took note of the widespread comment: "We never realized how much suffering actually took place." Thus: *It's important that we/they know what had happened.* This response was shared by most of the more critical viewers — both professionals and those who knew because they were there. But once the critical process began, many faults were uncovered, of varying degrees of severity.

Some dealt with facts: "The roundup in Warsaw was in the summer. I'll never forget the oppressive heat. And even if it had been in the winter, we'd never have been so well dressed, or so well fed. Did you ever see one fat survivor?"

Some dealt with nuances: John J. O'Connor of *The New York Times* found all the characters cardboard stereotypes, with epochal dilemmas reduced to soap-opera cliches, resulting in (as Elie Wiesel put it) a trivialization of a cosmic tragedy: The only member of the ill-fated Weiss family to survive is the poor-student, athlete-cum-partisan ... Time and again Nazi soldiers on the sidelines, watching Jews march benignly to their death, remarked, "See how cooperative they are? I told you they're sub-human!"

Some dealt with the focus of the program: Why depict the wiping out of an entire culture by telling the story of an assimilated, intermarried family? When Mrs. Weiss urged her young charges in a makeshift ghetto-school studying Western culture: "You must continue your (secular) education if you wish to make something of yourself," the irony was totally lost on the average viewer. For that matter, the script writer himself seemed oblivious of the fact that the "saving" culture was identical with the one responsible for their ultimate demise.

⇛ Reb Mechel's View

This distortion of focus was elaborated upon by Reb Mechel, an alumnus of Buchenwald, in a private conversation: "I had promised myself not to watch. But I had to. And with each new episode I wondered how any one could escape the inevitable death that awaited us. And then I silently congratulated myself for making it — thanking G-d with every breath."

"Was your reaction — your recognition of G-d's grace — implied in the TV presentation?" I asked him.

"Not at all. This was my personal celebration of making it,

triggered by the scenes on the screen. On the contrary, I found nothing to give my type of survival, or the death of others, any semblance of dignity. The submission of the masses — forced to disrobe and march to their death site, along an open pit — seemed like a puzzle, a cruel joke. We weren't submissive. We were starved. Our bodies were disease racked, broken. And yet we hoped. We could not imagine anything worse than what we had already endured. The roundup, the march — it could only be to better circumstances, we thought. And at the end — they whipped us, hounded us, made us run. To look over your shoulders meant certain death. Who could hesitate, let alone resist? But this was a small consideration. The main thing is that the people should know. Without 'Holocaust' and NBC — trivialization, commercials, and all — they would never have been aware."

ஃ But Others Say ...

Not everyone agreed with Mechel. Ari Weiss was visibly upset: "Why did they have to show an assimilated family? Why did the romantic leads have to live together and then get married — as though that were the norm for *anyone* in those days? Why should [Gerald] Green have to project that kind of counterfeit image of European Jewry for millions of viewers?"

"O.K., the image was false, and insulting to us. But do you think it was damaging as far as the general viewer is concerned?"

Ari's reply supplied me with half an answer to his own criticism: "It's hard to say. Last Thursday a telephone repairman was fixing our kitchen phone. He asked me, 'You any relation to the Weiss family on "Holocaust?"' I explained that the story and the family was fiction, but the circumstances depicted were true: 'Oh, I know that,' he said. 'But I never knew until the show how much the Weisses and all you people suffered. I just never realized.'"

"So you see," I told Ari, "the program did reach him. And I'd guess that it was only because he could relate to the Weisses, their sins and all, that he could identify with their suffering."

Ari thought a moment, and then "begged to disagree": "My mother was one of a group of girls in Auschwitz. The orderly in charge of dispensing food to the inmates was in the camp because his paternal grandfather had been Jewish — *a knappe Yid!* On Yom Kippur morning my mother pocketed her slice of bread and skipped her bowl of gruel. The orderly asked her why she was foregoing breakfast, so she told him about Yom Kippur. 'So *that's* why the other girls didn't take breakfast,' he said. 'If I'm here because they consider me Jewish, then I'm not going to eat today either!' he emphatically added.

"So you see," Ari said, "they appreciate us much more for being *us*, than for being carbon copies of *them*."

And I believe that he was right.

"Holocaust" left the impression that the real "heroes" were those who died with guns in their hands, the resisters. What nonsense. There were no heroes. It is natural for us, the spectators (and perhaps for the survivors too), to want to believe that some ways to die are "better" than others. But who says so? The idea that dying as a resister is more "courageous" is a medieval pagan idea borrowed by modern romanticism. Those who "went like sheep" were no less human, their deaths no less meaningful, their children no less precious. To focus on resistance was to make the real Holocaust into a cheap Jewish western.

Furthermore, the praising of resistance left the false impression that there was some hope, some way to "save" oneself from humiliation. That simply was not the case. Those who have survived say that it was not by virtue of any act of theirs, nor by virtue of any conviction that they survived. It was chance (*read: Providence — N.W.*). What hope existed was illusory, a tissue of love and lies. (That is one aspect of the real Holocaust that was portrayed well.)

And, if one must talk of heroism, what of the heroism of the religious? — The rabbis who led their people to a religious death, the students who were beaten for providing prayerbooks in the camps, and the strength of the evangelical Christians whose courage matched that of their religious Jewish counterparts.

In addition, "Holocaust" was misleading because it focused on the personal tragedies and "triumphs" of its characters. The real tragedy does not lie in the beatings (and the portrayal thereof was also pitifully inadequate). That is simply inhuman violence, repugnant though it is. The tragedy lies, at least in part, in the cessation of Jewish civilization in Europe. Dawidowicz ends Part Two of her book with the liquidation of the Warsaw Ghetto, not because it was heroic but because it was the end of the Jewish community of Poland. There is no more communal, institutional history of the Jews in Eastern Europe. The history of the Jew stops cold. The survivors of the real Holocaust always speak of "we."

— *From a critical review by David R. Blumenthal, Professor of Judaic Studies, at Emory University (Atlanta, Georgia), appearing in the InterMountain Jewish News.*

VIII.
In the Aftermath

Rabbi Avrohom Chaim Levine

The Phenomenon of Reconstruction

◆§ The Strength to Rebuild

THE JEWISH PEOPLE HAVE THE capacity to rebuild from the very depths of their suffering. I learned of this ability from both the words and the deeds of my *Rebbe*, Rabbi Elye Meir Bloch, זצ"ל, the late Telshe *Rosh Yeshivah*.

During the war years, Reb Elye Meir did not know for certain what had happened to his family. He only could guess that his wife and children had been murdered by the Nazis. He devoted his energy and talents to establishing the Telshe *Yeshivah* in Cleveland.

It was his practice to come to Detroit during the Spring *bein hazmanim* (intersession) to raise funds for the *yeshivah*. He would then stay on as the guest of my parents for Pesach.

At one *Seder*, he stopped at the passage from the *Haggadah*:

"*And I passed over you and saw you downtrodden in your blood and I said to you: 'Through your blood you shal' live! Through your blood you shall live!*

"The Jews had been enamored of the Egyptian culture," said Reb Elye Meir, "and wished to assimilate. But when the Egyptians actually pressed Jewish infants into the walls to fill gaps in the structure, and slaughtered them to provide blood for Pharaoh's baths, the Jews were so outraged and were so revolted by what they had seen, they totally rejected Egyptian culture. The brutality, the flow of blood, actually inspired them to return to Judaism, the source of life. At that point, where others would wallow in despair, we find the source of our integrity and cause for hope.

This essay appeared in *The Jewish Observer* of March 1985.

"The value attached to this is reflected in the use of the women's copper mirrors to construct the *kiyor* (laving pool for the *Mishkan*, the traveling sanctuary in the wilderness). These were very precious to G-d because they were donated by the women who had used them, when they were enslaved in Egypt, to beautify themselves so they would be attractive to their husbands: they elected to bring children into the world when a realistic look at their oppressive conditions would have dictated that no children should be born. Yet, they had the optimism to look beyond their suffering and to anticipate a time when they and their children would be redeemed.

"Today, too," continued Reb Elye Meir, "the Jews are seeing the Germans shedding the blood of their children, and their long-standing enchantment with German culture is growing sour. We are now on the threshold of a rebirth."

The words were spoken as a commentary on the *Haggadah*, but they were also a commentary on Reb Elye Meir's capacity for optimism and his ability to lead the rebuilding of *Klal Yisrael* during its darkest moments.

The Phenomenon of Reconstruction

Rabbi Elya Svei
prepared for publication by
Rabbi Mendel Kaufman

Waiting For Geulah: A Guide to Reconstruction

HOW DID THE SPIRITUAL giants that survived the destruction of World War II manage to rebuild the losses? What can we learn from their actions?

◆§ Unanticipated Immortality

> *Rabbi Yitzchok says, "The Torah teaches us, when a person performs a mitzvah he should do it wholeheartedly, for if Reuvein had known that the Torah would write (Bereishis 37:21) 'And Reuvein heard (the plan of his brothers to kill Yoseif) and he saved him from them,' then he would have carried Yoseif back to his father on his shoulders; And if Aharon had known that the Torah would write (Shemos 4:14) (in telling about Moshe at their first meeting before going to Pharaoh) 'And he will see you and he will rejoice in his heart,' then Aharon would have greeted Moshe with dancing and beating drums." ... Rabbi Yehoshua ben Levi says, "In days of yore when a person performed a mitzvah, the Prophet would record it (as part of Biblical history), but now if one performs a mitzvah, who records it? Eliyahu and Moshiach record it and G-d certifies it."*
> *— The Midrash*

This essay, based on a Yiddish address at a P'eylim gathering, appeared in *The Jewish Observer* of June 1976.

The midrash reveals to us a new dimension in the performance of a *mitzvah*.

Let us take the Midrashic interpretation of Reuvein's *mitzvah* first. Reuvein performs a great *mitzvah* in saving his brother's life. Not only is this an act of *hatzalah*, but it is also an act of great selflessness. Of all the sons of Yaakov, it was Reuvein who had the most to gain from the elimination of Yoseif. It was Yoseif who posed the greatest threat to Reuvein. Indeed, he eventually superseded Reuvein as *bechor*, in the right of primogeniture, and received an extra portion among his brothers, becoming two tribes (Ephraim and Menashe) among the twelve, Reuvein remaining but one.

Yet as great as these aspects of the *mitzvah* were, there was one aspect that Reuvein himself did not foresee: the aspect of immortality. Of this the Midrash tells us, had Reuvein foreseen that his act of selflessness would also be touched with immortality by being recorded in the eternal record of the Torah, then he would have performed the *mitzvah* on an even greater scale and he would have carried Yoseif back to his father on his shoulders.

The Midrash continues with the same analysis of Aharon's *mitzvah*. This *mitzvah* also has a number of aspects. First, Aharon was to play a vital role in the redemption of the Jewish People. Second, selflessly he rejoiced upon the appointment of his younger brother as the one who will lead this great exodus from bondage. However, just as with Reuvein, Aharon did not foresee the aspect of immortality in his *mitzvah*. Had he known that his great act of selflessness would be immortalized by being recorded in the eternal record of Torah, then he would have performed it on an even greater scale and he would have greeted Moshe with dancing and beating drums.

The Midrash continues with Rabbi Yehoshua ben Levi's question: In the days of the prophets a *mitzvah* would attain this added dimension of immortality by being recorded by the prophets in the eternal Biblical record, but today, how do *mitzvos* attain this added dimension? Rabbi Yehoshua ben Levi answers: By being recorded by Eliyahu and *Moshiach*. This means that each *mitzvah* is important not only for itself but also because it brings closer the *Geulah* as symbolized by Eliyahu and *Moshiach*.

This is the message of the Midrash. We must live with knowledge that every *mitzvah* we do transcends its immediate time and place. It becomes part of the ongoing process of ushering in the *Geulah*. This would serve to inspire us to greater heights of achievement, because as with Reuvein and Aharon, he who realizes that what he is doing will live on unto eternity, he will more likely expend maximum effort in this endeavor.

⋑ "Who Would Have Expected ...?"

We can gain a further insight into the importance of the fulfillment of a *mitzvah* from another Midrash (*Bereishis Rabbah*, end of *Sidrah Vayeishev*). This Midrash gives a list of incidents in Jewish history when the unexpected became reality. The Midrash says:

> Who would have expected that Avraham and Sarah, who were old, would have a son? Who would have expected that Yaakov, who crossed the Jordan on the way to his uncle Lavan's house with just his walking stick in his hand, would return wealthy? Who would have expected that Yoseif would go from prison to become Pharaoh's viceroy? Who would have expected that Moshe, who had been thrown into the river, would become what he became? ... (and the Midrash concludes) Who would have expected that the Diaspora would someday see glory and splendor? And who would have expected that the Sanctuary of David (the Temple) that had been destroyed would be rebuilt by G-d?

The obvious purpose of the Midrash was to console the Jewish People, who had seen their Temple destroyed and their remnants scattered throughout the world. The Midrash is telling the sorely pressed Jewish nation, no matter how heavy the burden of oppression may be and no matter how bleak the future may seem, Jews must never despair. Here are occasions in Jewish history when the unexpected became reality. No one expected to see the aged (Avraham and Sarah) give birth, nor the condemned to prison (Yoseif) or to death (Moshe) ultimately attain power. Yet miraculously their fortunes were reversed overnight from bad to good. So it is with the Diaspora and the rebuilding of the Temple: as impossible as it may seem, Jewish fortunes can and will be reversed from oppression to redemption.

⋑ "Who Waited ... ?"

There is however another interpretation that can be given to this Midrash. In the Hebrew original the Midrash begins each example with the words, *mi mechakeh*, which was translated as, "who would have expected?" *Mi mechakeh* could also be translated as "who waited?" so that now the Midrash may read:

"Who waited (to see) Avraham and Sarah, who were old, have a son? Who waited (to see) Yoseif, who was in prison, become Pharaoh's viceroy? Who waited (to see) Moshe, who had been thrown into the river, became what he become?"

And in each of these cases the Torah or the Midrash tells us who it was who waited. For example, in the case of Moshe the Torah tells us (*Shemos* 2:4) that it was his sister Miriam who waited: "And his sister stood from afar to see what would become of him." According to the Midrash, it was Miriam who prophesied that her mother Yocheved would bear a son who would be the redeemer of Israel. When Moshe was born and the whole house was filled with light, her father Amram kissed her on the head, for he saw that her prophecy was being fulfilled. When Moshe was placed into the river, her father then slapped her and said, "See what has become now of your prophecy!" But Miriam did not lose heart. She knew that her prophecy would be fulfilled. So she stood from afar to see what she could do to help the prophecy become reality. And in fact she was instrumental in bringing Moshe back to his mother that she would raise him.

This is what the Midrash is asking of each of these periods of history: *mi mechakeh*, who was waiting — who was striving and looking forward to the fulfillment of Divine prophecy? The list includes Avraham and Sarah waiting for the son they knew would come, Yoseif waiting in prison knowing that one way or another his dreams of leadership would someday be fulfilled, Moshe waiting in Pharaoh's palace for the redemption he knew would come.

⇨§ Some Who Waited

In this vein we can now understand the end of the Midrash, which asks: "Who waited to see the Diaspora someday develop into glory and splendor?" for the Midrash is challenging us to emulate great men of early generations. Similarly, the answer to this final "who waited" can be found in the stories of the great Torah personalities who dedicated their lives to implanting the glory and splendor of Torah wherever Jews were found. One such story would be that of the *Rosh Yeshivah*, Rabbi Aharon Kotler:

When the *Rosh Yeshivah* came to the United States during World War II, he found the level of Torah study in America very limited. Conventional wisdom had it that with the destruction of European Jewry and its Torah institutions, the future of Torah in

America was bleak. But he seemed to know that he had been saved from the fiery furnace for a Divine reason. He "waited" to see the golden Diaspora of America also attain the glory and splendor of Torah, as he had seen it in the Torah fortresses of Europe. With superhuman energy and courage, he first threw himself into rescue work, to save as many of the remnants of the *Churban* as he could. Then he threw himself into the task of building Torah in America. He selected Lakewood, New Jersey and founded his *yeshivah*, Beth Medrash Govohah, which produced Torah leaders and scholars who then went forth to bring Torah to the length and breadth of America. He was not deterred by obstacles, financial crises, or skepticism, because he "waited" to see the Diaspora once more attain glory and splendor in Torah. He knew that everything he did would lead to the fulfillment of the ancient prophecy, that through all times and in all lands, Torah must and will be the driving force of the Jewish nation.

In the same vein, we must appreciate how the Satmar Rav, Rabbi Yoel Teitelbaum, came to these shores broken in body after being interred in Nazi concentration camps, but not broken in spirit. *Mi mechakeh* — he succeeded in rebuilding his community, its *Kehillah* structure, its vibrant educational institutions, in the Williamsburg section of Brooklyn. This is the key to all great builders on the ashes: The *Roshei Yeshivah*, such as Rabbi Elye Meir Bloch of Telshe and Rabbi Yoseif Kahaneman of Ponevezh; the *chassidic* leaders, such as the late Gerrer Rabbi and יבדל לחיים the Bobover Rav; communal leaders, such as Reb Yitzchak Meir Levin, and rabbinical figures such as Rabbi Joseph Breuer.

◆§ The Power of a Mitzvah

It is now that we can understand the end of the Midrash which asks, "Who waited to see the rebuilding of the Sanctuary of David?" The Midrash is not merely consoling us. The Midrash is actually asking, as with the great men of the past, who waited and worked for the eventual fulfillment of the Divine prophecy of redemption: "Who is *today* waiting and striving to bring about the eventual rebuilding of the Temple?"

The responsibility of "waiting" devolves upon each of us, on his or her level. How does one go about "waiting"? As indicated by Rabbi Yehoshua ben Levi, the *mitzvos* a Jew fulfills are recorded by Eliyahu and *Moshiach* because they bring nearer the final redemption. As we raise our level of Torah study and fulfillment of *mitzvos*, so do we bring ever closer the ultimate and complete fulfillment of the Divine promise.

Were we to bear in mind that every *mitzvah* we perform has the power to bring the *Geulah* that much closer, how much more thought and care would we invest in every *mitzvah* that we do!

Rabbi Elya Svei

After the Churban: Being Judged by the Martyrs

A DESTRUCTION AS vast as *Churban* Europe forty years ago must have some implications to us regarding our conduct as Jews, both on the personal level and on a national scale. What steps are to be taken as we engage in reconstructing a world destroyed? What are the pitfalls to be avoided? Who can best judge if we are measuring up to the task?

Jewish history is an ongoing encounter with G-d, and every major experience contains a lesson. The ability to learn from specific events takes time and just as *Chazal* (the Sages of the Talmud) tell us that forty years must pass before one can fathom a lesson from a teacher of flesh and blood, so too may the passage of forty years be of help to us to truly learn from a historical event.

We are now approaching forty years since the end of World War II and the tragic horrors that befell our people in that era. Undoubtedly, there are many lessons one must learn from that *Churban*, and perhaps this passage of time will permit us to begin.

❧ After the Deluge

After a vast destruction, the first task on hand is to rebuild. Decisions must be made regarding what takes priority, and what is of secondary importance. We can find some guidelines from that most sweeping of disasters to befall mankind, the *mabul*, the deluge of Noach's time. Noach's first act after stepping out of the

---

This essay, based on a Yiddish address delivered at the 62nd national convention of Agudath Israel of America, appeared in *The Jewish Observer* of February 1985.

ark was to plant a vineyard. The Talmud finds fault with this, and notes that the Torah's narrative of Noach's vineyard, beginning with the word: וַיָּחֶל נֹחַ *"Vayochel Noach ... and Noach debased himself" (Bereishis 9:20)*, contains thirteen words with the prefix וַ, *vay*, [which may also be interpreted as a cry of woe]; thirteen *vays*, expressing cries of despair for Noach's downfall! *(Sanhedrin 70a)*.

What, one may wonder, was wrong with planting a vineyard? After all, its fruit — grapes and wine — certainly have their place in the scheme of a world restored: the wine is used for libation in the sacrificial order; it is used for *kos shel berachah*, on which countless blessings are pronounced; and as a beverage, wine "brings joy to man's heart" *(Tehillim 105)*. Nonetheless, the critique is obviously well founded.

Before planting the grapevine, Noach should have paused to consider the causes for the terrible decree that brought total destruction to the world: "And the earth was full of corruption," which refers to both robbery and immorality. As the Talmud says (in regard to the *sotah* — the woman suspected of infidelity), wine leads to moral decay *(Sotah 2b)*. Having personally witnessed the *mabul* and survived it, having known firsthand that wine was a crucial element in the hedonistic culture that brought it on, Noach should have avoided it, or at least given it a low place on his list of priorities. But he did not. He planted the grapevine first, and the Torah cried *"vay"* thirteen times.

We, too, during this age of reconstruction, must be certain that we are not guilty of replanting the seeds of the very weaknesses that precipitated the previous generation's destruction.

✥ Counter Anti-Semitism: The Netziv's Prescription

It would certainly be difficult for us to determine the specific causes of the fierce hatred that unleashed the massive destruction of *Churban* Europe, but beyond doubt, we would be wise to avoid anything that may have contributed to it — especially today, when anti-Semitism is surfacing with greater regularity and respectability in Europe, South America, and even in the United States. Let us, then, study the insights of the *Netziv* (Rabbi Naftoli Zvi Yehuda Berlin) — head of the famed *Volozhin Yeshivah* from 1852 through 1892 — who was one of the leading figures of Russian Jewry during some of the most oppressive years under the Czar's tyrannic rule. He wrote *Sefer Sh'er Yisrael*, on anti-Semitism, urging his fellow Jews to avoid its underlying causes: First and foremost, he wrote, the Jews are destined to be a nation apart, separate from all the others. If they do so out of their choosing, then they will be secure, in keeping with the passage: "Israel shall dwell securely alone ['*badad*,' in Hebrew] the eye of Yaakov" (*Devarim* 33:28) — meaning that this state of isolation represents Yaakov *Avinu*'s deepest aspiration, the vision in his eyes. This goal had once been realized, during the initial seventeen years that Yaakov and his children had spent in Egypt. Indeed, says the *Netziv*, G-d had assured Yaakov of this in His appearance to him on his descent into Egypt: "And Yoseif will place his hand on your eyes" (*Bereishis* 46:4): Yoseif will protect that vision of isolation that you cherish. And Yoseif did keep the Jews in Goshen, isolated from the rest of Egypt — alone, safe, and secure.

After Yoseif's passing, however, we are told that "the land was full of them" — the Jews left the confines of Goshen and assimilated with the Egyptian populace, even discontinuing *milah* (circumcision). It was then that "Their hearts (the Egyptians') turned against ... (the Jews) in hatred."

In sum, it is G-d's will that the Jews be a nation characterized by "*badad* — alone." If they choose aloneness out of their own volition, they will be secure. If not, the *badad* of hatred and rejection — the "*Eichah yashvah badad* — Alas! the city sitting in solitude" of Lamentations — becomes Jewry's lot. The greater wisdom, counsels the *Netziv*, obviously lies in choosing separateness over having it imposed on us.

In addition, the *Netziv* in his essay underscores two other factors that arouse anti-Semitism: conspicuous consumption, which arouses the envy of others, and a lack of scrupulousness in financial dealings. Only if these three pitfalls are eschewed, warns the *Netziv*, can we be safe from mounting anti-Semitism.

◆§ As Water to Fire

The *Netziv* continues, drawing from Scripture's comparison of the nations to water, "An abundance of water [a reference to persecution by the nations — *Rashi*] cannot extinguish the love" (*Shir HaShirim*; 8:7), and the Jews to fire, "And the House of Yaakov shall be a fire and Yoseif the flame" (*Ovadiah* 1:18). Each has its own characteristics: fire illuminates, water does not; fire heats, water cools. Water has much to gain from fire: for instance, when it is exposed to a fire's heat, water can radiate warmth, or

can radiate warmth, or cook food. So one might assume that the two would be compatible with each other. But when brought into immediate contact, the contrary is the case. Water douses fire, robbing it of its heat and light. All one is left with is unpleasant smoke. The key to a productive relationship between the two, then, is a barrier. For instance, when water in a pot is placed atop a fire, both gain from the interaction that results: the water absorbs the fire's heat, and the fire fulfills its purpose, using its power productively.

This analogy holds true in regard to Jewry and the Nations. They have much to contribute to each other, but a barrier between the two is absolutely essential. This separation permits the Jews to preserve their faith, their fidelity to Torah, and their singular way of life, which in turn can only be to the benefit of the other nations. Remove the barrier, and the resultant smoke and odor are suffocating.

A century has passed since the *Netziv* wrote his immortal words. Looking back at the way Jews were conducting their lives during the forty-fifty years that followed his cautionary essay, one notes no appreciable reduction in the three key causes of anti-Semitism ... and the *Churban* that followed, beginning in the 1930's, is now history.

What Would the "Kedoshim" Say?

The purpose of reviewing history is to learn from it: Can we, in our days, pass the same tests that previous generations faced? In terms of the tests of this past century, who could judge us better than the *kedoshim*, the millions who suffered martyrdom at the hands of the Nazis? Let us imagine for a moment that they, the *kedoshim* themselves, would pay us a visit, and evaluate how we are dealing with the very challenges that had confronted our predecessors. To be sure, they would be impressed with much of what they would see: our sons immersed in Torah study, our daughters committed to a life reflecting Torah values and permeated with personal modesty, our flourishing institutions dedicated to Torah scholarship and philanthropy. They surely would feel that their martyrdom was not in vain.

But should they drop into our homes and observe our life style, what would they think? ... the way we lavish money on our homes and furnishings ... the alien culture, the secular values, the moral degeneration that inundates our homes through periodicals and other channels ... If they would see how the very nations that bear responsibility, passively if not actively, for the death of the Six Million now serve as role-models for family life and for our attitudes toward the value of life, for us and our children — what would they say? ... If they would call on us in our business dealings and examine them in terms of integrity, would they find us clean?

Would they find us learning from the blood-soaked past, avoiding the basic causes of hatred of the Jews, or would they find us focusing our efforts on the very activities that brought destruction upon our people, repeating Noach's blunder, which called forth thirteen *vays* upon his head?

The Test of Reb Elchonon's Martydom

Amongst the *kedoshim* of World War II who could best evaluate us is Rabbi Elchonon Wasserman, revered head of the *Yeshivah* of Baranovich, Poland. Before he went to his martydom in the Seventh Fort in Kovno in 1940, he told his fellow captives: "We must be *tzaddikim* in the eyes of Heaven, if we were chosen to be His sacrifices. Let us sanctify ourselves and keep our minds free of disqualifying thoughts ... Perhaps in that way we will provide merit for our brothers and sisters in America." During his last moments, his concern was that we, safe across the ocean, should continue to survive!

Reb Elchonon had a very specific view regarding the major threats to Jewry's survival and how they should be met, which he analyzed with his customary depth: Over the millennia, Jewry has suffered from two types of perils — blood libels and false Messiahs. Each has an initial cause in our people's earliest years: When the sons of Yaakov sold Yoseif into slavery, they dipped his coat into goat's blood to deceive their father into thinking that he had been killed. As punishment for this, their children are accused of shedding gentile blood for ritual purposes. Forty days after receiving the Law at Sinai, the Jews worshipped the Golden Calf, saying: "This is your god, Israel!" As a result of this failing, we have never freed ourselves from our susceptibility to accepting false Messiahs.

When Reb Elchonon wrote these lines fifty-five years ago (in *Biurei Aggados*, published with *Koveitz He'aros*), history's worst "blood libel" was just on the other side of the horizon, five years away. Today, it needs no further description.

He identified the other fatal weakness — the contemporary "false Messiah" — as the ideology of the "well-known party" that presents a secular nationalism as the formula for ending Jewish suffering. It is as an inherently false premise, for totally ignoring the role of fidelity to Torah as the key to our security, totally sidestepping our estrangement from Torah as the cause for evil and oppression.

If Reb Elchonon would return and visit us today, if he would examine our allegiances, our thoughts and our inclinations, how would he assess them? Now that the Jewish State is in existence for over thirty-five years, and has saved so many Jews, the challenge is so much stronger. Under these heightened circumstances, would Reb Elchonon deem us free from trust in our contemporary false Messiah?

The key to understanding this particular challenge is found in G-d's words to the Prophet Shmuel when the Jews had demanded a king to replace Shmuel as leader: "They have not rejected you," said G-d, "but Me" (*I Shmuel* 8:7). True, their request seemed consistent with the Torah's command, "Appoint a king for yourselves" (*Devarim* 17:15), but they had added a revealing clause," ... a king to judge us, as is done amongst all the nations" (*I Shmuel* 8:5). To a Jew, the implication of *Malchus*, royalty, is *Malchus Shomayim*, the Heavenly Kingdom, but here they were rejecting *Malchus Shomayim* in favor of a king who will rule us "as all the nations." In effect, they were offering a pledge of allegiance to a symbol of "my prowess and the might of my hand."

Today, when people tend to attribute security and military successes to effective strategy, diplomatic skill and naked power, how would Reb Elchonon find us? What would he say? Would he deem us free from trust in our contemporary false Messiah?

⋑ Earth Consecrated by Avraham

Indeed, the hazard of misapplied trust is all the greater now, when millions of Jews are concentrated in *Eretz Yisrael*. This is borne out by the explanation offered by the late *Mashgiach* of Ponevezh, Rabbi Yechezkel (Reb Chaskel) Levenstein, regarding an incident recorded in the Talmud:

Nachum Ish Gam Zu was dispatched by his colleagues to represent the Jewish people before the Roman emperor, and he took along a chest of jewels to present as a gift. The keeper of the inn where he rested on the way stole the jewels and replaced them with earth. When Nachum arrived, the emperor opened the chest, and was shocked to see the earth:

"These Jews are ridiculing us!" he exclaimed, and decided to kill him.

Eliyahu Hanavi appeared in the guise of one of his advisors, and suggested: "Perhaps this is the earth that their Patriarch Abraham used when he defeated the four kings in battle. He threw clods of earth at them and the earth proved as lethal as swords and spears."

The emperor decided to test "Abraham's earth" against an enemy with whom the country had been locked in an unresolved conflict. It worked! They were defeated! In reward, the emperor filled the chest with precious stones and gave it to Nachum.

On his return trip to Eretz Yisrael, Nachum stopped at the same inn. When the larcenous innkeeper learned of Nachum's good fortune, he decided to cash in on the emperor's appreciation of his clods of earth. He leveled his house, filled a chest with the earth that lay beneath it, and presented it to the emperor as "more of the same earth."

The king tested it, and — not surprisingly — it proved powerless. The deceptive innkeeper was put to death (Taanis 21a).

Asks Reb Chaskel: Why did the innkeeper attempt to fool the emperor with his chest of dirt? He was well aware of its inefficacy. Obviously, answered Reb Chaskel, the innkeeper did not accept the miraculous story of Nachum Ish Gam Zu's chestful of earth. How could he, when he never believed in the prototype earth of Avraham *Avinu*, either? To his view, there were no metaphysical factors to consider anywhere, so *his* box of dirt was equal to any.

Today, added Reb Chaskel, there are those who fail to see the imprint of Avraham *Avinu* and his values on "a piece of earth." *Eretz Yisrael*, in their view, is a stretch of land, no more or no less invested with metaphysical powers than any other piece of real estate on the globe. Left in the hands of these skeptics, our planes and missiles are ultimately as worthless as clods of earth in defending ourselves against our mortal enemies. Only when we succeed in linking the Land with the forefather who consecrated it with his commitment to G-d and His Torah's values, only then do we benefit from the protection of living in Avraham's patch of earth, and only then are our protective forces invincible in battle, as jets and missiles can be.

Let us strive for clarity in our beliefs and fidelity in the object of our trust.

The Definitive Weapon

"With You (in Hebrew, *becha*) we will gore our enemies, with Your Name we will cut down those who rise up against us" (*Tehillim* 44:6). The Midrash quotes Rabbi Yitzchak who homiletically interprets the Hebrew word for "With You, *becha*." Written with letters having the numerical value of twenty-two, the implication is that we will overpower our enemies with the twenty-two letters of the *Alef Beis*, with which the Torah is written.

Twenty-two years have gone by since the passing of the great leader of the reestablishment of Torah after World War II. Rabbi Aharon Kotler, had headed Beth Medrash Govoha in Lakewood, chaired Agudath Israel of America's *Moetzes Gedolei HaTorah* (Council of Torah Sages), *Torah Umesorah* and *Agudas Harabonim*. Beyond doubt, he initiated a Torah revolution, employing the twenty-two letters of the *Alef Beis* as the prime weapon. As a result, America today is graced with *Yeshivos* and *Kollelim* of advanced Torah study — *lishmoh*, for its own sake — virtually from coast to coast, many of them inspired if not founded by Beth Medrash Govoha, representing second-generation fruits of his labors.

A young man connected with the administration of *Beth Medrash Govohah* in Lakewood approached me with a plan: Since virtually every community that hosts a *kollel* has undergone a complete metamorphosis, with more people than ever studying Torah, laymen making the *beis midrash* the focal point of their morning and evening, striving for ever-higher standards in Jewish commitment and practice, why not create a two-million dollar trust fund to fund the opening of a new *kollel* every year, making the countryside alive with Torah? Could there be a more fitting memorial to the Six Million than this, a more effective use of the definitive tool for reconstruction, the omnipotent twenty-two letters?

The Key to the Treasure

The passage from *Tehillim* quoted above concludes: "With Your Name we will cut down those who rise up against us." Said Resh Lakish in the name of Rabbi Yannai," G-d linked His Great Name with Yisrael" *(Yerushalmi, Taanis)*. *Korban Ha'aidah*, a commentary on *Talmud Yerushalmi*, says that when Yaakov's name was changed, it could just as well have become "*Yeshurun*" or "*Yashar-Elokim,*" instead. Why did the *malach* call him "Yisrael"?

He explains that the Name within Yisrael — which is one of G-d's Names of mercy — is similar to a key to a royal treasure chest that contains the king's secrets. The key must never be loose, lest it be misplaced and access to its precious contents be lost. The only way to insure that the key will always be available when needed is to secure it to the chest with a chain.

We Jews have been presented with a priceless treasure, G-d's Torah. If we are permitted to mix at random with other nations, our relationship with the Torah will surely be lost. Attached to G-d's Torah with His Name, we are secure. It is the only way in which we can ascertain that we will not be lost in *galus*. The incorporation of G-d's name in ours as the final syllable of *Yisrael's* name ties us to our heritage. But even after we find ouselves so linked, we must make use of the key.

The illumination from the fires that consumed the martyrs should light up our path: We should see the truth in life with the light of Truth, that all that exists is for His glory only.

Rabbi Avrohom Yaakov HaKohein Pam
prepared for publication by
Rabbi Shimon Finkelman

After the Churban: The Groundswell of Love

⋙ From Suffering to Love

WHEN WE ARE CAUGHT UP in the flow of history, especially now when we are still under the impact of the trauma of the *Churban* of European Jewry, it can be difficult to understand the direction of events and what is expected of us. The Torah provides us with the perspective with which to view the tribulations that *Klal Yisrael* has endured over the centuries. *"You are to know in your heart, that as a father instructs his son, so does* HASHEM, *your G-d, instruct you"* (Devarim 8:5).

The trials, though they are at times unbearable, actually stem from G-d's love and compassion for His children, and are intended to influence them to correct their ways so as to merit once again their status as His people. This concept, in itself, suffices for a simple understanding of the verse cited above. There is, however, a second aspect to the father-son analogy.

When a father is forced to reprove a child in a way that causes the child pain and anguish, the reproof is followed by a strong desire on the father's part to renew their loving relationship. Distressed over the hurt that his beloved son has endured, the father anxiously awaits a sign that misdeed has been replaced by true remorse; when the sign is given, the father then comforts the child and soothes his wounds.

Similarly, whenever G-d deems it necessary to inflict punishment upon *Klal Yisrael*, there follows a tremendous

---

This essay, based on a Yiddish address delivered at the 62nd national convention of Agudath Israel of America, appeared in *The Jewish Observer* of February 1985.

stirring of Heavenly love towards Jewry which translates into conciliation, consolation and ultimately redemption. This concept and the one mentioned above are both to be found in a *pasuk* in *Mishlei* (3:12), *"For he whom Hashem loves He reproves and He appeases as a father does his son."*

✌ A New Branch from the Truncated Tree

Indeed, there is pattern of *Churban* and rebuilding that is a part of Jewish experience over the years, and it can offer us many an insight. We find in *Tanach* that one of the most tragic events in Jewish history was followed by a tremendous surge of Divine love which could have resulted in the Final Redemption:

Sancherev, King of Ashur, ruler of the civilized world known at that time, conquered the Ten Tribes and sent them into exile, laid waste to most of Yehudah and besieged the city of Jerusalem where Chizkiyahu reigned. Then, in a single night, Sancherev's soldiers miraculously died and the city was spared.

The prophecies in the Book of *Yeshayahu* that deal with these events are immediately followed by *Perek HaMoshiach* (*Yeshayahu* 11), which speaks of the future Redeemer and the era that his arrival will herald. The juxtaposition of these prophecies indicates that in the wake of the tragedies of that time came a *z'man mesugal* (auspicious time) for *geulah*. *Chazal* do, indeed, tell us that *"Hakadosh Baruch Hu* desired to make Chizkiyahu the *Moshiach,"* but Chizkiyahu's failure to give full recognition to G-d for His salvation — he did not sing G-d's praises in a *Hallel* after the rescue of *Klal Yisrael* from Sancherev — had prevented this from occurring. (Still, G-d's mercy was showered upon His people, albeit in a different form: Under Chizkiyahu's reign, Torah flourished as never before or since, with men, women and children, from Dan to Beersheva, all expert in the most esoteric areas of Torah law.)

According to *Malbim*, this idea is to be found in the very words of Yeshayahu's prophecy: *"A branch will grow from the trunk of Yishai and a sapling will flourish from its roots"* (*Yeshayahu* 11:1).

The *Malbim* points out that the apparent repetition of phrases in the prophecy contains two messages: The tree of Israel, once axed down, will be restored as a new growth directly from the stump. This refers to the possibility, at that time, of immediate redemption, with the branch of *Moshiach* sprouting visibly from the trunk of the Davidic dynasty, in the form of Chizkiyahu, who stemmed from David. Should this not occur, as in fact it did not, the prophecy would still be fulfilled ultimately, as is implicit in the balance of the verse. The trunk may be hewn to the ground, with the termination of Davidic rule, but despair is still out of place. The root is still alive beneath the soil, and "a sapling will flourish from its roots." In time, *Moshiach*, a direct descendant of David, will reign.

After the Second Temple

This pattern of widespread destruction and merciful restoration appears repeatedly in the Jewish experience. After the destruction of the Second *Beis Hamikdash*, then, one could certainly anticipate some intimations of redemption. The Talmud records that Rabbi Akiva had put his hopes in Bar Kochva, believing him to be the *Moshiach*. He even bolstered his expectations with a passage from the Torah: "A star *(Kochav)* will emerge from Yaakov ..." *(Bamidbar* 24:17*)*. Contrary to popular assumption that he was somehow fooled, Rabbi Akiva was gifted with the clearest vision conceivable, with which he was able to penetrate the very Heavens. He knew that the time was propitious for the *Geulah Sheleimah* (total redemption), and that Bar Kochva was that person capable of fulfilling the role of the ultimate Redeemer. True, the Talmud does point out Bar Kochva's failings, but these only served to disqualify him during the ensuing course of events that followed. Rabbi Akiva perceived the pattern as it could have been fulfilled in his time.

From Spain with Hope

Similarly, 1492 witnessed the expulsion of the Jews from Spain, putting an end to a flourishing center of Torah study and a source of guidance for Jews the world over. Those Jews who remained behind were subjected to the tortures of the Inquisition. For certain, redemption was on the horizon, and out of his keen awareness of this, the *Arizal* (Rabbi Yitzchak Luria, sixteenth-century *kabbalist)* inspired his disciples to join him in yearning for its advent, as he led them on the mountains of Tzefas. It is clear from the writings of these *tzaddikim* that they sensed *Moshiach's* imminent arrival. Listen to the lyrical outpourings of the *Ari's* disciple, Rabbi Shlomo HaLevi Alkabetz, from the "*Lechah Dodi*" that he composed:

Hisna'ari: Shake off the dust — arise:
Don your splendid clothes, My people,

Through the son of Yishai, of Beis Lechem!
Draw near to my soul — redeem it!

Hiso'reri: Wake up! Wake up! for your light has come.
Rise up and shine:
Awaken, awaken, utter a song,
The glory of Hashem is revealed on you.

... *al yad ish ben Partzi:* Through the man descended from Peretz, we shall rejoice.

Somehow, the response of *Klal Yisrael* was not up to the call of the times, and *Moshiach* did not come.

World-Wide Upheaval

More recently, World War I uprooted virtually every Jewish community in Eastern Europe and destroyed the fabric of Jewish life where it had flourished for centuries. Within four years of the armistice that ended the war, England issued the Balfour Declaration, which declared the intention of establishing a national Jewish homeland in Palestine. At that occasion, the Chofetz Chaim said that this could well be a signal that G-d was presenting Jewry with opportunities for ultimate redemption. Care must be taken that the irreligious elements do not cause the redemption to be further postponed ... Tragically, his fears were realized; the World Zionist establishment was left in control of events, and succeeded in imposing a decidedly anti-Torah imprint on the national Jewish homeland ...

Just as the near-total destruction of European Jewry in World War II eclipsed any suffering endured until then, so too should the opportunity for *geulah* that followed exceed any that had come before. Indeed, only three years after the Allied victory, *Klal Yisrael* was presented with a wonderful opportunity to settle and develop *Eretz Yisrael*, on a firm basis of Torah values. This would have been an achievement that had not been available for centuries. Imagine an *Eretz Yisrael* where the sanctity of *Shabbos* reigns supreme, where the laws of the Land are rooted firmly in the *Shulchan Aruch*, where the sounds of Torah study echo from every corner! ... But, alas, this did not occur and the State of Israel was not established as a Torah state, to say the least ... Almost forty years later, clashes over religious issues are still an everyday occurrence. Topics such as legalized abortion and desecration of holy graves through archeological digs tear at the heart of all who harken to the word of G-d.

✎ Taking the Reins in Hand

Perhaps we can find an indication of a course of action to pursue from an exchange between the Chazon Ish and Ben-Gurion.

The then-premier of Israel visited the Sage of Bnei Brak because the Torah community had raised its voice in outcry against the law of compulsory military service for women.

"The majority of our country's people are irreligious," argued Ben-Gurion. "Yours are in the minority. Who should conform to whose way of life?"

The Chazon Ish was quick to reply by citing a halachah found in the Gemara (Sanhedrin 32b): "When two wagons, one laden with cargo, the other completely empty, travel towards each other on a road scarcely wide enough for one, the empty wagon must back up and allow for the full one to pass." The Chazon Ish continued, "Our wagon is laden with three thousand years of history, heritage and tradition. Yours, however, is empty, devoid of any real substance. Shouldn't you step back for us?"

Following this meeting, the draft of religious women was rescinded.

While the quick and direct reply of the Chazon Ish was nothing short of brilliant, in all probability it did not impress Ben-Gurion, who was not interested in the words of *Chazal* and who did not share the Chazon Ish's interpretation of the circumstances. In Ben-Gurion's view, his own wagon was full of ideological convictions and promise. That of the Chazon Ish, in his opinion, was outmoded, empty of contemporary relevance. The Chazon Ish replied in the way that he did because he was a man of truth, not because he intended to impress his adversary; Ben-Gurion most likely sidestepped in favor of the Chazon Ish to avoid a no-win confrontation with the religious *Yishuv*.

Let us return to Ben-Gurion's initial remarks. He did not attempt to convince the Chazon Ish of the value of his false ideology; he knew quite well that any such attempt would prove futile. Ben-Gurion had but one point to make: "... Yours are in the minority. Who should conform to whom?"

✎ While the Gates are Still Open

Force of numbers is an important factor in overpowering those opposed to Torah and can even impress them on their own terms. When we are the majority, we will prevail without question. More important, however, is that we reach each and every individual Jew and convince him of the truth of Torah. This will not happen through protests and demonstrations, which serve to distance even further those already estranged from the ways of our fathers.

The only conceivable way of achieving the goal we seek is by educating the masses, especially the young. The status of Torah in Israel has improved dramatically over the past thirty-six years, primarily because of dedicated efforts of *Chinuch Atzmai* to bring Torah education to children in every city, town, and village in Israel. In addition, *Reshet Shiurei Torah* is bringing Torah to all parts of the Land. *Yeshivos* that specialize in dealing with *baalei teshuvah*, *P'eylim*, *Mifal Torah Vodaath*, and other groups are devoting themselves to reaching out to our Sephardic brethren and deserve every measure of encouragement and every bit of support.

Rachmei Shomayim — Divine mercy and love — does not come and go in a flash. In view of the mammoth proportions of *Churban* Europe, we can certainly assume that the Gates of Mercy will not be quickly closed. *Hakadosh Baruch Hu* is waiting to console us and we can bring this about by inculcating our people with authentic Torah values.

Glossary

Glossary

All words are Hebrew unless otherwise indicated. Parenthesized words in entries indicate plural forms. It should be noted that since the essays were written by many different authors and during the tenure of various editors, the transliterations may not be entirely uniform throughout the book.

ACHARIS HAYAMIM
: the End of Days

ADMOR (ADMORIM)
: Chassidic rebbi(s)

AHAVAS YISRAEL
: love for the Jewish People

AKEIDAH
: sacrifice; specifically, the "sacrifice" of Yitzchak, Bereishis chap. 22

ALIYAH
: immigration to Israel

AL KIDDUSH HASHEM
: in sanctification of G-d's Name; specifically, dying in martyrdom

AMCHO
: in the expression "*amcho* man," an average religious person

AM HANIVCHAR
: Chosen Nation

AMOL'IGE KEDUSHA
: (Yid.) level of sanctity practiced in bygone days

AMUD
: lectern; especially, the chazzan's lectern

ARON KODESH
: Holy Ark

ASARAH HARUGEI MALCHUS
: ten Talmudic sages who perished horrendous martyred deaths at the hands of the Roman Government

AV[INU] BASHOMAYIM
: [our] Father in Heaven

AVEILUS
: mourning

AVEIRA
: sin

AVINU
: our father; used in the expression *Avinu Bashomayim*, "our Father in Heaven"; also appended to the names of the Patriarchs Avraham, Yitzchok and Yaakov

AVOS
: Patriarchs (Avraham, Yitzchak, Yaakov)

AVRAHAM
: the Patriarch Abraham

BAAL BITACHON
: person of powerful faith

BAAL TEFILLAH
: chazzan; prayer leader

BAAL(EI) TESHUVA
: returnee(s) to Judaism

BACHUR (BACHURIM)
: lit. boy; yeshivah student

BALLEBOSTE
: (Yid.) housewife

BEIS DIN
: religious court

BEIS HAMIKDASH
: Holy Temple in Jerusalem

BEIS MIDRASH (BATEI MIDRASH)
: study hall; synagogue

BEN TORAH (BNEI TORAH)
: lit. son of Torah; person devoted to Torah study and fulfillment

B'EZRAS HASHEM
: with the help of G-d

BIMAH
: Torah reading platform in center of synagogue

BITACHON
: trust in G-d

BNEI YISROEL
: Children of Israel

CHAZAL
: abbreviation for our Rabbis of blessed memory; specifically, the Rabbis of the Talmud

CHESSED
: kindness

CHILLUL HASHEM
: desecration of G-d's name

CHILLUL SHABBOS
: desecration of the Sabbath

CHINUCH
: education; especially, Torah education

CHIZUK
: strength, encouragement

CHUMASH (CHUMASHIM)
Pentatuech

CHURBAN (CHURBANOS)
destruction; the Destruction (n.)

DAVENING
(Yid.) praying

DRASHAH
homiletic exposition

EMES
truth

EMUNAH
belief in G-d; faith

ERETZ YISRAEL
Land of Israel

EREV
evening (also day preceding the Sabbath or Holy Days)

GADOL (GEDOLIM)
great man

GALUS
exile; diaspora

GAON
Torah genius

GEULAH
redemption

HACHNOSAS ORCHIM
hospitality

HAKADOSH BARUCH HU
The Holy One, Blessed Be He, i.e., G-d

HALACHAH
Torah law

HASHEM
G-d

HASHGACHAH
(Divine direction) guidance

HASHGACHAH P'RATIS
active force of the Hand of G-d in guiding the individual

HASHKAFAH
outlook

HASKALA
the "Enlightenment"

HATZALAH
rescue of life

IKVESA DEMESHICHA
the footfalls of the Messiah; i.e., the era immediately preceding the advent of Moshiach

ILLUY
genius

IMPRIMATUR
(Latin) Certification by Roman Catholic Church that document contains no misstatement of Church dogma

KABBALAH
mystical aspects of Torah

KADDISH
Memorial prayer

KADOSH (KEDOSHIM)
human sacrifice; martyr, willing or otherwise

KASHRUS
laws pertaining to kosher food

KEDUSHAH
sanctity, holiness

KEHILLAH (KEHILLOS)
community

KEIL MOLAY RACHAMIM
memorial prayers

KIDDUSH HASHEM
sanctification of G-d's name

KINOS
lamentations; elegies recited on Tishah B'Av

KLAL YISRAEL
the Nation of Israel

KNESSES YISRAEL
the Congregation of Israel

KOLLEL
post-graduate yeshivah, usually with a married student body

KORBAN (KORBANOS)
sacrifice; in this volume refers to the taking of innocent life

KRIAS SHEMA
reading of the *Shema*

LAMDAN
learned man

LISHMOH
Torah study and mitzvah observance for no reason other than in fulfillment of G-d's will

MAARIV
Evening prayer service

MAGGID
preacher; often officially appointed by a *kehillah*

MANHIGIM
leaders

MASHGIACH
dean, usually responsible for the ethical development of the students of a yeshivah

MECHALEL HASHEM
one who desecrates G-d's Name

MECHALEL SHABBOS
one who desecrates the Sabbath

MECHANECH (MECHANCHIM)
teacher

MEGILLAH
Scroll of Esther — read on Purim

MEGILLAS EICHAH
the Prophet Yirmiyahu's Lamentations on the destruction of the Beis Hamikdash

MEKADESH SHEM SHOMAYIM
lit., sanctify the Name of Heaven; sanctify G-d's name

MELAMED
teacher

MENORAH
candelabra; specifically, the Chanukah lamp

MENTCH
(Yid.) lit., a human being; loosely used to describe a person of admirable traits, reliability, compassion, honesty, etc.

MENTCHLICHKEIT
(Yid.) the character of a *mentch*

MESIRAS NEFESH
devotion to the point of risking one's life

MIDAH K'NEGED MIDAH
punishment or reward suited to the deed both qualitatively and quantitatively

MIDRASH
non-halachic portion of the Torah

MIKVEH (MIKVA'OS)
ritualarium

MINYAN (MINYANIM)
prayer quorum of ten adult Jewish men

MITZVAH (MITZVOS)
commandment

MOED
festival

MOLAY
memorial prayer

MOSER NEFESH
risk or give up one's soul

MOSHIACH
the Messiah

MUSSAR
ethics

NAVI
prophet

NESHAMA (NESHAMOS)
soul

NEVI'EI HASHEM
G-d's prophets

ORAYACH (ORCHIM)
guest

PARSHA[S] [HASHAVUA]
[weekly] portion of the Torah

PASUK (PESUKIM)
Biblical verse

PATERNOSTER
(Latin) Catholic prayer

PEYOS
side curls

RAMBAM (Maimonides)
R' **M**oshe **b**en **M**aimon

RAV
teacher

REBBAIIM
Chassidic Rebbis

RIBBONO SHEL OLAM
Creator of the world

ROSH YESHIVAH (ROSHEI YESHIVAH)
dean of a Yeshivah

RUACH HAKODESH
Divine spirit

SHECHINAH
G-d's illuminating presence

SEDER (SEDARIM)
(a) one of six orders of the Mishnah; (b) set time for Torah study; (c) the ritual meal eaten on the first (and outside of Eretz Yisrael the second) night of Pesach

SEFER
book

SEFER TORAH (SIFREI TORAH)
Torah Scroll

SHABBOS
Sabbath

SHALOM ALEICHEM
peace be upon you — traditional Hebrew greeting

SHAMASH
synagogue caretaker

SHE'EIRIS HAPLEITAH
survivors of Churban Europe

SHEHECHEYANU
 blessing recited on certain joyous occasions

SHELO LISHMOH
 Torah study and *mitzvah* observance for any reason other than for the simple fulfillment of G-d's will

SHEMINI ATZERES
 the final day(s) of the Succos festival

SHMUESS (SHMUESSEN)
 discourse — usually on ethics

SHOCHET
 ritual slaughter

SHUL
 (Yid.) synagogue

SIDDUR
 prayer book

SIFREI KODESH
 holy books

SIFREI TORAH
 Torah scrolls

SIMCHAS TORAH
 last day of Succos; the annual public Torah reading is concluded among great festivity on this day

SUCCAH
 booth used on the festival of Tabernacles

TALLIS
 prayer shawl

TALMID (TALMIDIM)
 pupil

TALMID CHACHAM (TALMIDEI CHACHAMIM)
 Torah sage

TANACH
 Scriptures

TEFILLIN
 phylacteries

TESHUVAH
 repentance

TIKKUN
 restoration

TISCH
 (Yid.) lit., specifically a gathering around the Sabbath or Festival table

TISHAH B'AV
 lit. the ninth day of the month of Av — the day the Temple was destroyed

TOCHACHAH
 rebuke, promise of punishment; portion of the Torah dealing with Divine punishment

TSAROS
 troubles

TZADDIK (TZADDIKIM)
 righteous man

TZEDAKAH
 charity

VAAD
 appointment, committee

VAAD HATZALAH
 American Orthodox Jewish Rescue Committee

VIDUY
 admission of wrongdoing and confessional of sins

YAAKOV
 the Patriarch Jacob

YAHRZEIT
 anniversary of day of death

YARMULKA
 skullcap

YECHEZKEIL
 the prophet Ezekiel

YESHAYAHU
 the prophet Isaiah

YESHIVAH (YESHIVOS)
 Torah academy

YESHUAH
 salvation

YETZER HARA
 evil inclination

YIDDISHKEIT
 (Yid.) Judaism

YIRAH
 fear; especially, of G-d

YIRAS SHOMAYIM
 fear of Heaven

YIRMIYAHU
 the prophet Jeremiah

YITZCHAK
 the Patriarch Isaac

YOM HA'ATZMAUT
 Israel Independence Day

YOM HASHOAH
 Holocaust Remembrance Day

YOMIM NORAIM
 High Holy Days

YOM TOV
 holiday

Z'CHUS merit